STANDARD CATALOG

of

Gem Values

SECOND EDITION

Anna M. Miller

John Sinkankas

GEOSCIENCE PRESS, INC.
TUCSON, ARIZONA

First published by Geoscience Press in 1994
Copyright © 1994 by Anna M. Miller and John Sinkankas
Library of Congress Catalog Card Number 94-076638
ISBN 0-945005-16-4

Printed in the United States of America

Published by Geoscience Press

Publisher's Cataloging in Publication
(Prepared by Quality Books Inc.)

Miller, Anna M., 1993–
     Standard catalog of gem values / by Anna M. Miller and John Sinkankas. — 2nd ed.
     p.   cm.
     Rev. ed. of work last published in 1988 under title: Sinkankas' standard catalog of gem values.
     Includes bibliographical references and index.
     ISBN 0-945005-16-4

     1. Gems—Catalogs. 2. Precious stones—Catalogs. I. Sinkankas, John. II. Sinkankas, John. Standard catalog of gem values. III. Title.

TS752.M55 1994   533'.8
                                                                                QBI94–888

16   15

PREFACE

SINCE FIRST PUBLICATION OF THIS WORK IN 1968, political events, social trends, and world economics have created dramatic gemstone price fluctuations from explosive highs to depressing lows. But through all these price peaks and valleys, the public's desire for gemstones has not diminished; in fact, it is stronger than ever. Part of the reason for the robust colored gemstone market can be explained by the vigorous marketing techniques used by gem dealers over the past two decades, along with mass media advertising by dealers' associations. Parallel to the dealers' marketing is the new and knowledgeable generations of buyers who know more about gemstone identification, treatments, alterations and value than their predecessors. Further, these buyers want more: more product knowledge, more insights into the mysteries of profitable buying and selling, more value for the money. While many collect gems as a hobby, some also see the investment value and note the easy transportability of such a store of value. Other collectors want to be first to display some of the exciting new gemstone discoveries.

This new edition reflects the latest prices and trends on rough material, faceted and cabbed gemstones, to which we have devoted hours of research and interviews in the appropriate markets. To inform you about new gemstones, we went to the source of discovery or to its discoverer. To provide an update and indispensable record of gem values, we called upon miners, wholesalers, jobbers and retailers. In all cases, however, the prices given are the latest *retail* prices available in 1993 from those who deal in these materials. And, while we realize that retail prices fluctuate to some degree across the country and around the world, prices in this book provide a guide to the current *average retail prices* quoted in the United States. In this way we hope to have taken some of the mystery out of gemstone pricing for our readers . . . while leaving intact the pleasure and magic of owning them.

Anna M. Miller

John Sinkankas

ACKNOWLEDGMENTS

Much of the information on rare gemstones and those of lesser value employed chiefly by amateur gem cutters was obtained from a study of advertisements in *The Lapidary Journal* and *Gems and Minerals* and other magazines expressly catering to the interests of the many earth science enthusiasts. Hundreds of price lists were ordered as a result of this study, and it would serve little purpose to acknowledge each one; however, of particular value were the extensive and detailed catalogs issued by International Gem Corporation of New York City and Grieger's Incorporated of Pasadena, California. Mr. Herbert Walters of Craftstones, Ramona, California, supplied prices for a large variety of first-class tumbled gems, mainly quartzes and other gemstones now used extensively in popular jewelry. Mr. Edward R. Swoboda of Los Angeles, California, most helpfully provided current price information on Japanese coral, shell products, and carvings; additional information on shell prices was supplied by John Q. Burch, conchologist, of Seal Beach, California.

In respect to more expensive gems, particularly those which are the classical stock in trade of professional jewelers, I wish to gratefully acknowledge the help of Mr. Richard T. Liddicoat, Jr., Director of the Gemological Institute of America, Los Angeles, California, without whose invaluable advice I would have had great difficulty in formulating meaningful price schedules for such important gems as rubies, diamonds, emeralds, and sapphires. Much information, both scientific and technical, on commercially important gems was also obtained from past issues of *Gems and Gemology*, published by the Gemological Institute under the editorship of Mr. Liddicoat. Certain tables appearing in this catalog which are owing to the work of members of the staff of the Gemological Institute are acknowledged separately. In this connection, I also wish to acknowledge the help I received from perusal of the extensive and sound article "Gem Stones and Allied Materials" by Dr. Richard H. Tahns, which appears in the third edition of *Industrial Minerals and Rocks*, published by A.I.M.E., New York, whose author, in turn, depended upon the Gemological Institute for reliable data. The interesting and useful price trend chart shown in Figure 3 is from that article.

Useful information was also supplied by Harry B. Derian, jeweler and gem carver of Los Angeles, California; Sol Shalevitz, diamond merchant, also of Los Angeles; Irwin Moed, expert in the irradiation of diamonds, New York City; Akbar Ouskouian, Persian turquois, New York City; Maurice Shire, emeralds, also of New York City. Information on the custom carving of fine cameos and intaglios was supplied by one of the few remaining expert practitioners of the art, Ewald Leyendecker of Idar Oberstein, Germany. Further information on charges for custom lapidary work in Germany was supplied by Ernest W. Beissinger of Pittsburgh, Pennsylvania.

The troublesome area of evaluating fine carvings in jade and other hardstones was made far less hazardous by frequent consultations coupled with examinations of the stocks of Kenneth Brown and John R. Siglow, dealers in oriental antiquities, of La Jolla, California. Both are discriminating and expert in their field and most cooperative in supplying information which would have been difficult to obtain otherwise.

Finally, I wish to acknowledge the help of O. D. Smith, photographer, of La Jolla, California, in the preparation of many of the photographs which appear in this catalog, including the color plate used for the cover; Miss Bonnie Swope of San Diego, California, who prepared most of the drawings in this book; and my wife, Marjorie, who supplied invaluable assistance in all phases of manuscript preparation.

1968

JOHN SINKANKAS

Most of the updated gemstone pricing information was collected and cataloged during 1992–1993 and into 1994. Many dealers, collectors, jewelers, and gemologists provided invaluable information and we offer a collective thank you to all of them. Some companies and individuals who should be acknowledged are Geoff Dominy, Richard W. Hughes, Richard Drucker—The Guide, Reynolds-McNear Amber Company, Lock's, House of Onyx, Dr. Bob Mallas, Bennett-Walls, Gerhard Becker, Si and Ann Frazier, Don Kay of Mason-Kay Company, Harriet Snare, and David Graham of the Cripple Creek Mining Company.

ANNA M. MILLER
JOHN SINKANKAS

IDENTIFICATION AND EXAMINATION

Neither the publishers nor the authors can undertake to examine, identify, or render an opinion on the condition or value of any cut or rough gemstone, due to the time and responsibility involved, but refer readers to the many reliable dealers, jewelers, and gemologists in public and private agencies who provide identification or appraisal services.

CONTENTS

INTRODUCTION TO GEMS

WEBSTER'S *UNABRIDGED DICTIONARY* (SECOND EDITION) DEFINES A GEM as "Any jewel, whether stone, pearl, or the like, having value and beauty that are intrinsic and not derived from its setting; a precious or, sometimes, a semi-precious stone cut and polished for ornament." Also, "A semi-precious stone of value because carved or engraved, as a cameo or intaglio." Interestingly, below these definitions appears, "In modern usage, GEM more frequently suggests a precious stone as cut or polished; JEWEL, a precious stone as set and worn for ornament. . . ."

The professional view differs somewhat as expressed in the Gemological Institute of America's *Jewelers' Manual* (1964): "**GEM.** (1) A cut-and-polished stone that possesses the necessary beauty and durability for use in jewelry; also, a fine pearl. (2) An especially fine specimen; e.g., *a gem diamond*. In this use, the meaning depends on the ethics and the range of qualities handled by the seller. (3) As an adjective, a prefix; e.g., *gem quality, gem crystal, etc.* (4) As a verb, to decorate with gems."

The definitions above agree that a gem must be beautiful and valuable, and that it must be cut and polished so that it can be used in jewelry. Webster's definition includes engraved gems since these are made from suitable material and are cut and polished. In fact, until about the turn of the century, the word gem meant an engraved stone more than anything else. Today the meaning has broadened until it embraces all kinds of cut stones, pearls, and even jewelry sets fashioned from organic materials such as amber, coral, jet, and ivory. However, for size reasons, it cannot apply to the large objects produced by the lapidary such as spheres, book ends, ashtrays, and carvings over an inch or two in length which are manifestly awkward to wear upon the person. However, it is emphasized that meaning (2) of the *Jewelers' Manual* cited above is still very much in use in the trade, that is, the word gem means a superlative specimen, generally of superb color, of best internal quality, finely cut, and otherwise head and shoulders above the vast majority of specimens cut from the same species. Thus the term "gem turquoise" as an example, refers to the finest grade of Persian material, *i.e.*, pure uniform blue of the highest possible intensity, and free of any defect whatsoever.

In this catalog, the term gem will be used principally to denote finished stones ready to wear in jewelry, but it will also be used in the sense of top quality as defined above. On the other hand, the term *gemstone*, or simply, *rough*, will be used only to designate rough material which has not had any lapidary work expended upon it.

The term *precious stone*, introduced above, now needs defining. At one time it was used in a narrow sense to signify one of a few very hard, durable, and beautiful minerals of considerable rarity which traditionally had enjoyed the highest esteem since antiquity, *i.e.*:

Diamond	Chrysoberyl
Corundum (Ruby and Sapphire)	Opal
Beryl (Emerald)	Pearl

Despite the fact that pearl is not a mineral, it was commonly ranked as a precious stone and included in the above list. All other gemstones were arbitrarily classed as *semi-precious stones*, a term which has lost favor because it is essentially meaningless. This becomes clear when one considers the very high prices for large specimens of superior quality which certain so-called "semi-precious" stones such as demantoid (andradite) or benitoite can command. While they may not be as durable or as beautiful in some respects as the classical "precious" stones listed above, they nevertheless are in demand as collectors' items. Also it is true that diamonds, rubies, sapphires, and other "precious" stones occur in poor specimens, which, in some instances, sell at much lower prices than those considered to be of lesser rank. It is largely for these reasons that the designations "precious" and "semi-precious" are being discarded.

Another term which is also losing ground but which has more to say in its favor is *ornamental gemstone*. It was coined as a classification for the massive or rock-like gemstones which found major employment in objects larger than jewelry gems, although some could be fine enough in quality to fall into the latter category. Included were such minerals as malachite, rhodonite, serpentine, jadeite and nephrite, chalcedony, and a number of others. Again the distinctions between such massive gemstones and others of higher rank are poorly defined and it is not at all uncommon to see fine examples of each of these minerals employed in jewelry as cabochons, small pendant carvings, beads, cameos, etc.

Another category of gemstones which is still in use is that of *rare* or *unusual gemstones*, generally meant to include those gemstones which occur so infrequently in gem quality that they are scarcely known except to connoisseurs. Here are included andalusite, axinite, cassiterite, iolite, and kornerupine, among others, all of which are reasonably durable and, in the better examples, quite attractive. In the last several decades a much greater number of species has been added to this category, including those gemstones which by no stretch of the imagination can be called "gemstones" if one of the criteria is to be durability when worn in jewelry. Into this group fall such fragile species as amblygonite, apatite, beryllonite, dioptase, and sphalerite. Some are so soft or so readily cleaved that cutting them is a severe test of the lapidary skill. Because of their inherent weaknesses, they must be forever consigned to soft folds of padding in a gem paper or in a cushioned mount in an exhibit case, never to be set in jewelry except as an empty gesture. Nevertheless, many of them are beautiful, and in terms of the amount of skill and effort expended on cutting them, they represent considerable value in a small package. Most of these species are cut by amateur lapidaries, particularly the more venturesome who become bored with cutting standard gemstones and eagerly seize the challenge of trying something new. Gradually these species are becoming acceptable to collectors, connoisseurs, and museums, and the demand for rough is increasing to fulfill a widening market for the finished gems.

Aside from the gemstones derived from the mineral kingdom there are those which owe their origin to organic creation. The most important example, touched on above, is the pearl. Pearls are concretions produced within shellfish and vary widely in shape and attractiveness, depending on which mollusk grows them. Their use in jewelry and ornamentation, at least among ancient civilizations accustomed to fishing in fresh or salt waters, may be even older than the use of mineral gemstones. By custom they have been considered as gemstones from time immemorial. Other organic materials classed as gemstones are mother-of-pearl, amber, coral, tortoise shell, ivory, and jet.

A final category of gemstones is one that is becoming increasingly important, namely, synthetics. Most synthetic materials are the laboratory equivalents of such valuable natural gemstones as ruby, sapphire, and emerald, but two, strontium titanate and cubic zirconium, have no known counterpart in nature, while another, synthetic rutile, has no natural match in respect to color and transparency. The commercial synthesis of gemstones and the creation of those without natural counterparts will probably increase as the necessary growth conditions are investigated and economical manufacturing techniques developed.

To summarize, there is no quick and easy definition for the term *gemstone* which is acceptable on all counts. It covers a wide range of materials, although most of them are minerals and rocks with only a few being organics. However, it is safe to say that *ornamentation*, whether it be of the person or otherwise, is the *principal theme pervading our esteem of gemstones*. Thus, when we think of gemstones, we think first of colorful and durable mineral materials obtained from the crust of the earth. This is the traditional restriction placed upon the term *gemstone* and accounts for the reluctance to accept into the fold a host of extremely attractive rare but soft minerals and organic materials beyond those few already mentioned.

Other special terms, such as cameos, intaglios, and faceted and cabochon gems, will be fully defined in later chapters. It is time to turn our attention to examining the factors which make gemstones valuable, for it is these which must be continually kept in mind if shrewd assessments of value are to be made.

FACTORS INFLUENCING ESTEEM

The factors influencing the esteem in which gems are held are few in number but extremely important because they so directly affect value. These are *attractiveness, durability, rarity, fashion,* and *size.* They are not fixed in scope by any means and the predominance of one factor may compensate for shortcomings in another.

ATTRACTIVENESS

The fascination felt for gems is mainly a visual appreciation of their beauty. There is little doubt that beauty is the most important quality that any gem can have, for without it no gem or other ornamental gemstone object will be highly prized, regardless of what else it has to recommend it. Beauty lies mainly in vivid coloration, as in the splendid red of the ruby or the glowing green of the emerald; it can also be in outline or shape, as in the symmetry of a well-cut faceted gem or the graceful lines of a tasteful carving; or it can exist in the special optical effects which the skilled lapidary is capable of developing in such gemstones as star sapphires, catseyes, or moonstones. Brilliance in a faceted gem is of course also highly important, especially if the sparkling reflections are combined with flashes of color in highly dispersive gems. All of these, and others too numerous to mention, influence the attraction we feel for gems.

COLOR

The importance of color cannot be overemphasized. It is one of the earliest impressions registered upon our senses when we fix our attention upon any object. Studies of human response to colors show that perception of hue is best in the central part of the spectrum and decreases toward either end. Thus, yellow-green, yellow, and yellow-orange will appear brighter as a rule than the hues which range from yellow-green to violet, and from yellow-orange to red. Further, as colors are observed in the decreased light of evening, those at the extremes of the spectrum, namely red and violet, seem to become darker while those near the center tend to retain their visibility. In terms of colored gems, this means that dark red, blue, or violet gems are less likely to "hold" their hues in evening illumination than yellow, orange, or yellow-green gems. For the person contemplating buying expensive colored gem jewelry meant to be worn mainly at evening functions, it would certainly be wise to "test" the jewelry under the expected lighting conditions rather than under those so carefully provided in the jewelry store. Grave disappointments may be avoided.

An interesting sidelight to modern studies of color perception is that hues toward the violet end of the spectrum, the so-called "cool" colors, tend to depress spirits, while those toward the other or "warm" end of the spectrum tend to excite. These human reactions to color have been amply demonstrated in workshop and office environments and may possibly play important roles in personal acceptance or rejection of certain colors in gems.

The preference of individuals for specific colors is well established, but not so well known is the relative attractiveness of colored gems in general. The most attractive colors appear to be those which are pure and rich in hue, such as red, green, blue, purple, orange, and yellow. Of these hues, the first three are most attractive, while purple and orange are slightly less so. There is a substantial drop of interest in yellow. Interest also rapidly wanes in all hues which become increasingly darker or lighter. The least interest is displayed in gemstones which are some shade of brown, particularly if they tend to be quite dark. Black and white gemstones are also unattractive as a rule, although they may be in vogue for brief periods as evidenced by the lavish use of jet in the Victorian era. Colorless gems are generally unattractive unless, as in the case of faceted diamonds, they display good brilliance, preferably with good dispersion or "fire" as an added feature.

The presence of color is important even in those gems which are offered primarily for their display of optical effects, *e.g.*, the sheen in moonstone, the spangles of aventurine, or the bright lines of reflected light which appear in star and eye stones. Between two moonstones, for example, one displaying a bluish light and the other a silvery light, the blue one will be preferred to the silvery one by the majority of persons. This preference holds true in virtually all kinds of lapidary objects, whether they be faceted gems, cabochons, or carvings.

DURABILITY

The ability of gems to resist normal wear while set in jewelry is a perfectly understandable requirement and needs no supporting arguments. Durability depends upon mineralogical *hardness*, or the ability to resist abrasion, and upon *toughness*, or resistance to fracture. Some cleavable minerals, such as topaz, while quite hard and easily capable of resisting normal abrasion, are sometimes split in two by relatively weak blows. Others, such as jadeite, whose single crystals are easily cleaved, occur in compact masses where this potential weakness is overcome by the interlocking of numerous minute crystals into a material of astonishing toughness.

The generally accepted rule of thumb for classifying gemstones as durable is that they be as hard or harder than quartz. The table below shows the Mohs Scale of Hardness which is used for gemstones as well as for ordinary minerals. It merely indicates which gemstones are harder than others and does not give absolute hardnesses.

MOHS SCALE OF HARDNESS

1. Talc (softest)	6. Feldspar: *moonstone*
2. Gypsum: *satin spar, alabaster*	7. Quartz: *amethyst, citrine, etc.*
3. Calcite: *cave onyx*	8. Topaz
4. Fluorite: *"blue john"*	9. Corundum: *ruby, sapphire*
5. Apatite	10. Diamond (hardest)

Many authorities state that all gems will eventually be abraded by atmospheric dust and the traces of soil unavoidably brought into homes and buildings because these contain fine particles of quartz (hardness 7), and unless gems are harder than quartz, damage will result. However, the severity of this kind of abrasion has never been convincingly demonstrated, and it is the view of other authorities that it is very minor in effect, if it has any effect at all, and that most damage to gems results from careless treatment while being worn, or from allowing gems to bump into each other in jewelry boxes or drawers.

While durability has its unchallenged virtues, exceptions to the rule are made if the gemstone happens to possess some other outstanding quality. Perhaps the best example is opal, which is both a soft and brittle mineral (hardness 5 to 6½). It is so liable to damage while being worn that jewelers are frequently called upon to demount an opal from a customer's ring and send it off for repolishing. Despite this handicap, opal commands very high prices in fine specimens because no other gemstone can match its distinctive beauty. Other soft and weak gemstones which are considered acceptable for wear because of their outstanding beauty are moonstone, peridot, tanzanite, and the synthetic gemstone strontium titanate.

RARITY

It is human nature to treasure the rare, sometimes for rarity's sake alone. Among gems, for example, synthetic ruby has never been as highly esteemed as natural ruby because it is made in relatively enormous quantities and is therefore much too common. On the other hand, synthetic star ruby, carefully controlled from manufacture to final retail sale in cut form, is able to command a good price because it is both beautiful and considerably rarer than ordinary transparent synthetic material. While synthetic gems can be fully as handsome as their natural counterparts, natural gems of equal quality or even of much lesser quality find a ready market and sell for much higher prices. The preference for the natural is a highly important human factor.

Paradoxically, rarity, as will be shown, can be a handicap if it goes too far. It is well known among dealers in art objects, antiques, and jewels that before any person can appreciate the worth of a masterpiece, he must have pointed out to him all of the factors which make such an item desirable. In the case of well-known gems such as diamond, ruby, sapphire, and emerald, nearly every prospective buyer has heard and read about them from childhood. By the time he becomes an adult, he has firmly fixed in his mind that these gems are precious, beautiful and desirable. He has even accepted one gem, the diamond, as an indispensable part of the engagement ring. The average jeweler does not have to convince the bridegroom-to-be that he should buy his fiancé a diamond engagement ring; this has already been done for him, and the sale negotiations merely need to settle such mundane details as quality, size, and price. This happy situation for the jeweler does not apply in the case of other gems, particularly if they are not well known. Thus, the transparent andalusite from Brazil, a handsome and durable gem, is readily salable only to connoisseurs or collectors of the unusual because it is so rare and its supplies so uncertain that no one in the trade wishes to risk a promotional campaign to acquaint the public with its virtues in the hope that profitable sales will result. Because of the problems briefly touched upon above, the vast majority of retailers in gems and gem-set jewelry avoid handling rare or unusual gemstones and stick to the "safe" standard gems which need no educational campaign to insure a supply of informed customers.

FASHION

The factor of fashion is closely related to those of attractiveness and rarity. What was considered attractive yesterday may not be attractive today, and today's standards may be displaced by others tomorrow. By today's standards, black gems are not attractive and are seldom worn except in the case of the small black-dyed onyx-chalcedony plaques sometimes seen in rings. But in the 19th century it became fashionable to wear jet jewelry for mourning, sometimes in incredible quantity. In the the same century, the opal, much maligned because of superstitious beliefs in its evil powers, became fashionable after Queen Victoria restored it to favor by wearing opal-set jewelry whenever it was appropriate to do so. Near the turn of the century and for about 15 years afterward, the *art nouveau* style reigned in the world of fine arts and influenced the design of jewelry. Because the naturalistic designs were better complemented by cabochon gems, they were used in much larger quantities than before and of course required the use of gemstones suited to cabochon cutting rather than those transparent kinds traditionally cut into faceted gems.

A curious instance of fashion turning against a gem because of the factor of rarity involves the pearl. At one time it was fashionable among the wealthy to wear chokers, necklaces, bracelets, rings, diadems, and chatelaines strung or set with natural pearls. In the early 1900s when Mikimoto and other Japanese perfected the techniques of producing cultured pearls in large quantities, the market in natural pearls suffered a disastrous setback from which it has never fully recovered. The extremely close resemblance of cultured pearls of good quality to natural pearls at once placed pearl in the category of common instead of rare and resulted in a greatly lessened demand for natural examples by those who wore them as symbols of wealth and position. While natural pearls are still highly esteemed, they no longer occupy their once exalted fashion position.

SIZE

The use of the expression "bigger and better" summarizes this human factor. Increasing size in gems is symbolic of greater wealth and higher position, with some exceptions of course. Frankly, few persons can look upon a ten-carat diamond worn in an engagement ring without being impressed, especially if the engagement rings of their friends carry diamonds of only one carat or thereabouts. Naturally, prices asked for such large gems are usually much more per carat than for much smaller gems. However, size is also esteemed for other reasons besides prestige. For example, in gemstones which occur in paler colors, such as aquamarine, very small gems, say about one or two carats, are so "washed out" in color that they simply are not as beautiful as those which are ten carats or more in weight. For this reason, the preferred size range for aquamarines is between ten and fifteen carats, and perhaps somewhat more. Such gems are sufficiently intense in color to be beautiful, yet are not so large that they become awkward to wear in rings. Conversely, some natural gemstones are so intense in color that excessively large cut specimens merely appear black, especially under evening light, and therefore the price demanded for oversized examples may actually be less per carat than for smaller sizes. A good example of a gem of this sort is dark green tourmaline.

Wearability must also be considered when choosing the size of a gemstone. Some popular gems like amethyst are available in enormous sizes, however, some of the oversized gems may be completely unwearable, even as pendants. While the public's desire for large smoky quartz, citrines, amethyst and aquamarine stones was high in the 1940s and 1950s in the Retro jewelry era, the pendulum has now swung to smaller, better quality stones.

II
SUPPLY AND MARKETING
INFORMATION

A LONG CHAIN OF EVENTS MARKS THE PROGRESS OF ROUGH GEMSTONES from the time they leave the mine to the time they are placed before a buyer, transformed into brilliant objects of beauty. At each stage the parcel of rough is examined by an expert whose livelihood depends on the infallibility of his judgment. Gradually the parcel is sorted out into various grades, from poor to superlative, and defective pieces removed. When at last the rough reaches the hands of the cutter it is subjected to the most critical scrutiny yet, for it is here that the promise in the colorful crystals is converted into gleaming, salable reality. The personal attention that each gemstone receives along the way contributes to the final cost and it is the purpose of this chapter to explain the workings of the system for the benefit of those who wish to deal in gems or wish to know how the gems they own came into being and why they are so costly.

NATURAL RARITY OF GEMSTONES

As mentioned before, most gemstones are minerals or rocks and occur in favored sites in the earth's crust or in the gravels that result from the weathering of rocks. It is truly remarkable how little of the millions of tons of minerals exposed to our view consists of beautifully crystallized minerals such as might be useful for gems. Of those that seem useful for gems, only a very few actually meet the standards, that is, are sufficiently beautiful, durable, rare, and large enough to be cut into salable stones. As a class of natural objects, gemstones are exceedingly rare while rarer still are those which will produce first-class gems. Thus one of the factors that makes gems esteemed, *rarity*, is already an inherent feature.

GEMSTONE MINING

Aside from the highly mechanized and efficient diamond-mining methods used in Africa, most gemstones are recovered from small pits sunk in gem-bearing gravel deposits or from short tunnels and shafts in hard rock. While extensive gem-bearing gravels containing rubies, sapphires, spinels, and other splendid gemstones occur in Sri Lanka, Thailand, and Myanmar (Burma), large quantities of topsoil and sterile gravel must be excavated before the layers containing gems are uncovered. After a pit is sunk with much labor and cost, the operators cannot be certain that they will find a productive deposit underneath. Many years ago it occurred to someone to mechanically mine, wash, and sort the gem-bearing gravels of the Mogok district in Myanmar under the reasonable assumption that modern methods and machinery could surely take the place of the traditional native labor and make mining far more efficient and profitable. Accordingly, the Burma Ruby Mines, Ltd. was organized and set in operation, but after some years of successful operation it was forced to dissolve in the face of vanishing profits. Gem mining in Myanmar is now back to the unmechanized state where it started and where it will probably remain for many years to come. In Sri Lanka, mechanical recovery and washing of gravels has never been tried extensively, due partly to the attitude of the people, who prefer that their native gemstone resources be exploited slowly over a period of many years instead of all at once. Naturally this prevents oversupply problems and assures that the miners will have gemstone resources to mine for generations.

A special kind of gemstone deposit is known as a *pegmatite*, or a very coarse-grained mass of quartz and feldspar usually occurring as a vein-like body enclosed in the country rock. Practically all aquamarines, morganites, topazes and tourmalines come from "pockets" or cavities in pegmatites, especially from those in Brazil, Madagascar, and California. Unfortunately, these gem-bearing deposits are not extensive as a rule, some being merely a few feet thick and containing only one or two productive pockets in which the crystals are of gem quality. Sometimes a pegmatite yielding good gemstones is exhausted in a few months, and the miners must abandon the deposit and search for another which shows signs of promising mineralization. Unfortunately, there is no way of being certain that gem-bearing pockets exist in a pegmatite unless the gemstones actually appear in the outcrop. Unless better means are found to detect the presence of gemstones beneath the surface, pegmatite gemstones will become increasingly scarce and more expensive. Many of the famous pegmatites of Brazil, Madagascar, and California are now exhausted, with fewer and fewer new finds being made every year.

In those mines where gemstones persist in depth, notably in the "pipe" diamond deposits of Africa, costs of mining steadily increase with depth, as is true of any underground mine. Only by the exercise of ingenuity in developing more efficient methods of mining has the De Beers Syndicate been able to provide diamonds at reasonable cost. Even so, costs in this area are rising as rapidly as they are in other segments of the economy and have been reflected in the recently imposed price rises for rough diamonds.

Mining for gemstones is, at best, a precarious business. Deposits are small, returns uncertain, and often profits so meager that discouraged miners leave the fields to enter other pursuits. While the gemstones themselves are "free" for the taking, it can be readily appreciated that all of the easily available deposits have long since been skimmed off, leaving those whose exploitation is possible only at considerable cost. In the long run, we may be certain that natural gemstones will become increasingly scarce and more costly.

DISPOSITION OF ROUGH

In nearly every gemstone deposit, the truly useful material is a very small percentage of the whole, on the order of two to five percent by weight of crystals which appear to be reasonably free of flaws, of good color, and of usable size. In order to make mining profitable, it is customary among miners to adopt one of several schemes for selling their production. One method is to lump all of the production into a "mine run" lot, containing all grades from bad to good, and sell the lot in toto. The other method is to grade the production at the mine and sell smaller lots at prices adjusted according to quality. The drawback to the first scheme is that very few buyers are able to pay for and dispose of large mine-run lots, forcing the miners to wait a discouragingly long time before the right customer comes along. The drawback to the second scheme is that buyers eagerly take top-grade rough but are reluctant to purchase lots of inferior material. Often the result is that the miners are "stuck" with considerable gem rough, which costs them as much to mine as the best grades, but for which there appears to be no market. If such miners had based their prices on the expectation of selling *all* grades, it is easy to see how their mining venture would become unprofitable. To avoid this disaster, miners usually place high enough prices on their readily saleable grades to assure themselves of at least recovering costs. Any further sales of poorer grades then become pure profit.

The same problem faces the field buyer who is usually headquartered in a large city, preferably with export facilities, and who sends his agents into the field to buy directly from the miners. Should he sell his purchases "as is" or should he classify the rough into parcels of various grades? In some instances, the decision is easy because of the nature of the gem material itself, as in the case of the tigereye quartz from Griqualand in South West Africa, which is remarkably consistent in quality and needs little sorting to be satisfactory to foreign customers. Other gemstones, usually massive types, also can be sold in nearly the same condition that they leave the mine, e.g., labradorite, amazonite, rose quartz, and rock crystal.

However, in a gem-producing region such as Minas Gerais in Brazil, where a bewildering variety of minerals and gemstones can be found in a single pegmatite, the field buyers purchase promising lots from the miners and ship them back to their city headquarters. Here the mine production is carefully washed and experts go over each piece, rejecting obviously unsuitable material, selecting suitable material, and placing the "doubtfuls" in a separate pile to be examined more closely at a later time. Well-crystallized specimens that have escaped damage are examined critically. Those that promise to bring more as rough gem material are ruthlessly broken up, to the distress of the mineral-collecting fraternity, while those which promise to fetch a better price as specimens are set aside.

FIG. 1.
Gem dealer Paulo Nercessian of Rio de Janeiro, holding a very large kunzite crystal.

By the time the sorting process is over, the field buyer has a series of parcels of (a) top-quality facet material, (b) lesser-quality facet material, either poorer in color or containing flaws, (c) cabochon or carving material, (d) specimen material, and (e) waste. While the dealer usually has no problem in disposing of all classes from (a) to (d), he realizes that his waste, if it can be sold, adds pure profit to his operation. If the waste consists of small chips, such as rock crystal, it can be sold to makers of fused quartz and glass; if it consists of colorful massive material or very small transparent gemstone bits, it can be sold to makers of tumbled gems who are thereby saved the trouble of crushing the rough material for themselves.

The above grades are not fixed by any means, and exceptional material may be placed in a "gem" category, usually a very small part of the whole, but so superior in quality and size that the sale of this one parcel may return the cost of the entire mine production lot. The same is true of large and fine mineral specimens such as undamaged crystals of beryl, tourmaline, spodumene, or topaz. Fig. 1 shows Paulo Nercessian, a buyer of Rio de Janeiro, holding an enormous crystal of gem-quality kunzite which was saved out from a large quantity of other kunzite and sold separately as a unique museum specimen.

COBBING AND TESTING

When time permits, the field buyer turns his attention to the pile of "doubtful" material mentioned above. This contains crystals and fragments of potential gem material which needs to be separated from waste. A typical example may be a large quartz crystal in which smoky quartz alternates with citrine, with the latter of course being much more valuable than the former. The crystal may also contain flawed areas which must be separated from the clean areas, and usually the base is milky quartz of no value whatsoever. Such a crystal is turned over to an expert "cobber," or a workman skilled in the use of small whippy hammers which he utilizes delicately to remove unsatisfactory material as shown in Fig. 2. Very large sections may be separated by the use of presses or diamond saws. Despite the loss of weight necessarily incurred in the cobbing process, the remaining material is

FIG. 2
Cobbing citrine quartz to remove flawed areas.

upgraded to such an extent that it brings a price which more than makes up for the weight loss and cost of labor.

Quartzes and other transparent gemstones are also tested by immersion methods, a technique which will be elaborated upon in a succeeding chapter. In brief, the crystals are immersed in an oil which enables the expert to see inside and detect the presence of flaws. This is important not only because of gem-cutting considerations but also because much quartz is sold for the making of electronic devices and needs to be free of flaws and other defects if it is to be useful. Much of our quartz gemstone production from Brazil is sold at reasonable cost only because it is a by-product of mining principally directed toward the recovery of electronic-grade quartz crystals.

HEAT TREATMENT

Another important test applied to certain rough gemstones is heat treatment to determine if colors can be improved thereby. Heat treatment is accomplished by the field buyer upon such gemstones as citrines containing smoky overtones (the smoky color is driven off), amethysts (changed to rich brownish-red or green), yellow topaz (changed to pink) and certain greenish aquamarines (changed to blue). He may test a few specimens out of each lot and then certify that the color change will occur, or he may heat-treat all specimens and charge more for the final product accordingly.

DISPOSITION OF ROUGH IN SRI LANKA, THAILAND, AND MYANMAR (BURMA)

Gemstone production in these countries is mainly in the form of single crystals found in extensive gem-bearing gravel deposits. All mining operations are small in scale, with numerous parties forming temporary companies to exploit limited patches of ground after the necessary licensing arrangements and financing have been accomplished. In Thailand and Myanmar, entire families and their relatives are engaged in mining, sorting of rough, and selling, usually financing their own operations from sales proceeds. In Sri Lanka, on the other hand, the financing is commonly provided by a gem merchant who receives all the rough, sells it, and divides the proceeds among all parties in the venture according to a traditional sharing procedure. In both countries, exceptional specimens may be saved out to be cut in behalf of the mining company and sold as cut gems in the anticipation of receiving a larger profit than would have been realized from the sale of the rough. The tendency in both countries, and, in recent years in Brazil, is to cut important rough rather than to sell it. Needless to say this means that buyers from abroad are finding it increasingly difficult to purchase good rough. However, while this has affected the cutting industry in such gem-consuming countries as the United States, England, France, and Germany, and has markedly increased the price of such rough as can be imported, the cost of finished gems has remained about the same. This is so because the increased duty levied against cut gems as compared to rough has been compensated for by the cheaper cutting charges prevailing in gem-producing countries. At present, rough supplies from Myanmar are almost nonexistent because of regulations imposed upon the miners who must sell their productions through government agencies. Visitors report that as a result of this policy the miners are hoarding their good material and supplying the government agents only with poor gem rough, which of course is virtually unsaleable. They also report that much high quality gem material is smuggled across borders into adjacent countries where reasonable prices are obtained for their stones.

EXPORT PROBLEMS

It would be exceedingly naive for any inexperienced in travel to a gem-producing country such as Brazil, Myanmar, Thailand, Madagascar or Sri Lanka and expect to bring back quantities of rough or cut gems at bargain prices. First of all, the local experts are fully aware of values, some of them having been born and raised in families whose business for generations has been buying and selling rough and cut gemstones. There is no reason to believe that they are ignorant, a view which unfortunately is held altogether too often by visitors from abroad. Second, the natives realize that the major portion of their income is derived from regular dealings with foreign customers who are trustworthy members of the gem trade. If they sold anything but trash to the casual visitor, they would imperil their relations with their important customers, and of course, this they cannot afford to do.

In the case of individuals who wish to import gems and rough on a permanent basis, numerous problems exist, which in variety and complexity are simply amazing to a person accustomed to dealing with the relatively simple customs procedures of his own country. Such complexities and associated problems are to be expected in Brazil and other Latin American countries, and also in Madagascar, Mozambique, Myanmar, Thailand, Sri Lanka, India, and others. Learning how to thread one's way through the maze of regulations is partially accomplished by obtaining the appropriate publication issued by the U.S. Department of Commerce for the country with which the dealer wishes to trade. But mastery of publications explaining regulations is only the beginning. In Latin American countries, particularly Brazil, customs regulations exist *between states*, and govern closely who can mine, sell, transport, and export gemstones, with licensing and fees required at virtually every turn, along with generous contributions to the appropriate official's personal welfare fund. Furthermore, chicanery and double-dealing are rife, until it becomes virtually impossible to do anything by one's self. It is for this reason that most successful importers seek out a trustworthy agent in the country concerned to do business in their behalf, partly as a legal expert, partly as a diplomat, partly as a gem expert, and partly as an exporter. Further complications arise as a result of currency exchange problems, especially in Brazil, where inflation has made the cruzeiro drop drastically in value, sometimes overnight.

The lot of the gemstone importer is not a happy one these days, and the rising prices of rough reflect the "squeeze" being put upon him by circumstances described above.

Disposition of Rough Gemstones in the United States

Gemstones are today imported by a number of small to large dealers, some acting as retailers, some as wholesalers, and others principally to supply their own cutting establishments. To assure themselves of quality, most importers make periodic trips to the gem-producing countries, sighting the various lots offered for sale and bargaining for those which appear satisfactory. These are immediately set aside and turned over to their local agents who then take on the responsibility of shipping the materials to the United States.

At home, the lots are again subjected to careful examination and resorting as necessary into smaller parcels for which the importer has customers. His pricing is once more based upon the probability of sale of choicer material and the possible sale of poorer grades. After prices are established, the material is offered to smaller rough gemstone dealers, to professional lapidaries, and to individuals, mostly amateur gem cutters. Some importers who are expert in mineral specimens make a practice of importing these also. A smaller number of importers specialize in only one kind of gemstone, such as emerald, opal, etc., which they may sell solely as rough or which they sell as finished gems after sending off the rough to professional lapidaries for necessary cutting.

Because of large variations in quality even within a graded parcel of rough, dealers offer two buying plans to customers, each presenting certain advantages. The first plan is to buy "grab" lots, where the dealer merely takes a quantity of rough from the parcel without further inspection, and sells it at a certain price.

The second plan is "selection," where a large quantity is sent to the buyer for inspection and selection, and the rejected material returned, or the buyer selects personally at the salesroom. Since the buyer is certain to choose only the best within the parcel, this privilege is charged for at a rate substantially higher than for "grabbing."

Sale of Cut Gems

Cut gems may be obtained from domestic professional lapidaries or imported from abroad already cut. The choice depends on cost and the cutting quality desired. If small gems are required as "side" stones or for pavé work, it probably pays to import them already cut because labor charges abroad are enough less to compensate for the higher duty which has to be paid on cut gems as compared to rough. This scheme is followed for such gems as small diamonds, rubies, sapphires, emeralds, and zircons. Excellent cutting work is done in Idar-Oberstein, Germany, in Thailand, Hong Kong, and a few other places, but unsatisfactory work is common in India and Sri Lanka, and it is from the latter places that faceted gems receive the dealer label "native cut," which is to say, "poorly" cut.

After gems are received, the dealer examines all of them carefully, checks weights and qualities, and then places them in specially folded paper packets called "diamond papers." Important gems are packaged individually with carat weight, dimensions in millimeters, quality, and price per carat or per piece marked on the flap of the packet. Mediocre quality gems are often lumped together in large numbers in the same packet.

The largest quantity of cut gems in the United States is sold by specialists in this aspect of the trade to other members of the trade. They are prepared to send out "approval" selections or single gems, depending upon the requirements of jewelers, or other cut-gem dealers who happen to have a call for a certain gem not in their own stocks. The prices are wholesale or "keystone," the latter term, when affixed to a price, meaning that it is 50 percent off to the retailer. The latter may then mark up the gems to assure himself a profit and dispose of them to individual buyers not in the trade, or send them to a manufacturing jeweler to be made up into jewelry.

Diamond Marketing

While there is considerable give-and-take in the entire colored-stone marketing process, such is not the case with the diamond whose fate is closely regulated from mining to cutting. About 85 percent of the world's production of diamonds is controlled by the De Beers Syndicate which began its remarkable career many decades ago in the Union of South Africa. Not only does the syndicate control production through a miners' association, with each mine being assigned an annual production quota, it also requires the miners to sell to a centralized buying organization which assembles all of the rough and markets it in a standard, undeviating procedure.

The problem of disposing of the poor as well as the good grades of gem-quality diamonds is solved by carefully estimating the demand for cut gems in world markets and the prospective consumption of diamond crystals by individual customers, for each of whom a parcel is prepared containing crystals of all sizes and qualities. The customers are notified when their parcel is ready and they travel to London to the selling organization headquarters to inspect their parcel in a ceremony known as a "sighting." Customers have the choice of accepting or rejecting the parcel, but mostly they accept. They may now cut all of the crystals or sell off parts of the parcel which they do not desire for themselves. Thus the rough is carefully released to precisely satisfy the demand and to prevent a glut of diamonds on the market which would depress prices.

While this monopolistic practice may be abhorrent to those who believe in free trade, it does have the merit of smoothing out fluctuations in prices and thereby confers a remarkable stability to the gem diamond industry and an assurance of a certain minimum value to each diamond sold. Specific rules formulated by the Federal Trade Commission to protect buyers of cut diamonds are discussed under that gem in Chapter IV.

INVESTMENT VALUES OF GEMS

Cut gems, especially diamonds, rubies, emeralds, and others equally valuable, are often considered to be "good" investments. It is true that a large amount of money can be placed in a few top-quality gems, and if the need should arise, they can be more easily transported and disposed of than bulkier items of equal value. During past wars or severe internal conflicts within certain countries this aspect of gems proved a godsend to persons who had to flee the borders with nothing but the minimum in personal possessions. Fortunately for most persons, this kind of "investment" is not necessary, and hopefully it may never have to be.

On a long-term basis, perhaps over a period of twenty-five to fifty years, high-quality gems do tend to appreciate in monetary value; that is, a fine gem bought years ago may fetch many more dollars than it cost. However, since the dollar has depreciated in buying power during the same period, the profit may be a "paper profit" instead of a real one. If there is an actual profit it has to be computed on the basis of the buying power of the dollar at the time of purchase compared to its buying power now. Some rarer gems, notably alexandrite chrysoberyl, catseye chrysoberyl, demantoid garnet, fine blue aquamarine, and fine peridot have appreciated in value so much that old gems sold now can often realize a real profit. However, for most gems, about the best that can be said for them is that they have retained considerable real value, perhaps about 50 percent of cost. More will be said about this in subsequent paragraphs.

RESALE VALUES AND PROFIT MARGINS

Closely connected with the discussion above are resale values and the profit margins of the dealers who sold the gems. These must be discussed together since one depends upon the other. Only the naive person could believe that a $2500 diamond bought today can be sold for the same price tomorrow. While some jewelry stores will give full value on a trade-in toward another purchase of higher value, or perhaps even stretch a point and give credit toward the purchase of an item of equal value, they cannot buy gems at retail value and expect to stay in business. This is not a unique situation by any means, even though the customer may argue that the diamond he wishes to sell is not damaged in any way, as would be the case with furniture, automobiles, or other items which suffer wear and tear. The jeweler must pay for his stock in trade, the services of his sales personnel, advertising, rent, upkeep, and a host of other expenses which are unavoidable. He cannot support all these expenses without requiring a profit on each sale.

The amount of profit varies considerably even within the same class of establishment, the tendency being to "mark up" fast-selling items at a lower rate than those which sell only occasionally. Markups on diamonds, for example, may be quite uniform over much of the country because a steady demand exists for those which are to be used in engagement rings; on the other hand, colored gems, such as the emerald, ruby, and sapphire, may bear variable markups because qualities are less standardized and the demand less steady. Keen competition exists among retail jewelers and the likelihood of getting a "steal" in one store as compared to another depends upon the individual jeweler's cash-flow needs, overhead, and the current state of the local economy.

Important variables in the amount of profit taken by the dealer are costs, as mentioned above, volume of business, overhead charges, and the class of clientele being dealt with. A popular fallacy is that small decrepit stores, with obviously cheap furnishings and low overhead, offer better bargains than the larger long-established stores doing business in handsomer environments and higher rent districts. The sad truth is that one is more likely to be fleeced in the smaller store than in the larger and more impressive one. Many small stores deliberately cater to clientele who represent less trustworthy members of the community, and usually, those less informed. To protect himself from bad debts, the proprietor handles merchandise upon which there is a large profit margin, and in many instances, he will not hesitate to ask prices fully as high as those being asked in higher-class establishments for precisely the same merchandise, despite the fact that his overhead and other costs must be much lower.

Particularly to be avoided are those stores which habitually use misleading advertising terms, some examples of which are "genuine synthetic" in reference to ordinary inexpensive synthetic ring stones, or "the home of the perfect, flawless diamonds," when perfect flawless diamonds are so rare that the average reputable jeweler neither has one in stock nor could find one if he were asked to do so. Advertising of this sort causes the prudent buyer to suspect the integrity of the shop owner. On the other hand, large, long-established stores have risen to their prominent positions mainly by fairness and honesty in their dealings, for only by these means can an enviable reputation be won and a steady clientele assured. Reputable stores commonly join self-regulating trade associations such as a gem society or retail jewelers association. By joining, they commit themselves to following rigid rules of business ethics and conduct, and customers may be more assured that they will be able to get better value for their money.

While profit margins are variable for the reasons mentioned above, some general statements can be made at this time in respect to the markups on individual gems, engraved gems, and other classes of finished lapidary objects. The markups are almost always on a sliding scale, with higher markups, in percent of cost, placed upon lower-priced items, and diminishing as the price of the item goes higher and higher. The most usual exception is when low-priced items sell quickly and in quantity. Another exception is when a dealer deliberately stocks a large variety of items in order to cater to the interests of as many persons as possible, but many of these items move only slowly. In such a situation it is usual to place much higher markups on the slow-moving items to compensate the dealer for the capital tied up in them. Such markups may be several hundred percent of cost, but for normal, steady-selling items, the markup is usually 100 percent for items costing about $200 to $300, decreasing to about 50 percent for items costing $1000 and to 30 percent or less for items costing about $2000. The markup is lower still for higher-cost items, but conversely may be more than 100 percent for items in the range of several dollars to $200.

It is emphasized that the above markups are only approximate and cannot be construed as being the rule for all sales of gemstones. However, it can now be appreciated that as far as resale values are concerned, one is more likely to recover a larger share of his costs from higher-priced gems than from lower-priced ones, in particular if the gems happen to be of very high quality.

Price Trends

While the prices of diamonds are carefully controlled, this is not the case with many other gemstones, which are commonly cast upon the market in a feast-or-famine fashion because of a big "strike" of rough in some gem-producing field. The resulting fluctuation in prices follows a definite pattern. When the news of the "strike" is broadcast, field buyers rush to the mine to purchase the production. The gem material is then placed into trade channels as quickly as possible to realize a quick profit. The glut of new material rapidly finds its way into the hands of cutters and soon thereafter the market receives the cut gems. In this game, the early birds reap quick profits because they can sell a considerable number of the gems at the older and higher prices if they were uncommon to begin with. But as the news spreads throughout trade circles, the gems quickly become unsaleable except at lower and lower prices, finally reaching some bottom figure which is so attractive to investment buyers or bargain hunters that the last of the gems are finally disposed of. For some time afterward prices remain depressed, but gradually they climb back to normal levels as the "floating" gems are absorbed by the public and the scarcity, which characterized the gem before, is once again restored.

In the long-range view, such events are only temporary in their effect and the fact remains that the general trend of gem prices is upward, closely following the world economy. The table below illustrates the remarkably steady rise in prices of good-quality gems, as compiled by the famous jewelry firm of Marcus & Company of New York and published in *Fortune*, December 1931. The sudden drop in the 1930 figures reflects the disastrous stock market crash of 1929.

Retail Values of Good-Quality One-Carat Gems
(in U.S. Dollars)

	1880	1890	1900	1910	1920	1930
Emerald	$150	$175	$250	$550	$800	$650
Diamond	125	125	175	275	750	500
Ruby	75	75	100	200	300	300
Sapphire	75	75	75	150	250	200

Another compilation, by G. F. Kunz, Vice President of Tiffany & Company, and published in *Saturday Evening Post*, May 5, 1928, is also of interest because it shows the very wide spread in retail prices between gems of best quality and those of fine quality. The first table refers to those exceptional specimens called "gems" by members of the trade, while the second table provides a per-carat price comparison. The sizes of the stones are not given, but presumably they are on the order of several carats or more.

VALUES PER CARAT-MOST EXCEPTIONAL SPECIMENS
1928

Name	Price per Carat
Emerald	$6,000
Ruby	4,500
Sapphire	2,000
Diamond, green	7,000
Diamond, red	8,500
Diamond, blue	6,850
Diamond, white	3,500
Pearl, 20-grain/5 cts.	20,400
Pearl, 10-grain/2½ cts.	2,600

VALUES PER CARAT-FINE QUALITY SPECIMENS
1928

Name	Price per Carat
Emerald	$ 1,000
Ruby	1,000
Sapphire	500
Diamond	700
Pearl, 10-grain	2,000

GEMSTONE PRICING TRENDS

The following prices for top quality cut gemstones, flawless or nearly so, of best color, are taken from recent lists and other sources, including the Richard H. Jahns chapters of gem materials in the *Industrial Minerals and Rocks* issues of 1960 and 1975 of the American Institute of Mining, Metallurgical and Petroleum Engineers, and from J. Sinkankas's *Gemstones of North America*, 3rd supplement, in preparation.

DOLLARS PER CARAT — PRICE TREND

Gemstone (cut)	Color Grade	Carats	1960	1975	1990
Aquamarine	good blue	3–15	$10–$75	$45–$750	$100–$475
Emerald	fine green	1–10	250–5,000	1,500–26000	6,000–30,000
Chrysoberyl	cat's eye	3–25	60–600	100–6,400	800–7,500
Alexandrite	fine color change	3–10	50–1,200	200–9,000	2,000–30,000
Ruby	finest pure red	1–10	40–7,000	250–35,000	5,000–50,000
Star Ruby	fine color and star	1–10	60–1,800	100–15,000	1,500–25,000
Sapphire	good blue	1–10	50–400	75–1,100	500–18,000
Star Sapphire	fine color and star	1–10	30–500	50–5,500	225–10,000
Garnets	demantoid	1–10	10–300	20–500	1,000–6,000
	Grossularite				
	(Tsavorite)	1–10		100–500	800–10,000
Opal	white-body and				
	play-of-color	1–10	10–150	10–1,450	150–2,000
Quartz – Amethyst	reddish violet	5–20	4–25	5–90	35–150
Kunzite	pink to lilac	5–20	12–60	3–90	40–180
Topaz	fine imperial color	5–15	10–100	20–900	600–2,000
Tourmaline, Red	fine medium color	5–15	15–50	12–350	6–1,500
Tourmaline, Green	fine medium color	5–15	5–30	5–80	200–2,000
Turquoise	fine blue	15–20	10–50	10–75	60–225

DIAMOND CUTTING AND CHARGES

Diamond cutting is a highly specialized form of lapidary work using accurate equipment but depending upon the skill of the cutters for satisfactory final results. The cutting trade tends to cluster its shops in only a few places in the world where the necessary talented workmen, equipment suppliers, and suitable rough are readily available. Principal cutting centers are established in Antwerp, New York, and in Israel, with smaller centers in Amsterdam, London, and San Juan, Puerto Rico. In the United States the largest center is located in midtown Manhattan, New York City, but several cutters operate shops in Chicago, Los Angeles, and a few other large cities. The United States cutters confine their work mainly to gems over ⅛ carat, the smaller gems being cut in Antwerp and Israel.

Cutting charges for gems of about one carat weight range from about $85 to $100 per carat in the United States, to $150 per carat or more, depending upon the volume of business brought to the cutter and the time spent in such preliminary work as cleaving, sawing, or other preparations prior to actual faceting of the crystals. If the cutting is contracted for through a jeweler, the charges will be somewhat more.

World Cutting Centers and Charges

Cutting centers devoted to all other gemstones are numerous. Practically every major country has at least one. The largest center is the Idar-Oberstein complex in Germany, which has been in continuous operation for centuries. Here all classes of work are accomplished, including diamond cutting, ordinary facet and cabochon work, gem engraving, sculpture, drilling of beads, making of ash trays, and other types of work too numerous to mention. A number of shops are family concerns, sometimes trading their participation in the lapidary arts through several generations. Many of the shops specialize. For example, one may handle bead-drilling especially well, while another is equipped and skilled in carving. Cutting charges range from several dollars per carat for faceted gems on small orders, to pennies per carat on very large orders. Charges are adjusted according to the complexity of the cutting, the nature of the material, and the size of the finished objects. Anyone interested in sending rough to Idar-Oberstein for cutting should inquire beforehand for a schedule of charges, stating as accurately as possible what the finished objects should be, their size, style of cut, and other details. Under no circumstances should flawed or defective rough be sent, because it costs just as much to cut poor material as it does the best. Unless the rough is carefully cobbed beforehand to eliminate areas which are defective, the customer may find himself paying for cutting charges on gems or other objects of indifferent quality, perhaps not worth the cost of the charges incurred. This advice applies equally to all other cutting centers.

Since World War II, an important center has developed in Hong Kong as a result of the influx of skilled lapidaries from the ancient lapidary centers in Canton and Peking in the mainland of China. Many classes of work are accomplished, including facet and cabochon cutting, beads, small to large carvings, and utilitarian objects. The specialty, of course, is carving, an art in which the Chinese have always excelled. However, if Western motifs are wanted, problems arise because of the ingrained tradition of turning out carvings in the highly stylized Chinese manner. The carvers are quite incapable of producing a true-to-life nude figure, for example, or a realistic animal unless an accurate model is supplied which they can copy. Needless to say, prior arrangements must be carefully concluded before material is supplied and permission given to go ahead.

A much older center than Hong Kong exists in Kofu, Japan, where family shops, much like those of Idar-Oberstein, ply their art with centuries-old traditions behind them. This center has been famous for its specialized work in spheres and carvings, formerly produced from Japanese rock crystal but now replaced by imported stones. Long familiarity with rock crystal is reflected in the faceted beads and the "pagoda" stones which are turned out very cheaply in the thousands. Larger carvings are also undertaken, but the results seldom achieve the spontaneity and imagination of the Chinese carvings unless the lapidaries are furnished with accurate models. Like the Chinese, they also cannot turn out life-like nudes, animals, and other objects because of being steeped in an art tradition which rarely allowed such faithful representations to be made.

Smaller cutting centers are located in various oriental countries, mostly to handle the gems mined from local deposits. Excellent faceted work is accomplished in Myanmar, but their cabochons are sometimes of poor quality when made from the cheaper materials. In Sri Lanka, particularly in Colombo, native lapidaries have paid far too much attention in the past to recovering as much weight as possible from the rough, following a tradition of centuries' standing. Many of their faceted gems are grotesque distortions, usually brilliant to be sure, but so deep or so deformed that many resemble carrots in shape. They are fond of certain cutting styles which repeatedly crop up on their faceted gems and are almost infallible hallmarks of Sri Lanka work. The preoccupation with weight also results in star gems which look like balls because the parts underneath are not cut away but left to add weight, or lopsided stars in which the crossing points of the light streaks are far off to one side. Similar asymmetry occurs in moonstones. However, in recent decades, formal instruction in faceting with modern machinery is now resulting in the production of faceted stones of acceptable workmanship. Indian work is inclined to be equally sloppy from the Western point of view, many faceted gems having facets applied in what seems to be only an approximation of symmetry. This irregularity certainly possesses a distinctive charm when the gems are set in the colorful gold mountings of native jewelry, but larger gems, imported into Western countries and meant for setting in

Western-style jewelry, often need to be recut. However, as remarked before in the case of Sri Lanka workmanship, quality of cutting is rapidly improving, especially for stones of several carats or more.

Important cutting centers are established in London, Paris, and elsewhere in Europe. The cutting of the locally-mined pyropes in Bohemia, once an impressive business, is now at a low point but is recovering. Excellent facet and cabochon work is accomplished in London and Paris, and also in the United States, in New York, Chicago, Los Angeles, and a few other major cities. Brazil is rapidly developing an impressive native cutting industry of considerable versatility and skill in the faceting of native gemstones. They have learned how to facet oval brilliants and other more demanding styles both in standard gemstones and in the difficult kunzite. Much agate is also being processed into ash trays and other large ornamental objects. In Australia, cutting centers exist for both facet and cabochon work, the latter specializing in the treatment of opals and the former in the sapphires found in several places on the continent. New Zealand has a small cutting center specializing in the cutting and carving of nephrite and bowenite. The famous zircons of Thailand are beautifully cut by native lapidaries who also now turn out enormous quantities of quartz gems at astonishingly low prices. Custom cutting is $1 to $2 per finished carat.

All centers mentioned above accept custom work, but due to varying costs of living, customs duties, and other factors, most small work of several carats or less is now being sent to the numerous Bangkok, Thailand cutting establishments, also to Hong Kong, and even more recently, to cutting centers in China and Korea. Precious material to be carved is mostly sent to Germany if Western designs and motifs are wanted while very elaborate carvings in hardstones, including jades, are usually manufactured in China and Hong Kong. Much of the nephrite jade carvings seen in curio shops everywhere is Alaskan or British Columbian material sent to the Orient for carving and then returned to other countries where it is commonly suggested that it is carved locally. Exceptionally complex and intriguingly designed fossil ivory carvings, utilizing Alaskan and Siberian materials, are now being carved in Malaysia whose native carvers have few peers, although most of their work has hitherto been made from wood.

It is reported by all dealers consulted that facet work in Bangkok is of exceptionally high quality and the prices for small stones, generally several carats or less, made from corundums for example, are low, about U.S. $ .80-1.25/ct. for ½ ct. stones and up to several carats weight. Melee, however, is not advantageously sent to any center for cutting unless it is truly valuable material. In all cases, it is strongly advisable for all shippers of rough to carefully inspect same, then preform all stones to insure that only the best material is actually cut. For larger corundums, charges in oriental centers may reach $2.00-3.00/ct. Valuable stones of from 5 carats or more may also be sent abroad, although most owners of such rough prefer to have it cut domestically.

In addition to commercial cutters, many amateurs in the United States and elsewhere do facet work, cabochon cutting, and carving as well as larger objects as book ends, polished petrified wood cross-sections, table tops, and the like. No standard pricing is in effect: each lapidary determining for himself how much effort he must expend upon any given project and how much he must charge to realize a profit. Thus, in the case of large slabs which are processed by machine, charges may run from $1.00 to several dollars per square inch. For facet work, amateurs often charge a minimum fee of perhaps $25.00-$65.00/stone, regardless of size, and perhaps a surcharge of several dollars per carat for exceptionally large or difficult stones. The latter, including very soft stones and those that cleave or fracture readily, are listed in the main body of this book and the generally high prices demanded for them reflect the very real difficulties faced by lapidaries in completing satisfactory gems. However, aside from these rarities, very little custom work is now being done by amateur faceters because commercial centers have not only learned how to handle the difficult gemstones but also can do the work at much lower cost. This is especially true in the case of cabochons, which are now sold at prices which would scarcely pay any amateur to match. Similarly, larger objects as agate ashtrays, bookends, eggs, and the like are produced in huge quantities in South America and sold very cheaply abroad. The only projects which can be advantageously executed by amateurs include extra-large faceted gems, generally requiring extra-large faceting machinery, carvings displaying genuine artistry, and special small carved forms that are much in vogue now as components of jewels and composite sculptures.

INTERNATIONAL MONETARY QUOTATIONS—1993

The following table gives the exchange rates for converting United States dollars into foreign currencies. Particular attention should be paid to those currencies marked with an asterisk (*) because their instability causes large changes in short periods of time; obtain latest quotations from a bank before contracting for materials or services.

WEIGHTS AND MEASURES USED IN THE GEM TRADE

Rough and cut gemstones are sold either by weight or size, the latter being used mostly for cabochon gems, and weight, in carats, for faceted gems. However, if cabochon gems are made from very precious material such as catseye chrysoberyl, emerald, opal, etc., they are sold by weight; conversely, very cheap faceted gems such as rock crystal, smoky quarts and some synthetics, may be sold by diameter size (expressed in millimeters).

Rough gemstones of the cheaper sorts are sold by the pound or by the kilogram. Somewhat more expensive types are sold by the ounce, and most faceting material and precious cabochon material is sold by the gram or even by the carat. Massive gemstones may also be sold in the form of slabs, generally about $\frac{3}{16}$" to $\frac{1}{2}$" thick, using the square inch as the cost unit.

Conversion Table of Weights and Measures

Unit	Equivalent
Pound, avoirdupois (lb.)	16 ounces .454 kilogram 453.60 grams 2268.0 carats
Ounce, avoirdupois (oz.)	28.53 grams 141.75 carats
Kilogram (kg.)	1000 grams 5000 carats 2.2046 pounds 35.25 ounces
Gram (gm.)	5 carats
Carat (ct.)	$\frac{1}{5}$ gram 100 "points"
Point (pt.)	$\frac{1}{100}$ carat
Grain (gn.)	$\frac{1}{5}$ carat
Inch (in.)	25.40 millimeters
Millimeter (mm.)	approx. $\frac{1}{25}$ inch

International Monetary Quotations

Country	Monetary Unit	Equivalent in $	$1 Buys
Argentina	Peso (100 centavos)	1.010	.99 centavos
Australia	Dollar (100 cents)	.6915	1.4461 dollars
Austria	Schilling	.08746	11.43 schilling
Bahrain	Dinar	2.6522	.3771
Belgium	Franc (1200 centimes)	.2994	33.39 francs
Brazil	Cruzeiro	.0000279	35,781.00 cruzeiros
Canada	Dollar (100 cents)	.7885	1.2683 dollars
Chile	Peso	.002544	393.05 pesos
China	Renminbi	.1749	5.7190
Colombia	Peso (100 centavos)	.001510	662.15 pesos
Czechoslovakia	Korun (100 hellers)	.0356	28.02 korunen
Denmark	Krone(100 ore)	.1606	622.69 kroner
Ecuador	Sucre	.000535	1870.03 sucres
Egypt	Pound (100 piastres)	.2994	3.3405
Finland	Markka	.18061	5.5368
France	France (100 centimes)	.18248	5.48 francs
Germany	Deutschmark (100 pfennige)	.6159	1.6237 marks
Great Britain	Pound (20 schillings)	1.5350	.6515 pounds
Greece	Drachma (100 lepta)	.004539	220.30 drachmas
Hong Kong	Dollar (100 cents)	.12939	7.7287 dollars
Hungary	Forint	.0115942	86.25 forints
India	Rupee (100 naye paise)	.03219	31.07 rupees
Indonesia	Rupiah (100 sens)	.0004811	2078.53 rupees
Israel	Shekel	.3746	2.6692 shekels
Italy	Lira (100 centesimi)	.0006779	1475.14 liras
Japan	Yen (100 sen)	.008973	111.45 yen
Jordan	Dinar	1.5874	.6723 dinar
Kuwait	Dinar	3.3272	.3006 dinar
Lebanon	Pound (100 piastres)	.000577	1734.00 pounds
Malaysia	Ringgit	.3891	2.57 ringgits
Malta	Lira	2.7027	.3700 lira
Mexico	Peso (100 centavos)	.3201024	3.1240 pesos

International Monetary Quotations (cont.)

Country	Monetary Unit	Equivalent in $	$1 Buys
Myanmar	Rupee	.0288	34.72 rupees
Netherland	Guilder (100 cents)	.5493	1.8205 guilders
New Zealand	Dollar (100 cents)	.5385	1.8570 dollars
Norway	Krone (100 ore)	.1455	6.8731 krone
Pakistan	Rupee (100 paisa)	.0375	26.68 rupees
Peru	New Sol (100 centavos)	.5287	1.89 new sols
Philippines	Peso (100 centavos)	.3788	26.40 pesos
Portugal	Escudo (100 centavos)	.006456	154.90 escudos
Saudi Arabia	Riyal (20 gurshes)	.26702	3.7450 riyals
Singapore	Dollars (100 cents)	.6184	1.6170 dollars
Slovak Republic	Koruna	.0356125	28.08 korunas
South Africa	Rand (100 cents)	.3138	3.1868 rands
South Korea	Won	.0012470	801.90 wons
Spain	Peseta (100 centimos)	.008083	123.71 pesetas
Sri Lanka	Kyat	.1447	6.91 kyats
Sweden	Krona (100 ore)	.1363	7.3391 krona
Switzerland	Franc (100 centimes)	.6764	1.4785 francs
Taiwan	Dollar (100 cents)	.038911	25.70 dollars
Thailand	Baht (100 satang)	.03964	25.23 bahts
United Arab	Dirham	.2723	3.6725 dirhams
Uruguay	New Peso (100 centesimos)	.253742	3.94 new pesos
Venezuela	Bolivar (100 centimos)	.01165	85.84 bolivars

III
ROUGH GEMSTONES

THE FOLLOWING SECTIONS DISCUSS IMPORTANT PROPERTIES and characteristics of rough gemstones which the buyer must take into consideration when making his purchases. It is not within the scope of this catalog to explain the causes of these properties and characteristics, or to describe the operation of the several gemological instruments which will be mentioned from time to time. The reader desiring more information should consult one of the gemological textbooks listed in the Bibliography. The last part of this chapter provides a complete and detailed listing of the gemstones which have been used by both commercial and amateur lapidaries. Each entry gives pertinent remarks designed to assist the reader in becoming a discriminating buyer.

FACET-GRADE MATERIALS

Obviously, the first consideration in choosing material for faceted gems is that it be transparent enough to permit the development of the brilliance for which faceted gems are mainly valued. Cloudy to translucent gemstones, and even those which are quite opaque, are sometimes cut into faceted gems, but they cannot be as spectacularly beautiful as those which are perfectly clear inside. Occasionally, highly translucent chrysocolla chalcedony, smithsonite, idocrase, serpentine, and other normally massive materials are facet-cut and show enough diffuse reflection from the back facets to make them glow in a rather pleasing manner.

Ideally, however, facet material should be completely "clean," or free of flaws of any kind such as cracks, partly developed cleavages, or solid inclusions or cavities containing liquids or gases. Common inclusions consist of layers of minute gas- or liquid-filled cavities, the shape of the layers suggesting the name "veil" or "veil-type" inclusions. Other common inclusions are hollow openings or solid inclusions, of small diameter and great length, often resembling bundles of hairs in parallel position. While inclusions of this kind serve useful purposes in cabochon gems, they are generally regarded as defects in facet-grade material.

EFFECTS OF FLAWS AND INCLUSIONS

Ordinary cracks and fissures are abundant in many gemstones but may also arise during trimming of the rough by miners and dealers. Whenever possible, cracked rough should be avoided for the reasons explained below. If the edge of a crack intrudes into a clean area, one may be sure that the base of the crack extends deeper than the eye can see, because its narrowest part is thinner than one wave length of light and thus becomes invisible. Despite its invisibility, the damage exists and it may happen that during cutting the crack will open farther. This is likely to occur in kunzite, topaz, tourmaline, and clear opal, but it could happen in other gemstones. In the case of kunzite, such cracks have been known to open progressively during cutting, despite all attempts of the lapidary to cut past them, until finally the partly finished gem falls in two. The small cracks around the periphery of transparent tourmaline crystals and those in the clear "cherry" and "honey" opals of Mexico are also likely to continually expand during shaping, until the stone is ground to a ridiculously small size or falls into pieces. For these

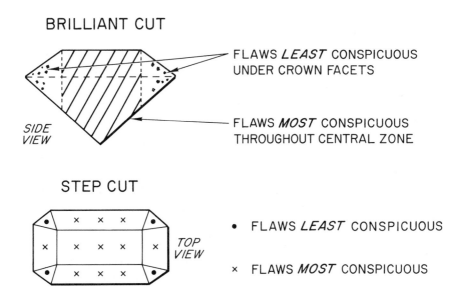

BRILLIANT CUT

FLAWS *LEAST* CONSPICUOUS
UNDER CROWN FACETS

FLAWS *MOST* CONSPICUOUS
THROUGHOUT CENTRAL ZONE

SIDE VIEW

STEP CUT

TOP VIEW

• FLAWS *LEAST* CONSPICUOUS

× FLAWS *MOST* CONSPICUOUS

FIG. 3
Placement of small flaws in round brilliant and step-cut gems to disguise their presence.

reasons, it is wise not to accept transparent rough in which well-developed cracks point toward clear interior areas.

Another drawback to leaving cracks in finished gems is that the slight surface openings may pick up polishing powder from the lap or create a series of small scores behind the crack opening which interrupt the smoothness of the polished facet. From the standpoint of brilliance and clean reflections, cracks are unsightly if allowed to remain near the center of the gem, because they will be repeatedly reflected until the gem seems to contain dozens of cracks instead of merely one or two. This effect is most disastrous in step-cut gems and least noticeable in round brilliants, particularly if the cutter places the flaws near the girdle facets as shown in Fig. 3. In some instances, notably in emeralds, numerous small, uniformly distributed flaws create acceptable gems which appear to "glow" rather than to sparkle. Such numerous inclusions are called *jardin*, or "garden."

If cracks or flaws cannot be avoided, the rough should be selected on the basis of (1) uniformity and small size of flaws, and (2) location of flaws near the periphery of the rough gemstone where they can be cut away or hidden beneath girdle facets. Under no circumstances should rough be accepted which contains

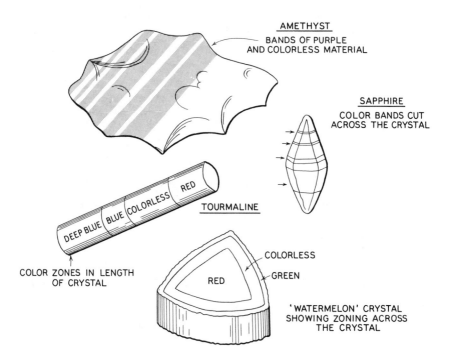

FIG. 4
Color distribution in gem rough.

flaws in the center of the clear area. This rough cannot be used unless it is sliced through the flaw itself and two smaller clean gems made instead of one large one.

COLOR AND COLOR DISTRIBUTION

In many gemstones, color tends to be uniformly distributed in the rough, and the lapidary's only concern is that of cutting the largest gem consistent with the shape of the rough. In other gemstones, however, the color may be unevenly distributed or even changeable in character from place to place as shown in Fig. 4. Amethyst is frequently an offender, with its color confined to narrow bands with colorless material between. If these bands appear edge-up as one looks down upon the gem, they will be easily noticeable and detract from the appearance. The skilled lapidary carefully notes their position and orients the rough in such a manner during shaping that the bands will lie approximately parallel to the top surface of the gem. Thus if one buys amethyst rough, it is necessary to look for this defect and select only those pieces in which it will be possible to place the bands correctly and still obtain a good yield.

Sometimes color occurs in only one spot or area, the rest of the rough being pale in hue or even colorless. If the rough is shaped as shown in Fig. 5, with the spot of color placed at the apex of the pavilion, the finished gem will be "flooded" with color and could appear quite handsome.

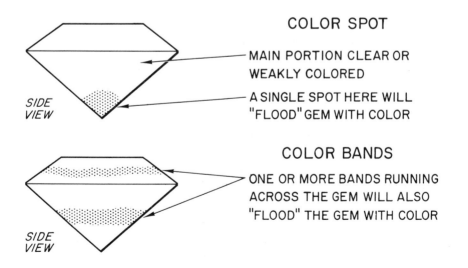

COLOR SPOT

MAIN PORTION CLEAR OR
WEAKLY COLORED

A SINGLE SPOT HERE WILL
"FLOOD" GEM WITH COLOR

SIDE VIEW

COLOR BANDS

ONE OR MORE BANDS RUNNING
ACROSS THE GEM WILL ALSO
"FLOOD" THE GEM WITH COLOR

SIDE VIEW

FIG. 5
Utilizing spots or bands of color properly when cutting gems.

A particularly troublesome color problem arises in gemstones which show marked differences in color depending upon the direction within the crystal. When two colors appear, the effect is called *dichroism* and may be present in such gemstones as tourmaline, beryl, apatite, benitoite, ruby, sapphire, and zircon. The effect is often so strong in tourmaline crystals that it can be easily detected with the unaided eye. The dichroic effect is shown diagrammatically in Fig. 6. Very commonly, the color along the length of the crystal, or the direction of the optic axis, is a disagreeable shade of olive which is sometimes so dark that it seems black. However, looking through the sides of the crystal, the color is a much more pleasing shade of yellow-green. Figure 6 shows how a step-cut gem must be placed in such a crystal if the final color is to be pleasing.

In some dichroic gems the lapidary reverses the procedure to obtain the best "face-up" color. For example, the best color in a pink tourmaline is seen looking *down* along the crystal axis instead of across; thus the gem has to be cut so that the top facets lie across the crystal instead of parallel to its length. Other dichroic gemstones that require this orientation are ruby and sapphire and some beryls. To be certain of the proper orientation, some cutters use a small instrument called a *dichroscope* which separates the two colors clearly and enables the skilled user to tell which direction in the rough gemstone would produce the best results.

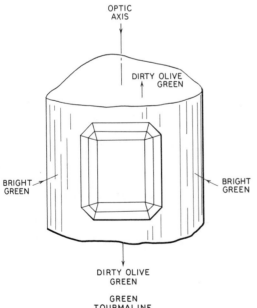

OPTIC
AXIS

DIRTY OLIVE
GREEN

BRIGHT
GREEN

BRIGHT
GREEN

DIRTY OLIVE
GREEN

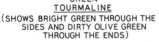

GREEN
TOURMALINE
(SHOWS BRIGHT GREEN THROUGH THE
SIDES AND DIRTY OLIVE GREEN
THROUGH THE ENDS)

Fig. 6
Dichroism in a tourmaline crystal showing how a gem is positioned to obtain the best finished appearance.

In still other kinds of gemstones, *three* colors occur in the crystals according to direction, and the effect then is given the name *trichroism*. It is more difficult to orient a gem properly in such crystals, but again the dichroscope is helpful. The cutter examines such crystals with care to observe the separate colors. Only two colors can be seen at one time, but by turning the crystal about he eventually detects the third color. He then makes a choice of direction based upon the most pleasing and strongest color, remembering that now at least two of the three colors will blend into a combined hue. Some experience is necessary in the cutting of such crystals, but once the tricks have been learned it is not a difficult procedure. Striking trichroic colors are seen in iolite (pale yellow, pale blue, deep blue) and in facet-grade andalusite (yellow, green, red).

It now only remains to say that in a third class of gemstones there is no color difference according to direction and of course no inspection of the rough is required with tile dichroscope, the lapidary needing merely to look for possible patchiness or zoning of color. Some gemstones in this class are garnet, opal, natural glasses (tektites), obsidian, and spinel. Those gemstones that would normally show dichroism or trichroism but are composed of a great many minute interlocked crystals also behave in this fashion, e.g., jadeite and serpentine. If highly translucent specimens of these gemstones are held before the dichroscope, no color changes will be detected.

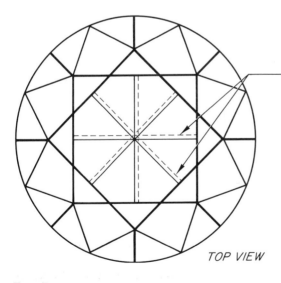

BACK FACET JUNCTIONS
APPEAR "DOUBLED"
AS VIEWED THROUGH
TOP OF GEM

TOP VIEW

FIG. 7
A faceted zircon gem showing how the back facets appear doubled due to double-refraction.

The table on page 39 shows the principal gemstones exhibiting pronounced dichroism or trichroism. Strong color differences require proper orientation if satisfactory gems are to result.

EFFECTS OF DOUBLE REFRACTION

The property of *double refraction* occurs in many gemstones, and when strong, must be taken into consideration when purchasing rough. In poorly cut zircons, sphenes, or synthetic rutiles ("titania"), a displeasing "blurry" appearance is seen as one looks down on the top of the gem because the junctions between facets seem doubled (Fig. 7). Double refraction is an inherent property which cannot be eliminated, but its effects can be reduced by skillful orientation of the rough, if the latter is of the proper shape to begin with. In some crystals, as in the zircon, there is only one direction along which double refraction is at a minimum, as shown in Fig. 8. If the faceted gem is cut so that its top facets lie *across* this direction, the least amount of blurring will be seen when one looks down upon the gem. In other crystals, there are several directions in which double refraction is least, sphene for example, and the knowledgeable buyer must examine each crystal very carefully to be sure that he picks those most likely to produce good results.

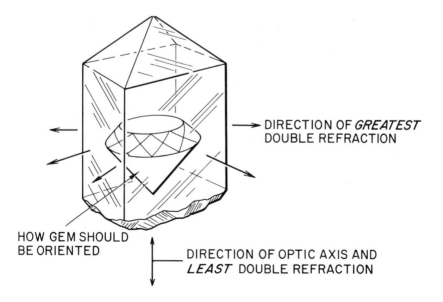

DIRECTION OF *GREATEST* DOUBLE REFRACTION

HOW GEM SHOULD BE ORIENTED

DIRECTION OF OPTIC AXIS AND *LEAST* DOUBLE REFRACTION

FIG. 8
How a faceted gem should be oriented within a zircon crystal to obtain least double-refraction.

COMMON GEMSTONES SHOWING
PRONOUNCED DICHROISM OR TRICHROISM

Name	Apparent Color	Colors Seen in Dichroscope	Contrast
Andalusite	brownish	green, red, yellow	strong
Axinite	brown	brown, violet, red	strong
Benitoite	blue	blue, colorless	strong
Beryl, aquamarine	blue	blue, colorless	distinct
Chrysoberyl, alexandrite	green (daylight)	green, yellow, red	strong
Chrysoberyl, alexandrite	red (artif. light)	green, reddish-yellow, red	strong
Corundum, ruby	red	red, orange-red	strong
Corundum, sapphire	blue	blue, pale green-blue	strong
Enstatite	brown	red-brown, green, yellow	strong
Epidote	brown	brown, green, yellow-green	strong
Iolite	blue	dark blue, paler blue, yellow	strong
Sphene	green	green, pale brown, pale yellow	distinct
Sphene	yellow	yellow, brown, pale green	distinct
Spodumeme, kunzite	lilac	violet, pink, colorless	strong
Tourmaline, rubellite	red	dark red, pink	strong
Tourmaline, indicolite	blue	dark blue, pale blue	strong
Tourmaline, green	green	olive-green, pale green	strong
Tourmaline dravite	brown	dark brown, pale red-brown	strong
Zircon	blue	blue, colorless	strong
Zoisite	brown	pale blue, dark blue, pink	distinct
tanzanite	blue		distinct

NOTE: For a complete list, consult one of the standard gemological texts listed in the Bibliography.

Except for the gemstones mentioned and a number of the rarely cut species, such as the carbonates, the effects of double refraction can be largely ignored when purchasing rough. In the case of synthetic rutile, however, it is extremely important, and every effort should be made to determine the optical axis before cutting begins. If a considerable number of synthetic gems are to be cut it is wisest to buy whole boules, because they lend themselves better to the axis-locating procedure described above than do sawed sections or the small angular pieces which are commonly sold for the cutting of small single gems. If small sections must be bought it is a good idea to ask the supplier to indicate with two opposed dots on the surface of the rough the position of the axis, which he should know if he has taken the trouble to saw the boule according to the axis position.

PRELIMINARY EXAMINATION OF FACET ROUGH

Perhaps the first question that the experienced lapidary asks himself when shown a parcel of facet rough concerns the *shape* of the gemstone crystals or fragments. If these are excessively thin, elongated, or grossly misshapen, the return in terms of finished carats against rough carats can be disappointingly low. Very slender pencils of tourmaline, for example, regardless of how lively the color or how elegant the crystal form, cannot yield gems any thicker than the pencil itself. Thin platy crystals, Montana Yogo Gulch sapphires for example, are also impossible to cut into anything except very small gems. Similarly, crystal fragments with deep hollows must be cut to eliminate such hollows, which means a drastic reduction in finished size regardless of how large the piece of rough appeared at the start. In general, best returns come from chunky or blocky pieces approximating spheres or cubes, and thus lending themselves readily to the cutting of brilliant or step cuts. In any case, the cutter must visualize what the rough can yield and buy accordingly, providing, of course, that the rough is satisfactory in terms of color, flaws, and the other considerations previously discussed.

Once the rough has been selected for shape, it should be critically examined for inner clarity, color and color distribution, cleavage traces, etc. Cracks or inclusions show up best in transmitted light, as shown in Fig. 9 where a desk lamp is being used for examination. The stone is placed at the edge of the shade in such a way that the strong light passes through the gem but does not blind the eyes. By slowly turning the rough, brilliant reflections arise from cracks, and to a lesser extent, from inclusions. Sometimes it is helpful to wet the stone with oil or with water because this allows a clearer view of the interior.

As an excellent alternative, a small pencil flashlight can be used to examine rough by holding the stone near the body at comfortable distance below the eyes and shining the light upwards through the stone. The best flashlight for this purpose is the kind fitted with a small bulb which is about the size of a match head. This puts a narrow but intense beam of light into the stone, which quickly illuminates blemishes.

IMMERSION OF ROUGH

A better way to examine the interior is to place a piece of rough in a liquid which nearly matches its refractive index. Everyone has observed the startling result when clear ice is placed in ordinary water; seemingly it disappears! Because ice is frozen water it has nearly the same refractive index as ordinary tap water; hence the "disappearance." Precisely the same effect is observed with gemstones, providing the right fluid is used. The trick is to obtain a closely matching fluid, the closer the better. A fluid may be of any kind, as long as it is not harmful. If an exactly matching fluid cannot be obtained, practically any fluid is better than nothing at all. Some commonly available fluids are fuel oils, kerosene, mineral oil, castor oil, salad oils, and clove oil. The following table lists those which are most

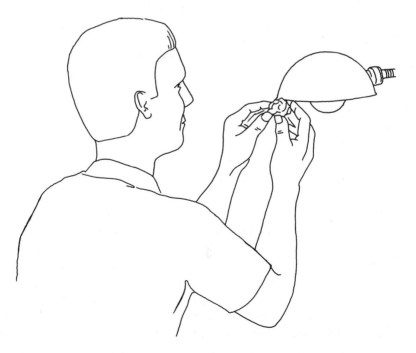

FIG. 9
Using a desk lamp to check for flaws in a transparent gemstone.

useful. Some of the unusual ones may be ordered from drugstores or chemical supply houses. Consult your local Yellow Pages.

OTHER MEANS OF EXAMINATION

One of the best ways to examine facet rough is to cut and polish a small "window" on the rough to look inside. Not much material is lost in the process and uncertainties as to internal quality can be resolved. Skilled cutters usually cut a single large facet on the rough where it will serve the double purpose of a window, and, if no defects are found, as the large table facet of the finished gem. It must be mentioned, however, that dealers do not permit gemstones to be returned to them if windows have been cut on the rough; buyers must make up their minds about the rough without damaging it in any way.

When a large quantity of rough is involved, especially if it is in the form of many small etched or abraded fragments or pebbles, individual examination becomes tedious and time-consuming. Sometimes it pays to make up an examination bench fitted with a frosted glass top, beneath which is an electric bulb. The pebbles are spread over the glass and the obviously clear ones separated from those which are just as obviously unsuited for facet work. Another method is to tumble the rough to a good polish, and from among the finished stones, select those of facet quality. This has been successfully employed with peridot rough from Arizona, rose quartz from Brazil, and other gemstones. While there is some loss of material, it is not as much as may be imagined and the ability to select top-grade, high-priced material may more than offset the loss in weight and the cost of tumbling.

CABOCHON MATERIAL

Flawlessness in cabochon material is not as crucial as it is in facet material; however, large flaws or surface cracks which tend to trap polishing powder, pores, soft inclusions which may pit during polishing, and other gross defects can result in unsightly gems. In very valuable materials such as star ruby and corundum, which depend for their value upon the inclusions creating the stars, great care is used in selecting the rough, because the brightness of the stars depends upon the baisic clarity of the gemstone. If dark-colored inclusions are present, or small cracks and other defects, the reflections will be interfered with and the gem will be less beautiful. Some specific recommendations on star rough follow.

IMMERSION FLUIDS

Name	Refractive Index	Suitable for
Kerosene	1.45	Opal
Glycerine	1.47	Opal
Mineral oil	1.48	Natrolite
		Moldavite
Cedar wood oil	1.51	Petalite
		Pollucite
		Leucite
Clove oil	1.54	Feldspar
Anise oil	1.55	Quartz
		Scapolite
		Beryllonite
Bromoform*	1.59	Beryl
Cassia oil	1.60	Topaz
Monochlornapthalene*	1.63	Topaz
		Apatite
		Tourmaline
		Andalusite
		Danburite
Monobromonapthalene*	1.66	Spodumene
		Phenakite
		Kornerupine
		Diopside
Monoidonapthalene*	1.70	Sinhalite
		Willemite
		Idocrase
		Kyanite
Methylene iodide*	1.74	Spinel
		Sapphire
		Garnet
		Chrysoberyl
		Benitoite
Methylene iodide with sulfur*	1.78	Garnet

*Avoid inhaling fumes; avoid skin contacts by using tweezers to immerse and remove rough.

SELECTION OF ASTERIATED, OR STAR, ROUGH

It is not an easy task to judge quality in star sapphire because most crystals, supplied by the gravel deposits of Sri Lanka and Myanmar, are heavily abraded and not properly shaped to show the star even if the crystals are immersed in a suitable fluid. The inclusions which cause the star, or *asterism*, lie in only one series of parallel planes, as shown in Fig. 10, with the optic axis at right angles to them. The first task is to determine the direction of this axis and to grind and polish away some material from one end of the crystal to impart the necessary spherical shape which allows the star to be seen. While some crystals are found which show a decided silky sheen at opposite ends, which mark the ends of the crystals and therefore the places where shaping should begin, this is not always the case, and some needless loss could occur unless the lapidary were sure. Fortunately, many crystals show some traces of crystal faces as shown in Fig. 10. These faces are usually striated parallel to the planes containing the inclusions. Using them as clues, coupled with the appearance of sheen on opposite ends of

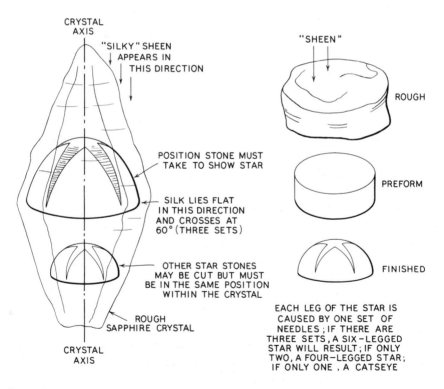

FIG. 10
How gems are cut from star sapphire crystals in order to place the star on top.

the rough crystal, it is possible to safely shape and polish one end to check for asterism. The material removed in this preliminary shaping and polishing operation needs only to be large enough to do the trick, sometimes a polished area of ⅛" across being sufficient.

Star rubies may be more difficult to orient because some of the crystals are less regular in shape than sapphire crystals. However, one excellent clue, if the crystals are not too badly worn, is to look upon the surfaces for triangular markings and ridges which occur only on the ends of the crystals.

In both ruby and sapphire, frequent wetting with methylene iodide helps to detect the silky shimmer of the star-forming inclusions. All checking for asterism should be under a pinpoint source of light and not under a fluorescent light or an overhead fixture containing several light bulbs. If the sun is available, it provides the best light of all.

Selection of Chatoyant Rough

The term *chatoyant* is used to designate the silky sheen caused by very small reflecting inclusions of a fibrous nature which lie in parallel position in certain gemstones. Strictly speaking, all star gems are chatoyant, but the chatoyancy occurs in several directions at once while in ordinary chatoyant gems, such as catseye chrysoberyl and catseye tourmaline, only one set of reflecting inclusions is present and therefore only one line of light crosses over the polished surface of the gem. The principles for selecting suitable chatoyant rough are the same as outlined above for star stones. Sometimes the selection task is easier because some chatoyant gems possess this property so strongly that even the briefest inspection is enough to convince one that the effect really exists. Good examples are tigereye from Africa, some chrysoberyls and tourmalines, and rarely, some beryls. Fig. 11 shows how a catseye gem is cut from chatoyant rough and indicates the proper shape of the rough if a good yield is expected.

In all star and catseye rough it is important to remember that the sharpest lines of light develop only if the finished cabochon is strongly curved over the top. If it is too shallow, the reflections tend to widen and become diffuse. A good rule of thumb is to select only those pieces of rough which are approximately ball-like in form. The finished cabochon should be approximately hemispherical, or broadly oval, with the thickness of the gem from ⅓ to ½ the breadth. If thicker gems are cut, they become grotesque, while thinner gems exhibit poorer optical effects. Further, the finest stars and eyes can only result if the inclusions are very slender, highly reflective, perfectly straight, sufficiently numerous to provide strong reflections, and evenly distributed throughout the crystal. It is very rare that all of these requirements are met in one gem, and naturally such a specimen commands a very high price.

Top-quality ruby, sapphire, and chrysoberyl rough displaying promising chatoyancy seldom leaves the country of origin without being cut locally and sold in this form. About the best that the amateur cutter can expect to obtain, or the professional for that matter, if he does not have direct trade connections into the countries producing such valuable rough, are smaller pieces of no more than several grams weight, or larger pieces which native cutters decided were too risky to cut because of uncertainties about the outcome. Lately, much cheap, nearly opaque red corundum, euphemistically advertised as "ruby," has come from India; it is a very poor approach to the real ruby in respect to quality, although it can be had in large crystals and in large quantities.

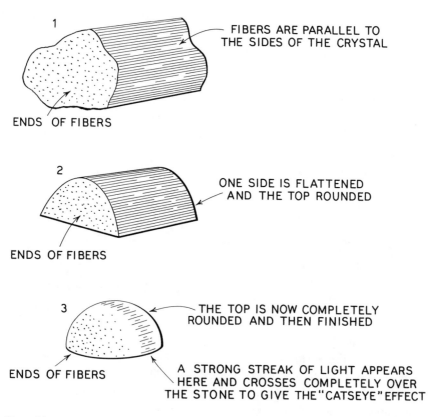

FIG. 11
How a catseye gem is cut from the rough in order to place the "eye" on top.

MOONSTONES

The finest moonstones are feldspar gemstones occurring in Myanmar and Sri Lanka. Both countries provide rough remarkable for its high degree of translucency, almost water-clear in some specimens, and the presence of minute inclusions which give rise to a beautiful silvery or blue sheen. Any rough requires careful inspection before purchase because of the tendency of native dealers to attempt to dispose of unsuitable material. Much of the rough is partly split along two prominent cleavage planes or sometimes into plate-like fragments which, at first glance, seem satisfactory for cabochons. Unfortunately, such thin pieces often display the moonstone sheen only on the thin edges. This means that any gem cut from them would have to be so small that it would scarcely pay for the cost of cutting. If these fragments are cut in any other way, with the idea of obtaining larger gems, the sheen will be badly off center.

Much less troublesome is the feldspar moonstone which has recently appeared from India in the form of large blocky fragments. While good-sized gems may be cut from them, they seldom compare in translucency or strength of sheen to the fine moonstones of Myanmar and Sri Lanka.

SUPERIORITY OF WATERWORM OR WEATHERED ROUGH

Much high-quality material occurs in the form of pebbles and boulders which have eroded from the rocks originally enclosing them. Sometimes they are found near the place of origin, but at other times they are washed into streams and rivers and subjected to severe pounding before coming to rest in it gravel cleposit. Only the soundest crystals and masses can survive this combined attack of weathering and stream wear, and it is for this reason that gravel beds rich in gems are the particular target of knowledgeable gem miners. It can be truly said that nature has tested each piece and destroyed those found wanting.

Stream-worn material is therefore likely to be of very high quality and includes the gem pebbles from Sri Lanka and Myanmar mentioned earlier, various durable gem species such as topaz, tourmaline, beryl, and chrysoberyl from alluvial deposits in Brazil and elsewhere, and waterworn agates such as those from the Montana river deposits. Nephrite jade and jadeite are famous for providing very fine material from pebbles and boulders. In fact, the older Chinese jade carvers vastly preferred alluvial material, either nephrite from the stream gravel deposits of Turkestan, or the jadeite boulders from Burma. These were viewed as having proved themselves tough enough to produce the most delicate carvings.

Weathering need not be connected with stream wear as is shown by the loose nodules of chalcedony found lying on the ground in many places in the world. The agate nodules and geodes of southern Brazil and northern Uruguay, vein sections of chryoprase in Australia, petrified wood in Arizona, and peridots and garnets in New Mexico and Arizona are some examples of gemstones weathered from their original deposits. Nature has destroyed the enclosing rocks in a gentle yet irresistible fashion, leaving behind the more durable gein material. As far as freedom from defects is concerned rough of this kind can be of top grade because it has been treated gently during the long cycle of erosion. However, if cracks existed in the material from the time of its formation, they may still be present after it has lost its enclosing rock and, as a general rule, the quality of the material is not as high as that found in stream gravel deposits where a more severe elimination process has taken place.

QUARRIED MATERIAL

Much cabochon rough is extracted from its host rock by the use of considerable physical force, perhaps even explosives. Sometimes the quarried blocks are so large that they cannot be easily transported and must be further broken down into manageable pieces by means of sledge hammers. If the material is valuable throughout, it may pay the operator of the mine to saw the larger masses into smaller blocks at the mine even if considerable difficulty is involved in doing so. In primitive countries, or in extremely remote areas, the use of power equipment may not be feasible and it then becomes necessary to break up the blocks as best one can. This necessarily involves considerable loss because the mere act of hammering means applying destructive stress to the stone and creating cracks which radiate in all directions from the points of impact. There is an art to breaking down large masses of rock so that the least damage is done except where it is wanted, but much good gem material has been destroyed by poor hammering techniques and later sold to the unwary who believe it to be sound.

Rough blocks can be a gamble unless they are carefully inspected for signs of hammering damage. One should look for the telltale whitish, crumbly places on the surfaces of blocks which are the remnants of hammer blows. Beneath each one is likely to be a network of cracks radiating deeply into otherwise sound material. Such damage is inclined to be particularly severe in brittle materials such as jasper, chert, petrified wood, rose quartz, and obsidian; or in cleavable or splittable materials such as feldspars, some types of nephrite jade, sodalite, and serpentine. On the other hand, granular materials such as rhodonite and jadeite tend to absorb the shock of misdirected blows a short distance below the surface and the damage is usually confined to smaller areas.

Cracked rough is not necessarily undesirable if meant for cutting into small articles, but it can be troublesome during slab sawing because of the tendency for sections to fall out prematurely and damage the blade. Cracked rough is definitely undesirable when large flawless masses are required for such items as book ends, spheres, and carvings.

Impregnation of Rough to Disguise Defects

Knowing that cracks detract from the value of rough, some overseas dealers in large parcels of rough, notably Brazilian and Indian dealers, sometimes practice a deception which the buyer should guard against. They soak the rough in an odorless and colorless or sometimes deliberately colored vegetable oil, which has two "improving" effects: (a) it heightens the color, and (b) it fills small cracks and pores, lending the impression that sound material is being bought While the use of oil for revealing true color has some justification—in fact, many materials offered for sale these days are customarily immersed in water for this purpose—the buyer must remember that small cracks, pores, and soft spots are also disguised by immersion and keen disappointments can occur after lapidary work begins. To be safe, it is wise to take a typical sample from a parcel of treated rough, wash it in soap and hot water, and then dry it off until all traces of water have disappeared. The sample will now appear in its natural state and the buyer will know what he is getting.

Sawed Blocks and Slabs

The great advantage of sawed blocks and slabs is that much guesswork as to quality is removed. The fresh, flat surfaces provide clear indications of color, pattern, texture, and presence or absence of defects. Another advantage is that sawed material is usually sounder because the mere act of sawing causes faulty rough to fall apart along the cracks created by natural forces or the hammer blows of the miner. This is an important consideration to the carver seeking good material.

Thin slices or slabs are sold in quantity to cabochon cutters. They should be about $\frac{3}{16}$" thick for ordinary cabochons, or perhaps somewhat thinner for small stones, and a little thicker for larger stones. Slabs that are much thinner or thicker are merely wasteful unless cut to order for some special project. Crudely cut slabs should be avoided; these can be recognized by pronounced grooves left upon their surfaces by an improperly operating saw. Particularly to be avoided are slabs with soft spots; these can be detected by merely wiping the surface with a wet cloth and noting if any places appear to dry much more quickly than the remainder of the slab; such places are probably porous and will refuse to take a polish. All sawed pieces and slabs cost more than mine-run rough because of labor and wear and tear on sawing equipment. A number of lapidary supply houses in the United States undertake custom sawing, charging at the rate of from twenty-five cents to fifty cents per square inch, depending on the volume of work and the type of material. Costs rise sharply if the rough consists of small nodules which are particularly troublesome to handle and require much attention during sawing.

Selection of Carving Rough

While it may seem that more latitude can be taken in respect to internal defects when choosing large rough for carvings, this is really not the case. As a matter of fact, it is far more difficult for the carver to obtain satisfactory rough than the cutter of gems. Because some types of carvings require sections to be quite thin, such as the arms or legs of a statuette, even the slenderest of cracks cannot be tolerated unless the carver is able to adjust his design to place such defects where they will not be conspicuous. The Chinese carvers are past masters in disguising cracks and other defects, but this is facilitated by the complexity of their carvings which makes it easy to change the design slightly to accommodate any defect which happens to appear during carving. On the other hand, the traditions of Western art generally call for more simplicity, which implies the freer use of broad, smooth areas. This, of course, allows much less opportunity to alter the design if a defect appears. Cracks, patchy color areas, soft spots, and other defects rre particularly undesirable whenever large smooth areas are to be part of the carvings. These remarks apply equally to material which is to be used in bowls, large ash trays, book ends, and other massive objects.

Rough Gemstone Prices

Rough gemstones, including certain organic materials, but not pearls, are listed alphabetically with cross references for varieties. Each entry is preceded by appropriate statements of characteristics, sizes, qualities, sources, etc. Not all varieties are included because so many of them, especially among the numerous members of the quartz family, are no more than trivial sub-varieties of little economic importance.

All prices are retail per avoirdupois pound (lb.), avoirdupois ounce (oz.), metric gram (gm.), or metric carat (ct.). Some items are priced by the piece (ea.) or square inch (sq. in.). Most prices are given in ranges according to improving quality. The variables upon which prices depend have been described for cut gems in a previous chapter and the same considerations apply to rough.

Prices asked for exactly the same material can differ appreciably from dealer to dealer due to suchi factors as dealer's volume, connections with direct sources of supply, expenses, and the amount of profit required to stay in business. The highest degree of price standardization occurs in the common, steadily-supplied gemstones and the least degree in the rare gemstones or those of extremely high quality and large size among the common jewelry-trade gemstones such as diamond, emerald, ruby, and sapphire. For the latter, exceptionally large and fine rough specimens may be negotiated entirely on the likelihood of getting someone with enough money to buy the rough, or to form a syndicate to cut up the rough, hoping to dispose of the cut gems at a profit. "Standard" prices for such rough gemstones are never fixed.

In this connection, the prices asked for expensive rough are not greatly below the prices asked for cut gems if it is apparent that the rough is clean and that the weight loss can be readily estimated. For example, a clean crystal of ruby of ten carats weight, well shaped, and obviously capable of being cut into an oval brilliant of five carats, will sell at a price not very far from the wholesale price of the cut gem. There is no gamble in the cutting because the clarity and color quality of the finished gem are assured while the cutting charges will be modest. For these reasons, the owner of the rough would be a very poor businessman to ask a price for it far below the wholesale price of the cut gem. On the other hand, rarer gems and collectors' gems are not disposed of as readily as the standard jewelry gems, and the element of chance becomes greater. Also, some rough is so fragile that it may break during cutting and result in serious weight losses. Dealers are therefore reluctant to pay as much for such rough, and as the reader will note when he compares rough to cut gem prices, exotic rough is generally priced lower in proportion than standard rough.

Many amateur cutters have been disappointed that they cannot always obtain top-quality rough and find it difficult to understand why this should be so. Some of the reasons have been touched on before, but it is worthwhile to say again that the largest and finest rough seldom passes beyond the borders of the country in which it was mined without being cut. In fact, the best specimens are bought up almost as quickly as they are mined. Thus many of the rough gemstones listed below, especially in the finest qualities, will appear on the market only rarely.

CATALOG OF ROUGH GEMSTONE VALUES

ABALONE, SEE SHELL

ABALONE PEARL, SEE PEARL IN CHAPTER VII

ACHROITE, SEE TOURMALINE

ACTINOLITE (SEE ALSO NEPHRITE)
Rarely in small crystals; hard but easily cleaved; collectors' gem only.
Madagascar, small dark green crystals, ¼"–1"   ea. $2.50-10.00

ADAMITE
Pink, facet grade crystals   ea.   5.00–15.00

AGATE, SEE QUARTZ

ALABASTER, SEE GYPSUM

ALBITE, SEE FELDSPAR

ALEXANDRITE, SEE CHRYSOBERYL

ALGAE, SEE QUARTZ

ALGODONITE
Irregular masses from Michigan copper mines furnish unusual cabochons of metallic luster;
rare; collectors' gem only.
Cabochon grade   lb.   4.00-10.00

ALMANDITE, SEE GARNET

AMAZONITE, SEE FELDSPAR

AMBER
Mostly supplied by East Germany, Russia, and Denmark in pieces to 4" diameter.
Dominican amber is now far more commonly offered in good to fine lapidary grade; avoid recent fossil resin *copal* which is much cheaper than true amber but also crazes quickly and has no
place in the lapidary arts.

Baltic, clear flawless yellow, 1.5–5 gram pieces	gm.	1.50
Baltic, clear scrap, .5–3 gram		6.00/oz. or 70.00/lb.
Baltic, carving grade, yellow to brownish	gm.	1.25–2.00
Baltic, cabochon grade, yellow to brownish	gm.	1.25–2.00
Baltic, with inclusions (not insects)	oz.	10.00
Dominican Republic, brownish-yellow to reddish-brown, 1–5 grams each	gm.	1.45
Dominican Republic, with insect inclusions, from $5 to several thousands depending on quality		

PRESSED AMBER
Small pieces of amber pressed together under moderate temperature into fused solid masses
of useful size; may have insect inclusions.

Denmark, beads, 8_20 mm	gm.	1.00
Denmark, blocks, with insects	gm.	15.00

AMBLYGONITE

Almost colorless to pale straw-yellow to rich yellow cleavage masses from Brazil affording clear areas suitable for faceting; supplies sporadic; soft; rare; collectors' gem only. Usual size faceted gems 3–15 ct.; record gem of about 70 ct. known.

Flawless, yellow, 1" crystal	ea.	90.00
Cabochon grade, small clear areas, to 5 oz.	oz.	2.50–5.00

AMETHYST, see QUARTZ

AMMOLITE

Fossilized ammonite shell, largely composed of aragonite and displaying splendid, opal-like reflections; from Alberta, Canada

Shells	ct.	50.00–150.00
Flakes	ct.	2.00–10.00

ANALCIME

A common mineral but very rare in transparent crystals sufficiently large to cut small faceted gems not over 1-2 ct.; soft, fragile; collectors' gem only.

Colorless, facet grade, crystals, not over ¼"	ea.	.50–5.00

ANDALUSITE

The clear variety provides beautiful dichroic gems in green-red or brown-red when properly cut; hard, durable, but too rare to be more than collectors' gems; supplied mainly from Brazil, also Ceylon, as waterworn pebbles and crystals; veil inclusions common; usual size ½", rarely to 100 ct.; cut gems to 5 ct. common but cut gems to 20 ct. rare and valuable.

Facet grade, clean, less than 5 ct.	ct.	2.50–11.00
Facet grade, clean 5–7 ct. size	ct.	3.50–14.00
Facet grade, clean, 10–15 ct. size	ct.	4.50–19.00
Facet grade, clean, over 15 c t.	ct.	5.50–24.00

CHIASTOLITE

Impure variety of andalusite in the form of cigar-shaped crystals to 1" diameter and displaying black cross-like figures against a white to tan background; soft; sometimes cut as a curiosity.

Crystals, ½–1¾" diameter	ea.	.25–2.00
Australia, crystals, all sizes	lb.	6.00

END OF ANDALUSITE SECTION

ANDRADITE, see GARNET

ANGLESITE

Extremely soft and fragile lead mineral; rarely in clear crystals large enough to facet; colorless to pale brown; collectors' gems.

Tunisia, 1"–4" crystals	ea.	2.00–12.00
Tsumeb, ½"–4" crystals	ea.	2.00–150.00

ANHYDRITE

Soft, fragile, rarely in facet-grade crystals; collectors' gem only.

Switzerland, pale purple cleavages to 2"	ea.	2.50–20.00
Ontario, massive cabochon grade	oz.	.50–8.00

ANTHOPHYLLITE
Sometimes displays a bronze iridescence but rarely available and seldom cut.

ANTHRACITE
Selected masses from Pennsylvania are suitable for carvings and ornamental items but seldom offered and then only at pound prices.

APACHE TEARS, SEE OBSIDIAN

APATITE
Popular among amateur cutters, but soft and requiring care in treatment; abundant vivid yellow crystals from Mexico yielding gems to 20 ct.; small fracture fragments of green and yellow-green available from other sources; Maine purple and Burma blue rare and highly prized; Mexican yellows can be heat-treated to colorless; greenish catseye available from Brazil; collectors' gem only.

Mexico, golden yellow, 1–10 cts.	ct.	.30–.80
Mexico, golden yellow, 10–20 cts.	ct.	.40–.90
Mexico, golden yellow, 30–40 cts.	ct.	.70–1.50
Madagascar, Ontario, green, facet grade, 1–10 cts.	ct.	1.00–2.00
Madagascar, Ontario, green, facet grade, 10–20 cts.	ct.	1.50–2.50
Madagascar, Ontario, green, facet grade, 20–30 cts.	ct.	2.00–3.00
Madagascar, Ontario, green, facet grade, 30–40 cts.	ct.	3.00–4.00
Zimbabwe, fine light green, 1–10 cts.	ct.	.40–1.50
Zimbabwe, fine light green, 10–20 cts.	ct.	.50–1.75
Zimbabwe, fine light green, 40–60 cts.	ct.	.70–2.50
Zimbabwe, fine light green, 60–80 cts.	ct.	.80–3.00
Zimbabwe, fine light green, 80 cts. up	ct.	.90–4.00
Zimbabwe, blue green, 1–10 cts.	ct.	1.00–3.00
Zimbabwe, blue green, 10–15 cts.	ct.	2.00–4.00
Zimbabwe, intense sapphire blue color, 1–5 cts.	ct.	4.00–8.00
Zimbabwe, intense sapphire blue color, 5–10 cts.	ct.	5.00–10.00

APOPHYLLITE
Soft, fragile; colorless crystal tips sometimes provide facet material; rare; collectors' gem only.

India, facet grade, crystal tips, ½"–4"	ea.	.50–8.00

AQUAMARINE, SEE BERYL

ARAGONITE
Rarely in facet-grade crystals only from Bilin, Czechoslovakia, as elongated pale straw-yellow prisms capable of cutting gems to 8 ct.; soft, fragile; collectors' gem only. Massive material sometimes offered for cabochons but most of this is actually calcite.

Bilin, straw-yellow, facet grade, ½"–4" crystals	ea.	.50–45.00

ARGILLITE
Soft gray slate-like rock from British Columbia used for carvings but under Indian monopoly and not usually sold.

AUGELITE
Soft, fragile; clear colorless crystals only from Champion Mine, Mono County, California; now unobtainable; collectors'gem only.

AVENTURINE, SEE FELDSPAR OR QUARTZ

AXINITE

Recently in large quantities from Calaveras, California, Baja California, and Mexico, as brown crystals with reddish purple overtones yielding faceted gems to 23 ct.; strongly trichroic; intensity of color makes gems larger than about 5 ct. appear dark; while classed as a collectors' gem the hardness and durability is sufficient for normal wear in jewelry.

Mexico, Grade "A" (lightly included), 3–33 cts.	ct.	12.00
Mexico, Grade "B" (moderate inclusions), 3–20 cts.	ct.	7.50

AZURITE

Small clean crystals facetable but finished gems must not be over ⅛" thick if any light is to be reflected; soft, fragile; collectors' gem only. Attractive cabochon material sometimes available but most material offered is too porous to permit good polish; alternate bands of azurite and malachite, sometimes called *azurmalachite*, are specially prized; cabochon material also too soft for jewelry.

Tsumeb, facet grade	oz.	.50–1.50
Cabochon grade, hard, compact, 3–20 lb.	lb.	8.00
Arizona nodules, 8-15 mm. diameter	oz.	4.00
Azurmalachite	lb.	20.00–40.00
Azurite, stabilized, color-treated, blocks	lb.	35.00

AZURMALACHITE, SEE AZURITE

BARITE

Very soft and fragile crystals provide small faceted gems for collectors; commonly available from South Dakota, Colorado, and England; massive barite rarely available.

South Dakota, golden brown, to 25 ct.	ct.	.25
Colorado, pale blue, 2" crystals	ea.	6.00–10.00
England, colorless, to 50 gm.	gm.	.25-.75
England, massive, brown-banded stalactitic pieces	lb.	4.00

BAYLDONITE

Bright chartreuse-green masses occasionally from the copper mines near Tsumeb, S. W. Africa, in cabochon grade; rare; collectors' gem only.

BENITOITE

Only known source of facet-grade crystals is at Dallas Gem Mine, San Benito County, California; rarely available except in small fragments seldom over 2-3 ct.; relatively soft; collectors' item. Largest gem known 15.42 ct.; cut gems under ½ ct. common; over 1 ct. rare and over 3 ct. extremely rare. Usually blue but a very few crystals have provided colorless faceted gems, and a ½ ct. pink stone is recorded.

Crystal fragments, ½–3 cts.	ct.	35.00

BERYL

Standard commercial gemstone; hard, durable, colorful; provides fine jewelry gems and small carvings. By far most expensive variety is emerald, ranking above diamond in large richly-colored examples; blue *aquamarine* highly prized but traces of green drastically reduce value (however, some rich yellow-green aquamarines are heat-treatable to fine blue) ; *golden beryl* and *morganite* only moderately valued, *goshenite* very low value. Most apricot- or peach-colored beryls, commonly called morganite, fade to pink upon exposure to strong light, the final hue depending on richness of original hue. Aquamarine sometimes contains plate-like brown inclusions capable of creating weak to moderately strong stars; catseyes occur in practically all varieties. Largest clean rough provided by aquamarine, sometimes in crystals of many pounds weight; also large clean crystals in golden beryl, more rarely in morganite and goshenite.

Emerald crystals rarely clean when over ¼" diameter, but reasonably clean crystals of nearly 1" diameter have been found.

AQUAMARINE

Supplied almost exclusively by Brazil; also from Madagascar, and sometimes from scattered deposits in the United States and Australia; occasionally in gem gravels of Sri Lanka and Myanmar. Finest blue grade, absolutely without trace of greenish tinge, is sometimes called "Fortaleza" after source in Brazil. Prices drop rapidly with smaller rough and as greenish tinges enter.

Fine blue, Fortaleza facet grade, 1–5 cts.	ct.	4.00–10.00
Fine blue, Fortaleza facet grade, 10–15 cts.	ct.	7.00–17.00
Medium blue, facet grade, 1–5 cts.	ct.	3.00–7.00
Medium blue, facet grade, 15–20 cts.	ct.	7.00–16.00
Medium blue, facet grade, 40–45 cts.	ct.	14.00–30.00
Light blue, facet grade, 1–10 cts.	ct.	1.00–2.00
Light blue, facet grade, 20–30 cts.	ct.	1.50–2.50
Blue-green, fine, facet grade	ct.	2.00–20.00
Light greenish colors	ct.	.60–2.10
Catseye, blue, strong eye	oz.	5.00–20.00

EMERALD

Principally from Colombia; also small crystals from Brazil, India, Rhodesia, the last of deep color and suitable for small cut gems; prices ascend steeply according to size and color, the prized color being a deep bluish-green or "Muzo" color, also deep yellow-green (Sandawana, Rhodesia).

Deep Muzo color, facet grade, ½–1 ct.	ct.	100.00+
Deep Muzo color, facet grade, 1–1½ ct.	ct.	200.00+
Deep Muzo color, facet grade, 2½–3 ct.	ct.	500.00+
Deep Muzo color, facet grade, 3½–4 ct.	ct.	700.00+
Medium green, facet grade, under 3 ct.	ct.	15.00–160.00
Medium green, facet grade, over 5 ct.	ct.	75.00–150.00
Pale green, various sizes	ct.	10.00–100.00
Cabochon grades, Muzo color, approximately 60% of facet grade prices		
Cabochon grades, medium color, approximately 40% of facet grade prices		
Catseye, medium green	ct.	20.00–100.00

NOTE: The so-called "tumbling" grade emeralds are virtually without value and should not be purchased.

SYNTHETIC EMERALD (CHATHAM CREATED)

Deep to medium green crystals grown by hydrothermal and flux-fusion methods; virtually indistinguishable from natural emeralds except through careful testing; growth methods are costly and slow, resulting in sustained high prices.

Chatham, dark green crystal clusters, to 20 cts.	ct.	22.00
Chatham, dark green crystal clusters, 21–40 cts.	ea.	550.00
Chatham, dark green crystal clusters, 41–60 cts.	ea.	650.00
Chatham, dark green crystal clusters, over 60 cts.	ea.	800.00

GOLDEN BERYL (HELIODOR))

Ranks low commercially because the color is not greatly favored for jewelry and resembles that of citrine; large color variations from greenish-yellow to golden yellow to pale yellow; a yellow with a reddish cast is more highly prized. A deep yellow kind has been called *heliodor*. Principally from Brazil, Zimbabwe, and Mozambique. Clean faceted gems seldom over 30 ct.

Very deep gold, facet grade, 1–30 cts.	ct.	4.00–31.00
Medium gold, facet grade, 1–40 cts.	ct.	2.00–19.00
Pale gold, facet grade, 1–30 cts.	ct.	1.00–7.00

GOSHENITE (Brazil, Zimbabwe, Mozambique)

This colorless variety is cut mainly for collectors; it is not used commercially.

Facet grade, 1–40 cts.	ct.	.50–2.75

HELIODOR (BRAZIL, ZIMBABWE, MOZAMBIQUE)

Golden yellow, light, 1–10 cts.	ct.	1.00–3.00
Golden yellow, light, 20–30 cts.	ct.	3.00–7.00
Deep golden color, 1–5 cts	ct.	3.00–9.00
Deep golden color, 10–15 cts	ct.	5.00–15.00
Deep golden color, 30–40 cts	ct.	8.00–24.00
Very deep golden color, 1–5 cts	ct.	4.00–10.00
Very deep golden color, 10–15 cts	ct.	6.00–17.00
Very deep golden color, 20–25 cts	ct.	8.00–26.00
Very deep golden color, 25–30 cts	ct.	9.00–31.00

GREEN BERYLS

This varietal name embraces deeper-hued green beryls, ranging from chartreuse to somewhat brownish-green types, some of which are capable of heat treatment to blue. Paler kinds are generally classed under aquamarine.

Deep yellow-green or brownish-green, heat treatable	ct.	4.00–28.00
Medium green, not heat treatable	ct.	1.60–15.00

RED BERYL (BIXBITE)

Found only in Wah Wah Mountains of Utah

Utah, Red Beryl, fine ruby red light inclusions .015–4 cts.	ct.	25.00–1,000.00+

MORGANITE

Includes true pink, also peach, apricot, and other orange tints which fade to pink or can be heat-treated to pirik; occasionally available in flawless rough large enough to cut gems over 100 ct.; veil-type inclusions common. Ranks low commercially because most cut gems are too pale.

From Brazil, Zimbabwe, and Mozambique,		
rich purplish-pink, when available	ct.	10.00–30.00
Brazil, medium pink color	ct.	.75–4.00
Brazil, rich orange-sherry color	ct.	12.00
Brazil, pink, catseye, coarse tubes	ct.	6.00–12.00
Brazil, cabochon grades	lb.	10.00–20.00

STAR BERYL

Aquamarine containing numerous very small plate-like crystals of brown hematite parallel to the basal plane and furnishing weak to good stars when properly cut; not all specimens produce stars; rare.

Brazil, brown star beryl, free of cracks	gm.	1.00–10.00

END OF BERYL SECTION

BERYLLONITE
An excessively rare phosphate mineral obtained only from one deposit in Maine as cleavable colorless crystals and fragments up to 2" diameter; soft, brittle; suitable only for collectors' gems. Cut gems over 5 ct. very rare.

Maine, crystal sections, ½"–1"   ea.   8.00–16.50

BINGHAMITE, SEE QUARTZ

BLOODSTONE, SEE QUARTZ

BOLEITE
Only from Baja, Calif. and Mexico, crystals ¼"–⅜"   ea.   15.00–25.00

BORACITE
Only from saline deposits of Germany as very pale bluish-green corroded crystals not over ⅜" diameter which provide attractive facet gems; very rare; collectors' gem only.

Germany, crystals, ⅛"–⅜"   ea.   2.00–20.00

BORNITE
Known as "peacock ore" because of iridescent tarnish film which quickly develops on fracture and cabochon surfaces; soft, brittle; collectors' item only.

Alaska, massive   oz.   1.50–3.00

BOWENITE, SEE SERPENTINE

BRAZILIANITE
Soft, cleavable phosphate mineral in greenish or pale yellow to rich yellow crystals; onlv from Brazil in cuttable specimens; collectors' item; largest gems 20-30 ct.

Fine rich yellow, or greenish-yellow, facet grade,
½"– 2" crystal   ea.   4.50–85.00
Cabochon grade, numerous flaws   gm.   1.00–8.00

BREITHAUPTITE
A sulfide mineral furnishing brilliant metallic luster cabochons, soft; collectors' gem onlv.

Ontario, massive, usually mixed with other sulfides lb.   2.50–25.00

BRONZITE, SEE HYPERSTHENE

BROOKITE
Very small crystals very rarely clean enough to facet; not commercially available.

BRUCITE
Gems of about 1 carat cut from transparent Jeffrey mine, Astestos, Quebec material; extremely rare

BURBANKITE, SEE REDMONDITE

BURNITE
An azurite, malachite, cuprite mixture

BYTOWNITE, SEE FELDSPAR

CACOXENITE, SEE QUARTZ

CALCITE
Clean crystals provide faceted gems of interest only to the collector; some colorless, twinned calcite, virtually flawless from New York and Ontario has been faceted into splendid stones dispersing all the colors of the rainbow. Some purplish-pink massive material of considerable

translucency has also been faceted; much massive, banded calcite is employed in ornaments ranging from wall panelling, counter tops, and pedestals, to book ends, desk stands, and spheres; such material is commoiily called *calcite onyx*; brownish types, usually obtained from cave deposits, are called *cave onyx*; some onyxes are available in blocks of several tons weight; chatoyant material is called *satin spar*.

Baja California, Mexico, brown, facet grade, crystals	ea.	6.00–10.00
Spain, purplish-pink translucent massive, select	gm.	1.25–2.00
Calcite onyx, various localities	lb.	2.00–3.00
Cave onyx, brown, various localities	lb.	2.00
England, fibrous satin spar, 6–80#	lb.	2.00
Michigan, Petoskey stone (coral replacement), pebbles	lb.	.20–.75

CALIFORNITE, SEE IDOCRASE

CANCRINITE

Bright yellow to orange-yellow massive, usually with blue sodalite; seldom occurs large enough to provide pure-color cabochon is over $1/2$" diameter; soft, brittle; collectors' item only. Recently blue gem quality massive cancrinite found in southeast Greenland in Kagssortog Fjord, but not commercially available.

Ontario or Maine, $1/2$" crystals	ea.	12.00

CARBORUNDUM, SEE SILICON CARBIDE

CARLETONITE

Very rare species in vivid to pale blue facet grade crystals from Mt. St. Hilaire, Quebec; a collector's stone only; usually less than 1 ct.

CARNELIAN, SEE QUARTZ

CASSITERITE

A highly prized collectors' item when faceted from colorless, flawless material; hard and tough but too rare to be used commercially; clear material only from outer zones of the dark brown crystals from Bolivian tin deposits. Massive fibrous variety known as *wood tin* sometimes cut cabochon. Faceted gems over 1–2 ct. rare; largest clean gems not over 4–5 ct.

Bolivia, facet grade, according to size & color	ea.	20.00–225.00
Mexico, wood tin, brownish nodules, $1/2$"–3"	oz.	.50–3.50

CATAPLEIITE

Very rare as colorless facet-grade crystals of small size, usually less tan 1 carat, from Mt. St. Hilaire, Quebec; a collector's stone only.

CATLINITE

Soft, easily carved stone containing pyrophyllite and usually brownish to reddish in hue; Indian "pipestone."

South Dakota; similar material from Arizona	lb.	.75–5.00

CATSEYE SHELL, SEE SHELL

CELESTITE

Soft, fragile strontium mineral sometimes faceted for collectors, usually blue. Also colorless or rare pink.

Mozambique, pale blue 1–5 cts.	ct.	.80–1.50
Mozambique, pale blue 5–10 cts.	ct.	.90–1.75
Mozambique, pale blue 20–30 cts.	ct.	1.10–2.50
Sicily, colorless crystals to $1/2$"x $1/4$"x $1/4$"	ea.	1.50–3.00

Ontario, small orange bladed crystals, in matrix,
per specimen, 2"x 3"   3.00–7.00

CERUSSITE
An extremely soft lead mineral, but capable of being cut into attractive faceted gems of considerable brilliance and dispersion; the best material is colorless; collectors' item only. Also in excellent catseye material, but very rare.

Tsumeb, colorless crystal to 20 cts.	ct.	.75–1.50
Tsumeb, colorless crystal to 20–40 cts.	ct.	.50–1.75
Tsumeb, colorless crystal to 40–60 cts.	ct.	.60–2.00
Tsumeb, colorless crystal to 60–80 cts.	ct.	.70–2.50
Tsumeb, colorless crystal to 80–100 cts.	ct.	.80–3.00

CHABAZITE
Rarely cut. Found in crystals less than 1 ct. near Victoria, British Columbia.

CHALCEDONY, see QUARTZ

CHAMBERSITE
A rare purplish-brown species yielding faceted gems of one or two carats; from Texas.

CHAROITE
Hydrous silicate of sodium, calcium, and potassium with black aegerine augites, gray transparent microline and rare orange tinaksite, a titanium mineral. Vivid purple color, discovered in 1976. Known from one location Chara River, Yakutsk, USSR. Hardness 6. Cuts into very colorful cabochons.

Good color   lb.   100.00–140.00

CHERT, see QUARTZ

CHIASTOLITE, see ANDALUSITE

CHIOLITE
Rarely faceted, colorless, from Lvigket, Greenland; a collector's stone only.

CHLORASTROLITE, see PUMPELLYITE

CHLOROMELANITE, see JADEITE

CHONDRODITE
Excessively rare orie-locality mineral from Tilly Foster iron mine, New York, as small transparent brownish-red crystals not over ⅛" thick; occasionally available from old collections; collectors' gem only.

Facet grade, to 4 ct.   ct.   2.00–12.00

CHROMITE
Black, massive chrome ore, sometimes cut as a curiosity.

Maryland, California, or Oregon   lb.   2.50–5.00

CHRYSOBERYL
Very hard and durable; provides excellent gems for jewelry such as catseyes, chartreuse to yellow faceted gems, and *alexandrites*, the last noted for their color change from green in daylight to bright red under artificial tungsten light, the value depending on how distinct the change is, how vivid the colors, and, of course, size, freedom from flaws, etc. The finest alexandrites came from the Urals and rough is no longer obtainable; those from Sri Lanka tend to be brownish and display considerably less attractive colors; recently in fair to good small crystals from Brazil. The best catseyes display a remarkably sharp silky white eye upon a highly translu-

cent green to yellow background, the greenish hues being more desirable; also in alexandrite type but seldom showing good color change. Brownish to yellowish facet grade chrysoberyls are not highly prized commercially because they resemble the cheaper gemstones, citrine and golden beryl; chartreuse-green faceted gems are much more esteemed and command good prices.

Brazil or Sri Lanka, yellow, facet grade, 1–3 cts.	ct.	2.00–5.00
Brazil or Sri Lanka, yellow, facet grade, 3–6 cts.	ct.	3.00–8.00
Brazil or Sri Lanka, yellow, facet grade, 6–9 cts.	ct.	10.00–15.00
Brazil or Sri Lanka, yellow, facet grade, 9–12 cts.	ct.	12.00–20.00

ALEXANDRITE

Brazil, color change greenish-blue to pale amethyst, to 10 ct.	ct.	20.00–70.00
Urals, green-red color change, 1–4 ct.	ct.	30.00–90.00
Urals, green-red color change, 5–10 ct.	ct.	50.00–350.00
Urals, green-red color change, over 10 ct.	ct.	100.00–500.00+
Ceylon, brownish-green to brownish-red, 1–4 ct.	ct.	25.00–75.00
Ceylon, brownish-green to brownish-red, over 10 ct.	ct.	50.00–300.00+
Rhodesia, fine color change, 1–4 ct., selected	ct.	100.00+
Rhodesia, fine color change, mine run crystals	lb.	150.00+

CATSEYE

Brazil or Sri Lanka, yellow body color, 1–4 ct.	ct.	5.00–25.00
Brazil or Sri Lanka, yellow body color, 5–15 ct.	ct.	10.00–65.00
Brazil or Sri Lanka, yellow body color, over 15 ct.	ct.	10.00–100.00+
Brazil, greenish body color, add 15%–20% to above prices		
Brazil, alexandrite-type, weak color change, 3–4 ct.	ct.	10.00–25.00

END OF CHRYSOBERYL SECTION

CHRYSOCOLLA, SEE QUARTZ

CHRYSOPRASE, SEE QUARTZ

CITRINE, SEE QUARTZ

CLEIOPHANE, SEE SPHALERITE

CLINOHUMITE
Similar to chondrodite, bright orange faceted gem of less than 1 ct. Cut from Pamirs, Mts., Asia material.

Bright orange	ct.	300.00

CLINOZOISITE
Sometimes available from Baja California as facet-grade crystals of brownish color; a collector's gem.

Brown to yellowish-brown, ½"–3" crystals	ea.	2.25–16.25

COAL, SEE ANTHRACITE

COBALTITE
Produces interesting metallic luster cabochons of pink-silver color.

Ontario, ½"–4" massive pieces	ea.	1.00–12.00

COLEMANITE

Soft, fragile, and slowly perishable facet-grade crystals obtained from the borate deposits of California; collector's gem only.

Colorless to faint yellow, ½"–4" crystals	ea.	3.00–35.00

CONCH, SEE SHELL

COPPER

Recently large masses of native copper from Keeweenaw Peninsula, Michigan, have been sectioned into book ends and ornamental blocks and slabs, then highly polished and lacquered to prevent tarnishing.

CORAL

Occurs in all shades from pale to dark pink or orange-pink, to various shades of red, to dark red ("ox-blood"); also brownish-red, and mottlings of several hues or with white; pure white is also commonly available. Mottled pieces are considered much less desirable. Flaws include worm borings and soft places, or discolorations due to decomposition in the case of coral fished up dead. Soft but fairly tough and capable of receiving fine detail in carvings and an excellent polish. Used in carvings, cabochons, beads, and as polished stem and twig sections set "as is" in jewelry or strung in necklaces in the case of slender twigs of about ¹⁄₁₆" thickness. Some large branches are sold for table ornaments; especially prized and very rare are sea-floor stones upon which a handsome growth of coral is attached; however, fakes are common, consisting usually of sections of branches, sometimes polished, set into soft rock which lacks the white calcareous deposits typical of true sea-floor pebbles. Values vary widely according to tastes developed in individual countries; *pelle d'angelo*, or "angel's skin," is highly prized in Europe and in the Orient, its color being a pure rose; also valued in the Orient is pure white, but yellowish-tinged varieties are unacceptable; intense pink appears to be valued by everyone, but darker hues to deep red ("ox-blood") are more esteemed in the United States. Large masses increase sharply in value because of the considerable rarity of old but perfect coral branches. Trade terms used for various grades of coral are: *Sardinian*, hard material of excellent quality; *Italian*, good quality in all shades from white to red; Moro, a fine-quality deep red Japanese type; *tosa*, average Japanese coral; *Sicilian* and *Algerian*, lesser qualities of Mediterranean coral; and *Japanese* coral, used to designate pieces that are mottled white and red.

Black coral is a different marine organism, lacking the calcareous skeleton of the true coral; its stems and branches consist of intensely black organic matter of great toughness; supplied from Pacific waters mainly, but also recently recovered from beaches of Atlantic side of Florida. In vogue for black, light-weight jewelry, accepts a fine polish; thick stem sections of about 1" are liable to split along annular growth rings.

Red, fine color, branch sections to ¾" thick	gm.	5.00–7.50
Red, good color, branch sections to ¾" thick	gm.	5.00–7.00
Red coral, bulk, all grades, sea-run	lb.	400.00
Pink sprays, 1½"–2¾"	ea.	5.00–25.00
Pink, *angel's skin*, fine grade	ct.	7.50–10.00
Orange & orange-reds, fine grade	ct.	1.25–1.75
White, fine grade	gm	2.50–4.50
White, branches, 3"–10"	ea.	2.50–10.00
Twigs, red, drilled, ¼"–⅝" long	ct	1.00
Twigs, red, ⅛" thick	ct.	1.00–1.25
Trees, red, 1½"–3" diam.	ct.	1.25–2.25
Black coral, stem sections, ½"–⅞" long	ct.	1.00
Black coral, stem sections, 1"–3" long	ea.	2.00–10.00
Black coral, cleaned, in bulk	oz.	5.00–20.00

CORAL (Petrified), see CALCITE (Petoskey Stone) or QUARTZ

CORDIERITE, see IOLITE

CORUNDUM

Includes *ruby*, *sapphire*, and star stones; red lines are called ruby but pinks and all other colors are called sapphire with the implication that the rough is suitable for gem purposes; otherwise it should be called by the species name. In recent years opaque to barely translucent red corundums have been sold as "ruby," particularly from India; needless to say they command but a very small fraction of the price received for real ruby in equivalent sizes. Finest sapphires are intensely hued, blue being the favored color; also prized are amethystine hues, orange, and rich pink; yellows are not as desirable for jewelry purposes while most greens tend to be somewhat dingy in hue, although very fine Australian stones have been found. Best star stones show distinct six-ray stars upon a richly-colored background whether red as in ruby or blue as in sapphire; as background colors depart from these hues the values drop sharply; the most abundant and cheapest star sapphires are only faintly blue, purplish, or merely pale gray to nearly white. In terms of size, star stones reach as much as 40 cts. in ruby and several hundred cts. in sapphire; faceted rubies over several cts. weight are rare but sapphires commonly occur in sizes of many carats. Hard, durable; a standard gemstone. Good rough always difficult to obtain because the best material in largest sizes is cut locally and only the leftovers are sold outside the country. Much rough is now customarily heat-treated to enhance color.

RUBY

The finest rubies occur in the gem gravels of Myanmar; good rubies also from Tanzania, Thailand, and pale rubies from Sri Lanka; very rarely, small rubies of good color from gravel deposits in United States and Australia. Extremely expensive in rich red color, costs increasing rapidly, with size and freedom from flaws. Some new material from Vietnam available.

Tanzanian, fine reds, $\frac{1}{4}$–$\frac{1}{2}$ ct.	ct.	200.00
Tanzanian, fine reds, $\frac{3}{4}$–1 ct..	ct.	300.00
Tanzanian, fine reds, $1\frac{3}{4}$–2 ct.	ct.	500.00
Tanzanian, fine reds, $2\frac{1}{2}$–$2\frac{3}{4}$ ct.	ct.	650.00
Madagascar, fine color, xls–1 oz.	oz.	30.00
North Carolina, pink to red xls–1–20 gms.	gm.	1.00

STAR RUBY

India, fine star, if available, 1 oz.	oz.	14.00–40.00
Indian, mine run	lb.	36.00

SAPPHIRE

The best rich blue sapphires occur in the gem gravels of Myanmar, sometimes in sizes large enough to facet gems of several hundred carats weight; fine rich blues also occur in Thailand but are usually much smaller; fine pale blues characteristic of Sri Lanka gravels; very small but fine colors from Yogo Gulch, Montana; fair to good sapphires from Australia especially in yellows and greens.

Myanmar, medium dark blue, facet grade, 1–4 ct.	ct.	5.00–60.00
Myanmar, medium dark blue, facet grade, 5–10 ct.	ct.	10.00–150.00
Myanmar, medium dark blue, facet grade, 11–30 ct.	ct.	20.00–250.00
Myanmar, medium dark blue, facet grade, over 30 ct.	ct.	20.00–500.00+
Myanmar, lighter blue, facet grade, 1–4 ct.	ct.	2.00–10.00
Myanmar, lighter blue, facet grade, 5–10 ct.	ct.	4.00–15.00
Myanmar, lighter blue, facet grade, 11–30 ct.	ct.	5.00–35.00+
Sri Lanka, pale blue, facet grade, 5–1 0 ct.	ct.	3.00–15.00
Sri Lanka, pale blue, facet grade, 11–20 ct.	ct.	5.00–20.00
Sri Lanka, amethystine, facet grade, 1–5 ct.	ct.	1.00–8.00

Sri Lanka, amethystine, facet grade, 6–15 ct.	ct.	3.00–30.00
Sri Lanka, pink, facet grade, 1–5 ct.	ct.	1.00–10.00
Sri Lanka, pink, facet grade, 5–10 ct.	ct.	3.00–20.00
Sri Lanka, orange, facet grade, 1–5 ct.	ct.	2.00–10.00
Sri Lanka, orange, facet grade, 6–10 ct.	ct.	4.00–20.00
Sri Lanka, orange, facet grade, 11–20 ct.	ct.	6.00–30.00
Sri Lanka, green, facet grade, 1–5 ct.	ct.	1.00–10.00
Sri Lanka, green, facet grade, 5–10 ct.	ct.	2.00–15.00
Sri Lanka, yellow, facet grade, melee	ct.	5.00
Australia, best blue, facet grade, 1–3 ct.	ct.	55.00
Australia, fine green, facet grade, 6–30 ct.	ct.	12.00
Australia, mixed colors, small, 4–6 cts.	ct.	6.00
Australia, dark blue, cabochon grade, 5–25 ct.	oz.	12.00–20.00
Australia, light to dark pink, 1–5ct.	ct.	10.00–45.00
Montana, Yogo Gulch, blue, 1½–2 cts.	ct.	2.00–12.00
Montana, Yogo Gulch, blue, 3–5 ct.	ct.	4.00–22.00
Montana, Yogo Gulch, 5+ ct.	ct.	16.00+
Montana, Yogo stones, sorted mine run	kg.	1,000.00–5,000.00
Tanzania, gray-blue to purplish, facet, 5–25 ct.	ct.	10.00–30.00

Star Sapphires

Myanmar, medium dark blue, 5–10 ct.	ct.	5.00–20.00
Myanmar, medium dark blue, 11–25 ct.	ct.	8.00–100.00
Myanmar, medium dark blue, over 25 ct.	ct.	8.00–125.00
Myanmar, medium blue, 5–10 ct.	ct.	2.00–10-00
Myanmar, medium blue, 11–25 ct.	ct.	3.00–40.00
Myanmar, medium blue, over 25 ct.	ct.	5.00–70.00
Sri Lanka, pale blue, 5–15 ct.	ct.	2.00–8.00
Sri Lanka, pale blue, 16–30 ct.	ct.	3.00–10.00
Sri Lanka, pale blue, over 30 ct.	ct.	3.00–15.00
Sri Lanka, bluish-gray, gray, etc., small pebbles	oz.	20.00–40.00
Sri Lanka, pale red to pink, small pebbles	oz.	40.00
India, pink, black, purple, mine run	lb.	10.00–18.00

Star Corundums

India, black star	oz.	8.00
Australia, blue star, 1 oz.	oz.	20.00
Australia, black star, 1 oz.	oz.	14.00–40.00
India, red star, crystals, selected sections	oz.	10.00–12.00
India, red star, mine run	lb.	36.00
Montana, lavender star, crystals	gm.	2.00–3.00

Synthetic Ruby and Sapphire

Star boules are not commercially available, all being used to cut finished gems in behalf of designated marketing companies; facet-grade boules available in any color and in any quantity. Synthetic ruby crystals grown by Chatham are no longer available.

Boules, ruby red, half, 145–175 cts.	ea.	22.50
Boule, ½–150 cts., blue sapphire	ct.	.35
Boule, ½ Padparadsha color sapphire	ct.	.18
Chatham Created ruby crystal – no longer available		

End of Corundum Section

COVELLITE
Soft, massive copper mineral; dark purplish tarnish as soon as polished; collectors' item only.

Alaska or Montana, massive	oz.	1.00–6.50
Alaska or Montana, massive	lb	10.00

CREEDITE
Faceted gems not over one or two carats cut form bluish/purple crystals found at Santa Eulalia, Mexico.

CROCOITE
Small, brilliant red-orange transparent crystals from Tasmania and Australia; faceted gems cut from them are far too soft to be used for any purpose except as collectors' items.

Prismatic crystal sections, ½"-4" long	ea.	15.00–425.00
Australia, 1"–2" long crystals	ea.	12.00–50.00

CROWN OF SILVER, see QUARTZ (Psilomelane Chalcedony)

CRYOLITE
Colorless gems faceted from clear areas on crystals and massive from Mt. St. Hilaire, Quebec.

CUPRITE
Very rarely, as small clear crystals suitable for faceting collectors' gems. Very rarely, as small clear crystals suitable for faceting collectors' gems, but in recent years, enormous, facet grade crystals have been found in the copper mines of Tsumeb and vicinity, Namibia; flawless cut gems have been cut in dozens of carats and larger. Sold as mineral specimens. The term "cuprite" is commonly used to designate a cuprite-stained epidote metarhyolite from Pennsylvania which has some use in cabochons and ornamental objects.

Pennsylvania, metarliyolite	ct.	8.00–10.00

DANBURITE
Hard gemstone suitable for transparent faceted gems but cut only for collectors; colorless to faintly pink crystals abundant from Mexico; rarely, pale yellow waterworn pebbles from gem gravels of Myanmar.

Mexico, colorless crystal tips, 3–10 cts.	ct.	1.00
Russia, large colorless crystal pieces, 10–20 cts.	ct.	3.00
Russia, large, fine xls, 20–30 cts.	ct.	3.50
Russia, large fine xls, 50–60 cts.	ct.	5.00

DATOLITE
Attractive faceted gems cut from very pale yellowish-green crystals; the finest are from Westfield, Massachusetts, and afford flawless gems to 5–6 ct. Unusual massive datolite, colored by copper and other minerals, occurs as warty nodules to 10" diameter in copper deposits of Michigan; these are prized according to size and color, the least valuable being white, increasing in value toward red, reddish-brown, orange, etc., and sometimes cut for cabochons but mostly sliced and polished as cabinet specimens.

Massachusetts, facet grade, ½"–3" crystals	ea	2.40–35.00
New Jersey, facet grade, to 4" crystals	ea.	2.50–40.00
Michigan, white nodules, according to size	ea.	.50–5.00
Michigan, nodules, according to size and color	ea.	4.00–100.00

DEMANTOID, see GARNET

DIAMOND

It is virtually impossible for anyone outside the established diamond cutting, selling, or trading organizations to obtain supplies of gem-quality diamonds except from Brazil, where a substantial quantity of diamonds is produced each year from river gravels by independent miners; the usual sources in Africa are closely controlled by the De Beers Syndicate, which grades the stones and places them on sale in London as lots, each lot containing various sizes and grades according to the established consumption records of the buyers who have traded with the syndicate in the past. Supplies are not abundant and few buyers of lots are willing to part with good stones if they can cut them themselves and realize a greater ultimate profit thereby. This situation, and the necessity for special lapidary equipment in order to cut diamonds, has resulted in few non-professional cutters attempting to cut this gemstone. Prices for rough rise very steeply with quality and size and the figures given below are only an approximate guide. A full discussion of qualities appears in the next chapter.

Crystals, Congo, 2–10 cts., cuttable	ct.	16.00
Crystals, better quality, 2–10 cts.	ct.	300.00
Crystals, "fair" quality, 2–4 cts.	ct.	80.00–100.00

DINOSAUR BONE, SEE QUARTZ

DIOPSIDE

Hard, durable, but seldom attractive colors; fairly steady supply of facetable dark green crystals from Madagascar; occasionally in pale green from Alpine localities and New York; also in attractive pale green waterworn crystals from gem gravels of Myanmar. The Madagascar material is so dark that gems over 5 ct. tend to be unattractive. Star diopside, but very dark, occurs in India. An intense chrome green comes from Russia.

Russia, chrome green, facet grade, 1–2 cts.	ct.	2.00
Russia, chrome green, 2–3 cts.	ct.	5.00
Russia, chrome green, facet grade, 3–4 cts.	ct.	6.00
Russia, chrome green, facet grade, 5–6 cts.	ct.	10.00
Finland, deep green chrome diopside, 1–3 cts.	ct.	1.50–10.00
India, very dark green, chatoyant, 2–8 gm.	gm.	.75
India, very dark green, chatoyant, 9–15 gm.	gm.	1.00
India, "black" star, 4-rayed, fine	lb.	18.00
India, "black" star, 6-rayed, 1–20 ct.	ct.	1.50–8.00
India, very dark green, facet grade, 1–5 ct.	ct.	.75–5.00

VIOLANE

Massive, purple variety of diopside, sometimes used in collectors' cabochons; rare; found in small patches in ore at Franklin, New Jersey, and at St. Marcel, Piemonte, Italy.

Massive, often admixed with other minerals	oz.	.50–.75

DIOPTASE

Vivid emerald-green crystals sometimes faceted into very small gems for collectors; soft, brittle; rarely clean. Largest clear gems about ½ ct.

Africa, ½"–3" crystals	ea.	25.00–400.00

DOLOMITE

An abundant rock-forming mineral, some types of which are used for large objects; rare in clear crystals suitable for faceting; soft, cleavable, a collectors' gem only.

New Mexico, colorless facet crystals to 15 ct.	ct.	.15–.75
New Hampshire, massive, tan, red & brown	lb.	1.00
Michigan, "Kona" dolomite, mottled & colored, massive	lb.	1.00

DRAVITE, SEE TOURMALINE

DUMORTIERITE, SEE QUARTZ

EMERALD, SEE BERYL

ENSTATITE

Sometimes available from India as corroded facet-grade crystals of dark greenish-brown to brown color; also showing 4-rayed star on nearly black background; faceted gems cut to 4–8 ct., but larger gems appear too dark; hard, tough, but cut only for collectors. Also from Tanzania. Facet-grade, dark green grains found with peridot in San Carlos Indian Reservation, Arizona furnish flawless but very dark gems up to 10 carats; smaller gems of one or two carats show green.

Tanzania, facet-grade 2–5 cts.	ct.	3.00
Tanzania, black star, 1–30 gm.	gm.	.75–3.00
India, greenish-black with white catseye	lb.	18.00

EPIDOTE

Abundant rock-forming mineral, sometimes cut in massive form for cabochons or for large ornamental items; facet-grade crystals cut for collectors, but while hard, are too dark to be attractive. *Piemontite* is a massive variety sometimes cut in cabochons of an attractive deep rose color.

Baja California, Mexico, crystals, small clear	gm.	.25–1.00
California, Kern Co., crystals with clear areas	gm.	.25–1.00
Austria, Salzburg, fine clear crystals	gm.	.50–2.50

ESSONITE, SEE GARNET

EUCLASE

One of the classic rarities: occurs in Brazil and Siberia in clear crystals ranging from colorless to pale straw-yellow, yellow, pale green, and blue; cleanable; cut only for collectors; cut gems over 5 ct. very rare.

Brazil, colorless, 1–5 cts.	ct.	3.00–5.00
Brazil, colorless, 5–10 cts.	ct.	4.00–6.00
Brazil, colorless, 10–15 cts.	ct.	5.00–7.00
Brazil, green and blue, 1–5 cts.	ct.	8.00–10.00
Brazil, green and blue, 5–10 cts.	ct.	9.00–11.00
Brazil, green and blue, 10–15 cts.	ct.	10.00–12.00

EUDIALYTE

Faceted gems of about ¼ carat have been cut from rose-red material found in Kipawa rocks, Termiscamingue Co., Quebec.

FABULITE, SEE STRONTIUM TITANATE

FELDSPAR

The feldspar group includes a wide variety of gemstones, cabochon and facet grade, which are noted for special optical effects: *adularescence* in moonstones, *peristerism* in *albite peristerite*, *schiller* in a number of species, *aventurescence* in sunstones, and *labradorescence* in *labradorite*. The finest moonstones are found in Sri Lanka and Myanmar, and may display either a silvery or blue adularescence, the latter being more highly prized. Blue peristerism, and sometimes peristerism in patches of different colors, is characteristic of some albites. Schiller, a spangly appearance due to minute separations along cleavage planes, is common in microcline, perthite, and albite. The bright spangles, or aventurescence, in oligoclase sunstone are due to very small, flat platelets of hematite. Very good material comes from Norway, India, and Oregon, the last containing minute flakes of copper. The labradorescence effect is best seen in labradorite from Finland, in the material from Labrador, and in a highly translucent variety of libradorite from Madagascar, which, unfortunately, occurs only in small pieces. *Amazonite*, the bright green to blue-green variety of microcline perthite, appears in very fine quality in Virginia and in a few deposits in Brazil, South Africa, and lately from Russia. Facet-grade feldspars include straw-yellow to pale yellow *sanidine* crystals eroded from lavas, and pale to vivid yellow orthoclase crystals from Madagascar, the latter sometimes furnishing clear gems to 100 ct. The silvery or blue orthoclase or microcline moonstones from Sri Lanka and Myanmar are always in demand in the jewelry industry, there is some demand for other feldspar gemstones, especially among collectors. All species and varieties are relatively soft for use in jewelry; some are easily cleavable and hence fragile.

ALBITE

Virginia, Amelia, white massive, blue peristerism	lb.	1.50–3.50
Virginia, Amelia, white massive, blue peristerism	sq. in.	.25–.75
Ontario, salmon-pink, massive, peristerite, various hues	lb.	.80

BYTOWNITE

Rarely occurs in small clear fragments suitable for faceted gems; probably most of the material sold for this species is actually sanidine.

Bytownite, light yellow, New York, ½ ct.	ct.	60.00

LABRADORITE

Pale to dark gray body color, displaying patches of colored reflections which are commonly blue but which may also be green, gold, bronze, red, and yellow; usually fractured and seldom capable of providing cabochons over 1" diameter; the best large masses come from Finland; exceptionally vivid effects observed in Madagascar variety but solid rough fragments seldom over ¼". Transparent grains of pale straw-yellow color and weathered from lavas are often sold under this species name but are probably sanidine. The name "spectrolite" is used for the labradorite from Finland.

Finland "spectrolite" red	lb.	380.00
Finland "spectrolite" 1st class	lb.	128.00
Finland "spectrolite" 2nd class	lb.	76.00
Finland "spectrolite" Slabs	lb.	165.00
Finland, rich labradorescence, black body color	oz.	15.00–20.00
Canada, rich labradorescence, good flash color	lb.	12.00
Labrador, fine labradorescence, gray 10–20#	lb.	7.00
Madagascar, intense hues, pieces not over 1½"	gm.	.75–1.50
Mexico, straw-yellow, facet-grade, to 200 ct.	gm.	.50–1.00
Texas, straw-yellow, facet-grade, to 25 ct.	gm.	.50–1.50
Oregon "sunstone" red body color	gm.	5.00–18.00
Oregon "sunstone" green and bi-color	gm.	5.00–18.00
Oregon "sunstone" peach body color	gm.	5.00–12.00
Oregon "sunstone" all color	gm.	.50–4.00

MICROCLINE

Includes *perthite*, a variety containing numerous streaks of albite; *amazonite* is green to blue-green perthite in which the microcline is colored but the albite streaks are white; some microclines provide moonstones while some perthites provide weak sunstones. Amazonite is popular for tumbled gems.

Amazonite, Virginia, Amelia, fine blue-green	lb.	3.00–8.00
Amazonite, South Africa, good blue-green	lb.	6.00
Amazonite, Colorado, fine blue-green, small slabs 1–2" sq.	lb.	12.00
Amazonite, Norway, good color	lb.	8.00
Amazonite, Ontario, deep green	lb.	5.00
Amazonite, Brazil, Grade A		.05/gm–22.50/lb.
Berthite, Ontario, salmon color	lb.	.90–1.50

| Berthite, Ontario, salmon color, weak sunstone | lb. | 1.00 |
| Berthite, Finland, salmon color | lb. | 1.00 |

MOONSTONE

For convenience, moonstones are discussed together although they may be orthoclase or microcline; the best stones are nearly transparent, the Myanmar blue sheen stones being more so than the blue or silver stones from Sri Lanka; after these come the silver and blue moonstones from New Mexico, which unfortunately are never large in flawless pieces; the moonstone from India, appearing lately in large quantities, is only translucent, although some of the greenish types show fair translucency and good sheen. Myanmar and Sri Lankan moonstones are becoming scarce. In all types, rough must be selected with care because the strongest sheen may appear upon thin edges, which would necessarily make cut gems much narrower than if the sheen appeared on broader surfaces. Moonstone is ordinarily cut cabochon, although it has been used very effectively for cameos and intaglios.

Myanmar, blue sheen, fine, 1–10 gm.	gm.	1.00–8.00
Myanmar, silver sheen, fine, 1–10 gm.	gm.	.75–5.00
Sri Lanka, blue sheen, fine, 1–30 gm.	gm.	.75–5.00
Sri Lanka, silver sheen, fine, 1–30 gm.	gm.	.50–3.00
Mexico, blue flash, select, 2½–5 cts.	ct.	3.00
India, silver sheen, choice select	oz.	2.50
India, silver sheen, mine run	oz.	3.00–5.00
India, other colors, mine run	oz.	.80–1.50
India, silver sheen, white body color	oz.	.50–2.00
India, yellow, 50–20 cts.	ct.	1.00

OLIGOCLASE

This species provides the best sunstones; the highest quality contains abundant uniformly distributed orange spangles uninterrupted by gray or white streaks; rare in sound pieces over ¾". Rarely, facet-grade oligoclase, in small sizes and colorless or faintly greenish.

Norway, sunstone, masses to 1" across, select	oz.	2.00
Norway, sunstone, masses to 3" across, mine run	lb.	3.00–6.00
India, sunstone, fine select grade	gm.	.10–.15
India, sunstone, select	oz.	.80–3.00
India, sunstone, in matrix ½–2 lbs.	lb.	5.00

ORTHOCLASE

The best facet-grade orthoclase is yellow material from Madagascar in crystals to several inches diameter, from nearly colorless to intense yellow; pieces with minute inclusions, which give the crystals a milky appearance, seriously reduce brilliance and should be avoided.

Madagascar, best yellow, 1–5 cts.	ct.	.60
Madagascar, best yellow, 5–10 cts.	ct.	.70
Madagascar, best yellow, 10–20 cts.	ct.	.80
Madagascar, best yellow, 20–30 cts.	ct.	.90

SANIDINE

Offered in formless fragments obtained from surface deposits and lightly etched or sandblasted; pale tan to straw-yellow; faceted gems to 14 ct.

Oregon, straw, to 0.3 ct.	ct.	250.00
Oregon, straw, ½"–2" crystals	ea.	2.00–8.00
Oregon, straw, mine run	oz.	1.00–2.50
Mexico, straw, to 0.3 ct.	gm.	.75–1.50
Mexico, straw, to 5 gm., mine run	oz.	1.00–2.00

END OF FELDSPAR SECTION

FIBROLITE see SILLIMANITE

FLINT, see QUARTZ

FLUORITE

Soft, cleavable, low refractive index, but occurs in many attractive hues and is commonly faceted for collectors; massive purple and white banded variety from England, known as "blue john," has been extensively employed for ornamental objects of considerable size, but the source of material appears depleted and the industry dormant. Facet grade available in colorless, pale blue green, purple, yellow, and, rarely, in pink or red; cut gems to several hundred ct.

England, green, purple, fine, 10–100 ct.	gm.	.50–1.50
Illinois, purple, yellow, fine, 100 ct.+	gm.	.25–1.00
Mexico, pale green	lb.	2.00
New Hampshire, fine green, to 200 ct.	gm.	.25–.75
Ontario, pale green, to 50 ct.	gm.	.25–1.50
S.W. Africa, pale green, to 60 ct.	ct.	.70–1.75
S.W. Africa, bi-colored, gree/rose, to 50 cts.	ct.	1.20–2.50

FRIEDELITE

Extremely fine-grained massive material from zinc mines of New Jersey; translucent; some resembles brownish carnelian in color; for cabochons and translucent faceted gems; rare except at localities named; a collectors' gem.

Seam material, ½"–1" thick	ea.	1.00–20.00

GADOLINITE

A heavy black rare-earth mineral sometimes cut as a curiosity.

½"–3" crystal	ea.	2.50–35.00

GARNET

The species and varieties of this group furnish many fine gems in a wide variety of hues; deposits widespread and some gem-quality garnets continually supplied to the market at relatively low cost; demantoids and spessartines in short supply; recently very fine rhodolite has appeared on the market from Tanzania and commands a high price in view of its beauty and the rarity of this variety in large sizes. Malaya, an orangy-brown stone was discovered in the 1970s in East Africa. The green garnet *Tsavorite* was found in 1974 in Kenya. It is mined n ear Tsavo National Park in Tanzania.

ALMANDITE

Many sources of facet-grade rough; star rough from Idaho in large sizes; colors from brownish-red and very dark to bright red to purplish-red of medium intensity.

India, facet grade, 10–30 ct.	ct.	.30–8.00
India, cabochon grade, to 100 gm.	oz.	4.00–8.00
Tanzania, facet grade, fine color to 40 ct.	ct.	.50–8.00+
Madagascar, facet grade, light red, 10–25 ct.	ct.	1.00–7.50
New York, dark brownish-red, 10–40 cts.	ct.	.50–8.00
Idaho, star rough, mine run	lb.	10.00–25.00
Idaho, exceptional 6-ray material	lb.	450.00
Idaho, fine cabs, 4-ray	ct.	15.00–25.00
Idaho, fine cabs, 6-ray	ct.	35.00–50.00
Idaho, facet gems	ct.	5.00–10.00
Idaho, star, dark purplish-red, 100 ct. lot	lot	25.00
Idaho, star, select grade	lb.	300.00

ANDRADITE

The classic variety of andradite is *demantoid*, noted for its beautiful intense yellow-green to emerald-green hues; rough formerly from Russia and now unobtainable; some rough from Italian alpine sources; rare.

Demantoid, Urals, when obtainable to 1 ct.	oz.	75.00–100.00

GROSSULAR

Also known as *hessonite* or *essonite*; facet-grade material resembles the orange-red to orange hues characteristic of spessartine, for which species grossular has been confused; additionally, in colorless to very pale orange facet-grade material, and massive, resembling jade or idocrase; largest hessonites supplied by gem gravels of Sri Lanka, yielding cut gems to 15 ct. Softer than other garnets. Also from Madagascar and Tanzania.

Hessonite: Madagascar and Tanzania, golden-red orange,
select, minimum of "traecle."

1–5 cts.	ct.	.75–2.00
5–10 cts.	ct.	1.25–3.00
10–15 cts.	ct.	1.50–4.00
15–20 cts.	ct.	2.00–5.00
20–25 cts.	ct.	2.50–6.00
25–30 cts.	ct.	2.75–6.25
30–35 cts.	ct.	3.00–6.50
35–40 cts.	ct.	3.10–7.00
Quebec, orange, facet grade, to 15 ct.	ct.	3.00–20.00
Malaya, East Africa, orangy pink, fine 2–4 ct.	ct.	30.00
Malaya, deep red with orangy pink, 2–5 cts.	ct.	2.00–8.00
Malaya, deep red with orangy pink, 5–10 cts.	ct.	1.75–6.00
Malaya, cinnamon with orangy red, 10–60 cts.	ct.	6.00–12.00
Malaya, pinkish red orange, 1–15 cts.	ct.	6.00–10.00
Tsavorite, good facet quality (some flaws) 1–1½ cts.	ct.	7.50
Tsavorite, clean/good green, 3–4 cts.	ct.	35.00
Tsavorite, clean/green color, 4–5 cts.	ct.	55.00
Tsavorite, blocky, facet grade, 5 cts. up	ct.	80.00+

PYROPE

Invariably as small smooth-surfaced grains in eruptive rocks or surface gravels; seldom over 1-2 gm.; best color dark uniform red; to be colorful, most faceted gems should not be over 1-2 ct. Deep red from Madagascar and Mozambique.

Madagascar and Mozambique, deep red, facet grade to 6 ct.	ct.	.80–2.50
Madagascar and Mozambique, deep red, facet grade 5–8 ct.	ct.	1.50–3.00
Madagascar and Mozambique, deep red, facet grade 8–11 ct.	ct.	2.00–5.00

RHODOLITE

Formerly quite rare but recently available in large fine rough from Tanzania; color range medium to pale purplish-red to pale reddish-purple, almost resembling some amethyst; produces fine brilliant gems.

Tanzania, facet grade, very fine, 8–14 cts.	ct.	4.00–20.00
Madagascar, Mozambique, Zimbabwe, and Tanzania,		
pink-lilac, select facet grade, clean, 1–3 cts.	ct.	1.75–3.00
3–5 cts.	ct.	2.50–4.50
6–8 cts.	ct.	3.00–5.00
8–10 cts.	ct.	4.00–7.00
10–15 cts.	ct.	4.50–9.00
very light lilac color, 1–3 cts.	ct.	2.50–4.00

6–8 cts.	ct.	4.50–7.50
10–15 cts.	ct.	6.00–12.50
25–30 cts.	ct.	11.00–20.00
pinkish-red color, 10–15 cts.	ct.	12.50
15–20 cts.	ct.	15.00
25–30 cts.	ct.	20.00
35–40 cts.	ct.	25.00
magenta-pink (Tanzania), 1–8 cts.	ct.	75.00

SPESSARTINE

Color range from pale orange to deep brownish-red; often flawed, such flaws most commonly observed in paler hues. Large gems to 30 ct. from Ceara, Brazil material, and lately to 25 ct. from Ramona, California. Ordinarily, clean gems of 10 ct. or less to be expected. New finds from Madagascar and Mozambique. Finest color and quality from California.

African, very fine orange-red, 1–20 ct.	ct.	1.00–5.00
Madagascar, bright orange, 1–5 ct.	ct.	.75–5.00
Brazil, orange to brownish-red, 50 ct.+	gm.	3.00–8.00
California, vivid orange to slightly red-orange		
Fine grade, cuttable to several ct.	ct.	8.00–10.00
Fine grade, cuttable over 10 ct.	ct.	25.00
Virginia, Amelia, various shades, 1–10 ct.	ct.	.50–5.00
Virginia, Amelia, cabochon grades	gm.	1.00–2.00

END OF GARNET SECTION

GOETHITE

Massive, fibrous material sometimes cut into ornaments or cabochons displaying bandings and weak chatoyancy; black with dark brown to yellow bandings.

Michigan	lb.	2.50–20.00

GOSHENITE, SEE BERYL

GRANITE

Various types of granite and granite-like rocks have been used for ornamental objects of large size and sometimes for cabochons and tumbled gems (see UNAKITE); *graphic granite* displays interesting patterns of grayish quartz upon white to pale tan feldspar and has been made into spheres, bookends, etc.

Granites, various localities	lb.	.30–5.50

GROSSULAR, SEE GARNET

GYPSUM

Ornamental objects made from compact varieties alabaster and satin spar, the latter chatoyant; white, pink, pale orange, pale brown, etc.; very soft but accepts a good polish; much worked in Italy into boxes, statuary, imitation fruits, etc.; accepts dye.

Alabaster, various colors	lb.	.75–9.00
Satin spar	lb.	1.00–10.00

HAMBERGITE

Very rare colorless gemstone; fairly hard but cut only for collectors; facet grade crystals only from Madagascar but this deposit exhausted, and material now comes only from old collections; clean gems to 5 ct. considered large.

Crystals, with small clean areas	gm.	2.00–10.00
Selected clean fragments, to 8 ct.	ct.	4.25–9.50

HELIODOR, see BERYL

HEMATITE
 Compact English and Brazilian material used for cabochons , faceted gems, and intaglios; sometimes called "Alaska black diamond." Sold in Alaska in highly polished small carvings, 1–2" size.

England, "kidney ore" masses to 15 lb.	lb.	9.00–25.00
Brazil, fine crystals, to 1⅞"–2"	ea.	20.00–25.00

HESSONITE, see GARNET

HEXAGONITE, see TREMOLITE

HIDDENITE, see SPODUMENE

HODGKINSONITE
 Very rare purplish-pink mineral in veinlets in ore from Franklin, New Jersey; sometimes clear enough to facet small gems not over ½ ct.: available only from old collections; collectors' gem only.

Facet grade, ½"–3" crystals	ea.	2.50–30.00

HOWLITE
 Soft borate mineral from California; solid white or lightly veined with black; in cauliflower-like nodules to 10 lb. but usually 1–4 lb.; useful for carvings and larger ornamental objects; can be dyed.

Massive, white, or white with black veins	lb.	.75–7.50
Massive, white, or white with black veins, slabbed	sq. in.	.25–.75

HYALITE, see OPAL

HYPERSTHENE
 Used in cabochons when displaying metalloidal sheen (bronzite); hard; rare in uncracked pieces over ½"; collectors' stone only.

Arizona, catseye or sheen material, to 40 ct.	ct.	.50–5.00

IDOCRASE (Vesuvianite)
 Relatively abundant in crystals but seldom providing clear areas for faceted gems of over 2 ct.; good cabochon material more common, jade-like material from California being called californite or, sometimes, "California jade." Fairly hard but mainly cut for collectors.

California, massive, bright yellow-green, translucent	oz.	.75–1.00
California, massive, bright yellow-green, highly translucent	gm.	.25
California, massive, ordinary greens	lb.	1.25–4.00
Ontario, brownish-yellow, facet grade, crystal fragments to 5 gm. ("Laurelite")	gm.	2.00–6.00

INDICOLITE, see TOURMALINE

IOLITE (Cordierite)
 Unique for strength and character of pleochroism: straw-yellow, blue, dark blue; effect obvious in rough pieces; pieces to 25 gm. common but veil inclusions abundant and clean faceted gems over 5 ct. rare; rarely contains oriented hematite crystals which impart aventurescent effect; more rarely, with silky inclusions giving star effect.

Brazil, pale blue, facet grade, 1–5 cts.	ct.	2.00–3.50
India, mine run, assorted sizes, 2.2 lbs. (1 kg.)	kg.	36.00
India, dark blue, facet grade, 3–10 cts.	ct.	2.00–5.00
India, dark blue, facet grade, 10–20 cts.	ct.	4.00–7.50

Madagascar, blue, facet grade, 5–10 cts.	ct.	3.00–5.00
Madagascar, blue, facet grade, 20–30 cts.	ct.	5.00–10.00

IVORY
Includes elephant, narwhal, walrus, and sperm whale (tooth) ivory; attractive brown-stained walrus ivory from Eskimo and Aleut burial sites in Alaska; soft but tough and easily carved.

Sperm whale teeth, 4"–6" long, 12–16 oz. each	oz.	.50–1.00
Walrus ivory, Alaska, fossilized	lb.	45.00

JADE, see JADEITE or NEPHRITE

JADEITE
Fine-grained massive pyroxene mineral much used for carvings and jewelry gems; classical source Upper Burma (Myanmar); also minor deposits of good material in Japan; fair material from Guatemala and other sources in Mexico or Central America of poor to fair coloration; poor material from California. Myanmar produces waterworn pebbles and quarry blocks in white, grayish-white, with areas of pale to rich emerald-green, red, brown, yellow, mauve, and black; the emerald-green variety, when intensely hued and translucent, is given the name imperial jade and is very costly; rich greens and rich pure reds are also costly, followed by mauve, yellow, and black; the whitish or grayish-white material, and the faintly greenish varieties which are very abundant in the Myanmar deposits are cheap; strangely, pure white translucent jadeite is rare and fetches a good price. A very dark green to nearly black jadeite is called chloromelanite; it has little value.

Emerald-green, highly translucent, 3–15 ct.	ct.	15.00–85.00
Emerald-green, fine, partly translucent, 3–50 ct.	ct.	3.00–25.00
Green, bright, but not vivid	gm.	5.00–8.00
Green, bright, carving grade	oz.	10.00–25.00
Green, pale, carving grade, streaked	lb.	15.00–60.00
Greenish streaked carving material, pale hues	lb.	8.00–25.00
Red intense, pure hue, translucent	oz.	15.00–25.00
Red, hues with brownish tinges	oz.	8.00–12.00
Mauve, pale, but uniform	oz.	10.00–15.00
Mauve, paler, streaked	oz.	3.00–6.00
Ordinary grayish-greenish material	lb.	4.00–9.00
Chloromelanite	lb.	5.00–12.00
Japanese material, green streaks on white	oz.	7.00–12.00
Japanese material, white	lb.	10.00–15.00
California, San Benijo	lb.	22.00

JASPER, see QUARTZ

JASPILITE, see QUARTZ

JET
Tough black lignite coal, capable of being carved or faceted; defects include splits and soft or porous places; best material from England but supplies meager; also from Spain, Japan, United States; once popular for mourning jewelry.

England	oz.	2.00–5.00
Utah, in pieces to 3" diameter	lb.	4.50
Colorado, in pieces to 3" diameter	lb.	7.00

KORNERUPINE
Hard, rare gemstone from gravels of Madagascar, Myanmar and Sri Lanka, and lately from Greenland; seldom available; a collectors' gem.

Madagascar, greenish, facet grade to 8 ct.	ct.	1.50–10.00

Sri Lanka or Myanmar, brownish, facet grade to 7 ct.   ct.   1.00-6.00

KUNZITE, see SPODUMENE

KYANITE

Abundant mineral but rare in facet-grade crystals; easily cleaved, difficult to cut; usually many inclusions; collectors' gem only.

Brazil, fine blue crystals, facet-grade areas	ct.	1.50-3.00
Brazil, pale green slender crystals, facet-grade	gm.	.50-.80
Kenya, pale to dark blue or green, facet-grade areas in crystals	gm.	.25-.75
North Carolina, green, facet-grade crystals	gm-	.75-1.50

LABRADORITE, see FELDSPAR

LAPIS LAZULI

Rock-like gem material in which the blue color is imparted principally by lazurite; also contains calcite as white streaks or spots and pyrite crystals; the finest grade is very fine-grained, uniform in color, lacks calcite, and if it contains pyrite, the latter is in evenly distributed pinpoint crystals; best material from Afghanistan; good mottled material from Lake Baikal region; fair from Chile and abundant; fair to good from California and Colorado but supplies meager. The most compact material can be faceted to a fine finish but most lapis is employed in cabochons, and in small to large carvings.

Afghanistan, finest deep blue grade, gem grade	oz.	12.00
Afghanistan, medium grade, some pyrite	oz.	1.00-5.00
Afghanistan, some mottling with white calcite	oz.	.75-1.00
Chile, best grades, bright blue, usually mottled with calcite	lb.	15.00-20.00
Chile, medium grades	lb.	12.00
Chile, tumbling grade	lb.	5.00
California, Colorado, various grades	oz.	1.00-3.00
Reconstructed, blocks, 2-3# 4x4"	lb.	35.00-39.00

LAPIS NEVADA

Compact, pinkish-greenish metamorphic rock composed of thulite, diopside, epidote, scapolite from Douglas Co., Nevada; useful for cabochons, carvings, beads, etc.

Mine run, per lb., $8.00/lb., per 10 lb. $5.00/lb, per 100 lb. $2.50/lb.

LAURELITE, see IDOCRASE

LAZULITE

A dark to medium blue mineral resembling lazurite but rare and seldom found in masses large enough to provide cabochons; very rarely, small clear crystals are found in some diamond-bearing gravels of Brazil.

California, ½"-2" crystals	ea.	20.00-240.00
California, massive, ½"-4" pieces	ea.	1.50-15.00

LAZURITE, see LAPIS LAZULI

LEPIDOLITE

Soft pink to mauve massive lithium mica rock occurring in pegmatites; has been used for spheres, bookends, and other ornamental objects; eventually fades.

California, Maine, etc.	lb.	2.00-8.00

LEUCITE

Faceting material from ⅛"-2" crystals occurring in lavas; very pale straw color; collectors' gem only.

Italy, to 3 ct.	ea.	1.25-7.50

LIBYAN DESERT GLASS, SEE TEKTITE

LINTONITE, SEE THOMSONITE

LLANITE, LLANOITE
Granite rock containing small blue chatoyant quartz grains in brownish groundmass; soft; useful for ornamental objects only.

Texas	lb.	.75-1.50

MAGNESITE
Rarely in clear facetable crystals from Brazil that provide faceted gems to 15-20 ct. Massive, very fine-grained material, mostly from Nevada, provides pure-white carving material; it is also dyed in the form of tumbled gems to simulate turquoise and other gemstones.

Brazil, colorless, facet, to 2 cts.	ct.	20.00
Brazil, colorless, ½"-4" crystals	ea.	8.50-500.00
Nevada, white, massive	lb.	3.00-12.00

MAGNETITE
Black magnetic iron ore sometimes cut as a curiosity.

½"-4" crystals	ea.	.75-10.00

MALACHITE
Bright green copper carbonate known from antiquity and extensively used for ornamental items and carvings, and for beads and other forms of jewelry; soft but dense and fairly tough in thick sections; attractively banded in shades of dark to pale green, the darker material accepting a better polish; often in large masses to many pounds in weight but seldom thicker than 4" with usual crusts being 1"–2" thick; slowly alters to a black coating, especially if excessively handled; classic sources in Russia exhausted; sporadic production from Arizona; principally supplied from copper mines in Africa.

Africa, fine, banded, pieces, exotic pattern, to 2 lb.	lb.	10.00-16.00
Africa, fine, banded, pieces, exotic pattern, over 2 lb.	lb.	12.00-20.00
Africa, small pieces for cabs	lb.	9.00

MARCASITE
Probably all small faceted gems used in buckles and the like and called "marcasite" are actually pyrite or a bright, non-tarnishing steel alloy.

	lb.	3.00

MARCASITE AGATE, SEE QUARTZ

MARIPOSITE
Foliated rock with bright green streaks of fuchsite mica in white ground-mass; soft; suitable for ornamental objects.

California	lb.	1.00-5.00

MEERSCHAUM, SEE SEPIOLITE

MESOLITE
White fibrous zeolite mineral sometimes cut into chatoyant cabochons; soft; collectors' item only.

Oregon, pieces to 2"	ea.	.75-6.00

METEORITES
Metallic meteorites are occasionally sliced and polished for unusual jewelry; very small "nuggets" have been set whole in tie clasps.

Texas, ½"-1"	ea.	5.00-10.00
Texas. 2-12 oz.	ea.	9.00-70.00

MICROCLINE, see FELDSPAR

MICROLITE
Extremely rare in facet-grade crystals which come only from the Rutherford mines near Amelia, Virginia; dark reddish-brown to pale brown; cut gems not over 3 ct.

Virginia, to 5 ct.	ct.	5.00-30.00

MIMETITE
Compact forms of this lead mineral have been cut into bright orange cabochons; soft; collectors' curiosity; occasionally available from Mexico.

MOLDAVITE, see TEKTITE

MOONSTONE, see FELDSPAR

MORDENITE
White fibrous zeolite mineral from Nova Scotia; sometimes cut into cabochons showing weak chatoyancy.

Nova Scotia, nodules up to ¾"	ea.	.50-1.25

MORGANITE, see BERYL

MORION, see QUARTZ

MOTHER OF PEARL, see SHELL

MOZARKITE, see QUARTZ (CHERT and FLINT)

MUSCOVITE
Massive, fine-grained rose material from New Mexico has sometimes been cut into cabochons; soft; collectors' item only.

New Mexico, to 2" pieces	ea.	1.75-3.00

MYRICKITE, see OPAL

NACRE, see SHELL

NATROLITE
Colorless slender crystals of this zeolite mineral provide small faceted gems, the largest of which, cut from New Jersey material, reach about 20 ct; also from California benitoite locality, from Ice River, British Columbia, and lately, from Mt. St. Hilaire, Quebec.

New Jersey, 1-5 ct.	ct.	4.00
New Jersey, 10-15 ct.	ct.	6.00
New Jersey, crystals with clear areas, to 10 gm.	ea.	5.00-50.00
California, small clear areas in crystals	ct.	4.00

NEPHRITE
Fibrous *actinolite* or *tremolite*; hard and extremely tough, the classical jade predating jadeite jade and much revered by the ancient Chinese; translucent to nearly opaque; many hues, but seldom as vivid as jadeite, include near-white, tan, yellow, brown, brownish-red, pinkish, yellow-green, olive-green, bluish, dark green to nearly black, etc. From Khotan, the ancient Chinese source, and from Siberia and Silesia. Currently supplied in large quantities from Alaska, British Columbia, Wyoming, California, and New Zealand. The prized green material from Siberia is also reappearing in the market. The Chinese prized the off-white Khotan "mutton fat" nephrite, but it is little esteemed in the West; the most valuable nephrites are now the bright greens from Wyoming, Siberia, and New Zealand without traces of olive; as the latter hue appears, the value decreases. "Black" jade from Wyoming and South Australia is also prized but in reality is a type of very dark olive-green nephrite. The Wyoming fine greens are now

very scarce. Unworked material from New Zealand prohibited from export. A deposit in Taiwan is now exhausted and probably green nephrite advertised from Korea, Taiwan, and China is British Columbia export material.

Alaska, dark greens, usually mottled	lb.	10.00-45.00
Alaska, dark greens, chatoyant streaks	lb.	15.00-25.00
Alaska, dark greens, good quality	sq. in.	2.00-5.00
California, Monterey, grayish-green , fine quality	lb.	12.00-22.00
California, Monterey, dark gray-green to olive-green	lb.	6.00-10.00
California, Monterey, slabbed	sq. in.	.50-5.00
California, Riverside Co., black	lb.	25.00
California, Riverside Co., black magnetite-hematite inclusions	lb.	25.00
California, Mariposa Co., dark green	lb.	3.00-5.00
Wyoming, finest light green, no inclusions	lb.	50.00-150.00
Wyoming, fine green	lb.	20.00-45.00
Wyoming, good green, some spots	lb.	15.00-20.00
Wyoming, olive-greens	lb.	12.00
Wyoming, fine black	lb.	10.00-14.00
Wyoming, pink and green	lb.	20.00
Wyoming, dendritic	lb.	25.00
Wyoming, blue	lb.	12.00
British Columbia, good green	lb.	25.00-up
British Columbia, ordinary greens	lb.	6.00-10.00
British Columbia, pink	lb.	25.00
British Columbia, greens, in blocks to 100 lbs.	lb.	3.50-20.00
British Columbia, stream pebbles, some cuttable	lb.	.75-1.00
British Columbia, modules	lb.	20.00
Taiwan, good green	lb.	30.00

NICCOLITE (NICKELINE)
Nickel sulfide mineral polishing to brilliant metallic luster and very pale copper color; collectors' gem only.

Ontario, massive cabochon grade	lb.	5.00-10.00

OBSIDIAN
A common glass-like volcanic rock used extensively for tumbled gems, small carvings, ornamental objects, and jewelry; brittle and weak; black most common but also brown, reddish-brown, and streaked material, the so-called "flow" obsidians; *Apache tears* are black to dark brown clear nodules weathered from perlite rock; *sheen* obsidians contain numerous minute spangly inclusions, the best being a *gold sheen* from Mexico; also *rainbow* obsidian with colored inclusions, sometimes in pronounced bands with or without spangling; also *spiderweb*, a brecciated type, and *snowflake*, a kind with grayish flower-like patches in a black groundmass. Available in large quantities and in large pieces to 10-25 lb. from California, Oregon, Nevada, Mexico.

Black	lb.	1.00
Snowflake	lb.	1.00-1.50
Mahogany sheen	lb.	1.00-1.50
Gold or silver sheen	lb.	1.00-1.50
Mexican gold sheen, large spangles	lb.	1.50-1.75
Rainbow	lb.	1.00-1.50
Apache tears, Arizona	lb.	8.00
Slabs of ordinary obsidians	sq. in.	.50-1.00
Tumbling grades of ordinary obsidians	lb.	.65-1.00
Mexico, pink snowflake	lb.	4.00

OLIGOCLASE, SEE FELDSPAR

ONYX, SEE CALCITE OR QUARTZ

OOLITE, SEE QUARTZ

OPAL

For a discussion of color and its bearing upon value in precious opal varieties such as *black, white* and *Mexican* types, see the following chapter; these value factors should be kept in mind when assessing rough. Additionally, rough sections should be turned over carefully under good light to see along which direction the most vivid color display occurs; in white opal, this direction is commonly upon the seam edges, but if gems were cut to put the best color "face up," the stones would necessarily have to be small. Check all translucent material against a strong light to detect opaque spots within; these may be areas of useless "potch" which will disfigure the finished gem. Check all Mexican, Nevadan, and Australian "jelly" opals against the light to see if cracks penetrate within otherwise clean areas; if so, these may enlarge with cutting due to relief of inherent stresses in the material; if possible, avoid buying such pieces. Examine all black opal scam material for thickness of seams; if such are too thin, the most delicate lapidary work may not be able to cut them into gems of sufficiently broad surface area. Use glycerine for coating surfaces to be examined; hold stone at about arm's length in a normally bright light. If the colors are quite apparent the finished gem will be bright and valuable. Most precious opal comes from Australia (whites & blacks); highly translucent to transparent colorless, faintly bluish, yellow, brownish, and reds from Mexico, with or without play of color, some being facetable; also colorless, white, and gray to black from Nevada, with or without play of color; colorless transparent non-precious *hyalite* from Mexico; common opal is abundant but seldom used for jewelry; *opalized wood* is used for specimen slices, bookends, etc. Blue and pink opal from the Andes mountain region of Peru is new to the market. Harder than Australian opal, the blue has a hardness of 7. The pink opal has a hardness of 6.

Australia, black opal, finest grade	oz.	500.00-2000.00
Australia, black opal, mintable, red, multicolors, crystal	oz.	750.00-1650.00
Australia, black opal, fair grades, thin seams	oz.	30.00-175.00
Lightning Ridge gem grade	oz.	560.00+
Lightning Ridge super gem grade	oz.	1000.00+
Australia, white opal, finest grade, large stones	oz.	175.00-350.00
Australia, white opal, good grade, large stones	oz.	60.00-100.00
Australia, white opal, good, small stones	oz.	30.00-50.00
Australia, white opal, good, chips	oz.	3.00-10.00
Australia, white opal, fair grade	oz.	3.00-40.00
Australia, white opal, fair grade small stones	oz.	12.00-45.00
Australia, white opal replacing shells or fossils	ea.	25.00-100.00
Australia, white opal replacing glauberite crystals, about 3" diam.	ea.	75.00-200.00
Australia, jelly opal, blue/green	gm.	26.00-90.00
Australia, boulder opal (seam opal)	ea.	5.00-250.00
Mexico, transparent precious, bluish body color	oz.	80.00-250.00
Mexico, transparent orange, yellow, red body color	oz.	40.00-90.00
Mexico, transparent mine run, some precious	lb.	12.00-25.00
Mexico, transparent mine run, precious opal in matrix	lb.	20.00
Mexico, transparent mine run, small chips precious opal	lb.	8.00-10.00
Mexico, facet grade hyalite, 2-10 ct.	ct.	.05-.25
Mexico, facet grade yellow, orange, red, 2-40 ct.	ct.	2.00-6.00
Honduras, precious seam opal	oz.	15.00-25.00
Honduras, precious matrix opal	oz.	10.00-25.00

Honduras, precious opal in nodules, $\frac{1}{2}$"-1"	ea.	10.00-45.00
Peru, blue, transparent, gem, facet quality	lb.	250.00-2000.00
Peru, pink, opaque, fine quality, cab grade	lb.	45.00
Nevada, Virgin Valley, black	oz.	15.00-25.00
Nevada, Virgin Valley, black, (rarely available)		
fine limb sections	oz.	50.00-100.00
Nevada, Virgin Valley, white, precious	oz.	15.00-25.00
Nevada, Virgin Valley, jelly, precious	oz.	20.00-40.00
Nevada, cabochon grade moss opal	lb.	1.25
Brazil, white precious opal, fine, red, blue, greens	oz.	25.00-75.00
Brazil, yellow to orange, facet grade	gm.	20.00
Oregon, cinnabar in opal, "myrickite"	lb.	30.00
Oregon, opal, facet grade	gm.	3.00
Common opal, includes "opalite"	lb.	3.00
Opalized wood, various types	lb.	.25-3.00

OPALITE, SEE OPAL

ORTHOCLASE, SEE FELDSPAR

PECTOLITE
Fibrous white compact masses sometimes cut into cabochons displaying a weak chatoyancy; collectors' gem only. Silky blue called *larimar* from the Dominican Republic.

California, seam sections to 1" thick	lb.	4.50-10.00
Dominican Republic, blue and white, slabbed	gm.	.75
Dominican Republic, chunks	gm.	.35

PENTLANDITE
Sometimes cut into cabochons for collectors; brilliant metallic luster.

Ontario	lb.	1.00-4.50

PERIDOT (OLIVINE)
Gem variety known as *peridot*; from dark brown to pale yellow-green, but only green hues used for gems; somewhat soft and brittle but customarily used in fine jewelry; finest crystals from St. John's Island (Zebirget) in Red Sea but now scarce; good to fine large crystals found in Myanmar but color somewhat darker than St. John's material; also, some contain swarms of very small inclusions which may deaden the brilliance of faceted gems; in other instances the inclusions are aligned and furnish good chatoyant gems; Myanmar material is now obtainable while small quantities of St.John's peridot reach the market from time to time, fair to fine material from San Carlos, Arizona, continues to be in abundant supply although seldom capable of cutting flawless gems over about 5 ct.

St. John's, facet grade, 3-6 ct.	oz.	10.00
St. John's, facet grade, 6-10 ct.	oz.	20.00
St. John's, facet grade, 11-20 ct.	oz.	30.00
St. John's, facet grade, over 20 ct.	oz.	40.00
Arizona, best facet grade, to 5 ct.	ct.	1.00-2.50
Arizona, best facet grade, 5-15 ct.	ct.	2.00-7.00
Arizona, best facet grade, 20-24 ct.	ct.	4.00-15.00
Arizona, mine run	lb.	16.00-20.00

PERISTERITE, SEE FELDSPAR

PERTHITE, SEE FELDSPAR

PETALITE

Rare pegmatite mineral; colorless to pink; sometimes facetable from clear areas in colorless crystals from New South Wales and Maine; fairly hard, brittle; inclusions common; collectors' item only. A recent material from Brazil is larger and flawless and in the best crystals produces brilliant, sparkling gems.

New South Wales, facet grade, colorless, 2-8 ct.	ct.	1.00-5.00
South West Africa, massive pink	lb.	5.00-7.00
Brazil, facet grade, colorless 1-10 cts.	ct.	1.50-3.00
Brazil, facet grade, colorless 10-20 cts.	ct.	2.50-4.00
Brazil, facet grade, colorless 20-30 cts.	ct.	3.50-5.00
Brazil, facet grade, colorless 30-40 cts.	ct.	4.00-6.00
Brazil, facet grade, colorless 40-50 cts.	ct.	4.50-7.00
Brazil, facet grade, colorless 50-60 cts.	ct.	5.00-8.00

PETOSKEY STONE, SEE CALCITE

PHENAKITE

Hard, colorless pegmatite mineral of considerable rarity; clear crystals sometimes cuttable to faceted gems of 5-10 ct. but usual sizes much less; also from Maine, Colorado, and New Hampshire. Inclusions common; collectors' gem only.

Brazil, facet-grade crystals to 2"	ea.	7.50-60.00
Urals, colorless facet-grade crystals to 2"	ea.	20.00-125.00

PHOSPHOPHYLLITE

Beautiful pale blue-green soft phosphate mineral found in cuttable crystals only in one Bolivian tin deposit; cleavable, fragile, difficult to process; very rare; collectors' gem only.

Bolivia, facet grade to 1" crystals.	ea.	55.00-125.00

PIEMONTITE, SEE EPIDOTE

POLLUCITE

Colorless to faintly straw-yellow, often with white inclusions; occurs as clear areas in form-less grains; medium-hard, brittle; collectors' gem only.

Maine, facet grade fragments to 10 ct.	ct.	1.00-2.50
Connecticut, facet grade fragments to 15 ct.	ct.	1.00-4.00

PRASE, SEE QUARTZ

PRASIOLITE, SEE QUARTZ

PREHNITE

Abundant in some lavas as crusts lining cavities; various shades of green, yellow, brown; rarely thick enough or colorful enough to provide good cabochon material; unusually translu-cent kinds are facetable; hard and tough but mainly cut for collectors.

New Jersey, fine green, cabochon grade	lb.	4.00-20.00
Australia, pale green, cabochon grade	lb.	3.00-15.00
Scotland, pale greenish-yellow, facet grade	oz.	1.00-5.00

PROUSTITE

Rare silver mineral of beautiful intense ruby-red color but very soft and difficult to polish; practically all facetable material comes from old specimens from Chanarcillo, Chile; collectors' gem only; surface tarnishes in a matter of months.

Facet grade, 2-20 ct.	ct.	5.00-45.00

PSILOMELANE, SEE QUARTZ

PUMPELLYITE (Chlorastrolite)
  Only the variety *chlorastrolite* is used for cabochon gems; it forms compact gray-green nodules in lavas and seldom exceeds ¼" diameter; highest-quality nodules accept a glass-like polish and display a pattern of small dark green to pale grayish-green chatoyant patches; rare in sizes over ½"; soft, mainly cut for collectors.

Michigan, spot-polished to show quality, nuggets ⅜"	gm.	.10-.20

PYRITE
  Solid crystals capable of being faceted or cabochoned into gems of brilliant metallic luster and pleasing brass-yellow hue; soft, brittle; collectors' gem only.

Various localities, crystals	oz.	.75-1.00
Various localities, crystals	lb.	3.00-8.00

PYROPE, see GARNET

PYROXMANGITE
  A pink manganese mineral sometimes cut into very small faceted gems; from one locality in Japan only; very rare; collectors' gem only.

Facet grade, ½ ct. pieces	ct.	1.00-5.00

QUARTZ
  The numerous varieties of this mineral provide more inexpensive gem material than all other species combined. *Crystalline* varieties are those with individual crystals large enough to see with the naked eye or under weak magnification; *cryptocrystalline* varieties require high magnification and typically contain minute fibrous or granular crystals, commonly arranged in parallel groupings forming bands. Varietal nomenclature of quartz has been made extremely complex and confusing by the tendency of miners and dealers to affix distinctive names to varieties which actually differ but little from well-established varieties; the result is a long list of names which have little meaning. The list below includes only the standard varieties or those which have been shown to be sufficiently different to deserve their own varietal names.

QUARTZ—CRYSTALLINE

Amethyst

  Customarily divided into three grades according to decreasing desirability: *Siberian*, *Uruguay*, and *Bahia*, the first being richest and purest in hue with decided change in color from blue-purple in daylight to red-purple under tungsten light; supplied mainly by Brazil with smaller amounts from Uruguay, Madagascar, and elsewhere; quality names above are appended to material from any source, providing it meets quality standards. Serious defects in rough include color-banding (usually as colorless streaks alternating with colored areas), variations in color intensity, smoky tinges, and veils of inclusions; attempts to remove smoky color may result in complete loss of amethystine hue as well as smoky tinge. Finest material is rare in sizes over about 1"–2" diameter. Mainly facet-cut, some being used for cabochons, tumbled gems, and larger pieces for carvings. Also from S.W. Africa, S. Africa, and Zambia.

Brazil, finest Siberian, facet grade, under 1-5 cts.	ct.	.50-2.00
Brazil, finest Siberian, facet grade, 10-20 cts.	ct.	1.25-2.50
Brazil, Uruguay facet grade, crystals	lb.	15.00
Brazil, very pale facet grade, 1-70 cts.	ct.	.10-.25
Brazil, cabochon and tumbling	lb.	4.50
Mexico, small, facet grade, medium color	gm.	1.25-2.50
Mexico, crystal tips, tumbling grade	lb.	4.50
Mexico, phantoms, terminated, cuttable	ea.	.50-1.00
Australia, crystals to 4", fair grade areas for faceting	lb.	28.00
Ontario, large crystals, tumbling grade	lb.	2.00-3.50

Tanzania, tumbling grade	lb.	10.00
S.W. African "Siberian" type, rich red tint, 1-5 cts.	ct.	.40-.80
S.W. African "Siberian" type, rich red tint, 5-10 cts.	ct.	.80-1.65
S.W. African "Siberian" type, rich red tint, 10-20 cts.	ct.	1.20-2.50
S.W. African "Siberian" type, rich red tint, 20-30 cts.	ct.	1.30-2.75
S.W. African "Siberian" type, rich red tint, 30-40 cts.	ct.	2.00-3.80
S.W. African "Siberian" type, rich red tint, 40-50 cts.	ct.	2.50-4.60
S.W. African "Siberian" type, rich red tint, 50-60 cts.	ct.	3.00-5.50
S.W. African "Siberian" type, rich red tint, 70-80 cts.	ct.	4.00-14.00

Greened Amethyst

Brazilian amethyst converted to peculiar grayish-green hues by heat treatment; the name *prasiolite* is sometimes applied to this material; faceted gems seldom over 10 ct.

Brazil, facet or cab grade	oz.	.60-5.00
Brazil, translucent, 6-18" saw sizes	lb.	4.00

"Star" Amethyst

Pale amethyst containing filaments of reddish hematite arranged upon the terminal faces of the crystals; when cut across the crystal tips a fixed six-ray pattern is seen, but the legs of the "star" are merely streaks where the hematite crystals fail to reflect light; apparently only from a single deposit in Mexico.

Single crystal tips	ct.	1.00

Ametrine

Amethyst and Citrine mix, Bolivia. Found in only one location in Bolivia, the site was discovered in 1964, west of the Paraguay River, a natural border with Brazil. Ametrine is naturally occurring material colored partly purple and partly yellow in the same crystal. Production is sporadic.

Bolivian, deep violet red and citrine, clean	oz.	29.00
Bolivian, deep violet mine run	kg.	5.00-20.00

Aventureine Quartz

Fine-grained quartzites containing numerous mica crystals which impart a spangled appearance when viewed in the appropriate direction; formerly in golden material from Russia but now the best is green material from India and Brazil; popular for tumbled gems, cabochons, carvings, and ornamental objects.

India, medium to light green, blocks to 20 lbs.	lb.	1.00-2.00
India, tumbling fragments	lb.	.75-1.00
India, slabbed	sq. in.	.25-.50
India, dark blue	lb.	3.00
Brazil, dark green, wiht mica inclusions	lb.	1.25-4.00
Brazil, blue, 5-20 lbs.	lb.	2.50

Binghamite, see Tigereye

Cacoxonite, see Goethite in Quartz

Cairngorm, see Smoky Quartz

Catseye Quartz

Contains numerous parallel fibers which are finer and less abundant than those in tigereye; cabochon gems show a good to fine straight streak of light; colors yellow, brown, rarely green; mainly from Sri Lanka; rough not available; also produced by bleaching of tigereye.

CITRINE

Much used in inexpensive jewelry as a substitute for genuine topaz and unfortunately often sold under that name; color ranges from faint yellow to deep pure yellow, to golden yellow, to reddish-yellow, and in various shades of yellowish-brown; heat-treated amethyst produces rich reddish material known as *Rio Grande citrine*, *Madeira citrine*, and *Palmyra citrine*, the deeper colored amethysts producing correspondingly deeper colors in the citrine; this material is more expensive than naturally-colored material. The terms *ox-blood* or *sang de boeuf* are sometimes used for natural dark citrines with a decided reddish hue. Virtually all citrine is produced in Brazil, but fine material occasionally appears from Madagascar. Ordinary citrine often occurs in sizes capable of cutting flawless gems over several hundred carats in weight. Most material is facet-cut but some is employed in cabochons and tumbled gems; large flawed pieces are desirable for carvings.

Brazil, Rio Grande, facet grade, 1½-3 cts.	ct.	1.50-3.75
Brazil, Rio Grande, facet grade, 3-5 cts.	ct.	3.50-6.50
Brazil, Rio Grande, facet grade, over 5 cts.	ct.	3.00-15.00
Brazil, fair to good grades of Rio Grande, to 70 cts.	ct.	1.00-5.00
Brazil, Madeira, & Palmyra facet grade, 1-3 cts.	ct.	.40-1.00
Brazil, Madeira, & Palmyra facet grade, over 3 cts.	ct.	1.00-2.00
Brazil, Madeira, & Palmyra facet grade, mine run	lb.	2.00-4.00
Brazil, ox-blood, facet grade, to 15 cts.	ct.	1.00-4.00
Brazil, rich yellow, facet grade, to 50 cts.	ct.	.50-.80
Brazil, medium yellow, facet grade, to 50 cts.	ct.	.50-.75
Brazil, pale yellow, facet grade, to 50 cts.	ct.	.20-.65
Brazil, yellow, tinged smoky, facet grade	ct.	.30-.75
Brazil, yellow, tinged smoky, facet grade	lb.	1.50-3.50

DUMORTIERITE QUARTZ

Fine-grained quartzite containing deep blue inclusions of dumortierite; also available in pink; generally used in larger ornamental objects.

California, blue	lb.	4.00
Nevada, pink	lb.	2.00-4.00

GOETHITE IN QUARTZ ("CACOXENITE")

The Brazilian material is commonly and erroneously called "cacoxenite" due to an early misidentification of the brilliant yellow to gold parallel goethite fibers and tufts which appear in this variety; the fibers are arranged in layers parallel to the terminal faces of large citrine-amethyst-smoky quartz crystals, the centers of which supply tumbling material, but only the outer zones provide the material herein described; when properly oriented, fair catseye and chatoyant effects are possible.

Brazil, good cabochon grade, pieces to 2"-3"	lb.	2.50-5.00
Brazil, good cabochon grade, slabbed	sq. in.	.50-1.00

GREEN QUARTZITE

A fine-grained pale green variety sometimes used for tumbled gems; available in large pieces from Brazil and Africa.

Pieces to 10 lbs.	lb.	1.00-4.00

GREENED AMETHYST, SEE AMETHYST

MORION, SEE SMOKY QUARTZ

PRASE

This varietal name was once applied to fine-grained quartzite colored dark green by inclusions of amphibole; some authorities believe it should also apply to green jaspers; the term is now rarely used and material using this name is very seldom sold.

ROCK CRYSTAL

Colorless quartz; very abundant in facet-grade crystals to several pounds weight; large flawless pieces capable of cutting spheres in excess of 3" are rare and cost rises sharply as size increases above this; electronic-grade crystals of 5-10 lbs. may realize over $50.00 per pound; much of facet material is left over from the extensive mining for electronic quartz in Brazil during World War II; Brazil continues to be the largest supplier, but good material is available from Arkansas as well as from many other places in the world.

Brazil, facet grade, to 100 cts.	ct.	.03-.05
Brazil, facet grade, to 200-300 cts.	ct.	.01-.03
Sphere blocks, for 3" spheres	lb.	5.00-12.00
Sphere blocks, for 4" spheres	lb.	10.00-25.00
Carving blocks, small flaws and inclusions	lb.	4.00-7.00

ROSE QUARTZ

Translucent to nearly transparent; from very pale pink to medium rose, sometimes with a bluish tinge; also chatoyant but rarely so pronounced that good star or catseye cabochons can be cut; favored for carvings. Value depends upon intensity of hue coupled with approach to transparency; mainly supplied by Brazil but also from Madagascar, South Dakota, and Canada.

Brazil, facet grade, good pink	oz.	3.50
Brazil, extra fine cabochon grade, dark pink	lb.	4.00
Brazil, fine star material, good pink, good chatoyancy	oz.	10.00
Brazil fine star material, pale pink	gm.	.15-.20
Brazil pale pink 20-80 lb.	lb.	.85-4.00
Madagascar, strong star material, gook pink	ct.	.10-.30
Madagascar, good pink, chunks	lb.	25.00
Georgia, facet grade, or star grade, good pink	oz.	5.00
Georgia, select facet grade	gm.	.25-.50
Georgia, tumbling grade	lb.	2.00-6.00
South Dakota, bright pink	lb.	4.00

RUTILATED QUARTZ

Recently in abundance from Brazil in fair to superb material containing brilliant coppery to golden rutile fibers in colorless to medium smoky quartz; some fibers occur in broad blades to $\frac{1}{2}$" wide, others appear in stellate patterns upon small black tabular hematite crystals; crystals to 10 lbs. weight. Used mainly for specimen pieces but also for cabochons, carvings, and ornamental items.

Brazil, golden rutile in quartz	lb.	7.50-8.50
Brazil, golden rutile in quartz, mine run	lb.	2.50-7.00
Brazil, golden rutile in quartz, tumbling pieces	lb.	2.50-5.00

SMOKY QUARTZ

Includes all varieties with hues from pale brownish smoky to rich brown to nearly black; *cairngorm* is rich brown material and *morion* is material of very dark color; can be heat-treated to lighten or drive off color completely; smoky quartz with yellowish tinge is commonly a mixture of smoky and citrine and can be heat-treated to remove the smoky hue and leave behind the pure citrine color. virtually all material is supplied commercially by Brazil but also available from Madagascar, California, Maine, and elsewhere. Favored for faceted gems which are often misleadingly called "smoky topaz." Also used in carvings, spheres, and other ornamental objects.

Brazil, medium smoky, facet grade, 1-100 cts.	ct.	.05-.07
Brazil, medium smoky, facet grade, 200-300 cts.	ct.	.03-.05
Brazil, medium smoky, facet grade, 1000 cts. up	ct.	.01-.03
Brazil, tumbling	lb.	.85-1.00

TIGEREYE

Narrow seams of an asbestos mineral replaced by quartz; the original fibrous structure is retained, resulting in chatoyancy in polished specimens; yellow, brownish-yellow, brown, red, blue, green, and streaked in these colors; yellow is by far the most abundant kind; supplied exclusively from South West Africa; Brown and yellow kinds turn red upon heat-treatment; they can also be turned to very pale yellow by bleaching in warm oxalic acid solution. *Binghamite* is a tigereye from the iron deposits of Minnesota; its fibers are much finer and chatoyancy sometimes greater. *Silkstone* is analogous to binghamite but the fibers are randomly oriented and it is not so highly prized. African tigereye used extensively in cabochons, engraved gems, tumbled gems, and ornamental items.

S. W. Africa, fine yellow, seams ½"-2" thick	lb.	6.50-15.00
S. W. Africa, dark blue	lb.	8.00-15.00
S. W. Africa, natural red	lb.	15.00
S. W. Africa, multicolored	lb.	8.00-15.00
S. W. Africa, fragments for tumbling	lb.	4.00-8.00
S. W. Africa, slabbed, 1"-1½"-2"	ea.	.90-1.30
Minnesota, binghamite, slabs	sq. in.	3.00
Minnesota, silkstone	sq. in.	.35-1.50

TOURMALINATED QUARTZ

Clear to smoky quartz containing slender black tourmaline needles; the value depends on uniformity of size of needles and even distribution throughout the quartz; the needles should not be too fine or too abundant; sometimes used for cabochons and carvings.

| Brazil | lb. | 4.00-7.50 |

END OF QUARTZ-CRYSTALLINE SECTION

QUARTZ—CRYPTOCRYSTALLINE

BANDED AGATE

Major source continues to be the Brazilian-Uruguayan basalt field producing nodules from walnut-size to 10"-12" in diameter; much is dull gray material but some is fairly colorful with good bands; finest colored material is being provided by the Mexican fields.

Brazil, nodules to 10" diameter	lb.	1.50-3.50
Brazil, nodules to 10" diameter, slabbed	lb.	4.50
Brazil, nodules to 10" diameter, slabbed, whole sections	ea.	1.50-15.00
Uruguay, small nodules and fragments, tumbling grade	lb.	.75-1.50
Mexico, Coyamito nodules, 1"	lb.	1.25-2.00
Mexico, Coyamito nodules, 1"-2"	lb.	1.00-5.00
Mexico, Coyamito nodules, over 2":	lb.	5.00-7.00
Mexico, Coyamito nodules, broken, tumbling grade	lb.	1.25-5.00
Mexico, Laguna nodules	lb.	2.00-5.00
Mexico, Laguna nodules, slabbed, whole sections	ea.	1.50-15.00+
Mexico, Laguna nodules, slabbed, whole sections	sq. in.	.50-1.00
Mexico, Moctezuma nodules	lb.	.45-2.50
Mexico, black & blue banded	lb.	1.50
Mexico, field run, various sources	lb.	.75

Mexico, field run, various sources, tumbling grade	lb.	.50-1.50
Botswana, slabbed	ea.	3.00-8.00
Botswana, slabbed	lb.	5.00
Montana, Dryhead, nodules & seam sections	lb.	7.50-12.00
Montana, Dryhead, tumbling	lb.	3.00-10.00
Idaho, blue and white, seam sections	lb.	4.00
New Mexico, seam sections	lb.	2.50-4.50
Nova Scotia, nodules & seam sections	lb.	6.00
Ontario, small nodules, ½"-2"	lb.	2.00
Oregon, Eagle Point, seam sections	lb.	4.00
Texas, blue and white, seam sections	lb.	.50-4.00

BLOODSTONE

An extremely dense, dark green moss agate in which appear more or less circular spots of dark red or so-called "drops of blood." India is virtually the only reliable source. Finest material shows a uniform green groundmass with evenly-spaced red dots.

India, bulk lots	lb.	6.00
India, very select	oz.	1.00-2.00
India, slabbed	sq. in.	.50-.75

CARNELIAN

Translucent chalcedony of brownish-red, red, or red-orange color; *sard* is dark reddish-brown, *sardonyx* is sard with white bands; natural brownish carnelian often improved in color by heat-treatment; most vivid red-orange material is heat-treated Indian carnelian; much carnelian from Idar-Oberstein is dyed.

Brazil, nodules and pieces to 7" diameter	lb.	2.00-4.00
Brazil, small pebbles for tumbling	lb.	1.50-2.50
Brazil, broken nodules for tumbling	lb.	2.00
Brazil, slabbed	ea.	3.00-7.50
Uruguay, small pebbles, field run	lb.	2.50-4.00
India, heat-treated, 1"-3"	lb.	2.00-3.50
Oregon and Washington, field run	lb.	2.00-3.50

CHALCEDONY

Mexico, blue, nodules to 2"	lb.	10.00
Mexico, amethystine, small pieces	lb.	1.25-3.50
South West Africa, blue, selected pieces	oz.	3.50
South West Africa, blue, selected pieces	lb.	16.00

DYED CHALCEDONIES

Finest grades dyed with permanent pigments and are uniformly colored, free of flaws, and mostly translucent; mainly supplied by Idar-Oberstein, Germany, in slabs; rough used is Brazilian agate and chalcedony.

Black, slabbed	sq. in.	.15-.25
Black, slabbed	lb.	28.00
Black & white banded, slabbed	sq.in.	.50-1.00
Black & white banded, slabbed	lb.	50.00
Red, slabbed	sq.in.	.50-1.00
Red, slabbed	lb.	38.00
Green, slabbed	sq.in.	.50-1.00
Green, slabbed	lb.	38.00
Green & white banded, slabbed	sq. in.	.50-1.00
Green & white banded, slabbed	lb.	50.00
Blue, slabbed	sq. in.	.50-1.00

Blue, slabbed	lb.	35.00-45.00
Blue & white banded, slabbed	sq. in.	.50-1.00
Blue & white banded, slabbed	lb.	50.00

CHERT AND FLINT

Chalcodonic materials of sedimentary origin; usually less translucent than chalcedonies deposited during volcanic activity; rarely display banding but may have attractive patterns and colors resulting from stains.

England, gray flint nodules	lb.	.65-1.25
Germany, brown flint nodules and pieces	lb.	.65-1.25
Iowa, banded chert	lb.	.50-1.50
Ohio, Flint Ridge chert, pieces, multicolor, slabs	ea.	5.00-12.00
Ozark Mountains, chert, "mozarkite", slabbed	ra.	10.00-25.00
Ohio Flint, tumbling	lb.	.50-.75

CHRYSOCOLLA CHALCEDONY

Translucent chalcedony colored attractive blue-green to green by copper minerals; finest material uniformly colored, free of inclusions, and highly translucent; some can be faceted into "sleepy" gems; principally from Arizona.

Arizona, finest "facet" grade	sq. in.	10.00-16.00
Arizona, finest "facet" grade, to 25 gm.	gm.	1.50-6.50
Arizona, good grade	sq. in.	15.00-30.00
Arizona, good grade, with some defects	oz.	3.00-15.00
Arizona, ordinary grade, some good areas	lb.	20.00
Arizona, soft, porous tumbling grade	lb.	2.00-7.00
Peru, finest gem quality	lb.	30.00

CHRYSOPRASE

Finest known material now comes from Australia and in respect to intensity of hue and quality far overshadows chrysoprase found elsewhere; the best Australian material is translucent, completely uniform in hue and texture, arid is free of pale spots or small quartz-filled vugs.

Australia, finest yellow-green, seam sections	oz.	12.00
Australia, select yellow-green, seam sections	lb.	96.00
Australia, good to fine grades	oz.	2.75-10.00
Australia, mine run lots	lb.	45.00
Brazil, pale green, good to fair quality	oz.	2.75-6.50
Brazil, pale green, good quality	lb.	3.80-9.75
Brazil, tumbling grades	lb.	2.00
California, medium green, good	oz.	2.00-4.00

CORAL (SILICIFIED)

Primarily supplied by Florida in the form of geodes lined with chalcedony of various colors; also solid coral showing coral markings, from Iowa and Utah; mainly used as polished specimens and for tumbling.

Florida, geode sections	lb.	1.00-1.50
Florida, whole geodes	lb.	2.00-5.00
Florida, yellow, solid, with markings	lb.	5.00
Iowa, solid masses, with markings		1.00-3.00
Utah, red horn coral, with markings, slabbed	ea.	3.00
Utah, red horn coral, with markings	lb.	15.00
Utah, red horn coral, with markings, polished	ea.	7.00-10.00

DENDRITIC AGATE, see also MOSS AGATE

Finest types display black, red, or brown inclusions resembling miniature trees, in translucent chalcedony; the best come from India but also occasionally fine from Montana and elsewhere.

Montana, Yellowstone River, slabbed	sq. in.	.75-5.00
Oregon, fine, surface polished, slabbed	ea.	6.00-10.00
Idaho, dendritic	lb.	3.00
Nevada, lavender, some brown, slabbed	ea.	5.00-15.00

DINOSAUR BONE

Dinosaur bones replaced by chalcedony and showing cell structure quite clearly; very variable in quality, solid material being quite rare.

Western U.S., choice cross-sections	lb.	8.00+
Western U.S., field run pieces	lb.	8.00
Western U.S., slabbed, ordinary grade	lb.	2.00-5.00
Western U.S., tumbling	lb.	.75-1.00

EYE AGATE

Two types of agate are called by this name: (1) any banded agate cut in such a manner that the exposed bands form circular rings, and (2) any agate containing tube-like structures which show rings when cut across in the proper direction; the first type is usually cut and polished as a first step and then dyed to impart color to some of the rings. The specimens are then used for display purposes.

Mexico, small eyes	lb.	1.00-1.50
Mexico, "luna" or "moon" agate, purplish-blue	lb.	5.00
Dyed display pieces, 3"-5"	ea.	3.00-18.00

FIRE AGATE

Chalcedonies which contain very thin bands of iridescent goethite; when properly cut the iridescence appears near the surface showing reddish, brownish, golden, and greenish colors; the best material is highly translucent because this detracts least from the iridescence; prices vary greatly depending on intensity of colors.

Southwestern U.S., nodules to 2" diam.	ea.	.75-2.50
Mexico, field run	lb.	12.00
Mexico, face-polished nodules	ea.	1.50-8.00

IRIS AGATE

Because the beautiful colors of this variety are seen only in transmitted light, this material seldom is used in jewelry but finds some employment in screens, lamp shades, or other transparencies through which light will be shown; the finest material is highly translucent, displays vivid colors, and the color bands are at least ½" wide; prices vary greatly depending on intensity of color, width of color bands, and if the slice is a complete nodule section.

Various sources, slabbed to less than ⅛" thick	sq. in.	.75-5.00

JASPER

A convenient catch-all term for all forms of impure chalcedony which contain so many inclusions that the material is usually translucent only on thin edges; many colors and patterns available; much jasper occurs in blocks of large size; common defects are hairline cracks, small quartz crystal-lined vugs, and porous spots which refuse to polish. Only a few varieties are listed below.

California, Morgan Hill, orbicular, excellent	sq. in.	.25-1.50
California, Morgan Hill, orbicular	lb.	7.00-8.50
California, Stone Canyon, brecciated	lb.	3.00

90 ✻ Standard Catalog of Gem Values

Oregon, "Morrisonite"	lb.	2.50-5.00
Oregon, Biggs	sq. in.	.50-1.00
Oregon, Biggs "picture"	lb.	12.00
Oregon, Bruneau	sq. in.	.50-1.00
Oregon, Bruneau	lb.	12.00-20.00
Oregon, polka dot, slabs	ea.	5.00-12.00
Arizona, fine red, slabbed	ea.	5.00-7.00
India, green	lb.	.75-1.50

JASPILITE
Dark reddish siliceous rock containing bands of hematite; the latter assume a bright metallic luster when polished; abundant from iron regions of Minnesota and Michigan.

Minnesota, Michigan	lb.	.90-2.25
Sweden	lb.	3.00

LACE AGATE
Applied to banded agate in which the bands zigzag on a small scale and resemble the scallops of lace edging; "crazy lace" from Mexico is porous and accepts organic dyes.

Alabama	lb.	1.25-3.00
Mexico, "black lace"	lb.	6.00-8.50
Mexico, "crazy lace"	lb.	2.00-6.00
Mexico, "lavender lace"	lb.	2.75
Mexico, broken pieces, assorted	lb.	.35-.50

LAKE SUPERIOR AGATE
Reddish, brownish, and greenish banded agate nodules and pieces found around the Great Lakes, particularly south of Lake Superior; colorful large nodules rare; usual size from 1" to 2"; commonly cracked.

Nodules and sections, ¾"-2"	lb.	.75-4.00
Specimen nodules	ea.	1.50-15.00
Select tumbling grade	lb.	2.00-3.50

MONTANA AGATE
Characterized by brownish-red bands and/or black (dendritic inclusions in translucent pale gray to bluish-gray chalcedony; nodules and fragments in gravels of Yellowstone River Valley, Montana; favorite ring-stone in Western U.S.

Choice nodules, 3" up	lb.	8.00-12.00
Medium grade nodules	lb.	2.00-6.00
Low grade nodules	lb.	1.00-3.00
Tumbling fragments	lb.	.50-1.50
Slabbed, various grades	lb.	2.00-4.00

MOSS AGATE
Contains dark green, brown, yellowish, or red wispy inclusions in translucent chalcedony resembling the filaments of moss; finest qualities display evenly spaced filaments which do not undercut during polishing; major supplies from India but common elsewhere.

Colorado, golden	sq. in.	.50-.75
India, green	lb.	1.00-1.50
India, slabbed	sq. in.	.50-.75
India, tumbling chips	lb.	.75
India, reddish-yellowish, in green	lb.	1.40-1.50
Mexico, "paisley"	lb.	2.00
Mexico, vaquilla," red & yellow	lb.	2.50
Mexico, vaquilia," red & yellow, tumbling chips	lb.	.75–1.50

Mexico, red	lb.	1.00-1.50
Mexico, black	lb.	1.50-2.50
New Mexico, yellow & brown	lb.	1.00-2.50
Oregon, red & yellow, slabs	ea.	6.00-10.00
Oregon, red & green, slabs	ea.	6.00-10.00
Texas, brown, yellow, red	lb.	.75-2.75
Texas, green	lb.	1.00-3.00

NOVACULITE

Gritty sharpening stone quarried in Arkansas and sometimes providing handsome cabochon material; difficult to polish to high luster.

Arkansas, various colors	lb.	.85-3.00

OOLITE AND ALGAE

Minute silica spherules (oolite), usually not over $\frac{1}{16}$" diameter; seldom attractive unless the spherules are distinctly colored; dark brown wavy patterns characterize algae.

Wyoming, brown and black patterns, picture algae	lb.	10.00

PETRIFIED WOODS

A large variety of silicified woods are available, ranging from enormous logs to branch and twig sections, and from dead-black or white to reds, yellows, tans, browns, and other hues; common defects are fractures, soft spots, and small quartz crystal vugs; some woods contain opal in addition to chalcedony and are difficult to polish well because of hardness differences; most specimens used for large ornamental objects but much is also tumbled; the region surrounding the Petrified Forest in Arizona supplies most market demands.

Arizona, Petrified Forest region	lb.	2.50-3.50
Arizona, Petrified Forest region, tumbling chips	lb.	.75-1.50
Georgia, brownish	lb.	1.00-1.25
Louisiana, brownish color	lb.	2.00
Oregon, tempskya, yellow-brown	lb.	1.50-2.00
Oregon, tempskya, yellow-brown, slabbed	sq. in.	.25-.75
Oregon, myrtlewood	lb.	3.00
Texas, palm, cross-sections	lb.	2.00-3.00
Wyoming, Eden Valley black, limbs, $\frac{1}{2}$"-2" dia.	lb.	4.00
Wyoming, North Fork black	lb.	2.00

PLUME AGATES

The finest grades provide very attractive cabochons if the feather-like inclusions are enclosed in translucent chalcedony; prized plume colors are red, yellow, orange, and black; the last is satisfactory only if the plumes are not too dense; quality depends on even spacing of filaments, absence of soft spots, brightness of plume colors, and degree of translucency of enclosing chalcedony; fine examples are not common.

Colorado, fair grade	lb.	2.50
Mexico, black	lb.	1.00-4.00
Mexico, red "Apache" or "flame"	lb.	.65-3.00
Mexico, "bird of paradise"	lb.	1.00
New Mexico, yellow-brown	lb.	.75
Oregon, Graveyard Point	lb.	2.00
Oregon, Carey red	lb.	1.50-15.00
Oregon, white, slabbed	ea.	5.00-15.00
Oregon, Priday Ranch, golden & red	sq. in.	.50-4.50
Texas, Woodward Ranch, select nodules, red	lb.	3.00-4.50
Texas, nodules, red, field run	lb.	2.50
Texas, nodules, black	lb.	.75-2.50

PSILOMELANE CHALCEDONY

Chalcedony containing abundant minute plumes of a black manganese mineral arranged in bands, some bands polishing to a brilliant metallic black; also called "crown of silver," and erroneously, "black malachite." Now used as a substitute for hematite.

Mexico, seam sections	lb.	5.50
Mexico, seam sections, tumbling grade	lb.	1.50
Mexico, seam sections, slabbed	sq. in.	.50-.75

SAGENITE

Chalcedony containing numerous straight needle-like inclusions, often radiating from common centers; rare in fine grades; commonly undercuts.

California, Nipomo, brownish needles, slabbed	ea.	8.00-20.00
Mexico	lb.	2.00-5.00

THUNDEREGGS

These nodules are mostly used as specimens when sawn into halves and polished; occasionally the interior material contains plumes and is then used for cabochons.

Idaho, Sucker Creek	lb.	.75-2.00
Mexico		.75-1.50
Oregon, Priday Ranch	lb.	.90-2.25
Oregon opal	lb.	20.00

TURRITELLA

Large numbers of conical spiral shells, about ¼" long, replaced by silica in a dark brown goundmass; principally supplied by Wyoming.

Slabby pieces to 3" thick	lb.	2.00
Slabby pieces to 3" thick, slabbed	sq. in.	.60

END OF QUARTZ—CRYPTOCRYSTALLINE SECTION

REMONDITE

Formerly misidentified as Burbankite; rare, the facet grade crystals of small size, yellow to orange-yellow in color; gems to about 5 carats; not commercially available.

RHODIZITE

Very rarely as small clear crystals and fragments up to ½" diameter suitable for faceting; pale yellow; from Madagascar only; extremely rare in facetable pieces.

Facet grade, areas in crystal fragments	ea.	7.50-15.00

RHODOCHROSITE

Beautiful massive material only from Catamarca, Argentina; used for cabochons, beads, and ornamental objects; rarely, facet-grade crystals from Colorado, some large enough to cut clean stones of over 50 carats. Soft and brittle but massive material fairly tough. Stalactite sections from Argentina are particularly prized as specimens because of their handsome concentric ring patterns. Also from South Africa in intense pink crystals.

Colorado, facet-grade crystals to 4"	ea.	25.00-525.00
Argentina, best quality, rich pink to pale red	lb.	10.00-12.50
Argentina, small pieces	lb.	5.00-10.00
Argentina, ordinary pale pink grade, all sizes	lb.	5.00-7.50
Argentina, tumbling fragments	lb.	.90-2.00
Argentina, stalactite cross-sections	sq. in.	4.50-6.00
South Africa, facet, intense pink crystals	ct.	2.50-20.00

RHODOLITE, SEE GARNET

RHODONITE
The richest colored material now comes in quantity from Australia; fine red from California no longer available; attractive pink available in quantity from Vancouver Island, Canada; very rarely, facet-grade crystals are found with galena at Broken Hill, New South Wales.

Australia, Broken Hill, facet-grade crystals to ½"	ct.	1.50-12.00
Australia, red, massive	lb.	5.00
Australia, red, tumbling fragments	lb.	.75-2.50
Australia, red, slabbed	ea.	5.00-12.00
California, pink, massive	lb.	4.00
British Columbia, pink, massive	lb.	1.00-7.00
British Columbia, pink, slabbed	sq. in.	.75-1.50
Colorado, pale pink	lb.	.1.25
Montana, Butte, pale pink	lb.	.75-1.50

RHYOLITE
Some silica-rich rhyolites are attractively banded in several colors, as reds, browns, tans, purples, etc., and take a fair to good polish; the name wonderstone has been applied to them. Used in small carvings.

California, blocks to 6"	lb.	.75-1.00
Nevada, blocks to 6"	lb.	.75-1.00
Mexico, blocks to 12"	lb.	.75-1.00

RICOLITE, SEE SERPENTINE

ROCK CRYSTAL, SEE QUARTZ

ROSE QUARTZ, SEE QUARTZ

RUBELLITE, SEE TOURMALINE

RUBY, SEE CORUNDUM

RUTILATED QUARTZ, SEE QUARTZ

RUTILE (Natural and Synthetic)
Natural rutile crystals are seldom large and clear enough to afford faceted gems; some have been cut from slender crystals from North Carolina and from twin crystals from Brazil. Synthetic rutile, commonly called *titania*, is rarely available in rough boules, boule sections, and preforms; full boules run 100–200 ct. and are usually very pale straw color.

Rutile, faceted gem, deep blood red, ¼-½ ct.	ct.	250.00
Synthetic rutile, boule sections, 10-50 cts.	ct.	.40-.60
Synthetic rutile, full boules, 70-100 cts.	ea.	.30-.40

SAGENITE, SEE QUARTZ

SAMARSKITE
A black, heavy, rare-earth mineral sometimes cut as a collectors' curiosity.

SANIDINE, SEE FELDSPAR

SAPPHIRE, SEE CORUNDUM

SARD, SEE QUARTZ

SARDONYX, SEE QUARTZ

SATIN SPAR, SEE CALCITE OR GYPSUM

SCAPOLITE
While somewhat soft for use in jewelry, clear scapolite provides attractive faceted gems, while catseye varieties provide handsome cabochons; rough crystals commonly deeply etched and should be examined carefully before purchase; facet-grade yellow available from Brazil; catseye rough from Myanmar sometimes available.

Brazil, pale to medium yellow, facet grade to 15 cts.	ct.	1.00-4.00
Madagascar, good yellow, facet grade, to 20 cts.	ct.	1.00-5.50
Kenya, rare purple-med. amethyst color	ct.	4.00-12.00
Kenya, very rare white	ct.	1.30-5.75

SCHEELITE
A sought-after collectors' item, providing highly refractive and dispersive gems; pale yellow, orange, or colorless; soft; clear crystals rare; largest faceted gems seldom over 15 ct.

California, Greenhorn Mts., colorless crystals to 15 gm.	ct.	2.50-20.00
Arizona, brownish crystals, small clear areas	ct.	2.00-5.00
Mexico, brownish-orange crystals to 4 gm.	ct.	2.00-5.00

SEPIOLITE (MEERSCHAUM)
White, porous material, much used for smokers' pipes and small carvings; usually sold to dealers by the box according to volume.

Turkey, pure pieces, shaped, about 4" diam.	ea.	1.25-21.75

SERANDITE
Rare reddish, pink, or salmon crystals from Mt. St. Hilaire, Quebec; faceted gems of less than 2 carats cut for collectors.

SERENDIBITE
Blue, massive cabochon material rarely from Johnsburg, New York; a collector's stone.

SERPENTINE
Embraces a wide variety of rock-like ornamental materials ranging from those used for decorative paneling in building interiors, to the finer and rarer kinds suitable for use in jewelry. *Verde antique* is a dark green rock much used for larger ornamental applications; *ricolite* is an attractively banded material of predominantly grayish to yellowish-green hues and available in large blocks; *bowenite* ("Soochow jade") is a fine-grained translucent type suitable for carvings and some jewelry cabochons; *williamsite* is the finest serpentine of all when it is highly translucent to nearly transparent, and colored a vivid pure green; some williamsite is clear enough to facet.

Rhode Island, yellow	lb.	2.00-3.00
New Jersey, yellow	lb.	2.00-6.00
New Jersey, greenish	lb.	.50-1.00

RICOLITE
Colorado, banded	lb.	.75-1.50
Colorado, banded	sq. in.	.25-.50

VERDE ANTIQUE
Various sources, various grades	lb.	1.50

WILLIAMSITE
Maryland-Pennsylvania, finest grade	lb.	10.00-25.00
Maryland-Pennsylvania, good, white inclusions	lb.	3.50-10.00
Maryland-Pennsylvania, fair grade, olive tinge, slab	sq. in.	.25-.50

END OF SERPENTINE SECTION

SHATTUCKITE

Arizona, Ajo, good blue, massive	lb.	3.00-6.50
Arizona, Ajo, tumbling grade	lb.	2.00-5.00

SHELL

The shells of a number of salt-water and fresh-water mollusks provide attractive material for inexpensive jewelry, ornaments, carvings, and utensils; the texture is fine and permits delicate carving and engraving; *mother-of-pearl* or *nacre* displaying pearly iridescence is prized for knife handles, small spoons, and carvings; non-nacreous shell provides cameo material if it contains layers of contrasting color. Shells listed below are seldom readily available to amateurs but may be obtained from dealers catering to shell collectors; however, samples bought from them are carefully selected for lack of damage and are therefore sold at much higher prices than the unselected commercial shells which are handled without regard to superficial damage. For further details on the species named and their uses in ornament, consult Julia Ellen Rogers' *The Shell Book* (1910, 1951).

Pearl Shell *(Pinctada)*

This is the standard pearly shell much prized for knife handles, veneers, inlays, and carvings, particularly because of its fine iridescence, thickness and breadth; large quantities are obtained in Australian waters but the finest specimens (*P. maxima*) are obtained from Tahitian waters; also fine is *P. margaritifera* from Australian waters.

Australian, *P. margaritifera* or *maxima*, large lots, fine grade	ea.	2.50-5.00
Australian, above, collectors' pairs, 6" diam.	pr.	10.00-25.00
Tahitian, *P. maxima*, collectors' pairs, 8" diam.	pr.	10.00-35.00

Fresh-Water Pearl Mussels *(Unio)*

These were formerly fished in large quantities from the rivers in the Mississippi drainage for the sake of pearl-button nacre, but the industry has now greatly declined; adequate supplies can still be obtained by visits to fishers still in business or from shell dealers; very many species available.

Typical U.S. *Unios*, shell pairs, 2-5"	pr.	10.00-20.00

Top Shell *(Trochus)*

Conical spiral shells with wide base 2½"-5" diameter; beautiful nacre; the *great top shell* listed below is much used for ornament manufacture in the South Sea Islands and for the making of small nacre articles; produced in large quantities from Australian waters.

Trochus niloticus, large lots	lb.	1.00-2.00
Trochus niloticus, specimens, about 4" diam.	ea.	2.00-10.00

Green Snail Shell (Turbo)

The *T. marmoratus* is also fished from Australian waters in large quantities and exported for the manufacture of pearl buttons and other articles; the nacre is thick and of good quality; up to 10" long.

Turbo marmoratus, to 8", large lots	lb.	1.00-2.00
Turbo marmoratus, specimens, small	ea.	2.00-4.00
Turbo marmoratus, over 7"	ea.	5.00-10.00

Abalone (Haliotis)

The beautifully colored and iridescent abalone shells have been used for centuries for decorative and utilitarian purposes; small bits are used for inlay work and in jewelry, particularly by the Indians of the Southwestern United States; the whole shells have been used as ornaments and ashtrays. Abundantly supplied from Baja California, Mexico, and California; principal species are the red abalone, *H. rufescens*, and the green abalone, *H. fulgens*; mature individuals attain shell sizes of 10"-12" and 7-8" respectively.

| Single shells, red abalone | ea. | 8.00-15.00 |
| Single shells, green abalone | ea. | 5.00-10.00 |

NAUTILUS SHELL

The chambered nautilus (*N. pompilius*) is a handsome pearly shell much used for ornaments, carvings of great delicacy, small containers, and for the manufacture of blister-like "coque de perles"; the latter are sections of inner whorls, cut off flat, and filled with wax or cement to simulate ordinary blister pearls; they are about ¼" x 1" in size and when set in jewelry are quite effective.

| *Nautilus pompilius*, Philippines, shells to 6" | ea. | 10.00-15.00 |
| *Nautilus pompilius*, specimens over 8" | ea. | 20.00+ |

HELMET SHELLS (*Cassis*)

The species of this genus are much favored for cameos because their white to near-white outer layers resting upon colored under-layers provides the necessary contrast for good cameo work; texture fine and capable of affording excellent detail; only one or two large cameos may be cut from one shell, plus several smaller ones; the first two species named below provide practically all of the material used in the cameo carving industry.

Cassis rufa, red helmet; Indian Ocean, Japan, 5"-7"	ea.	5.00-7.00
Cassis rufa madagascariensis, black or cameo helmet, W. Indies, to 10"	ea.	10.00-50.00
Cassis rufa tuberosa, sardonyx helmet; W. Indies, 6"-8"	ea.	10.00-20.00
Cassis rufa flammea, flame helmet; W. Indies, 4"-6"	ea.	10.00-25.00
Cassis rufa cornuta, horned helmet; Indian Ocean, W. Indies, to 12"	ea.	10.00-50.00

CONCH (*Strombus*)

The common queen conch (*Strombus gigas*) of Florida and the West Indies has been used for cameos in which the carved figures appear in pink against a white ground; the pink tends to fade in time; abundant and cheap when bought in quantity.

| *Strombus gigas*, 8"-10" | ea. | 10.00-25.00 |

"CATSEYES" (*Turbo petholatus*)

The snail-like South Pacific mollusk, *Turbo petholatus*, provides the so-called catseyes" which are cabochon-shaped calcareous trap doors used to protect the mollusk when the body is withdrawn into the shell. Many of these trap doors are handsomely colored and have been extensively used for ornament among the island natives.

| Green & white or red & white, 1"-1¼" | ea. | 5.00-15.00 |

END OF SHELL SECTION

SHORTITE

Rare, yellow facet grade from Mt. St. Hilaire, Quebec; colorless from Wyoming and Utah; faceted gems less than 1 ct.; collector's stone only.

SIDERITE

Brown to greenish-brown cleavable iron carbonate; rarely transparent and then sometimes used for small faceted gems for collectors; soft and weak.

| Portugal, Panasqueiros, cleavage sections to 5 gm. | gm. | 1.00-5.00 |

SILICON CARBIDE (CARBORUNDUM)

Sometimes thin crystal blades of this synthetic abrasive are pale enough in color to afford small attractive gems; hues brown, blue, green; very hard and tough; high refraction and dispersion; crystals rarely over ⅛" thick; collectors' item only; rarely available.

Crystal sections, facet grade to 1 gm.   ct.   .50-2.50

SILLIMANITE

Very rare; hard, but very easily cleaved and few attempts to cut succeed; as waterworn transparent pebble in gem gravels of Myanmar. Collectors' stone only. Fibrous type capable of cutting cat's eye-cabochons from South Carolina, Virginia, Idaho.

Myanmar, facet-grade pebbles, 2-10 cts.	ct.	1.00-5.00
South Carolina, fine sharp eye, brown	gm.	5.00-10.00
Idaho, cat's-eye	lb.	5.00-15.00

SILVER IN MATRIX

Dendrites of silver with sulfides occur in calcite matrix in some of the silver deposits of Ontario; suitable sections have been cut for cabochons and ornamental items; readily tarnishes; difficult to polish; soft; collectors' item only.

Ontario, calcite vein sections   troy oz.   4.00

SIMPSONITE

Facet-grade yellow-orange crystals from Brazil; hard, high refractive index; very rare; clear areas not over 4 mm.; collectors' gem only.

Facet-grade sections to 3 ct.   ct.   5.00-10.00

SINHALITE

Rare gem mineral found as waterworn pebbles in gravels of Sri Lanka; mostly pale straw-yellow to yellow-brown; pebbles to 1½" diameter; collectors' gem only.

Sri Lanka, waterworn pebbles, ½"-3" diam.   gm.   5.00-15-00

SMALTITE

Sulfide mineral providing attractive silvery cabochons; available in large masses from Ontario silver mines; collectors' item only.

Ontario, massive, to 3" diam.   lb.   7.50+

SMITHSONITE

Massive, fine-grained material in many hues as yellow, pale brown, reddish-brown, green, blue; translucent thick-banded types favored for cabochons; some highly translucent types are capable of being faceted into small "sleepy" gems; also in pale straw-yellow crystals of facet grade but very rare; soft but fairly tough when massive, brittle in crystals; massive types formerly cut for commercial cabochons but now mostly in demand by collectors; sources Greece, Sardinia, Mexico, New Mexico, South West Africa, Australia.

Mexico, blue-green massive crusts to 1" thick	lb.	15.00-25.00
New Mexico, Kelly Mine, fine blue-green crusts to 2" thick	lb.	20.00-35.00
South West Africa, deep fine green to 2", thick	lb.	25.00-45.00

SMOKY QUARTZ, SEE QUARTZ

SOAPSTONE, SEE STEATITE

SODALITE

Rich blue cabochon material; Ontario material veined with white, pink, cream, also with yellow cancrinite; recent Brazilian material blue with small white specks and much darker; soft and brittle but useful for heavier cabochons, carvings, and tumbled gems; available in large blocks from Brazil; very rarely, small (to ⅛") facet-grade areas in Ontario material. Hackmanite variety affording small faceted gems occurs at Mt. St. Hilaire, Quebec.

Ontario, fine grade	lb.	3.00-7.00
Ontario, ordinary grade	lb.	2.00-5.00
Ontario, slabbed	sq. in.	.50
Brazil, dark blue, high grade, 1-4 lb.	lb.	6.75

| Brazil, slabbed | sq. in. | .50 |
| Bolivia, blue | lb. | 2.85-5.75 |

SOOCHOW JADE, SEE SERPENTINE

SPECTROLITE, SEE FELDSPAR

SPESSARTINE, SEE GARNET

SPHALERITE
Despite softness and fragility, fine faceted gems are prepared from transparent crystals of yellow, orange, red, or green color; brown hues result in dull gems; abundant fine material from Spain and Mexico; very pale greens from Franklin, New Jersey (*cleiophane*), provide exceptionally beautiful gems, but material is extremely rare; lately, fine pale to olive green facet grade from Mt. St. Hilaire, Quebec, cut to as much as 55 carats but not commercially available. Largest faceted Spanish gems to about 100 ct., but most are less than 40 ct.; collectors' item.

Spain, fine yellow to orange, flawless, to 10 gm.	gm.	2.50-3.50
Spain, fine yellow to orange, facet grade, selected, to 60 cts.	ct.	2.75-4.50
Spain, green, rare	ct.	2.00-5.00
Mexico, Cananea, yellow-green, facet grade, select, to 10 cts.	ct.	.60-1.00
Mexico, Cananea, 20-30 cts.	ct.	.80-2.00
Colorado, dark greenish, small facet areas	oz.	1.00

SPHENE
Once classed as quite rare but recent supplies of material from Baja California, Mexico, and from Brazil have made rough occasionally available; soft and brittle but high refraction and dispersion provide extremely attractive faceted stones when color is pale yellow, green, or greenish-yellow; occasionally used in jewelry but mainly a collectors' item.

Brazil, yellow-green crystals to 5 gm., cuttable to 9 ct.	ct.	3.00-10.00
Mexico, brown, large crystals to 50 gm.+	gm.	1.00-5.00
Mexico, yellow-green, crystals to 5 gm.	gm.	10.00-30.00
Mexico, fine emerald-green, crystals to 1-3 ct.	ct.	10.00-30.00
Switzerland, yellow to pale green, thin crystals	ea.	5.00-15.00

SPINEL
Available only in small rough because large fine crystals arc cut in Sri Lanka and Myanmar as produced; in many colors including prized reds, red-oranges, and blues; also pink, grayish-purple, medium purple, dark wine-red, pale gray-blue; hard and tough; synthetics produced in great quantity. Blue and purple crystals, capable of yielding very small faceted gems less than 1 carat from Glencoe Island, Vt.; reputed dark greenish-black material form Mole Hill, Virginia; black, facet grade from peridot deposits in Arizona, New Mexico, and Nayarit.

Myanmar or Sri Lanka, reds, to 5 ct.	ct.	10.00-40.00
Myanmar or Sri Lanka, reds, 6-10 ct.	ct.	12.00-45.00
Myanmar or Sri Lanka, blue, to 5 ct.	ct.	1.00-5.00
Myanmar or Sri Lanka, blue, 6-10 ct.	ct.	1.00-6.00
Myanmar or Sri Lanka, blue, 11-20 ct.	ct.	1.00-8.00
Myanmar or Sri Lanka, gray-blue	gm.	.75-1.00
Myanmar or Sri Lanka, mine run, not over ¼"	oz.	6.00

SYNTHETIC SPINEL

Boules, various hues, to 200 ct.; also pieces	ct.	.04-.075
Preforms, ring-sizes	ea.	1.25-3.50
Preforms, doublets, ring sizes	ea.	7.50

END OF SPINEL SECTION

SPODUMENE

Because of difficulties in cutting and lack of strong colors, some varieties are not favored for commercial gems; pink to purple *kunzite* is the most attractive variety but suffers from color-fading; true *hiddenite* occurs only in very small crystals in North Carolina and is unobtainable; its name has becti applied carelessly to pale greenish varieties from Brazil and elsewhere which do not approach true hiddenite in color; Brazil also provides multicolored specimens, sometimes to hundreds of grams in weight and not infrequently flawless; readily cleaved but hard and quite durable; occasionally from San Diego County, CA.

Brazil, kunzite, fine pink to purple, 80-100 cts.	ct.	1.55-5.00
Brazil, kunzite, pale pink, to 100 cts.	ct.	.60-4.00
California, kunzite, purple	ct.	1.00-5.00
California, kunzite, pink	ct.	.75-3.00
Brazil, pale bluish-green, 1-60 cts.	ct.	2.00-6.00
Brazil, green bright	ct.	2.50-7.75
Brazil, yellow	ct.	1.00-6.00
Cats-eye kunzite, mauve, sharp eye	oz.	14.00
Afghanistan, kunzite, pink, chunks	gm.	1.75

STAUROLITE

Small cruciform crystals are cleaned and polished as good-luck charms; rarely in facet-grade crystals from Switzerland and then seldom capable of providing gems over $\frac{1}{2}$ ct.

"Cross stones," crystals to 1"	ea.	1.00-2.50
Facet grade, brown, some clear areas	ct.	2.00-5.00

STEATITE (SOAPSTONE, TALC)

Much used for carving, especially among the natives of the Far North who create naturalistic animal and human figure carvings of considerable artistic merit; deposits in North West Territories, Ontario, Saskatchewan, and a fine dendritic material from near Ennis, Montana and colorful material of carving grade from southern Oregon.

In various colors and sizes, blocks	lb.	1.00-2.00
Dendritic, good quality	lb.	8.00-16.00
Dendritic, fine quality, well-marked	lb.	17.00-32.00

STIBIOTANTALITE

A rare mineral and even more rarely providing small faceted gems from clear areas; reddish-brown to honey-yellow; hard; cut only for collectors; sometimes available from mineral dealers; from California or Mozambique.

Facet grade, usually with flaws, clear areas to 3 ct.	ct.	5.00-10.00

STICHTITE

Pale lilac to purple massive mineral forming narrow veinlets in green serpentine and sometimes cut in cabochons for collectors; soft and difficult to polish well.

Massive serpentine, with stichtite veinlets	lb.	1.50-3.25

STRONTIUM TITANATE ("FABULITE")

Colorless synthetic facet-grade boules provide beautiful gems to 50 ct. showing high refraction and dispersion; closest in appearance to diamond because of lack of color, presence of high dispersion, high refractive index, and lack of double refraction; soft and brittle; all output in United States channeled through one firm for cutting and distribution of gems under name of "fabulite"; some small boules have been produced in Japan.

Boule sections to 5 ct.	ct.	1.00-3.00

SUGILITE
Intense purple massive from Kalahari Managanese field, South Africa. Sugilite from Japan occurs with different mineralogical assemblage and is yellow-brown in color.

South Africa, fine purple, 1"-2" pieces	ea.	6.00-25.00
South Africa, purple, 1"-2" pieces	gm.	.50

SUNSTONE, see FELDSPAR

TALC, see STEATITE

TAAFEITE
An excessively rare mineral found in pebbles in the gem gravels of Sri Lanka: so scarce that rough is rarely offered for sale except in cut form.

TEKTITES
Glass-like materials of meteorite-impact or celestial origin; most are black but some are deep green and have been cut into faceted gems for collectors; fairly soft and brittle. Bright yellow-green glasses left over from assay tests for precious metals and resembling small spheres or cones of about ¼" diameter, usually with scaly outer layers, have been sold to the unwary as tektites; they quickly develop whitish powdery surfaces, even after polishing.

Czechoslovakia, *moldavite*, corroded masses to 1" diam.	gm.	4.00-5.00
Czechoslovakia, *moldavite*, fine, deep green	gm.	12.00-20.00
Libyan Desert, yellow impact glass, windworn masses to 3"	gm-	1.25-2.25
Far East types, black, ¼"-3" nodules	ea.	1.00-7.50

TEMPSKYA, see QUARTZ (Petrified Wood)

THAUMASITE
A fibrous white zeolite; when compact, forms dense fibrous masses capable of polishing into cabochons or beads; the latter are slightly chatoyant; soft; collectors' item only.

Virginia & New Jersey, masses to 6" thick	lb.	2.50-10.50

THOMSONITE
A fibrous mineral filling small cavities in eruptive rocks; sometimes beautifully colored in rings of pink, red, white, and green; quality depends on color contrast, patterns, and size of nodules; translucent grayish-green variety showing no patterns whatsoever is known as *lintonite*. Soft but fairly tough; used to limited extent in jewelry, particularly in Great Lakes region where produced.

Minnesota, Grand Marais, selected nodules	gm.	1.00-5.00
Minnesota, Grand Marais, field run	gm.	1.00-2.00
Minnesota, Grand Marais, lintonite	gm.	1.00-2.00

THULITE, see ZOISITE

THUNDEREGG, see QUARTZ

TIGEREYE, see QUARTZ

TITANIA, see RUTILE

TOPAZ
Most expensive when hues are purplish-red or strong reddish-orange, the latter often called "imperial"; also expensive when natural pink or purple; fine blue rough is costly when similar in color to fine blue aquamarine; sherry-color topaz crystals occur in cavities in rhyolite rocks and are seldom over 1½" in length, but similarly colored crystals from pegmatite pockets, while much larger in size, also fade upon exposure to strong light; colorless topaz crystals, very faintly yellow or very faintly blue, sometimes reach sizes in excess of 20 pounds, but the material is lit-

tle valued for cutting. Hard, but with one perfect cleavage, sometimes difficult to polish well; veil-type inclusions common; avoid pieces with cleavage traces.

Brazil, golden imperial, fine, clean 5-15 ct.	ct.	8.00-16.00
Brazil, golden imperial, fine, clean 15-25 ct.	ct.	10.00-20.00
Brazil, purplish or violetish-red crystals, 25-30 ct.	ct.	15.00-30.00
Brazil, pinked crystals, 3-15 ct.	ct.	2.00-10.00
Brazil, reddish-orange, fine, 5-10 ct. crystals	ct.	4.00-35.00
Brazil, reddish-orange, fine, 10-25 ct. crystals	ct.	2.25-40.00
Brazil, reddish-orange, fine, 25-50 ct. crystals	ct.	3.75-70.00
Brazil, yellow, 3-30 gm.	gm.	2.00-4.00
Brazil, fine blue, 5-50 cts.	ct.	2.00-8.00
Brazil, pale blue, 10-30 cts.	gm.	.70-2.00
Brazil, very pale blue, 1-80 cts.	ct.	.10-.40
Brazil, blue, cabochon grade	gm.	.30
Brazil, blue, tumbling grade	lb.	9.00-12.00
Brazil, colorless, 1-100 cts.	ct.	.07-.20
Brazil, colorless, 100-500 cts.	ct.	.08-.30
Colorado, sherry crystals (8-14 pcs. per oz.)	oz.	20.00
Mexico, golden-red, facet-grade crystals	ct.	.90-4.00
Texas, stream pebbles, pale blue	oz.	2.00
Texas, stream pebbles, very pale blue	oz.	1.00-2.00
Texas, stream pebbles, colorless, to 50 gm.	gm.	.10-.20
Utah, small colorless or sherry crystals, to ¾" long	gm.	.25-1.00
African, clean, facet quality, irradiated blue topaz	oz.	20.00
Irradiated blue topaz rough, dark indigo blue, 3-30 gm.	gm.	9.00-13.00
Irradiated blue topaz rough, medium blue, 3-30 gm.	gm.	4.00-6.00
Irradiated blue topaz rough, light blue, 3-30 gm.	gm.	1.35-2.50

TOURMALINATED QUARTZ, see QUARTZ

TOURMALINE

The following varieties commonly appear in the gem trade: *rubellite*, rich red to purplish red; *indicolite*, deep blue; *green*, in many shades and tints; *pink*, and *dravite*, a dark orange-brown variety. Bicolor crystals also occur, usually in green and red or pink; sometimes good specimens call be cut into very attractive emerald-cut gems. Numerous fine tubular inclusions also result in *catseye* varieties, mainly in greens but also in pink and blue. Rubellites are generally most expensive if relatively free from flaws and not too dark in color, the cost increasing as the color approaches that of ruby; also expensive are fine greens which are free of any trace of olive and which resemble the emerald in hue; pale blues are quite rare and also highly prized. *Achroite*, the colorless variety, is extremely rare but only in demand by collectors. Good yellows are also rare, especially in pieces large enough to cut gems of about 6 carats or over; however, the gems are not in demand because they too closely resemble citrine and golden beryl. Good sharp catseyes are in demand and suitable rough is quite expensive. Practically the sole commercial source of tourmaline is Brazil, but fine material occasionally comes from Madagascar, Mozambique, California, Tanzania, and Maine. A small quantity of green and dravite tourmaline is produced from the gem gravels of Sri Lanka.

ACHROITE

Brazil, Madagascar, etc., to 10 cts.	ct.	2.00-5.00

CATSEYE

Brazil, green, to 3 gm.	gm.	3.00-10.00
Brazil, blue, to 2 gm.	gm.	5.00-10.00
California, Mesa Grande, coarse tubes, 1-3 gm.	gm.	2.50-5.00

DRAVITE

Ceylon, waterworn pebbles, ½-5 gm.	gm.	4.00-8.00
New York, crystal fragments, ½-3 gm.	gm.	2.50-5.00

GREENS

Brazil, "emerald" color, Teofilo Ottoni, 4-15 gm.	gm.	18.00-50.00
Brazil, ordinary deep green, to 8 cts.	ct.	2.50-15.00
Brazil, fine blue-green, 3-18 gm.	gm.	5.00-35.00
Brazil, good yellow-green	gm.	2.00-15.00
Brazil, pale green	gm.	4.50-25.00
Brazil, green, olive shades	gm.	1.00-5.00
California, Mesa Grande, cab quality	dz.	3.00-5.00
Maine, fine blue-green to 4 gm.	gm.	5.00-25.00
Maine, fine blue-green 4-15 gm.	gm.	15.00-65.00
Tanzania, chrome green	ct.	16.00-22.00
Nigeria, chrome green, flawless	ct.	30.00-45.00

INDICOLITE

Brazil, fine blue, not too dark, to 15 gm.	gm.	5.00-15.00
Brazil, dark blue, for small cut gems, to 30 gm.	gm.	4.00-15.00
Brazil, pale blue, to 5 gm.	gm.	3.00-12.00
South West Africa, pale blue, to 5 gm.	gm.	5.00-15.00

PINKS

Brazil, rich pink, 1-6 gm.	gm.	10.00-25.00
Brazil, good pink,semi-facet, cab	gm.	1.00-3.00
California, Mesa Grande, pink	oz.	5.00-15.00

RUBELLITE

Brazil, deep red, finest grade, to 20 cts.	ct.	12.00-35.00
Brazil, deep red, finest grade, 5-10 cts.	ct.	10.00-20.00
Brazil, ordinary grades, 5-10 cts.	ct.	5.00-10.00
Brazil, ordinary grades, many inclusions, to 20 cts.	ct.	2.50-5.00
Nigeria, Mozambique, burgundy-red, facet grade	ct.	14.00-25.00

CABOCHON, CARVING, AND TUMBLING TOURMALINE

By far the greatest quantity of colored tourmaline contains numerous flaws, usually veil-type inclusions and small cracks, which render the crystals unsuitable for facet work but permit use for cabochons, carvings, and tumbled gems. The finest non-facetable material in large sizes is reserved for carvings, smaller sizes being used for cabochons. In general, the prices follow the trends noted above for facet-grade material in the several prized colors.

Best carving grades, crystals over 2" diameter	oz.	7.00-10.00
Best cabochon grades, fragments over ½" thick	oz.	4.50-6.50
Good cabochon grades, fragments over ½" thick	oz.	.50-3.00
Mine run, cabochon, and tumbling grades	lb.	9.00-18.00
Tumbling grades, usually less than ½" size	lb.	3.00-6.00
Bi-color, cab grade	oz.	3.00

END OF TOURMALINE SECTION

TREMOLITE (SEE ALSO NEPHRITE)

Rarely in small clear crystals which can be faceted; also in catseye-type crystals which produce weak streaks of light. The pink variety, *hexagonite*, from New York State, sometimes occurs in clear crystal grains capable of faceting into gems of about ½ carat. Rare; collectors' gem only.

New York, *hexagonite*, crystals to 4" long ea. .70-6.50

TURQUOIS

Large quality differences exist in turquois from different localities and even in the material mined from a single deposit. In general, seam or vein turquois is poorer in quality than nodular turquois, the latter usually being harder, less porous, and capable of taking a better polish. The finest turquois is still produced by the Iranian mines, but sometimes equally good material is found in some of the deposits of the Southwestern United States. Some fine production from the Cripple Creek, Colorado area, hardness of 6.7-7.7. Much porous material from the United States is plastic-impregnated after being tumbled to baroque form; the impregnated kinds can usually be recognized by their glassy polish, which is due to the plastic. Pale colors ordinarily mean that the material will refuse to polish well. Top-grade Persian material, especially in larger, "clear" pieces, is seldom sold in rough form.

Arizona, Bisbee, good blue, hard	oz.	12.50-25.00
Arizona, Bisbee, medium blue, hard	oz.	10.00-15.00
Arizona, Bisbee, nuggets, various grades	oz.	4.00-25.00
Arizona, Bisbee, spiderweb	oz.	12.50-25.00
Arizona, Bisbee, small fragments	oz.	2.00-10.00
Arizona, Morenci, good grade	oz.	10.00-25.00
Arizona, Kingman, best blue	oz.	10.00-25.00
Arizona, Kingman, medium blue	oz.	5.00-15.00
Arizona, Kingman, fair blue	oz.	1.00-5.00
Arizona, Kingman, large carving, best grade	lb,	700.00+
Mexico, Zacatecas, blue, best grade, hard	oz.	5.50-12.50
Mexico, Zacatecas, medium blue	oz.	4.00-10.00
Nevada, Fox Mine, dark blue	oz.	10.00-25.00
Nevada, Fox Mine, medium blue	oz.	10.00-12.50
Nevada, Fox Mine, pale blue	oz.	1.25-5.00
Nevada, Fox Mine, seam sections, blue	oz.	2.00-10.00
Nevada, Fox Mine, seam sections, blue	lb.	25.00+
China, 1"-2" nuggets (stabilized)	gm.	1.00
Cripple Creek, CO., mine run, blue-green	lb.	160.00
Persian, fair to good blue, small pieces to 3 oz.	oz.	14.00-25.00
Persian, fair to good blue, matrix	lb.	30.00-70.00
Persian, fair to good blue, spiderweb	oz.	8.50-10.00

TURRITELLA, SEE QUARTZ

ULEXITE

Too soft and too easily affected by atmospheric moisture to be considered a gemstone; nevertheless, attractive cabochons and spheres, showing catseye streaks, are prepared from chatoyant seam sections found in borate deposits of California; the same material provides the well-known "television stone."

California, seam sections, "TV" stone	lb.	2.50-9.50

UNAKITE

Granitic rock containing evenly-spaced patches of salmon-pink feldspar and bright green epidote with some quartz; a popular material for tumbled gems.

Virginia, North Carolina	lb.	.80-2.50
Virginia, North Carolina	sq. in.	1.00

VARISCITE

The beautiful pale green nodules from Fairfield, Utah, seldom appear on the market; major supplies are now coming from seam-type deposits in Utah and Nevada, of which the best grades are deep green, translucent, and take a good polish.

Fine, compact dark green, select	lb.	25.00
Fine, compact dark green, mine run	lb.	10.00-18.00
Fine, patterned slabs	sq. in.	6.00
Fine, solid color, slabs	sq. in.	6.00
Good, pale green color	lb.	6.00-10.00

VERDE ANTIQUE, SEE SERPENTINE

VERDITE

Occasionally offered from the Republic of South Africa; the original verdite is a compact rock consisting mainly of opaque green serpentine, but some new material, called by the same name, is apparently a quartzose rock colored by fuchsite mica. Called "transvall" jade.

Good green, some mottling	lb.	2.50

VESUVIANITE, SEE IDOCRASE

VIOLANE, SEE DIOPSIDE

WARDITE

Very small faceted gems have been cut from Yukon material.

WELOGANITE

Small faceted gems cut from Quebec material.

WILLEMITE

Massive, fluorescent material, usually mixed with fluorescent calcite and nonfluorescing franklinite and zincite, is still available from the zinc deposit at Ogdensburg, New Jersey; it finds some use for spheres, flats, and occasionally for unusual cabochons; solid willemite suitable for cabochons is rarer and costlier, while transparent willemite is very rare and is obtained only from old collections; a collectors' gem.

Facet grade, crystal sections to 4"	ea.	5.75-85.00
Massive, fluorescent material	lb.	1.00-12.50

WILLIAMSITE, SEE SERPENTINE

WITHERITE

Some fibrous masses are sufficiently translucent to provide "sleepy" faceted gems if not cut too large; abundant in pale straw-yellow crystal aggregates from Illinois and more translucent whitish aggregates from England.

Illinois, fibrous aggregates	gm.	.50-1.25
Illinois, fibrous aggregates, some translucent areas	lb.	5.00
England. fibrous aggregates	gm.	.75-1.50
England. fibrous aggregates, mainly translucent	lb.	6.00

WOLLASTONITE

Fibrous aggregates are sometimes compact enough to be cut into weakly cliatoyant cabochons; small faceted gems from asbestos, Quebec material.

WONDERSTONE, SEE RHYOLITE

WULFENITE

Clear areas in tabular crystals sometimes cut into small transparent faceted gems of very pretty color and fine brilliance despite the extreme softness and fragility of the mineral; a collectors' gem only.

Arizona, tabular orange or red crystals, ½"-3"diam.	ea.	3.00-40.00
Tsumeb, S.W. Africa, pale brown, crystals to 4" diam.	ea.	6.00-200.00
Morocco, yellow, 1"-2½"	ea.	30.00-65.00

ZEKTZERITE

Colorless to pink crystals from Washington state, cut stones to 10 cts. but rough not commercially available.

ZINCITE

Perhaps one of the rarest of all collectors' gemstones, the only source of clear material being the now-depleted zinc mine at Franklin, New Jersey, from which came a very small quantity of material in the form of bright orange-red seams in calcite-rich ore; the largest known clean faceted zincite is about 20 carats, but the vast majority of cut gems are less than 3 carats; collectors' gem only.

Facet grade, bright red, clean fragments, ½"-1"	ea.	25.00-100.00
Facet grade, blackish-red, ½"-3"	ea.	4.25-19.50

ZIRCON

Natural zircons predominantly some shade of brown, but colorless, very pale straw, pale brownish-orange, and blue zircons are obtained by heat treatment of suitable brown crystals; supplies mainly from Thailand and Sri Lanka, the latter providing a wide variety of green shades which do not change color upon heat treatment; faceted gems up to about 40 carats are known, but the rough ordinarily offered seldom provides faceted gems over several carats; hard but easily chipped. Also from Tanzania.

Africa, reds, orange-reds, 1-10 cts.	ct.	4.00-9.00
Africa, reds, orange-reds, 10-20 cts.	ct.	6.00-13.00
Purplish reds, 1-3 cts.	ct.	4.00-6.00
Purplish reds, 7-10 cts.	ct.	5.50-9.00
Sri Lanka, shades of green, usually slightly milky	ct.	3.00-10.00
Browns, various sources	ct.	2.50-12.00
Australia, red-brown	ct.	1.00-9.00
Tanzania, orange, yellow, clean, fine facet grade	ct.	5.00-25.00
Thailand, blue, heat-treated ½-3 cts.	ct.	2.00-4.00
Thailand, blue, 1½-3½ cts.	ct.	6.00
Thailand & Sri Lanka, colorless, heat-treated,	oz.	2.00

ZOISITE

The fine grained pink variety, known as *thulite*, is sometimes used for cabochons. A very beautiful facet grade variety was discovered in Tanzania of vivid trichroism: purple, blue, and red, or purple, green, and red. Flawless rough to 50 grams has been found, some in crystals and some in crystal fragments. A green facet grade variety is a recent discovery.

Norway, massive thulite, in blocks to 1 lb.	lb.	4.00
tanzanite, facet grade to 6 cts.	ct.	40.00
tanzanite, med. blue, good, 1-4 cts.	ct.	7.00-10.00

IV

FACETED AND
CABOCHON GEMS

THIS CHAPTER DEALS WITH THE TWO MAJOR TYPES OF CUT GEMS: *faceted gems* and *cabochon gems*. Faceted gems are covered with small flat surfaces called facets, while cabochon gems feature a top surface of smoothly rounded shape, and a bottom surface which is usually, but not always, flat. There are many variations in both types as will be seen.

The first part of the chapter takes up the mechanical aspects of the lapidary art, among them, attention to correct proportions and angles in the case of faceted gems, proper curvature in the case of cabochon gems, and perfection of polish in both. The next section deals with styles of cutting for both types of gems and gives numerous sketches to show the patterns of facets employed in faceted gems, the profiles of cabochons, and other features which appear in modern gems. The last section is a catalog of faceted and cabochon gems, arranged alphabetically by species and varieties as before, with comments on quality, size, and other considerations important to the prospective buyer.

FACETED GEMS

The effectiveness of faceted gems depends on the fact that the bottom part of the gem, or *pavilion*, acts like a mirror. The light falling on the top of the gem passes through the transparent material, strikes the pavilion facets, and is reflected upward to return to the eye. The use of many facets causes a dazzling display of individual sparkling reflections which change and shift as the gem is turned; these result in the effect known as *brilliance*.

Basic Cutting Styles

To achieve these reflective effects, two basic types of facet cuts are employed, the *step cut* (or *emerald cut* as it is also called) and the *brilliant cut*. Both are shown in Figure 12. From them, and from combinations of both styles, stem all of the many variations that have developed. The step cut consists mainly of parallel rows of strip-like facets, or *steps*. It has been used most effectively for emerald and other colored gemstones such as aquamarine, topaz, and tourmaline. It has also been used for colorless gemstones, including diamond and zircon, but not as frequently

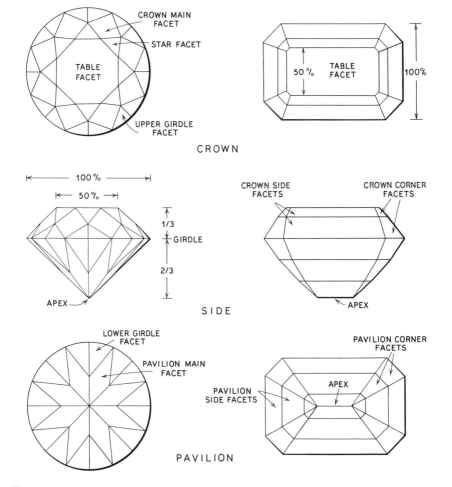

Fig. 12
The two most common facet gem cuts, the standard brilliant and the step cut.

as the brilliant cut. The latter is preferred for colorless or very faintly colored gems, because the greater number of facets in the brilliant cut creates more complex and, thus, more interesting reflections. In the case of the diamond, it brings out the property of *dispersion*, or the splitting of white light into its colored components, much like a glass prism splits a beam of sunlight into the vivid hues of the spectrum. Sometimes we see dispersion at work when a beam of light strikes a cut-glass vase or pitcher, or fleetingly, we see it along the beveled edge of an old-fashioned plate-glass mirror. In diamond, this optical property is very strong, and if the gem is faceted correctly, it results in numerous bits of vivid color flashing from the gem when it is held beneath a good light and turned in the fingers. It is for this reason that most persons are attracted to well-cut brilliant diamonds rather than to step-cut diamonds, which produce a less spectacular dispersion.

Another important consideration in choosing between a step or brilliant cut is the need to reduce or disguise the disfiguring reflections which arise from inclusions or defects within the gem. In general, very slight flaws can best be hidden in the general dazzle of reflections arising from the brilliant cut rather than in the relatively few strip-like reflections arising from the step cut. A notable exception to this rule is in the emerald. When it contains so many small, evenly-spaced inclusions, called *jardin*, or "garden," that no style of cutting will disguise their presence, the step cut is considered acceptable, although, of course, the brilliancy of reflections is greatly reduced and an attractive "glow" supplants the normal, sharp reflections.

REFRACTION AND ITS EFFECTS

The supreme considerations in transparent faceted gems are that the facets be placed at the correct angles to each other and that the finished gems have nearly the proportions shown in Figure 12. These angles and proportions were derived from many years of gem-cutting experience accumulated by lapidaries the world over and have been scientifically confirmed in modern times. The angles and proportions vary from one gemstone species to another because the property inherent in every gemstone, known as *refraction*, or the ability of a gemstone to reflect and bend light rays, also varies according to species. Each species has its own characteristic powers of refraction which the jeweler and gemologist measure on a small instrument called the *refractometer* when testing gems. The strength of refraction is given a number called the *refractive index*. The number is high in diamond, and low in opal. The effect of this difference in refractive power can be readily seen if two well-cut brilliant gems, one of diamond and one of opal, both clear, colorless, and flawless, are placed side by side. The enormous brilliance of the diamond far surpasses that of the opal.

Gems of lower refractive powers, such as opal, quartzes (amethyst, citrine, rock crystal, etc.), and beryls, must be cut somewhat deeper in the pavilion than those of higher refractive powers such as diamond, zircon, sphene, and strontium titanate. Thus, if one took two correctly proportioned round brilliant gems of the same diameter, one of diamond and the other of rock crystal, it would be apparent at once that the pavilion of the diamond was not as deep as that of the rock

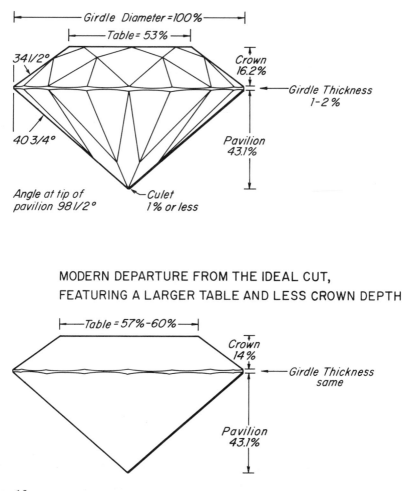

IDEAL OR AMERICAN BRILLIANT CUT

Girdle Diameter = 100%
Table = 53%
34 1/2°
Crown 16.2%
Girdle Thickness 1-2%
40 3/4°
Pavilion 43.1%
Angle at tip of pavilion 98 1/2°
Culet 1% or less

MODERN DEPARTURE FROM THE IDEAL CUT, FEATURING A LARGER TABLE AND LESS CROWN DEPTH

Table = 57%-60%
Crown 14%
Girdle Thickness same
Pavilion 43.1%

FIG. 13
Brilliant cuts commonly employed for diamond.

crystal. Lapidaries are well aware of the effects of refraction and take this property into consideration while cutting gems, adjusting the proportions and angles to suit the refractive index of each gemstone.

Slight departures from ideal angles and proportions can be made without serious harm to brilliance as shown in Figure 13, where the *ideal* brilliant cut for diamond and a modern variation are diagrammed. There are obviously substantial differences in them, yet if two diamonds of identical color and clarity are cut to the same diameter, one in the ideal cut and the other in its variation, it is virtually impossible, without special light-measuring instruments, to detect consistently which one is more brilliant.

In general, more liberties with angles and proportions can be taken with gemstones of higher refractive index than with those whose refractive powers are less. in the higher index gemstones there is a greater "reserve" of refractive and reflective power, and appreciable deviations from ideal cutting still provide excellent brilliance. This latitude narrows as the refractive index decreases, until for gemstones of low refractive index, the lapidary must be quite careful with angles and proportions if the finished gem is to look brilliant at all.

Drastic departures from proper angles and proportions result in equally drastic losses of light as shown in Figure 14. If the facets are angled too steeply, they fail to reflect the light within the gem and much is lost through the back facets of the

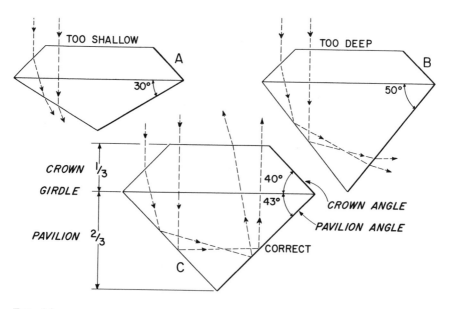

FIG. 14
Side views of faceted gems showing how incorrect angles will result in serious losses of light through the bottoms of the gems.

pavilion. A gem cut too shallow produces a gray area in the center called a "hole." A gem cut too deep results in a general loss of brilliance or a grayness; the gem is marked by feeble, rather than strong, reflections. Both of these effects are best observed by holding a gem underneath a good light and looking down upon the top.

EFFECTS OF INCLUSIONS ON BRILLIANCE

One or two spots, specks, minute crystals, small cracks, etc., do not greatly affect the total amount of light which is returned to the eye in properly cut gems, although they may be disfiguring because perfect inner clarity is established as the ideal for faceted stones. However, as the inclusions increase, they begin to scatter light, causing the rays to dart off at angles other than those desired. Many of these rays simply escape through the sides of the gems and contribute nothing to brilliance. Eventually the point is reached where so much light is lost that only a feeble glow appears on top, as in the jardin emeralds mentioned earlier. Extreme losses occur in those gemstone materials which are only translucent, such as chalcedonies, for example, which consist of very many extremely small crystals grown together in compact masses. As the size of the individual crystals grows smaller and the spaces between them grow smaller too, light has less opportunity to be deviated from its path and more returns to the eye; such material is highly translucent, and sometimes, as in the case of Williamsite serpentine, actually provides fairly satisfactory faceted gems. In gemstones that are normally transparent, such as ruby, sapphire, and quartz, very small inclusions commonly occur which, though abundant, are too small to be seen clearly with the naked eye. Nevertheless, they seriously interfere with the passage of light and cause much scattering; a faceted gem cut from this sort of material can be a great disappointment to the lapidary who expected a brilliant gem for his efforts. Other gemstones likely to have such inclusions are the blue sapphires of Kashmir, rose quartz, some heat-treated zircons from Thailand, and the green zircons of Sri Lanka. Sometimes the inclusions are so small that they cannot be seen under high-power magnification; nevertheless, their presence is easily detected by the glowing, "sleepy" look of the finished gems.

DELIBERATE DEPARTURES FROM IDEAL ANGLES AND PROPORTIONS

During the above discussion the reader may have gained the impression that there can be no excuse for cutting faceted gems in other than correct angles and proportions. Actually, there are good and sufficient reasons for departing from the ideal as will be seen, especially when it is considered that most gems are meant for setting in jewelry.

Consider the step-cut gem first. in this style of cutting, the bottom pairs of facets must be cut, like brilliants, at the proper angles if full reflection of light is to take place from them. If they are cut too shallow, a rectangular "hole" appears, and if several bottom pairs of facets are cut too shallow, the hole becomes even larger. Unfortunately, in order to be sure that these bottom-most facets are cut at the proper angles, the lapidary must cut all of the ones above at steeper angles. The net result is that any properly shaped step-cut gem must be considerably deeper than a standard brilliant-cut gem of exactly the same width. These relationships can be appreciated from the diagrams of Figure 12. In small stones, the increased depth is not a great drawback, but in large gems, especially those meant for rings, the increased depth results in a bulky gem which rises so high above the ring finger that it becomes top-heavy. This can, and does, result in the entire ring slewing sideways, to the discomfort of the wearer. For this reason, large step-cut ring stones are commonly cut under the proper pavilion angles. This makes the stone less brilliant, of course, but it also makes it less top-heavy and more comfortable to wear. The decision to buy such a gem is a matter of personal preference; if a great breadth is wanted, then brilliance has to be sacrificed to some extent.

In other instances, stones cut shallower than usual, or "spread," as the gem expert puts it, are intentionally shaped this way to obtain the maximum return from poorly shaped rough, especially if the latter is expensive. This is a common practice among diamond cutters, and if the departures from ideal proportions are not too great, satisfactory brilliance results, as shown in Figure 13. In still other instances, shallow cutting is used when colored gemstones would be too dark if cut to the proper depth; in this category are some very dark green or blue tourmalines, dark blue sapphires, and, among the rarer gemstones, blue iolites and dark brown axinites.

On the other hand, the principal reason for cutting gems too deep is merely to recover as much weight as possible from the rough and thus to exact a higher price for the finished gem on the basis of weight. Such excessively deep gems are particularly common among the sapphires cut locally in Sri Lanka, the elongated crystals of which lend themselves well to this exaggerated departure from accepted proportions. The appearance of some of these gems is sketched in Figure 15. In some specimens the length is so great that they resemble carrots in shape. The native cutters and the merchants who dispose of such gems to Western buyers know perfectly well that they must be recut if they are to sell in Europe or the United States, but they reason that if native customers, or those from India, are willing to accept such gems, then Western customers should be willing to do so

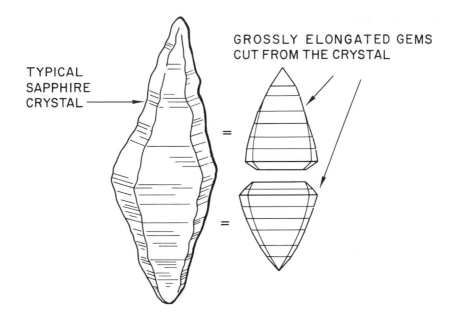

GROSSLY ELONGATED GEMS
CUT FROM THE CRYSTAL

TYPICAL
SAPPHIRE
CRYSTAL

FIG. 15
Poorly shaped faceted gems cut from Ceylon sapphire crystals by the native cutters.

too. It may be remarked in passing that Sri Lankan and Indian faceted gems are also remarkable for their lack of perfect symmetry in the placement of facets, sizes of facets, and even angles for opposed pairs of facets; in fact, they may be so sloppily cut that it is obvious the lapidary was only concerned with more or less rounding off the rough with facets, using minimum care to achieve a fair degree of brilliance. These hallmarks are so well known among members of the jewelry trade, that they can recognize these "native-cut" gems at a glance. However, as remarked before, cutters in Sri Lanka are new being instructed in the cutting of faceted gems in western proportions and using modern faceting machinery.

GIRDLES

The thin band which separates the *crown*, or top of the gem, from the *pavilion*, or bottom, is know as the *girdle*. It may or may not be polished, or covered with very small facets. A girdle which is too thin is likely to chip when the jeweler sets it in jewelry, as shown in Figure 16. If tile girdle is too thick, it results in a clumsy-looking gem. The proper girdle is neither too thin nor too thick, combining graceful thinness with adequate thickness to resist the stresses applied to it when seized by the prongs which secure the gem to its mounting.

Sometimes girdles are seen which are covered completely by a series of very small, evenly-spaced facets instead of the usual matte finish left by the initial grinding of the rough gemstone to give it its profile. The makers of such gems, usually diamond-cutters, claim that some light is reflected back into the diamond which would otherwise be lost. Others merely point out that the increased elegance of the gem is sufficient reason for employing such extra facets, especially if a rather large stone is to be set in a claw mount which would expose most of the girdle to view. There is no question that the latter reason is the better of the two, but another reason can also be advanced in support of polished, if not faceted, girdles—they are less likely to chip during setting.

The Girdle as an Indicator of Quality

By examining the accuracy with which the facets of the crown meet the facets of the pavilion along the girdle, even the inexperienced person is able to judge the relative skill of the lapidary. It goes without saying that the skilled workman will

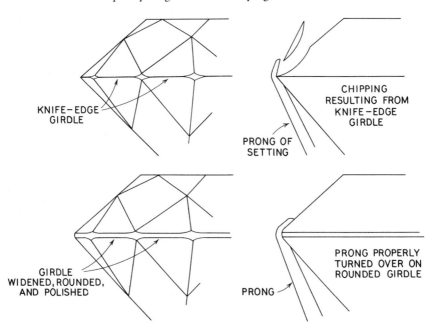

FIG. 16
Excessively thin girdles on faceted gems can easily result in chipping.

pay equal attention to all parts of the gem and not just to those which are most obvious. Offset or mismatched facets are shown in Figure 17 along with other cutting errors that can be easily detected with the naked eye or under low magnification. Such defects are seldom glaring but they depart from the ideal and are silent signs that the basic material of the gem was not considered worthy of the best cutting skill, or that the lapidary was sloppy in his work. *It is almost an invariable rule in the lapidary arts that the finest materials are sent to the finest cutters for treatment.* Only by doing this will it be possible to realize the fullest potential value of the rough. Thus, every indication of poor cutting should make the buyer suspicious of quality, and, of course, of real value. This rule is rigidly applied to the most expensive rough and relaxes as the rough becomes cheaper, until the most slapdash lapidary work generally appears upon gems cut from the poorest rough.

NATURALS

If one examines a parcel of round diamond brilliants, he is sure to see, sooner or later, a peculiarity which is confined *only to the diamond.* This is the existence of

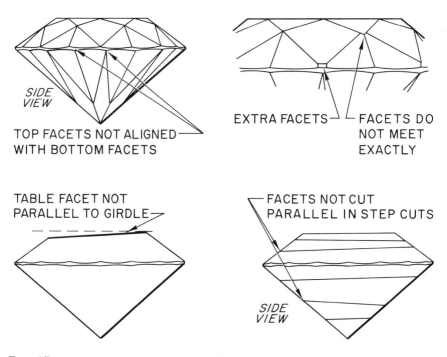

FIG. 17
Common faceting errors which decrease the value of gemstones.

small flat spots along the girdle, called *naturals*, which glisten brightly in marked contrast to the dull surface of the rest of the girdle. There may be one or, at the most, four such spots evenly spaced around the periphery. They are remnants of the natural faces of the diamond crystal, in this case, the octahedron. As shown in Figure 18, they result when the cutter grinds a section of the crystal into a circular outline, part of which is to become the girdle of the finished gem. To avoid loss of material, he grinds away the excess diamond until lie is on the verge of obliterating all traces of the original crystal faces. At this point he stops grinding and leaves behind one or more minute flat spots which are the naturals previously referred to. If these spots are quite small and inconspicuous, they can be hidden easily behind a prong or bead during setting, but if they are noticeable to the naked eye, the stone bearing them is not cut as well as it should be. Naturals *are* defects, although in the diamond trade they are considered relatively unimportant unless they are conspicuously large.

CULET FACET

A curious departure from logic in faceting occurs when diamond cutters place a small facet squarely upon the tip of the pavilion, as shown in Figure 19. This is

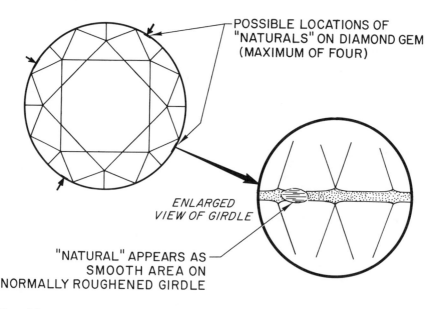

POSSIBLE LOCATIONS OF "NATURALS" ON DIAMOND GEM (MAXIMUM OF FOUR)

ENLARGED VIEW OF GIRDLE

"NATURAL" APPEARS AS SMOOTH AREA ON NORMALLY ROUGHENED GIRDLE

FIG. 18
Vestiges of natural crystal faces along the girdles of faceted diamonds.

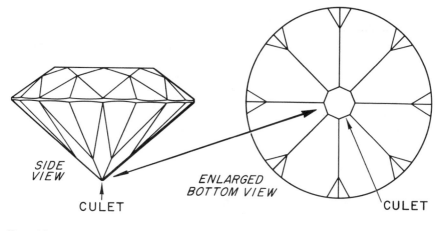

Fig. 19
The culet facet on cut diamonds.

called a *culet*. There is no question that this facet destroys the ability of a small area near the tip to properly reflect light, yet, through long-standing tradition, this culet is still placed on brilliant-cut gems. Several reasons have been advanced as to why it is there, among them, that it prevents splitting of the gem. But none of the reasons seem valid. However, the culet does serve as a check of the lapidary's skill because its outline forms a minute, more or less regular octagon. If the sides of the octagon are all of the same length and the angles between them are equal, it indicates that the large pavilion facets above are also very evenly and accurately cut. On the other hand, if the octagon is irregular or misshapen, it indicates poor cutting.

Surface Finishes

Maximum brilliancy in any faceted gem is achieved only when the facets are cut as flat as possible and polished to the highest degree of smoothness. The quality of surface finish is highly important in cabochon gems also, particularly in those displaying special optical effects such as star stones, catseyes, and moonstones. A perfect polish also greatly enhances the play of color in opal.

But to return to faceted gems, it is well known that the flatness of facets and the perfection of polish is best achieved on the hardest gemstones. Thus diamond, hardest of all, is capable of being cut and polished so perfectly that electron microscope photographs show scarcely any kind of surface irregularity even at magnifications of thousands of times. This superior flatness is not only attributable to the nature of the diamond itself, but also to the iron laps which are used for cutting and polishing. A careful diamond cutter keeps his laps in top condition so as to avoid any trace of irregularity on the facets caused by the grooves which appear on any kind of polishing lap after some use. Stones less hard than diamond very commonly show minute parallel polished grooves, particularly upon the large table facet, and indicate that the cutter allowed the stone to rest too long on the same place on the lap. In contrast to these "polish marks," as they are called, are the minute scorings with ragged edges which result from tearing of the surface of the gem. These tears may be due to small particles of grit caught in the surface of the lap or to minute fragments of the gem itself which have broken loose and ploughed through the facet under the force of the spinning lap.

Surface defects are most likely to appear upon the cheaper gemstones, where the rate of production must be high to keep lapidary charges low. Too much attention cannot be given to individual stones, and this usually shows up when the facet surfaces are examined with low-power magnification under a good light. Synthetic ruby, sapphire, and spinel often show a series of very small cracks on facet junctions which are due to the relief of stresses within the material created by the method of manufacture. They are commonly called "fire marks" because it is believed that they arise from polishing that is too rapid, and, hence, too hot. Many of these cracks are so small that a magnification of about 20x or more is required to see them well.

While "fire marks" and other surface defects may not be readily visible to the naked eye, they nevertheless cause scattering of light from the surfaces of the gem and decrease the total brilliance that could have otherwise been developed.

Softer gemstones, particularly those which are cut only for collectors, present many problems in polishing and are those most likely to show polishing defects. Some of them cannot be polished well except on soft and yielding laps, with the result that the facet junctions are noticeably rounded. While a good brilliance is obtained, the reflection usually lacks the crispness of well-cut gemstones of greater hardness.

Aside from the exceptions noted for soft stones, well-cut and well-polished faceted gems should display good proportions, flat facets of regular shape and all of the same size in any particular row of like facets, accurate junctions between facets without overlaps or gaps and a smooth, glassy polish, particularly on the large and highly important table facet. Scratches and polishing marks should not be visible to the naked eye. In the diamond trade, where quality grades are strictly defined, none of these defects should be visible under 10x magnification. Additional diamond trade practice rules, as promulgated by the U.S. Federal Trade Commission, are furnished under the Diamond listing.

CABOCHON GEMS

Because cabochons are entirely hand-shaped, the final curved surfaces depend for their geometrical perfection upon the skill of the lapidary. The ideal cabochon should be symmetrical in profile and outline, both of which can be easily determined by visual inspection. The base of the cabochon should have a slight bevel placed all the way around so that the jeweler will not chip the stone when he sets it into a mounting. The bevel is shown in Figure 20 along with some common shaping defects which detract from the quality of cabochon gems.

In mass-production cabochons, especially those from Idar-Oberstein in Germany, and some jadeite from Hong Kong, the form is achieved by grinding on hard-surfaced laps, leaving numerous small flat areas over the surface. Sometimes these are not entirely eliminated by subsequent smoothing operations and appear as vestiges upon the finished stones. These are also counted as defects, and one may be quite sure that their presence signifies an inexpensive material which the lapidary shop did not consider worthy of the additional labor required to make the surfaces truly smooth. On the other hand, more expensive materials, such as fine jadeite, chrysoprase, and catseye chrysoberyl, are treated with great care in respect to shaping and finishing.

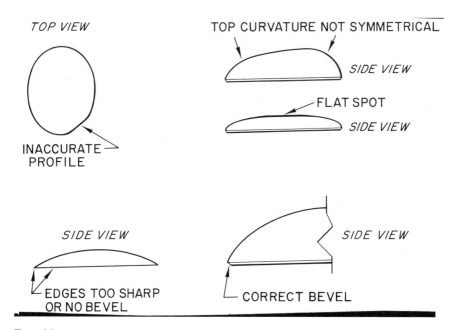

FIG. 20
Common shaping errors in cabochon gems.

A special defect of jadeite cabochons is the development of numerous small shallow pits over the polished surface because of improper polishing techniques. The appearance much resembles the slightly irregular surface of an orange or lemon peel, and, appropriately enough, is known among lapidaries as a "lemon peel" finish. The development of this kind of surface is difficult to avoid due to the nature of the gemstone itself, but the point is, it can be avoided, and when present, lessens the value of the gem.

PROPORTIONS OF CABOCHONS

The proportions of cabochon gems vary widely, some being quite thin in relation to their width, others being quite thick. Gemstones displaying star, catseye, and moonstone effects must be cut reasonably thick to "sharpen" the lines of light in the case of the first two and to induce strong sheen in the case of the last. Good star and eye effects require that the thickness of the cabochon be from $\frac{1}{3}$ to $\frac{1}{2}$ the width; good moonstoone effects are seen with the same proportions but do not lessen greatly until the thickness is reduced to about $\frac{1}{8}$ the width, depending on how strong the effect is in the rough used. Catseye gems, particularly chrysoberyl catseyes, often are cut with high tops and sharp curvatures at the crests, somewhat elongated along the streak of light, if the stone is elliptical. The sharp curvature narrows the line of light to a very thin, intensely bright line which enhances the gem's value. Very shallow curvatures must be used on gemstones whose optical displays or patterns of inclusions (e.g., tree agate) appear in planes; sometimes the curvature is so shallow that the top of the cabochon is nearly flat. Gemstones which must be cut this way are labradorite, sunstone, and tree agate. Precious opal is often shaped in this manner, especially black opal, whose rough mostly occurs in thin seam sections to begin with. On the other hand, the translucent Mexican-type opal appears best if the cabochons are shaped as proportionately thick as star gems.

The strength of material is also a major consideration in determining the depth of cabochon gems. For example, weak materials such as malachite and rhodochrosite must be cut fairly thick to prevent breakage during wear, but very tough materials such as jadeite, nephrite, and rhodonite can be cut quite thin. Another important consideration is tile total weight of the cabochon, especially if it is large in area. If cut too thick, it may weigh so much that it hangs heavily and awkwardly in a pin or pendant, much to the discomfort of the wearer.

ADDITIONAL NOTES ON STAR AND CATSEYE GEMS, MOONSTONES, ETC.

As previously explained, star- and catseye-causing inclusions, and those responsible for moonstone, sunstone, and other sheen or color effects, occur in certain planes in the host crystal. It is up to the cutter to examine the rough to determine how he can best cut it to place the special effect squarely on top where it belongs. If the optical display does not appear on top, it will be seen well only from one side instead of from all sides, depending on how much the ideal direction is deviated from. Because of the high value of star and catseye gems of good to fine quality, native cutters, particularly in Sri Lanka, attempt to make each gem as large as possible, even if it means a lopsided star or eye. These defects, and others, are shown in Figure 21.

If the star or eye effect is not greatly off to one side, the gem may be purchased with a view to recutting because too much weight will not be lost. However, if the effect is greatly displaced, the gem may be a very poor investment due to the large amount of material that must be removed to correct the position of the eye or star. The tendency to cut these gems as large as possible manifests itself in another irritating trick practiced by the Sri Lankan cutters. This is to cut the gems into nearly spherical balls even though only the polished top half can conceivably contribute to the star or eye effect. Native sellers attempt to assure the hesitant cus-

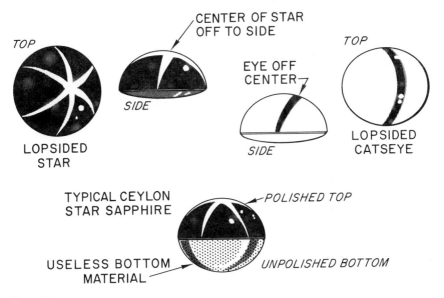

FIG. 21
Mistakes made in orienting star and catseye gems.

tomer that the bottom bulge is needed to "reinforce" the effect; this is simply not so. However, the bottom bulge may have good star or catseye material in it; if it does, the buyer may have the spherelike gem cut in half and the bottom recut into another gem. Unfortunately, in most instances, the lapidary has already satisfied himself that the bottom bulge is poor material whose only value is to add weight and inflate the price.

CHECKING POSITION OF OPTICAL EFFECTS

To determine the strength, perfection, and position of any special optical effect, stand beneath a single pinpoint source of light, e.g., a single electric bulb (*not* a fluorescent light) or the sun. Diffuse light, such as that found out-of-doors on a cloudy day, results in broad, diffuse reflections which are more confusing than re-

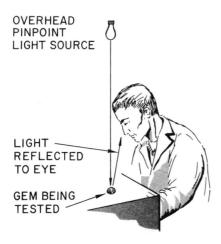

OVERHEAD
PINPOINT
LIGHT SOURCE

LIGHT
REFLECTED
TO EYE

GEM BEING
TESTED

FIG. 22
How a gem displaying an optical effect is examined.

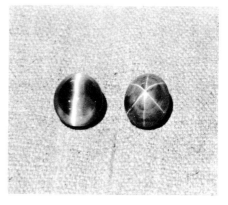

FIG. 23
Large and fine gems displaying the catseye effect on the left and the star effect on the right. The gem on the left is a catseye chrysoberyl weighing about 40 carats, while the gem on the right, weighing about the same, is a star ruby.
(Courtesy Smithsonian Institution)

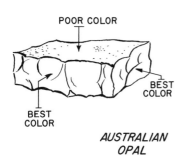

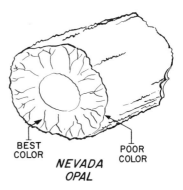

FIG. 24
Where the best play appears in rough opal.

vealing. As shown in Figure 22, the stone is held below the eyes in such a manner that the rays from the light source pass close to the forehead. Tilt the gem slowly from side to side, noting how much the optical effect appears to tilt with each movement. A few seconds' experimentation will show whether or not the optical and star gems are shown in Figure 23. The same technique is used for moonstone, sunstone, and labradorite gems. It may also be used for precious opal, particularly black opal, and certain classes of white opal which tend to display their strongest colors along the edges of rough seam sections instead of on top, as indicated in Figure 24. Because cutting the gems across the narrow dimension of the seam will obviously result only in small gems, many lapidaries succumb to the temptations of greater weight recovery and cut their gems the wrong way.

TUMBLE-POLISHED BAROQUES AND CABOCHONS

Large quantities of irregularly-shaped gems, known as *baroques* or tumbled gems, are now prepared very cheaply by tumbling pieces of rough in barrels along with suitable abrasives and liquids, and later, with polishing agents. the process takes many days or even weeks, depending on the kind of material, the size of the barrels, and other variables which are carefully considered by the manufacturers. Finished gems, with some applications in inexpensive but attractive jewelry, are shown in Figure 25.

While the principal tumbled-stone production remains baroques, an increasingly important segment has become the smoothing and polishing of geometrical shapes, including cabochons. Many of the jewelry gems sold today in clothing shops are tumbled. They begin as small sawed squares or other suitable shapes

FIG. 25
Typical tumbled gems showing their irregular shapes and some uses
in inexpensive jewelry.

and are merely placed in the tumbling barrels until they eventually emerge as polished gems. In the case of cabochons, the shaping must still be done by hand methods, but the tedious final smoothing operations can be accomplished by tumbling.
The drawback to this method of finishing is the tendency for all sharp edges to become severely rounded. In some kinds of jewelry mountings this is not of importance, but in others it is, and the traditional, completely hand-finished cabochons
are still employed in many kinds of jewelry. Balancing the drawback of rounded
edges is the fact that the tumbling operation often produces a vastly superior fin-

ish on certain gemstones which are hand-polished only with much difficulty and the expenditure of much time, for example, jadeite, certain jaspers, and rhodonite.

While it is true that flawed and cracked material can be fruitfully employed as grist for the tumbling mill, there is a falacy among some makers of tumbled gems that any rough, regardless of how poor it is, is suitable for tumbling. Unfortunately, in this field, as in other lapidary fields, there is no art of the lapidary that can improve the intrinsic quality of rough material. If it is poor to begin with, tumbling will only make this fact clearer.

Much of the charm of tumbled gems lies in their irregular shapes, but if the shapes are too irregular, it becomes nearly impossible to smooth those places which are deeply recessed or which follow large, open cracks. As with other lapidary objects, the best tumbled gems are made from colorful or attractively patterned material, free from unsightly cracks, flaws, and soft spots, and are polished to perfection. To be avoided are those pieces which have been tumbled so violently that they retain numerous surface cracks or rough spots upon protruding places. Other signs of poor workmanship are cracks filled with polishing compound, chipped places, and unpolished spots in deep recesses.

Tumbled gems must be fitted with attachment eyes. There are several suspension methods used: (a) a groove is cut around the gem and a thin wire is fitted into the grove and twisted into a suspension loop at one end; (b) an ornamental cap is cemented onto the stone with epoxy; and (c) a small, narrow groove is cut in one end of the stone and a metal ring is cemented into the groove with epoxy. The last of these methods is far superior in holding power to the others and should be specified where high-class stones are involved.

FACET AND CABOCHON GEM CUTS

Gem cutters have been particularly imaginative in devising new styles or "cuts" for faceted and cabochon gems, as will be seen in the drawings which follow shortly. Numerous variations have been invented by the lapidary artisans of Idar-Oberstein, Germany, and, more recently, by a host of amateur cutters in the United States. In the early 1980s German master cutter Bernd Munsteiner introduced a free cutting style that became known as "fantasy" cut. These highly interesting departures from conventional cuts resulted in faceted gems featuring deep, polished grooves, plane facets, seemingly placed at random, and curved surfaces combined with these features. These gems have now been accepted among jewelry designers and makers, especially when combined with sweeping curved metal areas, small diamond "sparks" and even other gemstones also carved to supplement and complement the fantasy cuts. The efforts of U.S. cutters appear in

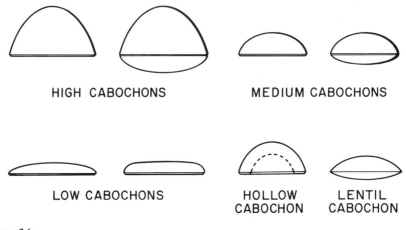

FIG. 26
Side views of various cabochon shapes.

the many carefully drawn diagrams furnished in past issues of *Lapidary Journal* and *Gems and Minerals* magazines. In some instances, the cuts are refreshing departures from old, well-established styles, but most are only slight modifications which offer the bored amateur something new.

In the gem trade and its special branch, the diamond trade, conservatism is the rule and serious departures from basic styles are seldom attempted. Sometimes a special piece of rough calls for an unusual cut, but mostly the standard brilliant and the step cut are used for faceted gems, and round or elliptical shapes for cabochons. An exception occurs when many small gems are needed to act as "side stones" to large gems in a ring or to cover entire surfaces of jewels in a blazing mass of brilliance. Many small bits of diamond, emerald, ruby, and sapphire can be used in such applications, faceted to shapes which will fit well into the design. However, it is seldom that large, good rough of the more expensive gemstone species is cut into other than conservatively styled gems, the advantage being that if such gems are ever unset from their mountings, they will sell more readily than others of equal weight and quality which have been cut in nonstandard patterns, possibly to fit special niches in unique pieces of jewelry.

If all faceted gems were examined it would be found that by far most are cut as *standard brilliants* of 57 facets, or its close relative, the diamond brilliant of 58 facets (counting the small culet facet), or as *step cuts*. Common variations on the basic brilliant style are the *oval brilliant, pendeloque, pear*, and *marquise*. Step-cut variations include the *octagon step cut* and the *cushion step cut*. A large number of gems are also faceted in *combination cuts*, which is the general term used to describe styles that combine features of both brilliant and step-cut styles. Some of

OVAL CABOCHONS
(BROOCH and COSTUME RING)

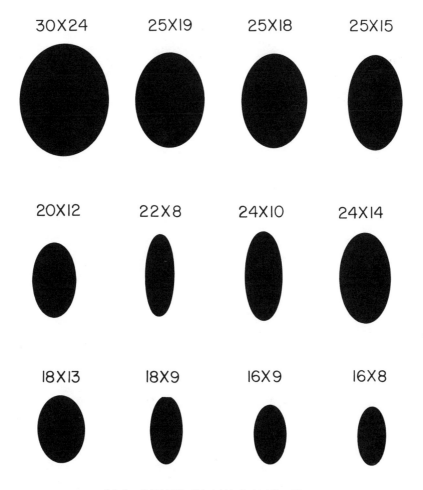

ALL SIZES IN MILLIMETERS

FIG. 27–A & B
Top views of oval cabochons in standard brooch, costume ring, and finger ring shapes.

the newer fancy cuts are complicated cuts to achieve a greater degree of brilliance in the finished gemstone such as the Jubilee cut with 80 facets, King cut—86 facets, Magna cut—102 facets, Royal cut—154 facets, Radiant cut—70 facets, Quadrillion—70 facets, Barion cut—62 facets. Some are trademarked like the Trielle cut, a triangle cut.

OVAL CABOCHONS
(RING)

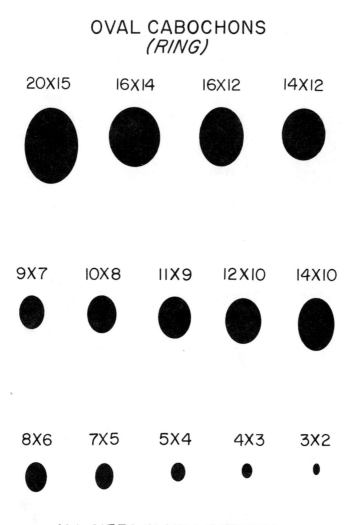

20X15   16X14   16X12   14X12

9X7   10X8   11X9   12X10   14X10

8X6   7X5   5X4   4X3   3X2

ALL SIZES IN MILLIMETERS

FIG. 27–A & B (continued)

Cabochons are also cut in a number of shapes, but those which are simply circular or elliptical are by far the most common. Some are faceted along the sides to add interest and a little sparkle, while others may be steeply beveled around the sides with nearly flat tops. An interesting combination of the cabochon and faceted gem is found in the *buff top* (Fig. 35), sometimes used for men's ring stones. In this style, the top is a low curved cabochon surface while the bottom is covered with facets much like the pavilion of an ordinary faceted gem.

CUSHION CABOCHONS
(FOR BOX RINGS)

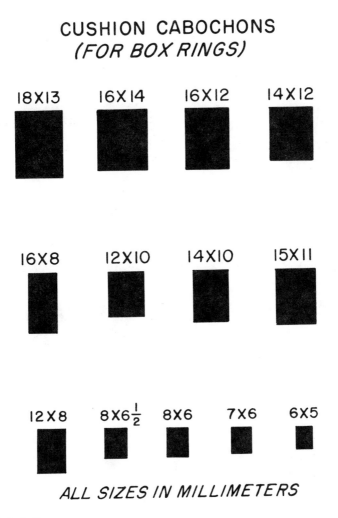

18X13 16X14 16X12 14X12

16X8 12X10 14X10 15X11

12X8 8X6½ 8X6 7X6 6X5

ALL SIZES IN MILLIMETERS

FIG. 28–A & B
Standard cushion cabochon shapes for box rings and octagon shapes for box or claw-mount rings.

DRAWINGS OF FACETED AND CABOCHON CUTS

Space does not permit including all of the styles in which gems have been cut, if indeed one could be sure that he had collected every known variation in the first place. However, the drawings do include the common cuts mentioned above and those variations of each which are of greatest importance. Also included are some common combination cuts and several simplified cuts which are employed for very small gems.

OCTAGON CABOCHONS

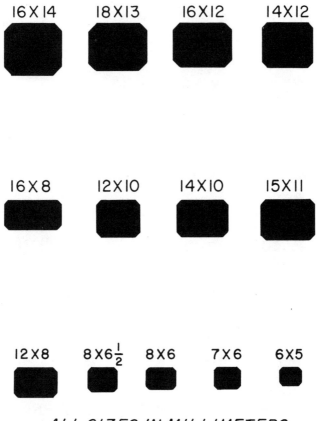

16 X 14 18 X 13 16 X 12 14 X 12

16 X 8 12 X 10 14 X 10 15 X 11

12 X 8 8 X 6½ 8 X 6 7 X 6 6 X 5

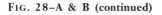

ALL SIZES IN MILLIMETERS

FIG. 28–A & B (continued)

FACETED AND CABOCHON GEM PRICES

Gems are listed alphabetically by species. Important varieties are placed under the species to which they belong. Where appropriate, each entry is preceded by brief statements of quality, size, defects, and other information designed to help the reader become a discriminating buyer of gems.

Prices are retail, by the carat (ct.) for most faceted gems and some cabochon gems, by the unit (ea.) for small gems, and by the ounce (oz.) or pound (lb.) for

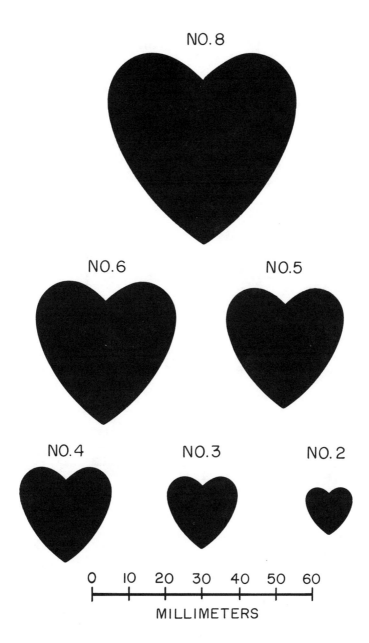

FIG. 29
Standard heart cabochon shapes used mainly in pendants. Suspension holes are usually out just below the bases of the "vees."

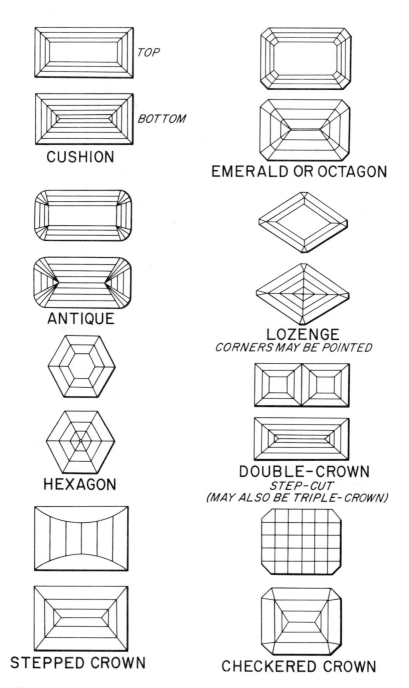

CUSHION

EMERALD OR OCTAGON

ANTIQUE

LOZENGE
CORNERS MAY BE POINTED

HEXAGON

DOUBLE-CROWN
STEP-CUT
(MAY ALSO BE TRIPLE-CROWN)

STEPPED CROWN

CHECKERED CROWN

FIG. 30
Some common and unusual step cuts for faceted gems.

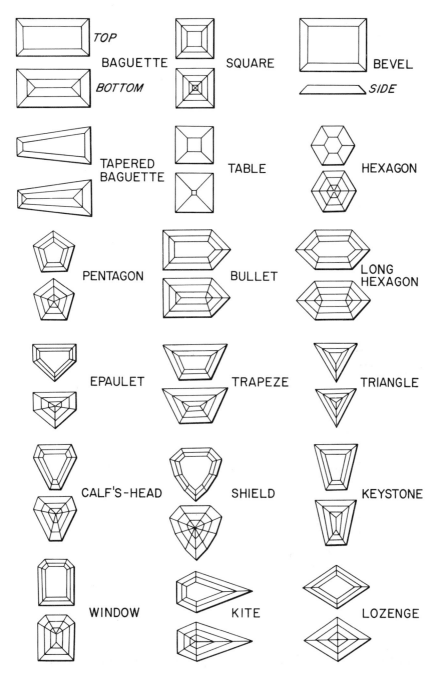

FIG. 31
Step cuts used for very small faceted gems.

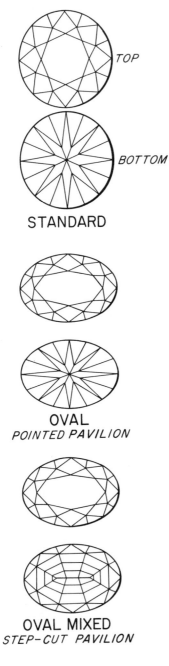

TOP

BOTTOM

STANDARD

DOUBLE

OVAL
POINTED PAVILION

OVAL
WEDGE PAVILION

OVAL MIXED
STEP-CUT PAVILION

PEAR

Fig. 32
Brilliant cuts used for faceted gems.

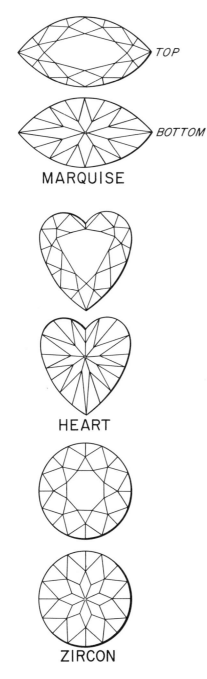

TOP

BOTTOM

MARQUISE

OLD-MINE

HEART

MAGNA

ZIRCON

PORTUGUESE

FIG. 33
Brilliant cuts used for faceted gems.

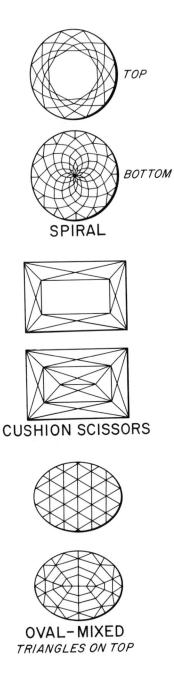

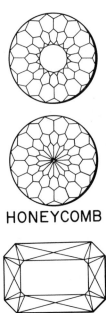

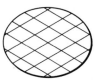

FIG. 34
Brilliant and mixed cuts used for faceted gems.

STAR

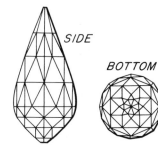

BRILLIANT-CUT BRIOLETTE

BUFF-TOP

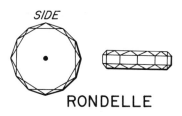

STEP-CUT BRIOLETTE

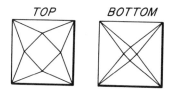

FRENCH

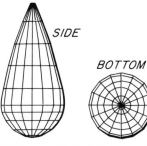

RONDELLE

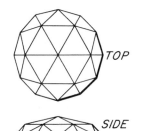

FULL DUTCH-CUT ROSE

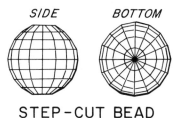

STEP-CUT BEAD

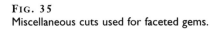

FIG. 35
Miscellaneous cuts used for faceted gems.

inexpensive tumbled gems. The *point* system is used for selling diamonds and some other gems of value weighing less than one carat, there being 100 points to the carat, with "25 points" meaning ¼ carat, "50 points," ½ carat, etc. The variables upon which the prices depend have been described in Chapter 1, but specific amplifying remarks on value factors are furnished under many of the species.

PRICES RANGES

Most prices are expressed in ranges, sometimes narrow, sometimes broad. In almost every instance, the increasing rarity of larger size rough is reflected in the higher prices asked for larger cut gems and, at the other end of the scale, by the lessened demand for very small gems, whose prices, per carat, may be much lower in proportion. In the case of small gems, the prices may reach a bottom per-carat figure, and then begin rising again for even smaller gems. This is explained by the fact that the amount of labor expended on the cutting of these very small gems is nearly the same as for larger gems, yet the yield is much lower in terms of carats per hour. Therefore it is necessary to charge more per carat for the cutting of these very small gems if the lapidary is to make this part of his work profitable. These very small gems are known as *calibre* or *melee* and range in diameter from 1 millimeter or less to several millimeters (see Fig. 31).

The great importance of color is reflected in the listings below, many of which are by color. Enormous differences in price can and do occur simply because some colors, or even certain shades of the same color, as in the ruby or emerald, are far more prized. Furthermore, among the paler-hued gems, such as the aquamarine, 10- to 15-carat gems are most in demand for ring stones because they are large enough to be impressive, yet not so large that they become awkward to wear. Smaller aquamarines tend to "wash out" in hue, which lowers their price per carat, while larger gems may rise only slowly in price per carat because they are not as much in demand.

Another factor which causes different prices per carat to be asked for gems that ostensibly are of the same color, quality, and size, is the presence or absence of flaws or other defects, such as color banding or zoning, and poor cutting.

A final factor, sometimes of importance, is the regard in which specific gems are held by individual dealers. One dealer may prefer an emerald which verges on the yellow side more than once which appears bluish; he may consciously or unconsciously price the yellow gem somewhat higher than the bluer one.

TREATMENTS

The majority of colored gemstones today are enhanced or treated in some manner to improve their appearance. Treatments are applied to both cut gemstones or rough and range from oiling and heat treating to sealing surface fissures with epoxy resins and colored glass.

Emeralds are both oiled and treated with epoxy resins; corundums, zircon, aquamarines, tourmalines, quartz, topaz, and tanzanite are routinely heat treated for color enhancement. Rubies and sapphires are also color enhanced with a high temperature penetrating diffusion process using iron and titanium oxide powder. Other color treatments include irradiation of topaz, quartz, tourmaline, corundum, pearls, and spodumene; dying of beryl, jade, lapis lazuli, and pearls; and cavity filling with glass of beryl, opal, and tourmalines.

Most of these treatments are permanent and accepted practices, however, new industry guides mandate treatment disclosure by the stone seller.

RULES FOR CHOOSING GEMS

As can be seen, the use of price ranges is mandatory; however, to aid the reader in evaluating gems, the following rules should be followed:

FOR COLORLESS GEMS

1. *Color Rule.* Ignore, except in the case of the diamond (see discussion for this species in the price list that follows).
2. *Clarity Rule.* Now supremely important; check for flaws, inclusions, spots, etc.
3. *Cutting Rule.* Examine gem for quality of cutting, i.e., proper proportions and angles yielding good brilliance and dispersion, symmetry of facets, even size of similar facets, accurate junctions between facets, sharpness of facet edges, lack of chipping or "knife edges" on girdles, and perfection of polish.
4. *Style of Cut Rule.* Consider this in relation to the use to which the gem is to be put; if the gem is capable of showing dispersion or "fire," is the cut suitable?
5. *Size Rule.* Consider use to which gem is to be put.
6. *Rarity Rule.* This consideration is mainly of importance to collectors of the unusual.

FOR COLORED GEMS

1. *Color Rule.* Usually of greatest importance except for very rare gems. Determine the order of color desirability by referring to the price lists that follow; determine if color is pure, vivid, and evenly distributed without being confined to bands, patches, spots, etc.; faint tints are usually less desirable than rich hues; check quality of color by examining gem under *normal* daylight, sunlight, tungsten light (ordinary electric bulbs) and fluorescent light, noting changes in color under each; for dark stones, be sure to examine under *normal* tungsten light and *not* under a strong spotlight such as is commonly present in salesrooms. *Note:* Colored gems, and even colorless gems, are commonly presented to customers in "diamond papers," or special folding paper wrappers which serve to store the gems and bear information as to their weight, species, cutting style, etc.; dark gray to black inner liners are commonly used for opals, faintly blue tinted liners may be used with diamonds, or colored liners with colored stones; *remove the gem and examine on ordinary white paper or white surgical cotton!*

2. *Clarity Rule.* Very desirable to have gems flawless, but exceptions may be made as in emerald, ruby, sapphire, etc.; evenly distributed flaws or inclusions known as "jardin" in emerald are acceptable, but naturally lower prices must be asked; avoid centrally located flaws in pale-hued gems especially.

3. *Cutting Rule.* Quality of cutting still important, but ideal proportions in the case of large step-cut gems may be deviated from slightly if gems meant to be worn in rings; very dark step-cut gems may depart even more from ideal proportions if this is necessary to prevent excessive darkness.

4. *Style of Cut.* More latitude allowed than for colorless gems, but in general step cuts are best; also popular are oval or round brilliants, hearts, pendeloques, etc.

5. *Size Rule.* Avoid excessive size in deep-hued gems.

6. *Rarity Rule.* This consideration is mainly of importance to collectors of the unusual.

Detailed discussions of color qualities and other considerations mentioned above are given in the following lists under BERYL, DIAMOND, CHRYSOBERYL, CORUNDUM, JADEITE, OPAL, etc.

PAPER WEAR

If a number of gems are stored in a single diamond paper, buyers should be alerted to the possibility that careless handling may have caused damage or "paper wear" due to mutual rubbing. While paper wear is most likely to occur among the softer gems, even the diamond and the corundum gems are susceptible; the most vulnerable places are the tips of pavilions, girdle edges, especially if very thin, and crown facets.

NOTES ON LIST BELOW

Unless otherwise noted all entries are faceted gems. The following abbreviations are used:

Carat (ct.)	Round (rd.)	Brilliant (brill.)
Cabochon (cab.)	Octagon (oct.)	Each (ea.)
Points (pt.)		

CATALOG OF
FACETED AND CABOCHON GEMS

ABALONE
Commonly offered in tumbled shell fragments; sometimes cut cabochon, an especially attractive type being composed of a thin layer of shell covered with rock crystal, but this type of doublet has not been offered commercially.

Cabochons, rds., 12-18 mm.	ea.	2.50-5.00
Cabochons, ovals, 16x12-20x15 mm.	ea.	2.50-10.00
Tumbled shell fragments, ½"- 2"	lb.	5.00-10.00

ABALONE PEARL, SEE CHAPTER VII

ACHROITE, SEE TOURMALINE

ACTINOLITE

Green catseye, weak	ct.	12.00-15.00

AGATE, SEE QUARTZ

AGNI MANI, SEE TEKTITE

ALBITE, SEE FELDSPAR

ALEXANDRITE, SEE CHRYSOBERYL

AMAZONITE, SEE FELDSPAR

AMBER
Because of softness, amber is principally used in brooches when cut in various cabochon styles; it is not suitable for rings; faceted gems, of the kind prepared from harder gemstones, are virtually unknown. Special pieces containing insects, or iridescent circular cracks, many of

which are induced in clear material by heat treatment, are cut into flattish cabochons or pendants. Clear yellow material commands higher prices than cloudy material. The best amber is Baltic, especially that retrieved from the sea. Sicilian amber is prized by connoisseurs because of its variety of colors.

Plaques or flat cabochons, with insects, ½"- 2"	ea.	25.00-125.00
Plaques or flat cabochons, with plant life, ½"- 2"	ea.	20.00-100.00
Yellow, clear, cabochons, ovals, 4-8 mm.	ea.	2.50-9.75

AMBLYGONITE
Very pale straw-yellow to medium-intensity yellow, the latter prized most; veil-type inclusions common; record step-cut gem 70 cts.; usual size 1½-15 ct.; prices increase steeply according to color and size. From Brazil only.

Rectangle cut, 1-2 ct.	ct.	55.00-120.00

AMETHYST, see QUARTZ

AMMOLITE
First mined in 1967, comes only fromthe south of Alberta, Canada. The stone has a dark body color marked with patchwork of opalescent colors. Mixtures of green, cold and red are common; blue, purple and solid red are rare. The stone is created through the fossilization and mineralization of squid-like creatures ammonites, estimated to be 70 million years old. It is found in between layers of iron shale in irregular shapes. Cabochons are often made into triplets. Both free form and calibrated cabochons are available.

Triplets, fine material, 8x6-10x8 mm.	ea.	36.00-65.00
Triplets, fine material, 11x9-14x120	ea.	77.00-110.00
Triplets, fine material, 14x12-16x12	ea.	125.00-150.00
Triplets, fine material, 18x9-20x15	ea.	125.00-230.00
Triplets, fine material, 25x18-30x22	ea.	345.00-510.00
Natural, solid material, 8x6-10x8 mm	ea.	50.00-85.00
Natural, solid material, 11x9-14x10	ea.	105.00-150.00
Natural, solid material, 14x12-16x12	ea.	180.00-210.00
Natural, solid material, 18x9-20x15	ea.	175.00-325.00
Natural, solid material, 25x18-30x22	ea.	482.00-715.00
Free form shapes (solid material)	ct.	12.00-40.00
Calibrated (solid material)	sq. mm.	.55-1.65

ANDALUSITE
Strongly dichroic pale reddish-brown and red, to olive-green and red, the latter most prized because differences in color more pronounced, but the first type of color is inclined to be more vivid; veil-type inclusions common; abundant in sizes to 3-4 ct. but scarce over 7 ct. and rare over 10-15 ct.; weak catseyes sometimes occur. From Brazil, also Sri Lanka and Myanmar.

Various facet cuts, ½-3 ct.	ct.	10.00-40.00
Various facet cuts, 4-7 ct.	ct.	52.00-95.00
Various facet cuts, 8-15 ct.	ct.	120.00-225.00
Catseye (weak), brown & red	ct.	25.00-75.00

CHIASTOLITE
All cabochons of this variety polish poorly due to softness, but some produce fair results; value depends mainly on strong color contrast between background, which should be white or nearly so, and the cross figures, which should be quite black and distinctly formed.

Cabs., rds., 4-6 mm.	ea.	6.00-25.00
Cabs., ovals, 16x12 mm.	ea.	15.00-18.00

END OF ANDALUSITE SECTION

ANDRADITE, see GARNET

ANGLESITE

Colorless faceted step-cut gems, sometimes prepared for collectors; very soft, fragile, but with high refraction and dispersion when properly cut.

Step cuts	ct.	80.00

ANHYDRITE

Colorless to pale pink-purple; soft and brittle; cut for collectors only.

Step cuts, 1-5 ct.	ct.	10.00-15.00

APATITE

Large variations in polish quality due to softness and differences in skill of individual cutters; best gems show sharp facet junctions. Bright, slightly greenish-yellow gems to 20 ct. abundant from Mexico but usual size range is 5-10 ct. with gems over this size quite scarce; record Mexican apatite about 25 ct.; rarest variety is rich purple from Maine, seldom over ½-1½ ct.; next comes fine aquamarine blue from Myanmar, sometimes yielding gems to 10 ct. although any over 1-2 ct. scarce; also yellow-green, olive-green, medium green, yellow, and rarely pink, the last inclining to fade to greenish under prolonged light exposure; some catseyes very fine with extremely sharp, bright eyes. Mexican gems can be heat-treated to colorless.

Maine, medium purple, to 1 ct.	ct.	200.00-250.00
Myanmar, fine blue, ½-1½ ct.	ct.	75.00-200.00
Myanmar, medium blue, ½-2 ct.	ct.	175.00
Myanmar, pale blue, ½-2 ct.	ct.	145.00
Myanmar, pale blue-green, 3 ct.+	ct.	100.00
Ontario, medium green, 3-11 mm rd.	ea.	10.00-160.00
Ontario, medium greem, oval-cut, 3x4–14x18 mm.	ea.	10.00-210.00
Colorless, round cut, to 5 ct.	ct.	25.00
Mexico, yellow, various facet cuts, 1-3 ct.	ct.	15.00-35.00
Mexico, yellow, various facet cuts, 4-1 0 ct.	ct.	20.00-40.00
Mexico, yellow, various facet cuts, 10-15 ct.	ct.	40.00-55.00
Brazil, rich blue	ct.	100.00

AQUAMARINE, see BERYL

ARAGONITE

Facet gems to 8 cts. cut only from elongated Czechoslovakian crystals; pale straw-yellow; with care, facet junctions can be made fairly sharp and surfaces smooth; sometimes with veil inclusions.

Various facet cuts, ½-2½ ct.	ct.	25.00-40.00
Various facet cuts, 3-8 ct.	ct.	25.00-45.00

AUGELITE

Colorless, soft, and brittle; extremely rare; cut for collectors only.

California, step cuts, ½-3 ct.	ct.	45.00

AVENTURINE, see FELDSPAR or QUARTZ

AXINITE

Attractive faceted gems only in 1-5 ct. range, inclining to be too dark when larger; flawless gems to 5 ct. common but over this size scarce, and over 10 ct. rare; cut examples relatively common with recent finds of fine facet-quality material in Baja California, Mexico; brilliant cuts usually more attractive; color red-brown with pale violet overtones.

Pear facet cuts, 5.2x3.5 (0.27) mm.		135.00

AZURITE

Faceted gems sometimes cut, but unless very thin (not over ⅛") they are merely blackish in appearance; good quality cabochons surprisingly rare, especially those showing layers of malachite (*azurmalachite*).

Cabs., octagon 8.5x4.5	ea.	35.00
Cabs., ovals, 7x5-30x20 mm.	ea.	.50-5.00

BARITE

Fine faceted gems cut from golden-brown North Dakota material; also from fine yellow material from British Columbia; large faceted gems to 45 ct. from colorless English material; small blue faceted gems from Colorado material but rarely over 1 ct.; very difficult to cut and most faceted gems show rounded facet junctions.

Golden brown, step cuts, to 5 ct.	ct.	60.00
Blue, step cuts, ½-1½ ct.	ct.	60.00

BEDIASITE, SEE TEKTITE

BENITOITE

Faceted gems relatively common in size range ¼-¾ ct., but 1 ct. size scarce and gems 1½-3 ct. rare; over 3 ct. very rare; color deep purplish-blue to pale blue to colorless, but colorless gems very rare; prices and demand holding up well.

Deep blue, rd. brills., clean, ¼-¾ ct.	ct.	1000.00-2500.00
Deep blue, rd. brills., clean, 1-2 ct.	ct.	850.00-2500.00
Deep blue, rd. brills., clean, 2-3 ct.	ct.	3000.00-4500.00
Good blue, rd. brills., clean, ¼ ct.	ct.	850.00-1500.00
Good blue, rd. brills., clean, 1-2 ct.	ct.	1000.00-1500.00

BERYL

Most prized variety is *emerald*, which in finest qualities exceeds all other gemstones in value in the range of 2-6 ct.; beyond that it is overtaken by fine rubies; much lower in value are fine blue aquamarines, and below the latter fall other beryl varieties; many common beryls occur in large sizes, for example, a beautiful yellowish-green step-cut gem in the Smithsonian of over 2000 ct. All beryls are hard, durable, and accept a fine polish.

EMERALD

Color, freedom from flaws, and size, in that order, determine value; the best color is an intense green, most persons favoring bluish-green but many liking intense, pure "leaf" green which inclines toward yellow-green; the terms *Siberian* and *Muzo* are commonly used to designate top color grades, although real Siberian emeralds are seldom offered; Sandawana (Rhodesia), Chatham synthetics, and some Indian emeralds are often very intensely colored in small sizes and make excellent melee. Flaws are usually, but not always, present in stones to 5 ct.; above that size flaws are invariably present; very small inclusion-type flaws are less disfiguring than fracture-type flaws, the latter tending to reflect light in spangles. Values ascend steeply for top-grade gems from 1 ct. to 6 ct., commonly exceeding diamond and ruby, but from this point values begin to "flatten" with increasing weight, ruby of top quality becoming more expensive per carat (see Fig. 3). Large emeralds are known up to and over 45 ct., but usually with many "jardin" type flaws. Old Indian gems commonly werecut from basal sections of large Colombian crystals, sometimes retaining the hexagonal outline and sometimes carved or cabochoned. Emeralds always retain value in top grades, even in small stones. Colombia virtually only source of larger emeralds. Step cut is preferred.

Finest Muzo bluish-green, essentially flawless, ½-1 ct.	ct.	4000.00-5000.00
Finest Muzo bluish-green, essentially flawless, 3 ct.	ct.	8500.00-12000.00
Finest Muzo bluish-green, essentially flawless, 5 ct.	ct.	14000.00-17500.00
Finest Muzo bluish-green, essentially flawless, 8 ct.	ct.	21000.00-25000.00

Finest Muzo bluish-green, lightly flawed, 1 ct.	ct.	2750.00-3500.00
Finest Muzo bluish-green, lightly flawed, 3 ct.	ct.	5000.00-6000.00
Finest Muzo bluish-green, lightly flawed, 5 ct.	ct.	7300.00-8500.00
Finest Muzo bluish-green, lightly flawed, 8 ct.	ct.	11000.00-15000.00
Finest Muzo bluish-green, moderately flawed, 1 ct.	ct.	2000.00-2750.00
Finest Muzo bluish-green, moderately flawed, 3 ct.	ct.	2900.00-4400.00
Finest Muzo bluish-green, moderately flawed, 5 ct.	ct.	6900.00-9200.00
Finest Muzo bluish-green, moderately flawed, 8 ct.	ct.	9900.00-13000.00
Medium Muzo bluish-green, essentially flawless, 1 ct.	ct.	1025.00-1500.00
Medium Muzo bluish-green, essentially flawless, 3 ct.	ct.	2200.00-2900.00
Medium Muzo bluish-green, essentially flawless, 5 ct.	ct.	5200.00-6500.00
Medium Muzo bluish-green, essentially flawless, 8 ct.	ct.	7250.00-9000.00
Medium Muzo bluish-green, lightly flawed, 1 ct.	ct.	550.00-1025.00
Medium Muzo bluish-green, lightly flawed, 3 ct.	ct.	1500.00-2200.00
Medium Muzo bluish-green, lightly flawed, 5 ct.	ct.	3500.00-5000.00
Medium Muzo bluish-green, lightly flawed, 8 ct.	ct.	4600.00-7000.00
Medium Muzo bluish-green, moderate flaws, 1 ct.	ct.	75.00-250.00
Medium Muzo bluish-green, moderate flaws, 3 ct.	ct.	150.00-600.00
Medium Muzo bluish-green, moderate flaws, 5 ct.	ct.	300.00-1000.00
Medium Muzo bluish-green, moderate flaws, 8 ct.	ct.	400.00-1500.00
Pale bluish-green, essentially flawless, 1 ct.	ct.	50.00-110.00
Pale bluish-green, essentially flawless, 3 ct.	ct.	150.00-425.00
Pale bluish-green, essentially flawless, 5 ct.	ct.	130.00-600.00
Pale bluish-green, essentially flawless, 8 ct.	ct.	500.00-700.00
Colombia, fine green, melee, step cuts, 2-4 mm.	ct.	50.00-150.00
Colombia, pale green, melee, step cuts, 2-4 mm.	ct.	20.00-50.00
Sandawana, intense yellow-green, essentially flawless, 1 ct.	ct.	560.00-2000.00
Sandawana, intense yellow-green, essentially flawless, 4 ct.	ct.	850.00-6250.00
Sandawana, intense yellow-green, lightly flawed, 1 ct.	ct.	400.00-825.00
Sandawana, intense yellow-green, lightly flawed, 4 ct.	ct.	250.00-1400.00
Sandawana, lesser color & perfection grades, 1-4 ct.	ct.	70.00-400.00
Sandawana, good green, melee sizes	ct.	60.00-150.00
India, medium green, melee sizes	ct.	50.00-125.00
Cabochons, according to color, flaws, etc., ½-20 ct.	ct.	225.00-1000.00
Cabochons, good color, moderately flawed, rds. 4-20 mm.	ea.	40.00-750.00
Cabochons, good color, moderately flawed, ovals, 7x5-20x15 mm.	ea.	40.00 +
Cabochons, "fixed star," 2-7 ct.	ct.	10.00-250.00
Catseye cabs., medium to light color, to 3 ct.	ct.	300.00-1500.00
North Carolina, emerald matrix cabs., 5-10 ct.	ct.	5.00-10.00

TRAPICHE EMERALD

Colombian, rare, displaying 6-rayed growth pattern.

1-3 cts.	ct.	1000.00-1250.00
3-6 cts.	ct.	1250.00-2000.00
6-9 cts.	ct.	2000.00-2500.00

SYNTHETIC EMERALD

Available in excellent intense bluish-green but seldom without serious flaws in sizes over 5 ct.

Best color, according to presence or absence of flaws, 1-2 ct.	ct.	490.00-550.00
Fine green, according to presence or absence of flaws, 1-2 ct.	ct.	300.00-380.00

Aquamarine

The finest gems are beautiful medium blue without trace of green, commonly called "Marta Rocha" or "Fortaleza" blue. the most beautiful faceted gems are those in the range 10-15 ct., which are large enough to display blue effectively and to appear impressive; smaller sizes are less in demand because the color pales; larger gems in the range 15-25 ct. tend to be bulky in finger rings and are less in demand. Values drop rapidly as greenish tinges appear or hues become excessively pale. Usually in step cuts, also ovals, brilliants, and hearts. Fine blues always in demand and now becoming scarce; flawless quality usually demanded.

Deepest pure blue, 3-6 ct., clean	ct.	375.00-575.00
Deepest pure blue, 10 ct., clean	ct.	475.00-650.00
Deepest pure blue, 15+ ct., clean	ct.	490.00-850.00
Medium blue, 3-6 ct., clean	ct.	250.00-375.00
Medium blue, 10 ct., clean	ct.	250.00-425.00
Medium blue, 15+ ct., clean	ct.	270.00-475.00
Light blue, 3-6 ct., clean	ct.	40.00-100.00
Light blue, 10 ct., clean	ct.	85.00-225.00
Light blue, 15+ ct., clean	ct.	100.00-250.00
Very light blue, 3-6 ct., clean	ct.	10.00-40.00
Very light blue, 10 ct., clean	ct.	15.00 +
Very light blue, 15+ ct., clean	ct.	20.00 +
Deepest greenish-blue, 3-6 ct., clean	ct.	20.00-40.00
Deepest greenish-blue, 10 ct., clean	ct.	50.00 +
Medium greenish-blue 3-6 ct., clean	ct.	15.00-25.00
Medium greenish-blue 10 ct., clean	ct.	30.00-65.00
Light greenish-blue, 3-6 ct., clean	ct.	5.00-10.00
Light greenish-blue, 10 ct., clean	ct.	15.00 +
Medium bluish-green, 3-6 ct., clean	ct.	5.00-30.00
Medium bluish-green, 10 ct., clean	ct.	15.00 +
Medium bluish-green, 15+ ct., clean	ct.	20.00 +
Light bluish-green, 3-6 ct., clean	ct.	10.00-25.00
Light bluish-green, 10-50 ct., clean	ct.	1.50-3.50
Light greenish-blue, catseyes, depending on color & brightness of eye, 5-10 mm.	ct.	8.00-15.00
Light blue, catseyes, fine sharp eyes	ct.	10.00-40.00

Morganite

Includes pinks, salmon hues, and orange; orange and salmon hues are unstable, fading rapidly to pink with exposure to light, especially daylight; the final pink intensity depends upon the initial intensity of salmon or orange; by far most pinks are pale and quite unprepossessing in small stones, but sometimes medium-intensity pinks are offered, which, in hue, are reminiscent of pink tourmaline. Madagascar has produced some exceptional purplish-pink gems to about 45 ct., clean. Usually from Brazil; also from California.

Finest purplish-pink, 3-6 ct., clean	ct.	60.00-100.00
Finest purplish-pink, 10 ct., clean	ct.	150.00-275.00
Finest purplish-pink, 15+ ct., clean	ct.	200.00-325.00
Medium purplish-pink, 3-6 ct., clean	ct.	30.00-60.00
Medium purplish-pink, 10 ct., clean	ct.	60.00-150.00
Medium purplish-pink, 15+ ct., clean	ct.	50.00-100.00
Light purplish-pink, 3-6 ct., clean	ct.	15.00-30.00
Light purplish-pink, 10 ct., clean	ct.	30.00-60.00
Light purplish-pink, 15+ ct. clean	ct.	25.00-50.00
Ordinary light pink, 3-10 ct., clean	ct.	5.00-15.00

Ordinary light pink, 15+ ct., clean	ct.	10.00-30.00
Pale salmon, 5-25 ct., clean	ct.	5.00-10.00
Orange, 5-25 ct., clean	ct.	10.00-25.00

GOLDEN BERYL

Very pale to medium-pure yellow but also ranging to greenish-yellow or brownish-yellow, sometimes fairly intense; much golden beryl resembles citrine too closely and this has perhaps contributed to the generally low esteem in which this gem is held; an exceptionally fine golden-yellow variety from South West Africa was called *heliodor* and this varietal name is still sometimes used; the brownish-yellow and some greenish-yellow (olive-tinged) varieties can be heat-treated to pure blues, the intensity of blue depending upon the intensity of the original hue (see heat-treatment note under GREEN BERYLS).

Finest golden yellow, 3-6 ct., clean	ct.	45.00-60.00
Finest golden yellow, 10 ct., clean	ct.	50.00-75.00
Finest golden yellow, 15+ ct., clean	ct.	75.00-100.00
Fine pure yellow, 3-6 ct., clean	ct.	30.00-40.00
Fine pure yellow, 10-25 ct., clean,	ct.	60.00-100.00
Pale yellow, 5-15 ct., clean	ct.	25.00-30.00
Pale yellow, 15+ ct., clean	ct.	50.00-60.00
Medium greenish-yellow, 3-6 ct., clean	ct.	8.00-30.00
Medium greenish-yellow, 10 ct., clean	ct.	8.00-35.00
Medium greenish-yellow, 15+ ct. clean	ct.	10.00-50.00
Light greenish-yellow, 3-6 ct., clean	ct.	10.00-15.00
Light greenish-yellow, 10 ct., clean	ct.	15.00-40.00
Light greenish-yellow, 15+ ct., clean	ct.	30.00-60.00
Madagascar, yellow-brown, 5-60 ct.	ct.	20.00 +
Good yellow, rd. brills., 3-12 mm. (to 6 ct.)	ea.	10.00-40.00
Madagascar, brownish-yellow catseyes, sharp eyes	ct.	20.00-60.00

GREEN BERYLS

Virtually all the hues included here are yellow-greens which verge on one hand toward the blues of aquamarine, and on the other, toward the yellows of golden beryl; very rarely some green beryls are found which are faintly tinged by the blue-green of emerald but seldom are such hues as intense as those found even in pale emerald. Sometimes green beryls are sold with the advice that they may be heat-treated to blues, but if this were really the case, such gems would have been heat-treated before being offered for sale because of the higher prices obtained for blue stones; it will be found that stones of chartreuse to olive-green can heat-treat to blue, but the typical pale greenish stones, found abundantly in Brazil, can not.

Medium yellow-green, 3-6 ct., clean	ct.	50.00-70.00
Medium yellow-green, 10 ct., clean	ct.	90.00-150.00
Medium yellow-green, 15+ ct., clean	ct.	75.00-100.00
Pale yellow-green, 5-15 ct., clean	ct.	15.00-35.00
Very pale yellow-green, 5-50 ct., clean	ct.	5.00-35.00
Greenish hues, catseyes, weak to fairly sharp eyes, to 45 ct.	ct.	10.00-40.00

GOSHENITE

Colorless, 1-25 ct., clean	ct.	10.00-20.00

RED BERYL

Discovered in the late 1970s in the Wah-Wah Mountains of Utah, Red Beryl is a unique American gemstone material. Crystals are found in white-colored volcanic rhyolite, and the red color is attributed to cesium as 0.2% Cs_2O and manganese as 0.3% MnO. Production of fine facet grade material is limited; most under 2 carats; some small cabochon material, non-transparent, highly included material is sometimes available.

Red Beryl, faceted, up to 2 cts.	ct.	2000.00-5000.00

END OF BERYL SECTION

BERYLLONITE

Colorless gems have been cut to 5 ct., clean, but are quite rare in this size; usual size for clean gems, brilliants, or step cuts is ½-3 ct.; only from Maine.

Colorless, ½-3 ct., clean	ct.	10.00-15.00
Colorless, 4-5 ct., clean	ct.	15.00-30.00

BILLITONITE, SEE TEKTITE

BLOODSTONE, SEE QUARTZ

BOLEITE

Deep blue, Mexico, ½ ct.	ct.	195.00

BORACITE

Pale greenish transparent faceted gems cut only from German crystals; very rare; all gems present a "sleepy" appearance due to interior optical imperfections; fairly hard but so rare that only a few cut gems exist.

Germany, very pale green step cuts, ⅛-2½ ct.	ct.	100.00-200.00

BOWENITE, SEE SERPENTINE

BRAZILIANITE

Very pale to medium golden-yellow hues; also greenish-yellow, the green verging on olive; small faceted gems to several carats are common, but gems over 5 ct., clean, are scarce, and over 10 ct., clean, rare; usually step-cut, also oval brilliants; only from Brazil.

Fine golden yellow, 1-5 ct., clean	ct.	70.00-115.00
Fine golden yellow, 6-10 ct., clean	ct.	80.00-125.00
Pale yellow, 1-5 ct., clean	ct.	50.00-60.00
Pale yellow, 6-10 ct., clean	ct.	50.00-75.00
Fine greenish-yellow, 1-5 ct., clean	ct.	40.00-80.00
Fine greenish-yellow, 6-10 ct., clean	ct.	45.00-85.00

CACOXENITE, SEE QUARTZ

CALCITE

Fairly attractive large faceted gems have been cut from brown material from Baja California, Mexico, and yellow from other localities; an unusual purplish-pink massive material, from Spain, has been faceted into step cuts displaying weak "glowing" reflections; very soft, fragile; for collectors only.

Spain, purplish-pink, 1-5 ct.	ct.	4.00-15.00
Deep yellowish-brown, step cuts, 5-45 ct.	ct.	5.00-10.00
Yellow, step cuts, 5-45 ct.	ct.	14.00
Colorless, step cuts, 5-45 ct.	ct.	3.50-5.00
Calcite onyx, cabs., ovals, 8x10-25x18 mm.	ea.	.80-12.00

CALIFORNITE, SEE IDOCRASE

CARNELIAN, SEE QUARTZ

CASSITERITE

Extremely rare in colorless gems without veil-type inclusions and traces of brown; the latter hue has a remarkable "deadening" effect on brilliance, and brownish gems seldom display the dispersion possible in this mineral; very small gems to about 1 ct. are not uncommon, but good-quality specimens over this size are quite rare; cut from Bolivian material only.

Colorless, clean, rd. brills., ½-2 ct.	ct.	40.00-130.00
Colorless, clean, rd. brills., 3-5 ct.	ct.	100.00-150.00

CELESTITE
Colorless to pale blue step-cut gems occasionally faceted for collectors, principally from Texas crystals; extremely soft and fragile; very difficult to cut.

Texas, colorless, step cuts, ½-3 ct.	ct.	10.00-30.00
Texas, pale blue, step cuts, ½-3 ct.	ct.	40.00-60.00

CERUSSITE
The best gems are colorless and clean, and may be had in sizes from 5 to 25 ct.; many gems are tinged brown and this hue greatly "deadens" the normally high dispersion and brilliance; usually step-cut, also cabochons and white, sharp catseyes.

Colorless, 5-15 ct., clean	ct.	6.00-40.00
Pale brown, 5-35 ct., clean	ct.	6.00-35.00
White, catseyes, 3-6 ct.	ct.	25.00-75.00

CHALCEDONY, SEE QUARTZ

CHIASTOLITE, SEE ANDALUSITE

CHLORASTROLITE, SEE PUMPELLYTTE

CHONDRODITE
Very rarely offered in small step- or brilliant-cut gems not over 2 ct.; color is brownish-red, very similar to dark almandite garnet; only from one locality in New York State.

Dark brown-red, ½-2 ct., clean	ct.	150.00-450.00

CHRYSOBERYL
The highly-prized *alexandrite* variety is scarce in good clean faceted gems up to 5 ct. and very scarce over this size; quality requirements are a decided color change, the stronger the better, and absence of the common veil-type inclusions which seriously reduce brilliance. The finest gems are Uralian, showing good emerald-green in daylight and rich purplish-red under tungsten light; gems from Sri Lanka tend to be less emerald-green and more brownish, as do those from Brazil. Despite the hardness and high durability of chrysoberyl, faceted gems other than alexandrite do not command very high prices; usual colors are bright yellow, golden yellow, brownish-yellow, greenish (olive)-yellow, and greenish (chartreuse)-yellow, the last being most prized; *alexandrite catseyes* are known but while displaying color change, the strength of change is usually feeble and the colors unattractive.

ALEXANDRITE

Urals, strong color change, 1-3 ct., clean	ct.	2000.00-20000.00
Urals, strong color change, 1-3 ct., clean, (or nearly so)	ct.	price negotiable
Urals, strong color change, 1-3 ct., lightly flawed	ct.	1500.00-6000.00
Urals, strong color change, 6 ct., lightly flawed	ct.	6000.00-20000.00
Urals, good color change, 1-3 ct., clean	ct.	1000.00-3000.00
Urals, good color change, 6 ct., clean (or nearly so)	ct.	3000.00-10000.00
Urals, good color change, 1-3 ct., lightly flawed	ct.	500.00-2500.00
Urals, good color change, 6 ct., lightly flawed	ct.	1000.00-4000.00
Urals, weak color change, 1-6 ct., clean	ct.	1000.00 +
Urals, good color change, heavily flawed, 1-6 ct.	ct.	25.00-500.00 +

Brazil, weak color change, 1-5 ct., clean	ct.	500.00 +
Sri Lanka, brownish, good color change, 1-6 ct., clean	ct.	250.00-1750.00
Sri Lanka, brownish, good color change, 10 ct., clean	ct.	600.00-2500.00
Melee, fair color change, 1-2 mm. rd. brills.	ct.	250.00 +
Catseyes, fair eye, fair color change, ½-9 ct.	ct.	500.00-2000.00

Yellow and Greenish-Yellow Chrysoberyls

Vivid greenish-yellow, nearly chartreuse, 1-3 ct., clean	ct.	150.00-200.00
Vivid greenish-yellow, nearly chartreuse, 4-15 ct., clean	ct.	200.00-250.00
Intense golden yellow, 1-6 ct., clean	ct.	150.00-240.00
Intense golden yellow, 7-15 ct., clean	ct.	150.00-300.00
Intense golden yellow, 15+ ct., clean	ct.	100.00-350.00
Pale golden yellow, 1-6 ct., clean	ct.	100.00-250.00
Pale golden yellow, 7-15 ct., clean	ct.	100.00-350.00
Pale golden yellow, 15+ ct., clean	ct.	200.00-400.00
Pale brown, or yellow-brown, 1-6 ct., clean	ct.	100.00-200.00
Pale brown, or yellow-brown, 7-15 ct., clean	ct.	150.00-275.00
Pale brown, or yellow-brown, 15+ ct., clean	ct.	150.00 +

Yellow and Greenish Catseye Chrysoberyls

Catseyes are at their finest when the minute inclusions are invisible to the naked eye and produce a brilliant narrow line of bluish-silvery light against a fine honey-yellow or greenish-yellow body color; grayish, gray-green, and brownish body colors are less desirable as are inclusions which are relatively coarse and produce rather broad eyes of less sheen or eyes that are white. Differences of opinion exist as to the most desirable body color; some dealers place a higher value upon deep yellow, verging slightly toward brownish, while others claim that a greenish body color is more desirable; all agree, however, that an olive-green tinge is less desirable than either of the hues mentioned.

Excellent sharp eyes, rich body color, 1-3 ct.	ct.	1000.00-1800.00
Excellent sharp eyes, rich body color, 6 ct.	ct.	1500.00-5500.00
Excellent sharp eyes, rich body color, 10 ct.	ct.	2000.00-5000.00
Good sharp eyes, good color, 1-3 ct.	ct.	600.00-3000.00
Good sharp eyes, good color, 6 ct.	ct.	1000.00-1500.00
Good sharp eyes, good color, 10 ct.	ct.	1500.00-3000.00
Fair eyes, fair body color, 1-6 ct.	ct.	300.00-1000.00
Fair eyes, fair body color, 10 ct.	ct.	800.00-1500.00
Fair eyes, olive-greenish body color, 1-3 ct.	ct.	300.00 +
Fair eyes, olive-greenish body color, 4-8 ct.	ct.	400.00 +
Fair eyes, olive-greenish body color, 15 ct.	ct.	300.00 +

End of Chrysoberyl Section

CHRYSOCOLLA, see QUARTZ

CHRYSPRASE, see QUARTZ

CITRINE, see QUARTZ

CLEIOPHANE, see SPHALERITE

CLINOHUMITE

Discovered in 1983, this rare gem was found in the Pamir Mountains in the south central part of Russia. With a hardness over 6, it is said to be reminiscent of hessonite garnet in its general appearanced. Colors range from dark, very slightly brown to orangy yellow. It is rare to ahve one over 1 carat; 2 carat stones are exceptionally rare.

Faceted ¼-1 ct.	ct.	300.00-1600.00

CLINOZOISITE

Step-cut gems, dark brown to green-brown, 1-3 ct., clean	ct.	50.00-150.00
Catseye, green-brown, weak eye	ct.	10.00-20.00

COLEMANITE

Colorless to faintly straw-yellow faceted gems sometimes prepared for collectors; soft and brittle; polish eventually disappears due to surface alteration.

California, step cuts, ½-5 ct.	ct.	60.00-68.00

CORAL

Commonly cut in cabochon form; also used in the form of polished twig and branch sections; see remarks on qualities in Chapter III.

Pink, ovals	ct.	6.00-10.00
Pink, angel skin ovals	ct.	3.00-6.00
Orange-red, ovals, 22x11-22x14 mm.	ct.	3.00-6.00
Ox-blood, ovals	ct.	20.00
Branch sections, ox-blood, dark pink, 2"-4", tumbled	ct.	1.00-2.00

CORDIERITE, SEE IOLITE

CORUNDUM

The supreme gem variety of corundum is the *ruby*, which, in its finest qualities, exceeds the diamond in value from about 3 ct. upward, and the emerald from about 6 ct. upward; the *star ruby* is the next most valuable variety, followed by fine blue faceted *sapphires* and *star sapphires*; other sapphire colors are generally less in demand and bring lower prices. All varieties are very hard, durable, and polish to a high luster; however, the poorly translucent red star-corundum from India is apt to pit during shaping and subsequent polishing may not completely remove these pits.

RUBY

Standards of quality are *Myanmar ruby*, finest vivid red, the best hue being rich red without trace of dinginess or "blackness" and red with a slight purplish tinge, sometimes called "pigeon blood"; followed by red which is orange-tinged as in *Siam ruby* (Thailand), or rich red that is somewhat darker in tone, sometimes with a faint brownish cast; and *Sri Lanka ruby*, applied to lighter-hued reds, which, by insensible progressions, change to varieties so pale as to merit the name *pink sapphire*. Following behind the finest rubies are *star rubies*, which, in the best grades, combine rich red body color, abundant, evenly-distributed "silk" inclusions, but not so profuse that the stone appears pink rather than red when cut, and polished cabochons showing stars with sharp streaks of light, and without serious gaps in the streaks due to thinness or absence of silk at critical points. Common defects in faceted gems are black inclusions, often with systems of radiating, mirror-like cracks, patches of silk which seriously reduce brilliance, and veil-type inclusions. Most gems are understandably cut to realize the largest clean weight, but often this means orienting the gem in such a manner that the orange tinge observed through the sides of the gem crystals is predominant instead of the more desirable purplish tinge which appears through the ends of crystals.

Myanmar and Vietnam, very slightly purplish-red, flawless or nearly so, ½-1 ct.	ct.	500.00-4000.00
Myanmar and Vietnam, very slightly purplish-red, flawless or nearly so, 1-2 ct.	ct.	2000.00-10000.00

Myanmar and Vietnam, very slightly purplish-red, flawless or nearly so, 2-5 ct.	ct.	5,000.00-10,0000.00
Myanmar and Vietnam, very slightly purplish-red, flawless or nearly so, 5+ ct.	ct.	10,000.00-225,000.00
Myanmar and Vietnam, very slightly purplish-red, light flaws, ½-1 ct.	ct.	300.00-3,000.00
Myanmar and Vietnam, very slightly purplish-red, light flaws, 1-2 ct.	ct.	1,000.00-4,000.00
Myanmar and Vietnam, very slightly purplish-red, light flaws, 2-5 ct.	ct.	3,000.00-10,000.00
Myanmar and Vietnam, very slightly purplish-red, light flaws, 5+ ct.	ct.	6,000.00-15,000.00
Myanmar and Vietnam, very slightly purplish-red, moderate flaws, ½-1 ct	ct.	200.00-2,000.00
Myanmar and Vietnam, very slightly purplish-red, moderate flaws, 1-2 ct	ct.	2,000.00-6,000.00
Myanmar and Vietnam, very slightly purplish-red, moderate flaws, 2-5 ct	ct.	5,000.00+
Thailand, Cambodia, ½-1 ct.	ct.	350.00-550.00
Thailand, Cambodia, 1-1½ ct.	ct.	550.00-1,100.00
Thailand, Cambodia, 4-5 ct.	ct.	1,375.00-2,000.00
Thailand, Cambodia, 5-8 ct.	ct.	1,650.00-3,000.00
Dark grades of above, ½-1 ct.	ct.	85.00-250.00
Dark grades of above, 1-1½ ct.	ct.	150.00-550.00
Dark grades of above, 1½-2 ct.	ct.	150.00-550.00
Dark grades of above, 2-3 ct.	ct.	200.00-825.00
Slightly orange-red, flawless or nearly so, ½-1 ct.	ct.	1,000.00-3,000.00
Slightly orange-red, flawless or nearly so, 3 ct.	ct.	3,000.00-4,200.00
Slightly orange-red, flawless or nearly so, 4-5 ct.	ct.	4,000.00-6,000.00
Slightly orange-red, flawless or nearly so, 8+ ct.	ct.	5,500.00-8,500.00
Slightly orange-red, light flaws, ½-1 ct.	ct.	550.00-1,000.00
Slightly orange-red, light flaws, 2-3 ct.	ct.	1,200.00-3,000.00
Slightly orange-red, light flaws, 4-5 ct.	ct.	2,000.00-4,000.00
Slightly orange-red, light flaws, 8+ ct.	ct.	3,000.00-5,500.00
Melee, fine, .02-.16 ct.	ct.	330.00-440.00
Melee, fine, .16-.36 ct.	ct.	450.00-750.00
Melee, fine, .36-.50 ct.	ct.	775.00-1,100.00
Melee, good, .02-.16 ct.	ct.	70.00-190.00
Melee, good, .16-.36 ct.	ct.	135.00-300.00
Melee, good, .36-.50 ct.	ct.	275.00-385.00
Melee, fair, .02-.16 ct.	ct.	45.00-70.00
Melee, fair, .16-.36 ct.	ct.	45.00 +
Melee, fair, .36-.50 ct.	ct.	55.00 +
Cabochons, fine red, rds. or ovals, 1-5 ct.	ct.	800.00-2,500.00
Cabochons, fine red, rds. or ovals, 5-8 ct.	ct.	1,500.00-3,500.00
Cabs., fair to good reds, rds. or ovals, 1-5 ct.	ct.	200.00-800.00
Cabs., fair to good reds, rds. or ovals, 6-10 ct.	ct.	300.00-1,500.00

Star Ruby

The colors given in the list above also affect the values of star rubies, but the differences in cost according to color grade are less pronounced than is true for faceted gems; the least desirable star rubies, if they can be dignified by that name, are the dark maroon to brownish-red gems from India which are translucent only in thin sections.

Extra fine medium color, ½-1 ct.	ct.	1,150.00-2,000.00
Extra fine medium color, 3 ct.	ct.	1,300.00-2,300.00
Extra fine medium color, 6 ct.	ct.	2,750.00-4,000.00
Extra fine medium color, 10+ ct.	ct.	6,750.00-8,000.00
Fine medium dark color, ½-1 ct.	ct.	575.00-1,150.00
Fine medium dark color, 3 ct.	ct.	900.00-1,300.00
Fine medium dark color, 6 ct.	ct.	1,650.00-2,750.00
Fine medium dark color, 10-20 ct.	ct.	3,300.00-6,750.00
Fine lighter hues, ½-1 ct.	ct.	200.00-575.00
Fine lighter hues, 3 ct.	ct.	300.00-900.00
Fine lighter hues, 6 ct.	ct.	800.00-1,600.00
India, dark red, 5-120 ct.	ct.	1.00-5.00
India, dark red, rds., 4-18 mm.	ea.	2.50-65.00
India, dark red, ovals, 8x6-20x15 mm.	ea.	2.50-65.00

BLUE SAPPHIRE

High quality *blue* sapphires consistently command higher prices than those of other colors; the most valued hue is a rich, slightly violet-blue which sometimes possesses the property of appearing violet-blue in daytime and purplish-blue under tungsten light and is medium dark in intensity; such gems are principally supplied by Myanmar. Fine pure blue gems rank next, followed by sapphires which are tinged with gray or purple. The *Kashmir* sapphire is pure blue, and when from the original locality in Kashmir, often somewhat milky in appearance because of numerous extremely fine inclusions. The designation *Ceylon* sapphire is applied not only to the typical pale violet-blue gems from that island, but also to those of other countries which resemble them; some Sri Lanka gems are medium dark in hue and command high prices. Large faceted gems of fine-quality sapphire up to several hundred carats are known but fine gems in the range 5-15 ct. are most likely to be sold, while smaller gems, cut from varieties which would be too dark in large sizes, are abundant as rounds and step cuts from melee sizes to several carats. Fine blues from Australia seldom exceed several carats; the excellent gems from Yogo Gulch, Montana, do not usually exceed 3 carats cut and most are considerably smaller. The *river* sapphires of Montana are very seldom intense or pure enough in color to be valuable; many contain centrally-positioned inclusions which seriously detract from brilliance and satisfactory cut examples seldom exceed several carats. The majority of blue, pale blue, and colorless sapphires are heat-treated to enhance the coloration and marketability of the stone.

Myanmar, Kashmir, Sri Lanka (untreated), slightly violet-blue, medium dark, flawless, ½-1 ct.	ct.	200.00-2,000.00
Myanmar, Kashmir, Sri Lanka (untreated), slightly violet-blue, medium dark, flawless, 1-2 ct.	ct.	800.00-4,000.00
Myanmar, Kashmir, Sri Lanka (untreated), slightly violet-blue, medium dark, flawless, 2-5 ct.	ct.	2,000.00-10,000.00
Myanmar, Kashmir, Sri Lanka (untreated), slightly violet-blue, medium dark, flawless, 5+ ct.	ct.	4,000.00-50,000.00
Same color, slight flaws, ½-1 ct.	ct.	100.00-1,000.00
Same color, slight flaws, 1-2 ct.	ct.	200.00-2,000.00
Same color, slight flaws, 2-5 ct.	ct.	400.00-4,000.00
Same color, slight flaws, 5+ ct.	ct.	800.00-5,000.00
Sri Lanka (treated), fine blue, flawless, ½-1 ct.	ct.	100.00-700.00
Sri Lanka (treated), fine blue, flawless, 1-2 ct.	ct.	500.00-2,000.00
Sri Lanka (treated), fine blue, flawless, 2-5 ct.	ct.	1,000.00-4,000.00
Sri Lanka (treated), fine blue, flawless, 5+ ct.	ct.	3,000.00-20,000.00
Same color, but very dark, slight flaws, ½-1 ct.	ct.	50.00-400.00
Same color, but very dark, slight flaws, 1-2 ct.	ct.	300.00-1,000.00

Same color, but very dark, slight flaws, 2-5 ct.	ct.	500.00-2,000.00
Same color, but very dark, slight flaws, 5+ ct.	ct.	1,000.00-5,000.00
Thailand, Cambodia, Australia, Nigeria, good blue, flawless (treated), ½-1 ct.	ct.	100.00-400.00
Thailand, Cambodia, Australia, Nigeria, good blue, flawless (treated), 1-2 ct.	ct.	200.00-800.00
Thailand, Cambodia, Australia, Nigeria, good blue, flawless (treated), 2-5 ct.	ct.	500.00-2,000.00
Thailand, Cambodia, Australia, Nigeria, (treated), 5+ ct.	ct.	1,000.00-4,000.00
Same color, but slight flaws, ½-1 ct.	ct.	30.00-150.00
Same color, but slight flaws, 1-2 ct.	ct.	100.00-300.00
Same color, but slight flaws, 2-5 ct.	ct.	150.00-500.00
Same color, but slight flaws, 5+ ct.	ct.	300.00-1,000.00
Medium dark blue, flawless, ½-1 ct.	ct.	550.00-800.00
Medium dark blue, flawless, 2-3 ct.	ct.	900.00-1,200.00
Medium dark blue, flawless, 5-6 ct.	ct.	2,300.00-3,200.00
Medium dark blue, flawless, 10-20 ct.	ct.	3,750.00-5,000.00
Same color, slight flaws, ½-1 ct.	ct.	300.00-550.00
Same color, slight flaws, 2-3 ct.	ct.	600.00-900.00
Same color, slight flaws, 5-6 ct.	ct.	1,400.00-2,300.00
Same color, slight flaws, 10-20 ct.	ct.	2,500.00-3,750.00
Grayish-blue, medium dark, flawless, ½-1 ct.	ct.	75.00-125.00
Grayish-blue, medium dark, flawless, 2-3 ct.	ct.	250.00-600.00
Grayish-blue, medium dark, flawless, 5-6 ct.	ct.	600.00-1,400.00
Grayish-blue, medium dark, flawless, 10 ct.	ct.	1,000.00-2,000.00
Same color, medium dark, slight flaws, ½-1ct.	ct.	50.00-75.00
Same color, medium dark, slight flaws, 2-3 ct.	ct.	100.00-250.00
Same color, medium dark, slight flaws, 5-6 ct.	ct.	200.00-600.00
Same color, medium dark, slight flaws, 10 ct.	ct.	400.00-1,200.00
Same color, but pale, various grades, ½-1 ct.	ct.	30.00-50.00
Same color, but pale, various grades, 3 ct.	ct.	60.00-100.00
Same color, but pale, various grades, 6 ct.	ct.	75.00 +
Same color, but pale, various grades, 10 ct.	ct.	100.00 +
Thailand, dark blue melee, 1-3½ mm. rds.	ct.	180.00-360.00
Sri Lanka, light blue melee, native cut, 1-3½ mm. rds.	ct.	100.00-180.00
Violet-blue melee, various color shades	ct.	40.00-100.00
Blue melee, various color shades	ct.	25.00-60.00
Gray-blue melee, various color shades	ct.	16.00-40.00
Montana, Yogo Gulch, fine blues, ½-2 ct.	ct.	70.00-500.00
Montana, river sapphires, ½-4 ct.	ct.	40.00-100.00

PINK SAPPHIRE

Some specimens are remarkably brilliant and attractive in color; however, it is uncommon to find large gems with uniform coloration; most cut gems are only several carats.

Medium dark, various grades, ½-1 ct.	ct.	350.00-800.00
Medium dark, various grades, 1-2 ct.	ct.	650.00-1,200.00
Medium dark, various grades, 4-5 ct.	ct.	1,400.00-3,000.00
Medium dark, various grades, 5-7 ct.	ct.	1,600.00-3,500.00
Pale pink, various grades, ½-1 ct.	ct.	25.00-60.00
Pale pink, various grades, 3 ct.	ct.	75.00 +
Pale pink, various grades, 4-5 ct.	ct.	85.00 +
Pale pink, various grades, 5-7 ct.	ct.	100.00 +

GREEN SAPPHIRE

Fine pure green gems from Australia, also from Sri Lanka and Myanmar; values drop sharply as gems become olive-tinged or grayish, also if mottled in appearance because of color zoning.

Medium dark, various grades, ½-1 ct.	ct.	20.00-45.00
Medium dark, various grades, 1-3 ct.	ct.	45.00-70.00
Medium dark, various grades, 3-5 ct.	ct.	70.00-90.00
Medium dark, various grades, 10-20 ct.	ct.	150.00-200.00
Medium color, various grades, ½-1 ct.	ct.	10.00-20.00
Medium color, various grades, 1-3 ct.	ct.	20.00-45.00
Medium color, various grades, 5-10 ct.	ct.	70.00-100.00
Pale color, various grades, ½-1 ct.	ct.	5.00-10.00
Pale color, various grades, 3 ct.	ct.	10.00-50.00
Pale color, various grades, 6-10 ct.	ct.	20.00-70.00

YELLOW SAPPHIRE

As is usual among gems, various yellow sapphires do not command very high prices; golden-yellows and orange-yellows are worth somewhat more than pure yellows; some Sri Lanka and Myanmar gems attain cut sizes over 45 carats; some Australian golden-yellow gems are very fine.

Medium yellow or golden yellow, very fine, 1-3 ct.	ct.	250.00-425.00
Medium yellow or golden yellow, very fine, 3 ct.	ct.	500.00-625.00
Medium yellow or golden yellow, very fine, 5-10 ct.	ct.	625.00-850.00
Medium yellow or golden yellow, very fine, 10-20 ct.	ct.	900.00-1,100.00
Pale yellow or golden yellow, various grades, 1-3 ct.	ct.	10.00-60.00
Pale yellow or golden yellow, various grades, 3-6 ct.	ct.	20.00 +
Pale yellow or golden yellow, various grades, 10 ct.	ct.	10.00-50.00
Medium orange-yellow, various grades, 1-3 ct.	ct.	60.00-125.00
Medium orange-yellow, various grades, 3-5 ct.	ct.	125.00-300.00
Medium orange-yellow, various grades, 5-10 ct.	ct.	250.00-425.00
Pale orange-yellow, various grades, ½-1 ct.	ct.	8.00-25.00
Pale orange-yellow, various grades, 3-6 ct.	ct.	20.00 +
Pale orange-yellow, various grades, 10 ct.	ct.	50.00 +

ORANGE (*Padparadschah*) SAPPHIRE

Reddish- to somewhat brownish-orange, sometimes resembling the brownish to reddish-orange "imperial" topaz or some spessartine garnets; rare in large sizes.

Sri Lanka, various grades & shades, 1-7 ct.	ct.	325.00-6,600.00

PURPLE SAPPHIRE

The finest specimens resemble the best grades of amethyst but are inclined to be more brilliant, purer in hue, and somewhat redder; rare in cut gems over several carats.

Sri Lanka, fine, 1-5 ct.	ct.	150.00-650.00

STAR SAPPHIRES

The finest blue gems occur in the gem gravels of Myanmar and Sri Lanka; the latter country additionally furnishes a considerable variety of star gems in other colors, among them, a great many indifferent grayish to nearly white, or very pale blue, pink, or purplish gems, most of which are sold very cheaply as compared to the rich-hued gems; as a rule, the prized body colors of facet-grade sapphires are also prized in star stones. Fine-quality star sapphires have been cut to sizes well in excess of 150 carats. The gems from Sri Lanka are very often cut to realize maximum weight; thus they will be found to be so deep upon the bottom that they resemble spheres (see Fig. 21); this surplus material adds nothing to the star and its sole purpose is to bring more money into the hands of the original native dealer; for the same reason, other star gems are cut lopsided so that the star appears some distance from the geometrical center of the top, thus requiring such gems to be recut before they can be mounted. Other common defects are interrupted streaks of light because of absence of fibrous inclusions at critical points, too few inclusions resulting in weak stars, and also too many inclusions, causing gems to appear whitish. Hexagonal zoning of inclusions is also common in star sapphires, and if too evident, detracts from value.

Slightly violet-blue, medium dark, best grades, 1 ct.	ct.	150.00-225.00
Slightly violet-blue, medium dark, best grades, 1-3 ct.	ct.	700.00-1,200.00
Slightly violet-blue, medium dark, best grades, 5-10 ct.	ct.	2,500.00-4,600.00
Slightly violet-blue, medium dark, best grades, 10-20 ct.	ct.	3,400.00-5,000.00
Same color, good to fine grades, 1 ct.	ct.	85.00-150.00
Same color, good to fine grades, 3-5 ct.	ct.	575.00-1,200.00
Same color, good to fine grades, 5-10 ct.	ct.	900.00-2,500.00
Same color, good to fine grades, 10-20 ct.	ct.	1,700.00-3,400.00
Same color, medium hue, good to fine grades, 1 ct.	ct.	40.00-85.00
Same color, medium hue, good to fine grades, 3-5 ct.	ct.	285.00-575.00
Same color, medium hue, good to fine grades, 5-10 ct.	ct.	350.00-900.00
Same color, medium hue, good to fine grades, 10-20 ct.	ct.	575.00-1,700.00
Same color, light hues, good to fine grades, 1 ct.	ct.	20.00-115.00
Same color, light hues, good to fine grades, 3-5 ct.	ct.	50.00 +
Same color, light hues, good to fine grades, 5-10 ct.	ct	50.00 +
Same color, light hues, good to fine grades, 15 ct.	ct.	50.00 +
Grayish-blue, medium dark, good to fine grades, 1 ct.	ct.	20.00-100.00
Grayish-blue, medium dark, good to fine grades, 6 ct.	ct.	50.00-185.00
Grayish-blue, medium dark, good to fine grades, 10 ct.	ct.	150.00-450.00
Same color, dark, good to fine grades, 1-6 ct.	ct.	100.00-150.00
Same color, dark, good to fine grades, 10-15 ct.	ct.	150.00-225.00
Same color, medium light hues, good to fine grades, 1-6 ct.	ct.	100.00-200.00
Same color, medium light hues, good to fine grades, 10-15 ct.	ct.	125.00-150.00
Bluish-gray, light to medium hues, good to fine grades, 1-6 ct.	ct.	120.00-155.00
Bluish-gray, light to medium hues, good to fine grades, 10-15 ct.	ct.	115.00-190.00
Purplish, medium to medium dark hues, good to fine grades, 1-6 ct.	ct.	125.00-200.00
Purplish, medium to medium dark hues, good to fine grades, 10-15 ct.	ct.	200.00-600.00
Pink, pale to light hues, good to fine grades, 1-6 ct.	ct.	100.00-300.00
Pink, pale to light hues, good to fine grades, 10 ct.	ct.	150.00-350.00
Black, gold-brown star, best quality, 1-6 ct.	ct.	40.00-100.00
Black, gold-brown star, best quality, 10-15 ct.	ct.	80.00-155.00
Black, brown to grayish-brown star, various grades, 1-6 ct.	ct.	80.00-150.00
Black, brown to grayish-brown star, various grades, 6-10 ct.	ct.	80.00-200.00
Black, brown to grayish-brown star, various grades, 10-15 ct.	ct.	100.00-225.00

SYNTHETIC STAR CORUNDUMS

Excellent synthetic star corundums are readily available, the principal types being Linde (blue, red, white, and black) and Gemma (Star of Freyung), the last made in Germany and furnished in blue cabochons with less sharp stars than those in corresponding Linde stones; all are fully controlled from manufacture and cutting to sale of cut gems by designated wholesale distributors. Recently, Linde has placed the letter "L" upon the base of each cut stone. Compared to natural stars, the synthetics are so perfect that they usually can be reliably identified on this basis.

Linde, rd. cabochons, 5-12 mm.	ea.	6.50-60.00
Linde, oval cabochons, 8x6-16x12 mm.	ea.	12.00-148.00
Linde, pear cabochons, 6x4-7x10 mm.	ea.	8.50-35.00

SYNTHETIC STAR DOUBLETS, BACKED

Blue, oval cabochons, 1-2 cts.	ea.	7.00-20.00

SYNTHETIC SAPPHIRES

Large quantities of synthetic sapphire boules are cut into faceted gems for costume jewelry and rings; mass-produced gems are cut rapidly, the stresses developing minute cracks along facet junctions; better-grade gems are cut more slowly and produce beautiful results; in no case are faceted synthetic sapphires expensive; the alexandrite-type is one of the most popular and appears to be sold throughout the world, often without clearly stating to unwary customers that it is a synthetic sapphire and not the much more valuable chrysoberyl variety.

Rd. brills., various flues, well-cut, 3-10 mm.	ea.	.75-5.00
Ovals, octs., cushions, various hues, well-cut, 3-18 mm.	ea.	1.50-15.00
Hearts, various hues, well-cut, 2-20 mm.	ea.	1.50-18.00
Pears, various hues, well-cut, 5x3-9x7 mm.-	ea.	2.00-6.00
Alexandrite-type, ring stones, generally	ct.	2.00-8.00
Melee, various lines, rd. brills., 1-3½ mm.	ea.	.75-2.00

END OF CORUNDUM SECTION

DANBURITE

Abundant colorless faceted gems from Mexico and Russia of 1-3 ct.; available in ranges 3-5 ct., and larger.

Russia and Mexico, colorless, ½-1 ct.	ct.	100.00-150.00
Russia and Mexico, colorless, 10-25 cts.	ct.	150.00-200.00

DATOLITE

Finest faceted gems cut from large Massachusetts crystals; small gems of 1-2 ct. from Paterson, N.J., material; massive material from Michigan seldom sold in cabochon form.

Mass. or N.,I., clean, very pale green, ½-1½ ct.	ct.	40.00-60.00
Mass. or N.,I., clean, very pale green, 2-5 ct.	ct.	60.00-80.00

DEMANTOID, SEE GARNET

DIAMOND

Aside from the usual price rise with weight, the principal factors affecting value are (a) color, (b) clarity, and (c) cut or "make." Each factor is carefully judged in arriving at the retail value of any gem.

The factor of *color* is given an importance unequalled in the evaluation of any other gem. By far most diamond gems appear colorless to the untrained eye and only a few gems display decided hues such as one expects to see in varieties of corundum, for example; these are "fancy" diamonds, very rare and very costly. The apparently colorless gems are painstakingly subdivided into numerous, if somewhat artificial, color grades, the nuances between which are seldom apparent when gems are mounted in jewelry. Nevertheless, some color-grading system is employed by every dealer in diamonds, and affects directly and substantially the price that is charged. As Robert Crowinngshield of the Gemological Institute of America states: "The grading of most diamonds for color is the art of classifying them on a scale from colorless to obviously yellow." This statement is based on the fact that most diamonds encountered in the trade range from absolutely colorless to some tinge of yellow or faint brown. Those that are decidedly yellow or brown in hue are fancies and sold as such. There are numerous color-grading systems in use, three of which are shown below with some intermediate steps omitted:

DIAMOND COLOR-GRADING SYSTEMS

Colorless . . . . to . . . . Pale Yellow etc.													

G.I.A. system	D	E	F	G	H	I	J	K	L	M	N	0	P etc.
American Gem Society	0		II		III		IV		V		VI		etc.
Old system	River		Wesselton		Crystal		Capes		etc.				

Since the FTC banned the use of the term in 1979 as a general description term, overly-free use of "blue-white" is much less evident now. Several decades ago when jewelers used this term more freely in their advertisements and were rightly regarded with suspicion because of the very real rarity of diamonds which actually display some tinge of blue. A survey by the Gemological Institute of America some years ago showed that only one diamond out of 500 examined under scientifically-adjusted lighting conditions actually qualified for the term "blue-white." Needless to say, diamonds of this hue command very high prices. Even higher prices are asked for fancies, particularly those which are blue to rich blue, red, pink or green, with lesser prices asked for golden, yellow, and rich brown gems. Some of these colors appear in irradiated gems, namely yellows, browns, greens, and blues.

The factor of *clarity* refers to the absence of inclusions or flaws. The term "perfect" is now seldom used; instead, those diamonds which do not reveal inclusions or flaws when examined by an expert eye under 10-power magnification rate the term "flawless." From flawless downward, various grading systems are in use but the terms in the table on page 166, with their meanings, are approved by the Gemological Institute of America and are widely used.

The final factor of *cut* refers to the mechanical shaping and polishing of a diamond crystal into a faceted gem, giving due regard to proper proportions, symmetrical outlining and placement of facets, accurate meets or junctions between adjoining facets, proper girdling and culeting, and surface finish upon facets. Good proportions, as shown in Figure 16, are necessary for development of brilliance and dispersion ("fire"), the optical properties for which colorless diamonds are most noted. Diamonds too deeply or shallowly cut are less brilliant than they could be, sometimes seriously so. Excessively thin crowns ("swindled" crowns) cut down dispersion substantially, although brilliance can be quite satisfactory. In general, overlapping facet junctions, extra facets, or uneven facets do not seriously detract from brilliance and dispersion, providing that the basic proportions are nearly correct; however, careless work is usually a sign of poor material and should also be cause for rejection of any stone in which it is glaringly evident. Careless polishing, usually shown by scores or "wheel marks" on facet surfresults in some loss in brilliance and dispersion. Excessively thick or thin girdles are also signs of poor cutting, thick girdles being used by some cutters to realize as much weight from the rough as possible. Excessivbely thin girdles, coming to sharp edges, are unsatisfactory because they may break during setting of the gem or chip if the gem hapens to strike a hard surface. especially after it is set into a ring. The culet facet at the tip of the pavilion should be as small as possible and not at all readily visible with the naked eye.

The *style of cut* is of considerable importance because some cuts are more optically effective than others, although large variations in prices seldom occur among gems of the same quality and weight because of differences in style, providing of course that the style is an acceptable one. From the standpoint of brilliance and best display of dispersion, coupled with an intriguing shift in reflections as gems are turned about, the *standard round brilliant* style is best, and by far most diamonds are cut in this fashion; other modifications of the brilliant style, such as ovals, pears, pendeloques, and marquises, suffer more losses of light because of their geometry. Step cuts are very brilliant but dispersion is seldom as effectively displayed in them and the simplicity of their strip-like reflections is not as pleasing to many prospective buyers as the scintillating, triangular reflectiosn of gems cut in brilliant styles. The old style mine cut in actually a nearly square brilliant cut, but the proportions employed make the gems excessively deep and much less brilliance is realized from them. Soimetimes they can be recut into a modern style, and, providing the basic gem is of high quality to begin witih, made to increase in value despite the substantial weight loss involved in the process.

Very small gems are called melee or calibre, and may be cut into full brilliants, simplified brilliants, step cuts, or step cuts with specific outlines for setting into corresponding openings or recesses in jewelry as shown in Figure 31; such small stones are often seen as complementary gems or "side" stones in rings, surrounding or setting off larger gems. The price per carat depends on quality, of course, but also upon the amount of labor expended in their cutting, the styles with more facets naturally commanding higher prices. As with other very small gems, the price per carat in diameters of about 4-5 millimeters is somewhat higher than for ordinary diamonds.

G.I.A. DIAMOND CLARITY-GRADING SYSTEMS

Term	Meaning	Remarks
Fl	Flawless	No imperfections visible under10x magnification.
IF		Internally flawless
VVS 1	Very, very slightly included	Difficult to see any imperfections under 10x magnification.
VVS 2	Very, very slightly included	Somewhat less difficult to see imperfections under 10x magnification.
VS 1	Very slightly included	Imperfections not obvious but easy to locate under 10x magnification.
VS 2	Very slightly included	Same, imperfections somewhat easier to locate under 10x magnification.
SI 1	Slightly included	Imperfections very readily visible under 10x magnification, but not large enough to be seen by naked eye when diamond is "face up."
SI 2	Slightly included	Same, but imperfections easier to see under 10x magnification.
I 1, I 2, I 3	Imperfect grades	Imperfections increasingly visible to the naked eye when gem is "face up."

Price Trends: During the 1980s the diamond market in the U.S. soared. The total retail value of diamonds sold increased enormous 120% from $5.2 billion in 1980 to $11.3 billion in 1987 according to NW Ayer the U.S. New York advertising agency for DeBeers. All categories of diamonds nearly doubled sales in dollar terms.

The importance of the diamond in the general economy is considerable, while in the jewelry trade it is very important. This is reflected in the "Guides For The Jewelry Industry," issued by the Federal Trade Commission, Washington, D.C., and promulgated February 27, 1979, with revisions April 15, 1986. The rules define the term "diamond," deal with misrepresentations and misuses of various terms intended to mislead prospective buyers, and otherwise clearly specify the bounds of ethics in the selling of diamonds. Of particular interest to prospective buyers and sellers are the sections dealing with the misuse of the word "perfect," the true significance of the term "blue-white" in connection with diamond colors, misuses of the terms "brilliant," "full cut," "clean," etc. Any buyer or seller of diamonds should be familiar with these rules and it is urged that a copy be obtained for guidance, and in the case of sellers, for compliance. Reputable jewelers selling diamonds will have a copy available to customers for reference should they so desire. Copies may be obtained by application to the FTC.

The prices below are for good- to fine-quality stones, the extreme prices for each weight being for flawless, colorless gems, cut to ideal or very nearly ideal proportions (American cut), while the lower prices are for gems which may be somewhat off-color, flawed to some degree, or cut to proportions departing substantially from the ideal. Much lower prices can be asked for badly flawed gems, those decidedly off color, etc., and conversely, higher prices may be asked for flawless, perfectly proportioned gems.

⅛ carat (12½ points) – DEF – V S	ct.	900.00
¼ carat (25 points) – F – VVS1	ct.	1,700.00
½ carat (50 points) – G – VVS1	ct.	3,900.00
¾ carat (75 points) – H – VVS1	ct.	3,900.00
1 carat (100 points) – G – VVS1	ct.	6,000.00
1½ carats – H – VVS1	ct.	6,100.00
2 carats – H – VVS1	ct.	8,300.00
2½ carats – I – VVS1	ct.	7,000.00
3 carats – I – IF	ct.	10,500.00
Melee, single cut rds., good quality, VS, .005-.03 DEF	ct.	500.00
Melee, single cut rds., fine quality, IF, .005-.03 DEF	ct.	600.00
Melee, full cut rds., good quality, VS/DEF .04-.07	ct.	775.00
Melee, full cut rds., fine quality, IF/VS DEF .04-.07	ct.	875.00

IRRADIATED DIAMONDS

Nondescript color diamonds are now commonly irradiated with deuterons and neutrons in cyclotrons and atomic piles to produce attractive green, blue, gold, canary, coffee, and even black gems; there may be slight residual radioactivity. Gems whose only fault may have been poor color can often be made far more beautiful and valuable; most starting gems are some shade of very pale yellow or brown. However, such gems should be sold with the clear understanding on the part of the buyer that they are not naturally colored. Gemological methods exist to distinguish natural fancies from irradiated diamond. The prices below have been recently asked for good-quality yellow stones; considerably lower and higher prices may be asked according to flawlessness, richness of hues, quality of cut, etc.; blues and greens are higher, while coffees and blacks are lower.

Yellow, ¼ ct. (25 pts.) – VVS1	ct.	400.00-700.00
½ ct. (50 pts.) – VVS1	ct.	1,000-1,100.00
1 ct. – VS1	ct.	2,000.00-2,400.00
2 ct. – VS1	ct.	2,600.00
3 ct. – VS1	ct.	4,200.00
Blue, ¼ ct. (.23-.29) – VS2	ct.	850.00-1,000.00
Blue, ½ ct. (.45-.55) – VS2	ct.	1,000.00-1,200.00
Blue, 1 ct. – VS2	ct.	1,600.00-1,800.00
Green, ¼ ct. (.23-.29) – VS2	ct.	770.00-850.00
Green, ½ ct. (.45-.55) – VS2	ct.	800.00-1,000.00
Green, 1 ct. – VS2	ct.	1,200.00-1,500.00

Irradiation charges, less than 1 ct.	ct.	100.00
Irradiation charges, over 1 ct.	ct.	100.00-150.00
Laser drilled, 1-3 cts.	ct.	75.00-100.00

End of Diamond Section

DIASPORE

A rare gemstone from Turkey, medium yellowish-green with rose tint under changing light. hardness 6.5-7. Facet quality material to about 10 carats size; larger gems have been reported, e.g., a 157.66 ct. and others of 26.97 and 10.63 ct.

Diaspore, 1-3 cts.	ct.	300.00-900.00
Diaspore, 3-6 cts.	ct.	800.00-1,500.00
Diaspore, over 7 cts.	ct.	1,800.00

DINOSAUR BONE, SEE QUARTZ

DIOPSIDE

The green faceted gems from Madagascar are usually too dark to be effective above 4-5 carats; attractive green from Myanmar, but rare.

Myanmar, medium dark green, 1-10 ct.	ct.	5.00-15.00
Madagascar, dark green, clean, 1-15 ct.	ct.	4.00-7.00
New York, yellow-green, clean, 1-5 ct.	ct.	8.00-26.00
Italy, fine green, 1-5 ct.	ct.	8.00-20.00
USSR, emerald-green, 1 ct.	ea.	200.00
Sri Lanka, olive green, catseyes, 3 ct.	ct.	17.00
Sri Lanka, olive green, 4-ray star cabochons, 3-15 ct.	ct.	1.00-5.00

DIOPTASE

| Deep emerald-green, $\frac{1}{4}$-1 ct., step cuts | ct. | 45.00-55.00 |

DRAVITE, SEE TOURMALINE

EMERALD, SEE BERYL

ENSTATITE

| India, yellow-green | ct. | 125.00-150.00 |
| India, brown | ct. | 160.00 |

EPIDOTE

A much overrated gem, which, in the usual very dark green varieties, scarcely shows a glimmer of reflected light except in gems less than 1 carat; rarely, pale brownish varieties yield small gems which are somewhat attractive.

| Austria, very dark green, step cuts, 1-15 ct. | ct. | 10.00-15.00 |
| Mexico, brownish, step cuts, 1-2 ct. | ct. | 15.00-20.00 |

EUCLASE

Very rare; colorless, pale to light blue, faint purple, straw-yellow, yellow, green; cut gems only from Brazilian crystals mined many years ago.

Medium blue, clean to lightly flawed, $\frac{1}{4}$-1 ct.	ct.	12.00
Pale blue, clean to lightly flawed, $\frac{1}{4}$-1 ct.	ct.	100.00-400.00
Good yellow, clean to lightly flawed, 1-8 ct.	ct.	25.00-75.00
Colorless, clean to lightly flawed, 1-8 ct.	ct.	20.00-40.00

FABULITE, SEE STRONTIUM TITANATE

FELDSPARS

The finest faceted gems are cut from the yellow orthoclase of Madagascar; other species and varieties furnish interesting and sometimes attractive faceted gems. The best cabochon gems are the exceptionally transparent Burmese *moonstones*, displaying bright blue reflections in an almost transparent matrix, sometimes with a fairly sharp silver eye in conjunction with the blue; next best are the fine blue moonstones from Sri Lanka, followed by the silvery kinds; fair to good moonstones are cut from Indian material as are good sunstones, but the latter may be cracked or flawed; interesting catseye and star gems are also furnished by India, sometimes of high quality.

ORTHOCLASE

Madagascar, fine yellow, clean, step-cut gems, 1-5 ct.	ct.	20.00-30.00
Madagascar, fine yellow, clean, step-cut gems, 5-25 ct.	ct.	40.00-60.00
Madagascar, pale yellows, clean gems, 3-10 ct.	ct.	25.00-60.00

SANIDINE

Oregon, Mexico, Texas, brown, clean, step cuts	ct.	60.00

OLIGOCLASE

North Carolina, colorless to faintly greenish, facet gems, 1-4 ct.	ct.	2.00-20.00
Norway, India, *sunstone*, oval cabs., 8x6-22x14 mm.	ea.	5.00-60.00
Norway, India, *sunstone*, rd. cabs., 4-15 mm.	ea.	5.00-75.00
India, *sunstone*, to 30 ct. cabs.	ct.	25.00

ALBITE

Colorless faceted gems, clean, to 3 ct.	ct.	10.00-15.00
India, catseye, strong eye, 3-40 ct.	ct.	5.00-10.00

MICROCLINE

Amazonite, oval cabs., 7x5-30x20 mm.	ea.	1.50-18.00
Amazonite, rd. cabs., 4-25 mm.	ea.	1.50-10.00
Perthite, dyed various hues, tumbled gems	lb.	10.00-20.00

LABRADORITE

Finland, fine blue or dark gray groundmass, oval cabs, 8x6-22x14 mm.	ea.	20.00-225.00
Finland, fine blue or dark gray groundmass, oval rd. cabs, 4-25 mm.	ea.	10.00-120.00
Madagascar, red	ct.	175.00
Labrador, various colors, gray groundmass, oval cabs., 7x5-30x20 mm.	ea.	5.00-30.00
Labrador, same rd., cabs., 4-20 mm.	ea.	5.00-30.00
Oregon, spinel-red, fine	ct.	1,750.00

MOONSTONES

Myanmar, fine blue, 1-3 ct.	ct.	20.00-30.00
Myanmar, fine blue, 4-9 ct.	ct.	25.00-50.00
Myanmar, fine blue, 10+ ct.	ct.	40.00-60.00
Sri Lanka, fine blue, 1-3 ct.	ct.	10.00-20.00
Sri Lanka, fine blue, 4-9 ct.	ct.	15.00-25.00
Sri Lanka, fine blue, 10+ ct.	ct.	20.00-40.00
Fair to good blues, 1-3 ct.	ct.	7.00-10.00
Fair to good blues, 4-9 ct.	ct.	10.00-15.00
Fair to good blues, 10+ ct.	ct.	10.00-20.00

Sri Lanka, fine silver-white, 1-3 ct.	ct.	8.00-10.00
Sri Lanka, fine silver-white, 4-9 ct.	ct.	15.00-20.00
Sri Lanka, fine silver-white, 10+ ct.	ct.	15.00-25.00
Sri Lanka, fair to good, silver-white, 1-3 ct.	ct.	2.00-10.00
Sri Lanka, fair to good, silver-white, 4-9 ct.	ct.	2.00-15.00
Sri Lanka, fair to good, silver-white, 10+ ct.	ct.	5.00-25.00
Sri Lanka, silver-white, ovals, 7x5 mm.	ea.	5.00-7.00
Sri Lanka, silver-white, rds., 3-4 mm.	ea.	1.00-5.00
India, various hues, oval cabs., 8x6-22x16 mm.	ea.	1.00-35.00
India, various hues, rd. cabs., 4-25 mm.	ea.	1.00-40.00
India, star & catseye gems, 5-50 ct.	ct.	2.00-10.00
India, green cabs., weak stars, 5-15 ct.	ct.	1.00-15.00

END OF FELDSPAR SECTION

FIBROLITE (Sillimanite)

Very rarely offered as small faceted gems of fine pale blue color from Myanmar; normally not over several carats in weight; an astonishingly large faceted gem of 35 carats is in the British Museum; extremely difficult to cut because of easy cleavage.

Myanmar, blue, 1-5 ct.	ct.	150.00-500.00

FLUORITE

Low refractive index prevents faceted fluorites from being very brilliant, but satisfactory results are possible if gems are correctly cut and polished; faceted gems of large size are known (about 200 ct.); common imperfections are minute inclusions which scatter light. Purples most abundant, followed by pale yellows; fine blue gems scarce, also pinks and reds.

Various hues, step cuts or brills., 1-50 ct.	ct.	20.00-50.00
Green cabs., ovals	ct.	25.00
Purple ovals	ct.	50.00

GARNET

Hard, durable, and much used in jewelry, e.g., faceted *almandite* and *rhodolite* in rings, *pyrope* in pavé-type pendants and pins. Emerald-green to rich yellow-green andradite (*demantoid*) most sought after by collectors and most expensive; also expensive are *rhodolite* and *spessartine*; star *almandites* are sometimes most attractive, but many display very weak stars which do not compare in quality to those displayed by star gems of other species, e.g., corundum.

Almandite

Wide color range, from inexpensive dark brown-reds to costlier medium intensity purplish-reds; prices rise as hue lightens. Ordinary dark material supplied in large quantities by India.

Brown-red, faceted, generally	ct.	5.00-10.00
Purplish-red, faceted, very fine, medium hue, 1-5 ct.	ct.	20.00-30.00
Purplish-red, faceted, very fine, medium hue, 5-10 ct.	ct.	30.00-40.00
Purplish-red, faceted, very fine, medium hue, 11-30 ct.	ct.	25.00-50.00
Purplish-red, faceted, medium dark hue, 1-5 ct.	ct.	6.00-12.00
Purplish-red, faceted, medium dark hue, 6-10 ct.	ct.	8.00-15.00
Purplish-red, faceted, medium dark hue, 11-15 ct.	ct.	15.00-20.00
Purplish-red, faceted, medium dark hue, 1-5 ct.	ct.	5.00-12.00
India, facet rds., well cut, 3-10 mm.	ea.	.50-15.00
India, facet rds., native cut, 3-10 mm.	ea.	.50-10.00
India, facet octs., ovals, 7x5-16x12 mm. (1-10 ct.)	ea.	4.50-50.00
India, facet hearts, well cut, 4x4-10x10 mm.	ea.	1.40-12.00
India, facet ovals, well cut, 6x4-12x10 mm.	ea.	1.00-16.50

India, facet ovals, native cut, 6x4-12x10 mm.	ea.	1.00-15.00
India, rose-cut melee, 1-3½ mm.	ea.	1.00-5.00
India, facet squares, 1-3½ mm.	ea.	1.00-5.00
Madagascar, medium pinkish-red	ct.	5.00-10.00
India, cabochons, ovals, 7x5-20x15 mm.	ea.	2.00-30.00
India, cabochons, rds., 4-20 mm.	ea.	1.00-35.00
India, tumbled gems, ¼"-½"	oz.	1.00 +
Madagascar, tumbled gems, dark red, small, ⅛"-¼"	lb.	10.00 +

STAR ALAMANDITE (Idaho)

Although star garnets are abundant in Idaho, most cut examples can only be classed as fair quality with weak, interrupted legs, numerous inclusions, etc.; exceptionally good specimens are truly rare.

Four-ray, exceptionally fine, 1-3 ct.	ct.	15.00-50.00
Four-ray, exceptionally fine, 4-7 ct.	ct.	25.00-60.00
Four-ray, exceptionally fine, 8-15 ct.	ct.	30.00-120.00
Four-ray, exceptionally fine, 15+ ct.	ct.	40.00-150.00
Four-ray, good, 1-3 ct.	ct.	10.00-30.00
Four-ray, good, 4-7 ct.	ct.	10.00-40.00
Four-ray, good, 8-15 ct.	ct.	10.00-45.00
Four-ray, good, 15+ ct.	ct.	10.00-60.00
Four-ray, fair, 1-3 ct.	ct.	2.00-15.00
Four-ray, fair, 4-15 ct.	ct.	5.00-25.00
Four-ray, fair, 15+ ct.	ct.	6.00-30.00
Six-ray, fair to good	ct.	35.00-50.00
Tumbled star material, ½"-¾"	gm.	.50-.75

ANDRADITE

Prized gem variety, now quite rare, is transparent *demantoid*, ranging in color from rich emerald-green to various shades of yellow-green, the first being most in demand; the best gems approach the emerald in hue; as traces of yellow appear, values drop. Transparent gems in brown or brownish-green also available.

Demantoid, emerald-green, medium dark, ¼-1 ct.	ct.	1,000.00-2,000.00
Demantoid, emerald-green, medium dark, 1-2 ct.	ct.	2,000.00-4,000.00
Demantoid, emerald-green, medium dark, 2-3 ct.	ct.	4,000.00-6,000.00
Demantoid, emerald-green, medium, ¼-1 ct.	ct.	500.00-1,000.00
Demantoid, emerald-green, medium, 1-2 ct.	ct.	700.00-2,000.00
Demantoid, emerald-green, medium, 2-3 ct.	ct.	3,00.00-4,000.00
Demantoid, yellow-green, medium dark, 1 ct.	ct.	300.00-500.00
Demantoid, yellow-green, medium dark, 1-2 ct.	ct.	400.00-700.00
Demantoid, yellow-green, medium dark, 2-3 ct.	ct.	1,000.00-3,000.00
Demantoid, yellow-green, medium, 1 ct.	ct.	120.00-300.00
Demantoid, yellow-green, medium, 1-2 ct.	ct.	200.00-400.00
Demantoid, yellow-green, medium, 2-3 ct.	ct.	500.00-1,000.00
Demantoid, yellow-green, light, 1 ct.	ct.	100.00-125.00
Demantoid, yellow-green, light, 1-2 ct.	ct.	100.00-200.00
Demantoid, yellow-green, light, 2-3 ct.	ct.	200.00-300.00

GROSSULAR

Faceted gems have been cut from brownish-orange (*hessonite*), pale orange to orange-yellow, ind colorless material, but mostly from the first named: massive material has been cut into cabochons of attractive bright green or pink shades (Transvaal), or white; faceted gems often display a characteristic "swirled" internal appearance which slightly decreases the sharpness of internal reflections.

Quebec, orange, facet grade	ct.	20.00-50.00
Large, top grade	ct.	200.00
Medium dark orange, ½-1 ct.	ct.	25.00-30.00
Medium dark orange, 5-10 ct.	ct.	90.00-150.00
Medium orange, 1-3 ct.	ct.	20.00-35.00
Medium orange, 3-5 ct.	ct.	35.00-50.00
Light orange, 1-3 ct.	ct.	5.00-20.00
Light orange, 3-5 ct.	ct.	10.00-35.00
Orange hues, rd. brills., 3-12 mm. (to 6 ct.)	ea.	5.00-50.00
Orange hues, octs., ovals, 7x5-16x12 mm. (1-10 ct.)	ea.	10.00-150.00
Massive, green ("Transvaal jade") cabs., rds., 4-20 mm.	ea.	5.00-35.00
Massive, green ("Transvaal jade") cabs., ovals, 7x5-30x20 mm.	ea.	5.00-35.00
Massive, pink cabs., prices generally equiv. to massive green		

Tsavorite is the trade name for green grossularite found in the Tsavo Park region of Kenya, and in Tanzania in East Africa. The material was first discovered by a miner/explorer Campbell Bridges in the 1960s. Tsavorite has an isotropic crystal system and the chemical composition is calcium aluminum silicate. There is no cleavage, and the fracture is subconchoidal, often brittel. R.I. 1.73-1.75; S.G. 3.3-4.3; hardness 7 plus on Mohs Scale.

Top Kenyan color, almost flawless, to ½ ct.	ct.	200.00-500.00
Top Kenyan color, almost flawless, 1-2 ct.	ct.	900.00-1,500.00
Top Kenyan color, almost flawless, 2-3 ct.	ct.	1,500.00-2,000.00
Top Kenyan color, almost flawless, 3-5 ct.	ct.	2,200.00-4,000.00
Top Kenyan color, almost flawless, 5-10 ct.	ct.	4,000.00-6,000.00
Top Kenyan color, lightly flawed, 1-2 ct.	ct.	600.00-900.00
Top Kenyan color, lightly flawed, 2-3 ct.	ct.	900.00-1,500.00
Top Kenyan color, lightly flawed, 3-5 ct.	ct.	1,500.00-2,200.00
Top Kenyan color, lightly flawed, 5-10 ct.	ct.	2,500.00-4,000.00
Good color, almost flawless, 1-2 ct.	ct.	300.00-600.00
Good color, almost flawless, 2-3 ct.	ct.	500.00-900.00
Good color, almost flawless, 3-5 ct.	ct.	800.00-1,500.00
Good color, almost flawless, 5-10 ct.	ct.	1,000.00-2,500.00
Commercial color, lightly flawed, ½-1 ct.	ct.	80.00 +
Commercial color, lightly flawed, 1-2 ct.	ct.	100.00 +
Commercial color, lightly flawed, 2-3 ct.	ct.	200.00 +
Commercial color, lightly flawed, 3-5 ct.	ct.	300.00 +

PYROPE

Extremely dark red hues are characteristic, the intensity often being so great that few faceted gems over several carats display obvious color; most gems must be cut to less than one carat; this is particularly the case with the Bohemian pyropes which are commonly rose cut and set pavé in many classes of jewelry; very rarely, large gems of medium dark hue are found and these command high prices, but there is reason to believe that most of these are compositionally intermediate between almandite and pyrope.

Pyrope, pure medium dark red, faceted, 1-5 ct.	ct.	15.00-20.00
Pyrope, pure dark red, faceted 1-5 ct.	ct.	12.00-20.00
Alm.-pyrope, medium dark red, faceted, 1-5 ct.	ct.	12.00-30.00
Alm.-pyrope, medium dark red, faceted, 10 ct.	ct.	10.00-40.00
Alm.-pyrope, medium dark red, faceted, 15 ct.	ct.	10.00-50.00
Alm.-pyrope, dark red, faceted, 1-5 ct.	ct.	10.00-20.00

Alm.-pyrope, dark red, faceted, 10 ct.	ct.	16.00-25.00
Alm.-pyrope, dark red, faceted, 15 ct.	ct.	25.00-50.00
Alm.-pyrope, rd. brills., 3-12 mm. (to 6 ct.)	ea.	1.00-24.00
Alm.-pyrope, oval brills, 7x5-16x12 mm. (1-10 ct.)	ea.	2.20-75.00
Arizona pyrope, tumbled gems, about ¼"	oz.	2.00-5.00

RHODOLITE

One of the most beautiful garnets; finest colors are medium to relatively light purplish-red, resembling some amethysts, but richer in hue and set off better by the considerably higher brilliance in faceted gems; large gems are rare, but recent finds of fine quality material in Tanzania introduced cut gems of unprecedented size.

Rich purplish-red, 1-5 ct.	ct.	25.00-90.00
Rich purplish-red, 10 ct.	ct.	80.00-135.00
Rich purplish-red, 15+ ct.	ct.	130.00-200.00
Light purplish-red, 1-5 ct.	ct.	20.00-45.00
Light purplish-red, 10 ct.	ct.	50.00-80.00
Light purplish-red, 15+ ct.	ct.	75.00-130.00
Medium color, rd. brills., 2-12 mm. (to 6 ct.)	ea.	5.00-150.00
Medium color, octs., ovals, 7x5-12x10 mm. (1-5 ct.)	ea.	10.00-150.00
North Carolina, or Sri Lanka, light hue, ½-3 ct.	ct.	10.00-75.00
North Carolina, or Sri Lanka, light hue, 3-10 ct.	ct.	10.00-100.00

SPESSARTINE

One of the rarer garnets; color range from pale orange to deep brownish-red; the "gem" color is a beautiful rich red-orange; seldom flawless over 5 carats; large cut gems to over 20 carats have been cut from Brazilian and Virginia material, but are brownish-red; small veil inclusions common, especially in pale to medium orange types. The rich red-orange gems of Ramona, California, are probably the best available; also from Brazil and Madagascar.

Finest red-orange hue, ½-3 ct.	ct.	15.00-2,000.00
Finest red-orange hue, 4-5 ct.	ct.	75.00-100.00
Finest red-orange hue, 6-10 ct.	ct.	100.00-250.00
Medium orange, ½-3 ct.	ct.	35.00-75.00
Medium orange, 4-5 ct.	ct.	75.00-150.00
Pale orange, ½-3 ct.	ct.	20.00-75.00
Pale orange, 4-5 ct.	ct.	45.00-80.00
Brownish-red hues, 1-5 ct.	ct.	8.00-25.00
Brownish-red hues, 6-10 ct.	ct.	15.00-35.00
Brownish-red hues, 11-25 ct.	ct.	20.00-45.00

END OF GARNET SECTION

GOSENITE, SEE BERYL

GROSSULAR, SEE GARNET

HAMBERGITE

Faceted colorless gems now very rare and seldom over 4-5 carats; sometimes with tubular inclusions.

Madagascar, colorless, 5x2.3 mm. rectangle	ea.	32.50
Madagascar, colorless, 4.8x2.1 mm. rectangle	ea.	10.00

HELIODOR, SEE BERYL

HEMATITE
Massive material used extensively in intaglios, faceted gems, beads, and cabochons; always dead-black with brilliant submetallic luster; some *psilomelane chalcedony* now being used as a substitute.

Faceted rds., flat backs, 4-12 mm.	ea.	1.00-3.50
Faceted cush. flat backs, 8x8-16x12 mm.	ea.	8.00-30.00
Faceted ovals, flat backs, 12x10-15x20	ea.	12.00-45.00
Cabochons, rds., 3-12 mm.	ea.	.75-3.00
Cabochons, ovals, 4x6-8x10 mm.	ea.	1.00-8.00
Faceted, various full cuts	ct.	7.00-24.00

HESSONITE, SEE GARNET

HOWLITE
White, opaque, fine-granular massive, sometimes with narrow black veinings, sometimes cabochoned but now mostly tumbled and dyed turquois color.

Tumbled gems, dyed intense turquois blue, ½"-1½"	lb.	5.00-15.00

IDOCRASE (VESUVIANITE)
Transparent gems are rare despite the abundance of the mineral in nature; fine small gems to about 1-2 carats have been cut form clear crystals from European sources; also fine gems but often with small veil-type inclusions, from greenish-golden material from Laurel, Quebec, once known as *"laurelite"*; also handsome faceted gems, with diffuse reflections, from bright apple-green crypto-crystalline material from California (Pulga).

Quebec, rich greenish-yellow, ½-1 ct.	ct.	40.00-75.00
Quebec, rich greenish-yellow, 2-4 ct.	ct.	75.00-150.00
California, Pulga, fine green, faceted, 3-15 ct.	ct.	5.00-10.00
California, massive, mottled green, cabochons, 10x12 mm.	ea.	5.00

INDICOLITE, SEE TOURMALINE

IOLITE (CORDIERITE)
Faceted gems available in deep violet or blue-violet, through various paler shades to relatively pale violet or gray-violet; strongly pleochroic; care must be exercised in orientation to avoid mottled hues or yellowish hues; rarely in flawless gems over 8 ct. most examples containing abundant veil-type inclusions; also in cabochons, sometimes displaying reddish aventurescence or pronounced, whitish, 4-ray star.

Fine blue, clean, 3 m. round	ea.	10.00
Fine blue, clean, 3.5 mm. round	ea.	12.00-14.00
Fine blue, clean, 4.0 mm. round	ea.	14.00-18.00
Fine blue, clean, 4.5 mm. round	ea.	16.00-20.00
Fine blue, clean, 5.0 mm. round	ea.	18.00-25.00
Fine blue, clean, 6.0 mm. round	ea.	20.00-25.00
Fine blue, clean, 7.0 mm. round	ea.	35.00-45.00
Fine blue, clean, 8.0 mm. round	ea.	50.00-65.00
Various hues 7x5-16x12 mm. (1-10 cts.)	ea.	25.00-250.00
Cabochons, 10x8 mm. oval	ea.	95.00
Cabochons, 4-ray star, 6 ct.	ct.	20.00-45.00
Fine med. violet, 1-5 ct.	ct.	60.00-80.00
Fine med. violet, 5-10 ct.	ct.	100.00-150.00

JADE, SEE JADEITE OR NEPHRITE

JADEITE

Finest gem jadeite (Myanmar) is *imperial jade* when the color is an intense pure green, evenly distributed and without mottling, veining, or other conspicuous defects, and the cabochon (or small carving) is semi-transparent; value decreases as translucency decreases, even if the color is excellent, also when the grain size becomes apparent or veinings or areas of paler green or colorless jadeite appear; further decreases occur which the color becomes excessively dark or takes on grayness, or tinges of olive-green. Other colors are less prized, but pale pure greens are highly prized, also rich reds, mauves, yellows, oranges, etc.; the least desirable gems are dark olive-greens, gray-greens, or vaguely-tinged gems, and blacks. As in the case of imperial jade, quality depends on intensity and purity of color, degree of translucency, evenness of texture, and absence of veinings, mottlings, etc. jadeite cabochons are usually sold by the stone.

Imperial jade, finest grades, 18x14 mm. oval cabs.	ea.	5,000.00-25,000.00
Imperial jade, excellent grades, 18x14 mm. oval cabs.	ea.	5,000.00-20,000.00
Fine, even green, translucent, 18x14 mm. oval cabs.	ea.	3,000.00-17,500.00
Fine green, translucent, some mottling with white, same size	ea.	1,000.00-2,500.00
Uniform vivid yellow-green ("Apple-green"), same size	ea.	1,000.00-4,000.00
Apple-green, mottled with white, same size	ea.	750.00-1,500.00
Uniform darker green, olive-tinged, same size	ea.	500.00-875.00
Uniform darker green, olive-tinged, mottled white, same size	ea.	550.00-700.00
Fair-quality greens, oval cabs., 18x14 mm.	ea.	600.00-750.00
Medium greens, oval cabs., 18x14 mm.	ea.	375.00-500.00
Mauve, uniform, light to medium dark, 18x14 mm. oval cabs.	ea.	1,250.00 +
Blue, uniform, light to medium dark, 18x14 mm. oval cabs.	ea.	1,000.00-3,000.00
Above hues, mottled, also with green, 18x14 mm. oval cabs.	ea.	750-1,250.00
Above hues, mottled with white, 18x14 mm. oval cabs.	ea.	500.00-750.00
Red, uniform, medium to medium dark, 18x14 mm. oval cabs.	ea.	350.00-550.00
Brownish, reds, uniform, medium to medium dark, 18x14 mm. oval cabs.	ea.	200.00-290.00
Orange, uniform, medium, 18x14 mm. oval cabs.	ea.	200.00-250.00
Yellow, uniform, light to medium light, 18x14 mm. oval cabs.	ea.	150.00-175.00
Black, uniform, 18x14 mm. cabs.	ea.	100.00
Pure white, translucent, 18x14 mm. cabs.	ea.	75.00-100.00
Faintly-hued whites, 18x14 mm. cabs.	ea.	50.00-75.00
Sets, one ea., red, green, mauve, yellow, black, 10x8 mm. ovals	set	145.00
Sets, one ea., red, green, mauve, yellow, black, 18x13 mm. ovals	set	195.00
Turkey, nat. purple	ct.	22.00-25.00

Cat's Eye Jade (Actinolite), an unusual jade which exhibits a fine eye. Colors range from light to dark green; semi-transparent. Collector's stone.

Cat's Eye Jade	ct.	10.00-15.00

JASPER, SEE QUARTZ

KORNERUPINE

Very rare, almost invariably faceted but also in cabochon; best gems are cut from greenish Madagascar material; the brown gems from Sri Lanka or Myanmar are less desirable.

Madagascar, good greenish, ½-4 ct.	ct.	30.00-60.00

Madagascar, dark green, ½-3½ ct.	ct.	25.00-45.00
Sri Lanka, reddish-brown, ½-4 ct.	ct.	20.00-45.00
Catseye, 8mm. rd. cab.	ct.	25.00-30.00

KUNZITE, SEE SPODUMENE

KYANITE

Has been faceted into step-cut gems to about 15 carats, but gems over 5 carats are seldom free of tube-like inclusions, minute splits, or zones of varying color; finest gems intense violet-blue, but very fine examples also known of pale blue or medium green. Not durable.

Nepal, fine blue, ½-2 ct., clean	ct.	20.00-60.00
Nepal, fine blue, ½-4 ct., slightly flawed	ct.	20.00-45.00
Pale blue, 1-10 ct., usually mottled in hue	ct.	10.00-20.00
Brazil, medium green, 1-5 ct., clean	ct.	50.00-60.00
Pale green, 1-5 ct.	ct.	20.00-30.00
Pale green, 6-15 ct., mottled, slight flaws.	ct.	10.00-20.00

LABRADORITE, SEE FELDSPAR

LAPIS LAZULI

Finest gems are cabochoned or sometimes facetecl from perfectly uniform, fine-grained material of intense violet-blue color, and lacking inclusions of calcite (white) or pyrite (gold); quality of material is judged by the evenness and luster of polished surfaces; pittings or dimplings indicate poorer material; somewhat less desirable is material in which hue is paler or approaches pure blue but the other attributes remain the same. Far more common, and less valued, are gems prepared from good solid material of fine color, but evenly speckled with small, uniform-size pyrite crystals. the presence of calcite drastically lowers the price; the best Chilean material is poor compared to even fair grades of Afghanistan material; it is usually patchy, difficult to polish well, and commonly contains areas of disagreeable grayish material.

Afghan. finest grade, oval. cabochon, 16x12 mm.	ea.	200.00
Afghan. fine grade, cabs., 1-3 ct.	ct.	20.00-40.00
Afghan. fine grade, cab. 3-5 ct.	ct.	40.00-75.00
Afghan. fine grade, cab. 5-10 ct.	ct.	75.00-100.00
Afghan. medium grade, cab. 1-3 ct.	ct.	10.00-20.00
Afghan. medium grade, cab. 3-5 ct.	ct.	20.00-40.00
Afghan. medium grade, cab. 5-10 ct.	ct.	50.00-75.00
Afghan. lesser grade, oval cabs. 3-5 ct.	ct.	10.00-20.00
Afghan. lesser grade, oval cabs. 5-10 ct.	ct.	25.00-50.00
Chile, cabochons, oval, 3-5 cts.	ct.	5.00-10.00
Chile, cabochons, oval, 5-10 cts.	ct.	10.00-20.00
Chile, tumbled gems, ¼"-1½"	lb.	40.00

LAURELITE, SEE IDOCRASE

LEUCITE

Provides colorless to faintly straw-yellow transparent gems with a slight milkiness and considerable "fire" which is clue to diffraction effects within the gems.

Italy, ¼ ct.	ea.	25.00

LIBYAN DESERT GLASS, SEE TEKTITE

MALACHITE

Quality depends on color, a medium green being best, also on attractive bandings and a good polish free of pits. Mostly used in large ornamental applications. Excessive contact with skin results in loss of polish and black surface alteration.

Cabochons, rds., 4-25 mm.	ea.	2.00-24.00
Cabochons, ovals, 5x7-18x30 mm.	ea.	1.50-12.00
Tumbled gems, ½"-¾"	lb.	40.00

MICROCLINE, see FELDSPAR

MOLDAVITE, see TEKTITE

MOONSTONE, see FELDSPAR

MORGANITE, see BERYL

MOTHER-OF-PEARL, see SHELL

NATROLITE

Colorless, transp. facet gems, step cut, ½-1½ ct.	ct.	15.00-35.00

NEPHRITE

In general, no nephrite gems approach the beauty and intensity of color the best jadeite gems, the intense greens, reds, yellows, and oranges of jadeite having no counterparts in nephrite; however, some very good yellow-greens occur in Wyoming and New Zealand nephrites, while the black nephrite of Wyoming is superb and produces better cabochons and beads than black jadeite. Variations in texture in nephrite commonly cause polishing difficulties, resulting in cabochon surfaces that may be pitted, dimpled, or variably brilliant in luster. Quality depends on color, freedom from dark specks, inclusions, partially developed splits, and surface defects. The finest greens of Wyoming and New Zealand are about on par; as olive tinges appear, values drop rapidly; mottled varieties are much less valuable. Rarely, small whihtish-green catseyes have been cut from Alaskan material.

Wyo. or N.Z., fine yellow-green, 18x14 mm. oval cab.	ea.	50.00-100.00
Wyo. or N.Z., good yellow-green, 18x14 mm. oval cab.	ea.	40.00-65.00
Wyo. or N.Z., med. yellow-green, 18x14 mm. oval cab.	ea.	25.00-50.00
Good quality, medium dark green, rd. cabs., 4-25 mm.	ea.	12.00-15.00
Good quality, medium dark green, oval cabs., 7x5-25x18 mm.	ea.	10.00-20.00
Good quality, medium dark green, cush. cabs., 6x6-14x12 mm.	ea.	10.00-18.00
Good quality, medium dark green, drilled hearts, 14x14 mm.	ea.	15.00-18.00
Good quality, medium green drilled hearts, 30 mm.	ea.	8.00-10.00
Wyoming, black, oval cabs., 10x8-18x13 mm.	ea.	8.00-10.00
Wyoming, mottled jade ("snowflake"), hearts, 18x18 mm.	ea.	6.00-10.00
Calif., medium dark green, oval cabs., 30x13-38x22 mm.	ea.	5.00-10.00
Calif., black, magnetite inclusions, ovals, 18x13-40x30 mm.	ea.	10.00-15.00
Wyo., medium dark green, tumbled gems, ½"-1½"	lb.	30.00
Various, drops, 20x6-40x25 mm.	ea.	5.00-15.00
Various, heart cabs., 10-25 mm.	ea.	8.00-22.00

OBSIDIAN

Enormous quantities now used for tumbled gems, ornamental objccts, and plain or partly sculptured cabochons (black or gold sheen) prepared in Mexico and set in native silver jewelry.

Black, rd. cabs., 4-25 mm.	ea.	1.00-5.00
Black, oval cabs., 7x5-30x20 mm.	ea.	2.00-8.00
Snowflake, oval cabs., 14x10-40x30 mm.	ea.	1.50-10.00

Gold sheen, rd. cabs. 4-25 mm.	ea.	1.50-10.00
Gold sheen, ovals, 7x5-30x20 mm.	ea.	1.00-12.00
Stars, faceted, 5-pt., 14-28 mm. dia.	ea.	10.00-15.00
"Apache tears," tumbled, fine quality	lb.	10.00-12.00
"Apache tears," tumbled, medium quality	lb.	8.00-10.00

OLIGOCLASE, SEE FELDSPAR

OPAL

Cut opals may be divided into two broad types, those which display brilliant flashes of color and are known as *precious opals*, and those which do not, known as *common opals*. Commercially, the first are of utmost importance and the greatest attention will be placed upon them here. Value in precious opal depends on color intensity, color distribution, kinds of colors, number of colors, and shape of cabochons. the best opals display extremely intense colors, unrivalled in purity by any other gemstone; only the brilliant hues seen upon the wings of certain tropical butterflies are comparable. The colors are seen best only if the opal matrix in which they appear suspended is nearly transparent; as the matrix becomes cloudier or milkier, the flushes lose intensity, sometimes becoming only feeble in poor-quality gems. Color distribution refers to the separate patches of hue, their size, shape, and the way they appear over the exposed area of the gem; the best dualities display patchcs of about the same size, at least 2-3 mm. in diameter in gems of about 18x14 mm., and preferably larger in larger stones; the entire surface must bc covered uniformly by these patches as in a mosaic; very broad patches or very small patches reduce value; also less desirable are patches which appear striated, elongated into streaks, nonuniform in size, or otherwise departing from the perfect "mosaic" type pattern previously mentioned. the kinds of colors are extremely important, the most desirable being pure "exciting" lilies, preferably reds, blues, greens, intense purples, golds, etc.; preferably at least two colors should be present and, better yet, three; the colors will appear even more intense and vivid if they consist of " warm" colors adjacent to "cool" colors, that is, red plus green or blue, orange plus blue or green, etc. Any kind of *uncolored* patchiness, inclusions of clay or white opal ("potch"), cracks, etc., seriously detracts from value. The shape of cabochons is of lesser but still considerable importance-outlines should be symmetrical, ellipses are preferred in the shape of an 18x14 mm. oval (see Fig. 27); solid gems should be low-crowned in order to present the broadest possible display surface but should not be flat, nor should the cabochon be so thin that it may break if acidentally knocked; opal doublets should especially have sufficient precious material on top to withstand some abuse.

For purposes of classification, the following types of precious opal are recognized in the trade: *black opal*, body color gray (Australia) to quite black (Nevada); *white opal*, body color white to off-white (Australia); *Mexican opal*, body translucent to transparent, colorless, faintly bluish, pale to deep yellow, brownish-yellow, orange, red and brownish-red. Highly translucent to nearly transparent material from Australia and Nevada of whitish body color is often called *jelly opal*. White opal also occurs in Mexico and Nevada, but only rarely is it cut into gems. Opals are generally sold by the carat, but the typical black opal doublets from Australia are sold by the stone because of variability in weight of the valueless backing material. White jelly opals are sometimes faceted as curiosities, non-precious Mexican opals are commonly faceted into handsome gems for collectors and sometimes for use in jewelry. However, all opals are soft and brittle and must be carefully protected from excessive abrasion or bumping into hard objects.

The general rule for determining satisfactory color intensity in precious opal is to hold the gem at arm's length, or about a distance of two feet from the eye, in ordinary illumination (not direct sunlight or under an intense spotlight) and observe if the color flashes atre clearly visible; if the stone appears merely dark (black opals), white (white opals), or some other undistinguished hue reflecting the body color, the gem is of low quality.

Black Opal

The queen of all opals; the finest specimens are unbelievably beautiful but also extremely rare despite recent aggressive mining for new supplies and the fairly large total quantities produced; gems of high quality over thumbnail size are particularly scarce, especially in solid vein sections sufficiently thick for nondoubletted cabochons.

Highest quality, 1-5 ct. oval cabochons	ct.	3,350.00-12,000.00
Highest quality, 5-10 ct. oval cabochons	ct.	3,350.00-12,000.00
Highest quality, 10-15 ct. oval cabochons	ct.	2,650.00-9,500.00
Fine quality, 1-5 ct. oval cabochons	ct.	575.00-3,350.00
Fine quality, 5-10 ct. oval cabochons	ct.	675.00-3550.00
Fine quality, 10-15 ct. oval cabochons	ct.	575.00-3,650.00
Medium quality, 1-5 ct. oval cabochons	ct.	100.00-575.00
Medium quality, 5-10 ct. oval cabochons	ct.	125.00-600.00
Medium quality, 10-15 ct. oval cabochons	ct.	150.00-750.00
Fair quality, 1-5 ct. oval cabochons	ct.	50.00 +
Fair quality, 6-10 ct. oval cabochons	ct.	50.00 +
Good quality, rd. cabochons, 4-15 mm.	ea.	24.00-150.00
Lightning Ridge, black-dyed, 10x8-25x18 mm.	ea.	25.00-75.00

Black Opal Doublets (Australian)

Oval cabochons, thin prec. opal top,10x8-16x10 mm.	ea.	23.00-36.00
Rounds or cabochons, 6 mm.	ea.	10.00

"Black Opal," Dyed

Some rather porous white opal from Australia, usually displaying small specks of play of color, "pin fire," has been successfully dyed along the minute fissures and openings to impart an artificial black hue, possibly through sugar-sulfuric acid techniques.

Cabochons, ovals, 10x8-25x18 mm.	ea.	15.00-60.00

White Opal

Virtually all gems cut from Australian material; very fine qualities are rare and extremely beautiful; rnuch poor-quality material is cut up into cheap gems, some of which require close examination under strong light to detect any color play at all.

Highest quality crystal opal, 1 ct. oval cabochons	ct.	400.00-600.00
Highest quality crystal opal, 2 ct. oval cabochons	ct.	400.00-600.00
Highest quality crystal opal, 5 ct. oval cabochons	ct.	600.00-1,400.00
Highest quality crystal opal, 10 ct. oval cabochons	ct.	600.00-1,200.00
Highest quality crystal opal, 10+ ct. oval cabochons	ct.	600.00-950.00
Fine quality, 1 ct. oval cabochons (semi-crystal)	ct.	85.00-175.00
Fine quality, 2 ct. oval cabochons (semi-crystal)	ct.	85.00-180.00
Fine quality, 5 ct. oval cabochons (semi-crystal)	ct.	90.00-200.00
Fine quality, 10 ct. oval cabochons (semi-crystal)	ct.	100.00-225.00
Fine quality, 10+ ct. oval cabochons (semi-crystal)	ct.	100.00 +
Fair to medium qualities, 1 ct. oval cabochons white base	ct.	25.00-75.00
Fair to medium qualities, 2-5 ct. oval cabochons white base	ct.	25.00-75.00
Fair to medium qualities, 6-10 ct. oval cabochons white base	ct.	50.00-110.00
Fair to medium qualities, 10+ ct. oval cabochons white base	ct.	50.00-110.00
Fair quality, oval cabs., 7x5-25x18 mm.	ct.	8.00-25.00
Fair quality, rd. cabs., 4-25 mm.	ct.	8.00-25.00
Fair quality, small rd. cabs., 2-3½ mm.	ct.	4.00-8.00

Better quality, oval cabs., 7x5-25x18 mm.	ct.	8.00-25.00
Better quality, rd. cabs., 4-25 mm.	ct.	8.00-110.00
Fine Australian "jelly," with play of color, oval cabs.	ct.	50.00-110.00

MEXICAN OPAL

Generally held in lower esteem in the trade; factors in this lower position are the widely held but not fully justified assumption that Mexican opals will dehydrate and crack over a period of time (this also happens to some Australian opals), and the lower demand for many of the Mexican opals which appear in various shades of yellow or orange body colors; these shades, plus intense reds and brownish-reds, no doubt lessen the effectiveness of the color flashes, such as red flashes in red opal (cherry opal), or yellow flashes in yellow opal; however, some Mexican opals, particularly those which are faintly bluish in body color, are superb and rival the finest and most translucent white opals from Australia. Because the intensity and abundance of color patches in Mexican opal are seldom as great as in Australian opal, it is customary to cut gems in rather deep cabochons, sometimes presenting a bulky appearance and less spread for a given weight.

Best grades, 1 ct. oval cabochons	ct.	60.00-100.00
Best grades, 2 ct. oval cabochons	ct.	60.00-100.00
Best grades, 5 ct. oval cabochons	ct.	60.00-100.00
Best grades, 10+ ct. oval cabochons	ct.	75.00-150.00
Fine grades, 1 ct. oval cabochons	ct.	40.00-60.00
Fine grades, 2 ct. oval cabochons	ct.	40.00-60.00
Fine grades, 5 ct. oval cabochons	ct.	40.00-60.00
Fine grades, 0+1 ct. oval cabochons	ct.	50.00-75.00
Fair to good grades, 1-5 ct. oval cabochons	ct.	10.00-40.00
Fair to good grades, 6-10 ct. oval cabochons	ct.	10.00-50.00
Rhyolite matrix, prec. opal areas, oval cabs., 8x6-20x15 mm.	ea.	3.00-20.00
Honey, facet, no play of col., rd. brills., 4-12 mm.	ea.	3.00-20.00
Red, facet, no play of col., rd. brills., 4-12 mm.	ea.	5.00-40.00
Brazil, honey to orange, facet, no play of col., 3-15 ct.	ct.	3.00-15.00

CATSEYE OPAL

Australian, yellow-green, sharp eyes, 5-15 mm.	ct.	5.00-9.00

END OF OPAL SECTION

ORTHOCLASE, SEE FELDSPAR

PERIDOT (OLIVINE)

In general, the finest faceted gems, cut from St. John's Island peridot, are pure yellow-green and free of inclusions; those from Myanmar are a deeper green, somewhat less vivid, and in some gems marred by very small inclusions arranged in layers and imparting a "sleepy" or slightly fuzzy appearance to the reflections; Arizona peridot ranges from rather pale yellow-green through all shades up to brown; brownish tinges are much less desirable; it is difficult to obtain Arizona gems over 5 carats that are free of inclusions. Rarely, good aventurescent gems from Myanmar material, showing strong pale green sheen. Most, if not all, peridot gems sold in Hawaii, and claimed to be local, are Arizonan in origin.

Rich pure green, 1-6 ct., clean	ct.	40.00-60.00
Rich pure green, 7-10 ct., clean	ct.	100.00-135.00
Rich pure green, 11-25 ct., clean	ct.	150.00-225.00
Medium green, 1-6 ct., clean	ct.	25.00-40.00
Medium green, 7-10 ct., clean	ct.	60.00-100.00
Medium green, 11-25 ct., clean	ct.	100.00-150.00

Yellow-green, 1-6 ct., clean	ct.	12.00-25.00
Yellow-green, 7-10 ct., clean	ct.	20.00-60.00
Yellow-green, 11-25 ct., clean	ct.	40.00-100.00
Brownish-green, 1-6 ct., clean	ct.	4.00-12.00
Brownish-green, 7-10 ct., clean	ct.	10.00-20.00
Arizona, tummled gems, ⅛"-½"	oz.	5.00-10.00

PERTHITE, see FELDSPAR

PETALITE
Colorless gems of small size rarely available; sizes usually to 3 carats; white inclusions and small cracks commonly present.

Rd. brilliants, flawless, ½-3 ct.	ct.	10.00-25.00

PHENAKITE
Colorless gems occasionally available from material mined many years ago in Brazil; clean round brilliants and step cuts to 5 carats; small flaws or inclusions usually present in gems of 5-10 cts.

Faceted, clean, ½-3 ct.	ct.	100.00-125.00
Faceted, clean, 4-5 ct.	ct.	100.00-125.00
Faceted, slight imperfections, 6-10 ct.	ct.	90.00-100.00

POLLUCITE
Faintly straw-yellow gems, not over 2 carats, have been cut from Maine material; also colorless from Connecticut in faceted gems to 10 carats but rarely without whitish inclusions.

½-3 ct., clean	ct.	50.00-130.00
4-10 ct., clean to slightly included	ct.	50.00-130.00

PRASIOLITE, see QUARTZ

PROUSTITE
Very rare; practically all faceted gems have been cut from crystals collected in Chile many years ago; intense pure red with strong adamantine luster on polished surfaces which increases to semi-metallic as inevitable alteration occurs; this may be reduced by keeping gems away from the light; luster can be restored by gentle rubbing with lens paper, but small scratches may appear as a result; extremely difficult to cut and polish; very soft.

Flawless, step cuts, 1-4 ct.	ct.	25.00-35.00
Flawless, step cuts, 5-10 ct.	ct.	40.00-50.00

PSILOMELANE, see QUARTZ

PUMPELLYITE (Chlorastrolite)
Finest material provides fascinating small cabochons, seldom over 10 mm., displaying "turtleback" pattern of light to very dark olive-green patches which appear to "shift" as the gem is turned under the light due to the fibrous nature of the mineral; best quality shows this effect clearly, and is compact material, highly polished, and lacking soft places or inclusions; good specimens relatively rare.

Oval cabochons, 6-12 mm.	ea.	5.00-12.00

PYROPE, see GARNET

QUARTZ
The standard gem varieties commonly sold in jewelry stores are *amethyst*, *citrine* (often misleadingly sold as "topaz"), *smoky quartz* (often misleadingly sold as "smoky topaz"), *rock crystal*, *rose quartz*, and, in recent years, *greened amethyst*; the foregoing are usually sold as transparent faceted gems, or sometimes, cabochon gems. the following massive varieties are also sold: *aven-*

turine, chrysoprase, chrysocolla chalcedony, bloodstone, tigereye, dyed chalcedony (very common), and a large variety of *agates*; these are sold mainly as cabochons but sometimes as faceted gems.

AMETHYST

The finest quality is rich purple, showing a characteristic change of color according to the kind of light under which it is observed, i.e., reddish-purple under tungsten light, and bluish-violet under daylight or daylight fluorescent tubes; the color must be pure and not made murky by traces of smoky coloration; other grades are progressively weaker in hue and color change, until some are so pale that the hue is merely a purplish-pink. In the trade, dealers assign the following names to various color grades: *Siberian*, the best color, deep and rich in quality, excellent color change; *Uruguay*, very good, medium intensity, lesser color change; *Bahia*, paler color, weak color change. The terms "Rose de France" and "lilac" have been recently used to describe pale purplish-pink stones. Color banding, unfortunately, is common in amethyst and only skillful work on the part of the lapidary can prepare satisfactory gems from such material; if bands appear on the top of the gem where a slight tilting shows streaks of colorless material within the purple, the value of the gem sharply declines. Top-quality gems to about 20-25 carats should be flawless or very nearly so, lack apparent banding, and should be accurately cut; gems of this quality over 25 carats become increasingly valuable because of scarcity of good rough.

Siberian grade, very fine, intense hue, 3 ct.	ct.	10.00-25.00
Siberian grade, very fine, intense hue, 5 ct.	ct.	18.00-35.00
Siberian grade, very fine, intense hue, 10 ct.	ct.	25.00-40.00
Siberian grade, very fine, intense hue, 20 ct.	ct.	35.00-50.00
Siberian grade, medium dark, 3-5 ct.	ct.	8.00-20.00
Siberian grade, medium dark, 6-10 ct.	ct.	15.00-25.00
Siberian grade, medium dark, 11-20 ct.	ct.	20.00-35.00
Uruguay grade, medium colors, 3-20 ct.	ct.	5.00-20.00
Bahia grade, medium to dark, weak dichroism, 3-20 ct.	ct.	4.00-20.00
Bahia grade, paler hues, weak dichroism, 3-20 ct.	ct.	1.50-20.00
Pale "lilac" or purplish-pink, 3-20 ct.	ct.	.50-.60
Light to medium hues, rd. brills., 3-12 mm (to 6 ct.)	ea.	1.00-6.00
Light to medium hues, octs. ovals, 7x5-16x12 mm. (1-10 ct.)	ea.	1.00-8.00
Medium dark melee, rd. brills., 1-3½ mm.	ea.	1.00-3.00
Cabochons, generally	ct.	1.65-2.60
Cabochons, medium color, 4-12 mm.	ea.	2.00-7.00
Cabochons, medium color, ovals, 8x6-20x15 mm.	ea.	3.00-25.00
Cabochons, good color, rds., 4-12 mm.	ea.	2.00-40.00
Cabochons, good color, ovals, 8x6-20x15 mm.	ca.	5.00-40.00
Tumbled gems, good color	lb.	24.00-30.00
Tumbled gems, medium color	lb.	15.00-25.00
Tumbled gems, fair color	lb.	12.00-20.00
Tumbled gems, "lilac," nearly flawless, to ¼"	lb.	24.00-35.00

GREENED AMETHYST

This is amethyst subjected to careful heat-treating which changes purple hues to various shades of pale to medium green, the latter having a slight olive tinge; the name "prasiolite" has been applied to this variety.

Various facet styles, 3-15 ct.	ct.	7.00-10.00
Rd. brills., 3-12 mm. (to 6 ct.)	ea.	5.00-25.00
Faceted octs., ovals, 7x5-16x12 mm. (1-10 ct.)	ea.	6.00-85.00

Aventurine Quartz

Medium intensity bluish-green material from India; poor yellow-green from Brazil; also a medium blue Brazilian material recently placed on the market. Most cabochons suffer from pitted surfaces where minute mica inclusions have plucked out during polishing. Available in very large sizes.

India, green, oval cabs., 8x10-13x8 mm.	ea.	7.00-45.00
India, green, small round cabs., 2-3½ mm.	ea.	1.00-8.00
India, green, 5-pt. stars, 14-28 mm. dia.	ea.	5.00-20.00
Brazil, blue, oval cabs.,10x8-40x30 mm.	ea.	10.00-20.00
India, green, heart cabs., 10-40 mm.	ea.	1.50-20.00
Tumbled gems, India, green, ½"-1½"	lb.	8.00-20.00
Tumbled gems, Brazil, green, ½"-1½"	lb.	6.00-20.00

Catseye Quartz

May be cabochoned from natural fibrous material, or bleached and dyed afterward as is the case with much straight-fiber tigereye now being cut into catseyes; some of the straw-to-yellow gems resemble poorer grades of catseye chrysoberyl; also in green, red, gray.

Oval or round cabochons, from 6-25 mm.	ct.	3.00-25.00
Colored, rd. cabs., 4-20 mm.	ea.	2.50-15.00
Colored, oval cabs., 7x5-20x15 mm.	ea.	3.00-25.00

"Cacoxenite" Quartz

In reality, clear quartz containing parallel inclusions of rich yellow *goethite* fibers; also sometimes in citrine and/or amethyst matrix.

Catseye gems, fine quality, to 10 ct.	ct.	3.00-20.00
Cabochons, rounds, 4-25 mm.	ea.	2.50-20.00
Cabochons, ovals, 18x13-25x18 mm.	ea.	7.50-25.00
Faceted, to 10 ct.	ct.	3.00-20.00
Tumbled gems, ½"-1½"	lb.	8.00-15.00

Citrine

The best qualities must have strong hues, either rich yellow with orange tinges, or rich orange-red, the latter always with some brownish tinge and ranging from medium to medium dark in intensity; pale yellows, yellows with tinges of smoky hue, or stones approximating intermediate hues between yellow citrine and smoky quartz are considerably less valuable. Large rough is available and consequently flawless gems to several hundred carats in yellow hues are available; however, the prized reddish hues are produced from heat-treatment of amethyst and are limited in size to about 25 ct. Among gem dealers the following varietal names are commonly used: *Rio Grande or Madeira*, designating heat-treated amethyst turned to reddish-yellow or reddish-brown hues, also *Palmyra* for those which have become more orange-yellow after heat-treatment; the fanciful terms *sang de boeuf* or *ox-blood* are sometimes used for gems which are naturally very deep reddish-brown. Very rarely, exceptionally fine citrines may command prices between $15 and $20 per carat, but the vast majority of gems are sold well below these figures.

Very exceptional orangy-yellow or orangy-red gems	ct.	20.00-30.00
Rio Grande grade, dark hues, clean, to 15 ct.	ct.	18.00-25.00
Rio Grande medium to medium dark, clean, to 15 ct.	ct.	10.00-28.00
Madeira & Palmyra grades, clean, to 10 ct.	ct.	8.00-35.00
Rich golden yellow, clean, 5-50 ct.	ct.	7.00-10.00
Fine yellow, 5-50 ct.	ct.	6.00-10.00
Pale yellow, 5-50 ct.	ct.	2.00-7.00
Smoky yellow, 5-50 ct.	ct.	2.00-7.00
Smoky yellow, dark, rd. brills., 10-25 mm.	ea.	6.00-10.00

Smoky yellow, dark, oct. step cuts, 12x10-25x25 mm.	ea.	5.00-12.00
Smoky yellow, dark, oval brills., 12x10-25x18 mm.	ea.	6.00-15.00
Smoky yellow, dark, brill. hearts, 10-18 mm.	ea.	5.00-10.00
Good yellow melee, 1-3½ mm.	ea.	1.00-3.00
Cabochons, dark yellow, rds., 4-25 mm.	ea.	1.25-20.00
Cabochons, dark yellow, ovals, 8x6-20x15 mm.	ea.	1.25-12.00
Cabochons, bright yellow, rds., 4-25 mm.	ea.	1.00-7.00
Cabochons, medium yellow, ovals, 8x6-20x15 mm.	ea.	2.00-12.00
Cabochons, generally	ct.	5.00-10.00
Tumbled gems, citrine-amethyst admixture, ½"-1¼"	lb.	6.00-12.00
Tumbled gems, smoky citrine, ½"-1¼"	lb.	8.00-15.00
Rio Grande grade, ¼"-⅝"	lb.	24.00

AMETRINE

Color half amethyst and half citrine, usually cut into larger stones to optimize the color of the stone, seldom cut in oval or pear shapes. From Bolivia:

Fine color, emerald cut, flawless, 1-20 cts.	ct.	4.00-15.00
Fine color, emerald cut, flawless, 20-50 cts.	ct.	9.00-12.00
Fine color, emerald cut, flawless, 50-100 cts.	ct.	8.00-10.00

ROCK CRYSTAL

This colorless variety is exceptionally abundant in nature and the prices of gems reflect mainly the cost of lapidary work, handling, and other trade charges.

Faceted, various standard cuts, 10x8-25x18 mm.	ea.	3.00-10.00
Faceted, fancy cuts, about 20x20 mm.	ea.	10.00
Faceted, generally	ct.	1.50-10.00
Faceted 5-pt. stars, drilled, 14-28 mm. dia.	ea.	2.00-10.00
Faceted 6-pt stars, drilled, 14-28 mm. dia.	ea.	2.00-10.00

ROCK CRYSTAL, REPLICAS OF FAMOUS DIAMONDS, ETC.

Fairly accurate replicas of famous diamonds are regularly sold either as individual pieces, partial sets, or complete sets; the colored diamonds may be glass, citrine, or synthetic spinel. Also available are sets which illustrate the steps in cutting faceted gems.

Inidividual replicas, according to size & type	ea.	125.00
Replicas of Cullinan diamonds, set of 9	set	225.00
Replicas of fifteen famous diamonds, wgts.	set	350.00
Cullinan Rough replica	ca.	140.00
Replicas of 31 famous diamonds, some colored	set	590.00
Cutting steps, 7 stones	set	205.00

ROSE QUARTZ

Abundant, with low prices being asked for cut gems; by far most material is pale pink to pink, and only exceptionally are gems offered which are rich pink, sometimes with a slight tinge of purple; all rose quartz is somewhat milky because of microscopic inclusions, but nearly clean material is faceted into attractive gems; some, containing oriented inclusions, are capable of providing star and catseye gems; the finest of the latter show a fairly brilliant white eye of surprisingly high quality.

Faceted gems, medium clarity to nearly transparent, to 50 ct.	ct.	1.00-15.00
Round brilliants, 3-12 mm. (to 6 ct.)	ea.	1.00-5.00
Oval brilliants, 7x5-16x12 mm. (1-10 ct)	ea.	1.25-12.00
Oct. step cuts 7x5-16x12 mm. (1-10 ct)	ea.	1.25-12.00
Cabochon catseyes, fine strong eye, good color, 10-25 ct.	ct.	1.50-8.00
Cabochon catseyes, ordinary grades	ct.	1.00-3.00

Cabochon catseyes, doublets	ct.	2.00-10.00
Cabochons, 18x13 ovals	ea.	6.00
Tumbled gems, medium hue, ½"-1½"	lb.	12.00-18.00
Tumbled gems, good hue, ½"-1½"	lb.	16.00-20.00
Tumbled gems, fine hue, many with flawless areas	lb.	24.00 +

RUTILATED QUARTZ

Finest gems are fairly large cabochons containing brilliant yellow to gold silky shafts of rutile in crisscross patterns; of somewhat lesser value are those with smoky quartz as the matrix and those in which coppery or brownish rutile needles are present; in any case, value depends mainly upon the brilliance of the inclusion reflections; occasionally step-cut into fairly attractive gems.

Brazil, exceptionally fine, 25 mm. cabs.	ea.	15.00-35.00
Brazil, medium quality, cabs., rds., 4-25 mm.	ea.	4.00-10.00
Brazil, medium quality, cabs., ovals, 7x5-30x20 mm-	ea.	5.00-25.00
Brazil, step cut, 10-45 ct.	ct.	.75-8.00
Tumbled gems, colorless to smoky matrix, ½"-1½"	lb.	5.00-12.00

SMOKY QUARTZ

There is not much variation in color quality in this variety, by far most smoky quartz being the same brownish hue, but the intensity ranges from pale smoky to very dark, the latter sometimes being called morion, while medium dark, lively hues are sometimes called cairngorm; the abundance of smoky quartz in nature reflects itself in the low paces asked for cut gems and also in the very large variety of faceted gem shapes. Most prices below are for flawless faceted gems in which the only variables arc complexity of lapidary work and intensity of color. Commonly, and misleadingly, sold as "smoky topaz."

Round brilliants, clean, medium to medium dark, 5-40 mm.	ea.	1.50-15.00
Oval brilliants, clean, medium to medium dark, 10x8-40x30 mm.	ea.	1.50-12.00
Oct. step cuts, medium to medium dark, 10x8-40x30 mm.	ea.	1.50-12.00
Hearts, faceted, clean, medium to medium dark, 10-40 mm.	ea.	1.50-25.00
Square step cuts, clean, medium to medium dark, 12x12-20x20 mm.	ea.	2.00-20.00
Pears, faceted, clean, medium to medium dark, 13x18-22x15 mm.	ea.	2.50-20.00
Pears, faceted, clean, same hues, drilled, 13x18-22x15 mm.	ea.	2.50-10.00
Faceted large clean gems, generally	ct.	1.00-10.00
Cabochons, ovals, 8x6-25x18 mm.	ea.	3.50-12.00
Cabochons, rounds, 4-25 mm.	ea.	3.00-12.00
Tumbled gems, light to dark, ½"-1½"	lb.	6.00-15.00

STAR QUARTZ

Gems may be cut either from flawless rock crystal and backed with a striated colored mirror on the base, which results in a weak star appearing upon the surface of the finished cabochon, or from rock crystal filled with numerous inclusions resulting in natural stars; however, very few specimens of the latter are so strong that they are effective by themselves and it is usual to back them with a reflecting base, often pigmented to simulate star corundum colors.

Natural, blue-backed, oval cabs., 9x7-12x10 mm.	ea.	4.50-12.00
Natural, blue-backed, round cabs., 5-12 mm.	ea.	2.50-10.00

Natural, black, unbacked ovals, 8x6-14x12 mm.	ea.	10.00-20.00
Rock crystal tops, star-backing, blue, ovals, 8x6-20x15 mm.	ea.	10.00-22.00
Rock crystal tops, star-backing, red, ovals, 8x6-20x15 mm.	ca.	10.00-35.00
Rock crystal tops, star-backing, blue, rds., 4-15 mm.	ea.	12.00-20.00
Same, but red, 4-15 mm.	ea.	13.50-25.00

TIGEREYE

Very abundant and inexpensive in any form; slight increases in value for hues or mixtures of hues other than the common yellow-brown hue; the last can be bleached to pale straw-yellow, or heat treated to brownish-red; blue or green types tend to polish poorly.

Cabochons, rounds, yellow, 4-25 mm.	ea.	1.60-14.00
Cabochons, rounds, yellow, sharp eye, same sizes	ea.	2.00-15.00
Cabochons, rounds, blue, same sizes	ea.	2.00-15.00
Cabochons, rounds, blue, sharp eye, same sizes	ea.	2.50-20.00
Cabochons, ovals, yellow, 7x5-30x20 mm.	ea.	8.00-35.00
Cabochons, ovals, yellow, sharp eye, same sizes	ea.	9.00-35.00
Cabochons, ovals, blue, same sizes	ea.	3.00-18.00
Cabochons, ovals, blue, sharp eye, same sizes	ea.	3.50-20.00
Small, yellow rds., 2-3½ mm.	ca.	1.30-1.60
Tumbled, fine grade, yellow or red, ½"-1½"	lb.	8.00-15.00 +
Tumbled, medim grade, yellow or red, ½"-1½"	lb.	6.00-15.00

TOURMALINATED QUARTZ

Rock crystal or smoky quartz containing jackstraw aggregates of black tourmaline needles, the quality depending on thickness of needles (about 1 mm.), uniform distribution in matrix, color of matrix (colorless being preferred), and freedom from small cracks surrounding the needles.

Cabochons, ovals, 18x13 mm. generally	ct.	1.00-5.00
Tumbled, sparse to medium-density needles, ⅝"-1½"	lb.	5.00-10.00

BLOODSTONE

Finest grades are dark green Indian moss agate in which the "moss" is so fine and so densely packed that close inspection is needed to detect textural differences; in this matrix appear deep red spherules of "blood"; ordinary grades show variations in color of the matrix, obvious moss filaments, and irregular spots, some too large and others too small; poor grades display slight pitting of surfaces where the moss-like inclusions are too soft to polish well.

Round cabochons, fine grade, 4-12 mm.	ea.	3.00-10.00
Oval cabochons, fine grade, 7x5-13x18 mm.	ea.	7.75-20.00
Round cabochons, ordinary grades, 4-12 mm.	ea.	3.00-9.00
Octagon cabochons, ordinary grades, 7x5-13x18 mm.	ea.	8.90-21.00
Tumbled gems, ordinary to fair grades, ½"-1⅝"	lb.	8.00-20.00

CARNELIAN, SARDONYX, ETC.

Best carnelians are rich orange-red verging on deep orange, and have been cut chiefly from heat-treated material from India; excellent carnelians, sometimes attractively banded in white, are also cut from Brazilian and Uruguayan agate, but the best are almost invariably enriched in hue by heat treatment which has the effect of changing original brownish colors to dark reds and brownish-reds; the white banded kinds are called sardonyx. As with other common chalcedonies, prices are determined mainly by lapidary and handling costs.

Carnelian, fine oranges, oval cabs., 16x12 mm.	ea.	5.00
Carnelian, good grade, round cabs., 4-15 mm.	ea.	2.50-8.50
Carnelian, good grade, oval cabs., 7x5-18x25 mm.	ea.	1.25-6.00
Carnelian, good grade, small rds., 2-3½ mm.	ea.	.80
Carnelian, good grade, heart cabs., drilled, 20 mm.	ea.	4.50

Carnelian, good grade, faceted 5-pt. star, 40 mm.	ea.	5.00
Hearts, cabs., 10-40 mm.	ea.	1.40-20.00
Brazil, tumbled gems, fine color, ½"-1½"	lb.	8.00-12.00
Brazil, tumbled gems, sardonyx, ½"-1½"	lb.	12.00-20.00

MISCELLANEOUS CHALCEDONIES

Common banded agates, rd. cabs., 4-25 mm.	ea.	1.00-4.50
Common banded agates, oval cabs., 7x5-30x20 mm.	ea.	.35-4.50
India, assorted types, 9-17 mm. rd. cabs.	ea.	1.00
Banded agates, drilled 5-pt. facet stars, 14-28 mm.	ea.	1.50-5.00
Common jaspers, rd. cabs., 4-25 mm.	ea.	1.00-5.00
Common jaspers, oval cabs., 7x5-30x20 mm.	ea.	1.00-4.50
Cabochon hearts, drilled, 10-40 mm.	ea.	2.50-20.00
Mexico, fine colored cabs., according to hue & pattern	ea.	2.00-25.00
Mexico, psilomelatie chalcedony, oval cabs., 18x13-25x18 mm.	ea.	1.00-7.00
Dinosaur bone, oval cabs., 25x18-40x30 mm.	ea.	2.50-20.00
Petrified woods, oval cabs., 18x13-40x30 mm.	ea.	2.50-20.00
Tumbled ordinary grade agates, jaspers, etc.	lb.	5.00-20.00
Tumbled colorful & patterned agates, jaspers, etc.	lb.	10.00-20.00

DYED CHALCEDONIES

Black, blue, green or red cabochons readily available; black-dyed clialcedoiiy is commonly called "onyx" and is much used in inexpensive rings; "Swiss lapis" is porous, brownish jasper dyed blue and, unlike most dyed chalcedonies whose colors are permanent, it tends to fade with time or develop mottled or discolored areas.

Various hues, rd. cabs., 4-25 mm.	ea.	2.50-5.00
Various hues, oval cabs., 7x5-30x20 mm.	ea.	1.50-8.00
Various hues, small rd. cabs., 2-3½ mm.	ea.	1.00-2.50
Blue-dyed jasper, "Swiss lapis," rd. cabs., 4-25 mm.	ea.	2.00-4.50
Blue-dyed jasper, "Swiss lapis," oval cabs., 7x5-30x20 mm.	ea.	2.50-15.00

CHRYSOCOLLA CHALCEDONY

The finest cabochons arc perfectly uniform in texture and hue, decidedly translucent, and pale to medium blue ill color; lesser grades are less translucent, may show uneven color distribution, colorless areas, or contain inclusions of malachite or minute quartz-lincd vugs or veinlets. Exceptionally translucent material is sometimes faceted.

Arizona, highest quality, cabs.	ct.	2.00-12.00
Arizona, highest quality, faceted gems, 5-15 ct.	ct.	2.50-15.00
Arizona, medium grade, rd. cabs., 4-25 mm.	ea.	1.00-10.00
Arizona, medium grade, oval cabs., 8x6-2x16 mm.	ea.	2.00-10.00

CHRYSOPRASE

Former standards of quality in this apple-green chalcedony have becn displaced completely by the new chrysoprase from Australia which ranges in hue from medium to medium-dark apple-green to intense yellow-green, with some approaching intense pure green; cabochons in excess of 30 mm. are easily possible from rough of unprecedented perfection of texture, evenness of color and good translucency.

Australia, fine grade, oval cabs.	ct.	10.00-30.00
Australia, medium grade, rd. cabs., 4-10 mm.	ea.	3.00-8.00
Australia, medium grade, oval cabs., 10x8-18x13 mm.	ea.	7.50-25.00

MOSS AGATE

Ordinary moss agate consists of slender, dark-hued filaments, complexly intertwined in a groundmass of translucent chalcedony, as notably displayed in the common lapidary material; the cost of gems is mainly for the lapidary work and subsequent trade handling. *Dendritic agate*, or *tree agate*, is another type in which the filaments form fantastic growths resembling minia-ture trees or the flat fronds of ferns and certain sea organisms known as "sea fans"; large and fine specimens of this kind, to several inches in diameter, often command several hundred dol-lars per stone. Ordinary Indian moss agate is always inexpensive, but the costlier "tree" types are priced according to perfection of fronds, translucency of enclosing chalceclony which per-mits them to be seen clearly, and absence of fractures or inclusions which may be infiltrated with black or red material.

India, green moss, cabs., rds., 4-25 mm.	ea.	.50-2.50
India, green moss, cabs., ovals, 7x5-30x20 mm.	ea.	.50-4.50
India, green moss, cabs., hearts, 10-40 mm.	ea.	1.50-20.00
India, green moss, tumbled gems, ½"-1½"	lb.	8.00-12.00
Black moss in clear to milky matrix, round cabs., 4-25 mm.	ea.	.50-2.50
Black moss in clear to milky matrix, oval cabs., 7x5-30x20 mm.	ea.	.50-4.50
Montana, black moss in clear matrix. various cabs.	ea.	2.50-25.00
Texas, black moss in white matrix, various cabs.	ea.	1.50-15.00
Texas or Oregon, red moss in clear matrix, cabs.	ea.	2.50-50.00
Oregon, large black "trees" in translucent matrix, to 50 mm.	ea.	2.50-150.00
India, large black "trees" in translucent matrix, to 50 mm.	ea.	3.00-200.00

END OF QUARTZ SECTION

RHODOCHROSITE

The faceted gems from Colordao material are usually slightly to badly flawed but are con-sidered acceptable in view of the great rarity of transparent material; sizes to about 6 carats have been cut. Massive banded material from Argentina ranges from pink to deep pink, sometimes to red; it is soft and weak and seldom accepts a polish without some surface irregularities.

Colorado, faceted, step cut, 1-8 ct.	ct.	20.00-100.00
Argentina, round cabs., 4-25 mm.	ea.	1.00-10.00
Argentina, oval cabs., 8x6-40x30 mm.	ea.	15.00-75.00
Argentina, fine, faceted 3-6 cts.	ct.	60.00-150.00

RHODOLITE, SEE GARNET

RHODONITE

Very rarely a small faceted gem appears upon the market, cut form one of the transparent brownish-red crystals from New South Wales; maximum size about 2 carats. Quality in ordi-nary massive material depends on intensity of color, the most desirable being pale red to red, on perfection of finish, and on pleasing patterns of black "spiderweb," if such are present.

New South Wales, faceted, step cut, ½-2 ct.	ct.	50.00-150.00
Australia, fine hues, rd. cabs., 4-25 mm.	ea.	10.00-25.00
Australia, fine hues, oval cabs., 7x5-30x20 mm.	ea.	10.00-45.00
Australia, tumbled gems, black-veined pink	lb.	10.00-20.00
Australia, tumbled gems, rich pink	lb.	16.00-25.00
Colorado tumbled gems, pink	lb.	8.50-25.00

RICOLITE. SEE SERPENTINE

ROCK CRYSTAL, SEE QUARTZ

ROSE QUARTZ, see QUARTZ

RUBELLITE, see TOURMALINE

RUBY, see CORUNDUM

RUTILATED QUARTZ, see QUARTZ

RUTILE (Natural and Synthetic)
Very dark red natural rutile is sometimes faceted, but traces of color appear only in gems of melee sizes, larger ones merely appearing black; synthetic rutile ("titania") has been furnished in red, blue, and very pale straw-yellow boules, but practically all gems are cut from the last; quality depends mainly on proper orientation to eliminate effects of double refraction, the worst gems being obviously "fuzzy" while the best present sharp reflections; another important factor is finish, poor quality gems displaying rounded facet edges, scratches, inaccurate facets, etc., because of difficulties in polishing. Synthetic rutile displays very strong dispersion.
Natural, very dark red, rd. cuts to 3.5 mm. dia.   ct.   1,000.00-2,100.00

SANIDINE, see FELDSPAR

SAPPHIRE, see CORUNDUM

SARDONYX, see QUARTZ

SCAPOLITE
Faceted gems, usually step-cut, in colorless to medium yellow, to about 10-15 ct.; also very attractive catseye gems, commonly white, also pink, and rarely blue.

Brazil or Myanmar, faceted gems, yellow, 1-5 ct.	ct.	20.00-45.00
Brazil or Myanmar, faceted gems, yellow, 6-15 ct.	ct.	40.00-75.00
Myanmar, faceted gems, colorless, 1-3 ct.	ct.	35.00-80.00
Myanmar, catseyes, blue, 2 ct.	ct.	300.00
Myanmar, catseyes, pink, 3-8 ct.	ct.	100.00-125.00
Myanmar, catseyes, purple, 1 ct.	ct.	100.00

SCHEELITE
Faceted gems to about 20 carats have been cut from colorless California material, and very attractive gems, to about 15 carats, from orange-yellow Mexican material; brilliant cuts are favored but step cuts are also effective; the colorless gems display considerable dispersion.

California, colorless, 1-15 ct.	ct.	30.00-60.00
Mexico, orange-yellow, ¼-5 ct.	ct.	35.00-75.00
Mexico, orange-yellow, 6-10 ct.	ct.	45.00-85.00

SERPENTINE
Very translucent types sometimes acet-cut as collectors' gems; cabochons often attractive but seldom used in jewelry; finest cabochon material is intense green to somewhat bluish-green translucent *williamsite* variety from Maryland Pennsylvania; other varieties include *bowenite*, an exceptionally compact material with medium to high translucency, and *ricolite*, a banded variety.

Various translucent bowenites, oval cabs., 18x13-40x30 mm.	ea.	1.50-5.00
Williamsite, rich green, oval cabs., 18x13-40x30 mm.	ea.	7.00-18.00
Williamsite, dark green, oval cabs., 18x13-40x30 mm.	ea.	1.50-5.00

SUGILITE
A grape-colored massive material from Africa used for carvings and cabochons. Promoted under the trade names "Royal Lavulite" and "Royal Azel."

Sugilite, per carat for cabochons, good color material	ct.	10.00-25.00

SHELL

Mother-of-pearl, cabochons, ovals, 6x4-25x18 mm.	ea.	.65-2.00
Mother-of-pearl, black, cabochons, ovals, 2x4-22x8	ea.	.75-1.00
Mother-of-pearl, pink, cabochons, ovals, 2x4-22x8	ea.	.70-1.20

SILLIMANITE, SEE FIBROLITE

SINHALITE

Because of the demand for this recently-identified gemstone, faceted specimens are hard to locate and costly; pale yellow-brown to rich brown, also greenish-brown to black; faceted gems resemble yellow or brown chrysoberyl and some are known in excess of 100 carats.

Sri Lanka, brownish-yellow, step cuts, 2-5 ct.	ct.	100.00
Sri Lanka, brownish-yellow, step cuts, 6-15 ct.	ct.	100.00-150.00
Sri Lanka, brownish-yellow, step cuts, 16-40 ct.	ct.	100.00-150.00

SMITHSONITE

Pale yellow faceted gems have been cut from Australian and South West African material.

Faceted, pale yellow, ¼-4 ct.	ct.	300.00-415.00
Faceted, white	ct.	300.00-400.00

SMOKY QUARTZ, SEE QUARTZ

SODALITE

Very rarely, extremely small faceted gems have been cut form dark blue transparent material from Ontario. Most sodalite is opaque or poorly translucent and is used in cabochons, tumbled gems, and large ornamental objects; material from Ontario or Maine ranges from medium to dark blue with white mottlings and veinings, to medium to pale blue speckled with inclusions of yellow cancrinite, white feldspar, and black magnetite or mica; the material from Brazil, a recent arrival on the market, is dark blue with minor white specklings and veinings. Rather soft and brittle.

Ontario, dark blue, faceted, ¼-½	ct.	15.00-20.00
Ontario, oval cabochons, 10x8-25x18 mm.	ea.	1.50-10.00
Brazil, oval cabochons, 8x6-30x20 mm.	ea.	1.50-10.00
Brazil, rd. cabochons, 4-25 mm.	ea.	1.00-15.00
Brazil, tumbled gems, dark blue, ½"-1½"	lb.	8.00-20.00

SPESSARTINE, SEE GARNET

SPHALERITE

Popular among collectors and amateur cutters because of its beauty in faceted form. The finest type, resembling a diamond when cut but now almost unobtainable, is very pale green cleiophane from Franklin, N.J., a locality which also produces an olive-green material. The most consistently available fine gems are cut from Spanish material, which provides splendid brilliants and step cuts of rich golden yellow color, many nearly flawless, and others which range in hue from yellow through orange to red; very good pale greens, reminiscent of some green sphenes, are cut from Cananea, Sonora, Mexico, material. Faceted gems are known to about 100 ct., but those over about 25 ct. are seldom entirely free of veil-type inclusions or sharp color bandings; soft and difficult to cut with sharp-edged facets and scratch-free finishes; occasionally cut cabochon.

Spain, bright yellow to orange, faceted, 5-10 ct.	ct.	150.00
Spain, bright yellow to orange, faceted, 11-45 ct.	ct.	200.00
Spain, dark red, faceted, 5-25 ct.	ct.	75.00-150.00
Mexico, fine yellow-green, 3-20 ct.	ct.	50.00-100.00

SPHENE

Favored among collectors of beautiful and unusual gems, but too soft to find serious application in jewelry; many fine faceted gems recently supplied from material produced at numerous points in Baja California, Mexico, in dark brown, green-brown, yellow-green, greenish-yellow, bright green, and even emerald-green, the last being very small with cut gems reasonably free of inclusions seldom over 1 carat; the other Mexican gems have been cut to about 14 carats, quite clean, with a large number of flawless gems in the range 1 to 5 carats. Recently, in clean to fairly clean faceted gems up to about 3 carats, green to yellow-green and yellow, from two sources in Brazil. Very small gems, not over 3-4 mm. diameter, cut from very dark brown Ontario crystals can be heat-treated to dark orange; brownish gems from Mexico can also be considerably lightened by prolonged heat treatment at red heat.

Mexico, emerald-green, ½-1½ ct., fine	ct.	300.00
Mexico, yellow-green, 1-3 ct., moderate inclusions	ct.	50.00
Mexico, eye-clean, 1-7 cts.	ct.	100.00
Mexico, eye-clean, fine, green, 1-6 cts.	ct.	150.00

SPINEL

Natural spinels present a very wide range of hues: red, orange-red, brownish-red, purplish-red, purple, and blue, also purplish-, reddish-, or bluish-gray; the finest hues are vivid, but as grayish components enter gems become darker, lack the liveliness of the best color grades, and are priced much lower; inclusions may be veil-type or scattered small dark crystals. Excellent gems to 45 carats have been cut from gem gravel material of Myanmar and Sri Lanka; prized colors are intense orange-red, red, or purplish-red; less prized are purples and blues unless they happen to be exceptionally vivid; mainly cut as faceted gems. Star spinels are known but are extremely rare.

Orange-red, fine color, medium intensity, 3 ct.	ct.	1,100.00-1,950.00
Orange-red, fine color, medium intensity, 6 ct.	ct.	1,350.00-2,300.00
Orange-red, fine color, medium intensity, 7-10 ct.	ct.	2,800.00-4,500.00
Red, purplish-red, fine medium color, 3 ct.	ct.	400.00-800.00
Red, purplish-red, fine medium color, 6 ct.	ct.	675.00-1,100.00
Red, purplish-red, fine medium color, 7-10 ct.	ct.	1,650.00-2,800.00
Red, purplish-red, fine dark color, 3 ct.	ct.	100.00-400.00
Red, purplish-red, fine dark color, 6 ct.	ct.	300.00-675.00
Red, purplish-red, fine dark color, 7-10 ct.	ct.	750.00-1,650.00
Red, purplish-red, fine light color, 3-10 ct.	ct.	40.00-150.00
Purple, fine medium color, 3-6 ct.	ct.	125.00-400.00
Purple, fine medium color, 5-10 ct.	ct.	300.00-500.00
Purple, dark or light colors, 5-10 ct.	ct.	60.00-300.00
Blue, fine medium color, 3 ct.	ct.	150.00-400.00
Blue, fine medium color, 6 ct.	ct.	200.00-500.00
Blue, fine medium color, 5-8 ct.	ct.	225.00-600.00
Blue, dark color, 3-6 ct.	ct.	35.00-150.00
Blue, dark color, 5-8 ct.	ct.	75.00-225.00
Blue, light color, 5-8 ct.	ct.	35.00-75.00

SYNTHETIC SPINEL

Available in many colors; faceted gems much used as inexpensive ring stones; the blue type is noted for distinct red flashes which fleetingly appear as the gem is turned beneath a strong light source; also used for doublets and in cabochons.

Round brilliants, all colors, 3-20 mm.	ea.	1.00-4.00
Octs., ovals, cushion, all colors, 3-20 mm.	ea.	1.00-5.00
Hearts, all colors, 2x2-20x22 mm.	ea.	1.00-10.00
Melee, various hues, 1-3½ mm.	ea.	1.00-2.00

Doublets, green, purple, yellow, etc., faceted, 2-14 mm. rds. ea.   1.50-10.00
Doublets, same hues, step cuts, 10x8-18x13 mm.   ea.   15.00
Tumbled gems, various colors, ½" average   ct.   1.00

END OF SPINEL SECTION

SPODUMENE

Faceting varieties include *kunzite* in various shades of violet or purple, with some being almost pink; *hiddenite*, a rich emerald-green variety from North Carolina, found only in small crystals and now extremely rare; and various color varieties without special names (green, colorless, and yellow). Large numbers of faceted kunzites have recently appeared on the market from Brazil, some weighing hundreds of carats and flawless; there is considerable demand for richly-hued gems but prices asked have been rather low due to oversupply and the probability that, like previous kunzites, the colors will fade; yellow and green spodumenes do not fade. Some dealers call pale, slightly bluish-green spodumene "hiddenite," but most authorities prefer that this name be reserved for the unique chromium-bearing North Carolina variety. Most spodumene gems are flawless, but some lower-grade kunzites from Brazil and elsewhere contain etch cavities resembling slender inclusions of rutile. Occasionally, massive fibrous spodumene furnishes weak catseyes.

Kunzite, rich purple or violet, 5-50 ct.   ct.   35.00-125.00
Kunzite, medium purple or violet, 5-50 ct.   ct.   22.00-90.00
Kunzite, pale purple or violet, 5-50 ct.   ct.   12.00-60.00
Pale yellow-green, 5-150 ct.   ct.   12.00-55.00
Pale, slightly bluish-green, 3-10 ct.   ct.   25.00-45.00
Very pale yellow, 5-150 ct.   ct.   5.00-20.00
Pale yellow, 5-150 ct.   ct.   2.00-6.00
Medium yellow, 5-75 ct.   ct.   5.00-12.00
Colorless, 5-50 ct.   ct.   1.00-5.00
Kunzite, round brilliants, 3-12 mm. (to 6 ct.)   ea.   2.00-70.00
Kunzite, oct. step cuts or oval brills., 7x5-16x12 mm.   ea.   7.50-350.00
Yellow-green, round brills., 3-12 mm. (to 6 ct.)   ea.   1.00-45.00
Yellow-green, oct. step cuts, oval brills., 7x5-16x12 mm.   ea.   7.50-150.00

STAUROLITE

Clear facet-grade crystals are very rare and gems cut from them are apparently confined to staurolite from Switzerland; these are always dark and very small; cleaned and oil-impregnated cross-twin crystals have been used for charms.

Switzerland, brown, faceted, to 2 ct.   ct.   45.00-75.00

STRONTIUM TITANATE ("FABULITE")

Within the united States production of boules of this synthetic gem material and cutting and marketing of gems are controlled completely, the gems being marketed under the trade name of "fabulite"; some synthetic material has come from Japan but only small gems have been cut from it; ordinary fabulite can be cut to order in gems in excess of 50 carats which are absolutely clean and display the enormous dispersion and absence of any body color for which this material is noted. Soft; must be worn and handled with care (when available).

Fabulite, round brills., or other cuts, 1-10 ct.   ct.   35.00-50.00

SUNSTONE, SEE FELDSPAR

TAAFEITE

Light pink, rare, Sri Lanka, 1-5 ct.   ct.   1,200.00

TEKTITES

Moldavite, the dark "bottle-green" transparent tektite found in Czechoslovakia has been faceted for many years in brilliants and step cuts to about 10-20 carats; straw-yellow to yellow *Libyan Desert glass* has also been faceted but seldom in clean gems over 5 carats in weight; it is much rarer than moldavite. Very dark brown or very dark green tektites, such as the *bediasites* of Texas, *billitonites* of Java, and others from Asia and Australia, have also been faceted as curiosities but appear merely black and have very little value; *agni mani* tektites are of this type.

Moldavite, dark green, faceted, 1-20 ct.	ct.	5.00-35.00
Libyan Desert glass, yellow, faceted, 1-20 ct.	ct.	6.00-35.00
Black types, faceted, 1-100 ct.	ct.	4.00-8.00
Black types, cabochoned, 10x8-25x18 mm. ovals	ea.	5.00-15.00

THOMSONITE

The best cabochons of this attractively-patterned fibrous material are cut from small nodules found in Minnesota; quality depends on color patterns, strongly contrasting colors arranged in concentric bands being the most desired, e.g., pink or salmon with deep green; prices rise steeply according to size. Soft; accepts a good polish.

Fine quality, colorful markings, ¼"-½"	ea.	15.00-35.00
Fine quality, colorful markings, ¾"-1"	ea.	20.00-45.00

THULITE, SEE ZOISITE

TIGEREYE, SEE QUARTZ

TITANIA, SEE RUTILE

TOPAZ

A hard gemstone, used for hundreds of years for faceted gems. Prized hues in order are: purples, reds, oranges, deep yellows, medium dark blues, pale yellows, pale browns, colorless. the so-called "imperial" topaz is a medium red-orange hue with slight brownish tone. The reddish-brown, or "sherry," and pale brown hues of topazes from pegmatite pockets and from cavities in trachytic rocks are fugitive in most specimens, paling with exposure to light, eventually to colorless. Naturally purplish or violet crystals are very rare; pale purplish or violet tinges are sometimes imparted by heat treatment ("pinking") of red-orange gems, the depth of final color depending on depth of initial color. Because of easy cleavage, faceted gem girdles should be closely examined to see that they are not too thin and thus liable to suffer damage during setting or wear.

Purplish, or violet-red, medium light, 1 ct.	ct.	125.00-175.00
Purplish, or violet-red, medium light, 5 ct.	ct.	425.00-625.00
Purplish, or violet-red, medium light, 10 ct.	ct.	475.00-800.00
Purplish, or violet-red, medium light, 15 ct.	ct.	750.00-1,100.00
Pink, pale, 1-10 ct., for clean gems, generally	ct.	125.00-475.00
Slightly brownish or orangy-red, medium, 1 ct.	ct.	50.00-125.00
Slightly brownish or orangy-red, medium, 5 ct.	ct.	225.00-400.00
Slightly brownish or orangy-red, medium, 10 ct.	ct.	300.00-475.00
Slightly brownish or orangy-red, medium, 15 ct.	ct.	500.00-700.00
Yellow-oranges, rich yellows, reddish-browns, medium, 1 ct.	ct.	90.00-150.00
Yellow-oranges, rich yellows, reddish-browns, medium, 5 ct.	ct.	400.00-600.00
Yellow-oranges, rich yellows, reddish-browns, medium, 10 ct.	ct.	600.00-850.00
Yellow-oranges, rich yellows, reddish-browns, medium, 15 ct.	ct.	700.00-1,100.00

Yellow-oranges, reddish-browns, light, 1 ct.	ct.	40.00-90.00
Yellow-oranges, reddish-browns, light, 5 ct.	ct.	150.00-400.00
Yellow-oranges, reddish-browns, light, 10 ct.	ct.	100.00-275.00
Yellow-oranges, reddish-browns, light, 15 ct.	ct.	150.00-350.00
Blue, medium dark, 1-5 ct., color treated	ct.	6.00-20.00
Blue, medium dark, 10 ct., color treated	ct.	15.00-30.00
Blue, medium dark, 15 ct., color treated	ct.	18.00-40.00
Blue, medium, 1-15 ct., color treated	ct.	2.00-25.00
Blue, light, 1-15 ct., color treated	ct.	2.00-10.00
Yellow, medium, 10-15 ct.	ct.	75.00-125.00
Yellow, light, 1-50 ct.	ct.	40.00-60.00
Yellow, very light, 5-200 ct.	ct.	1.50-25.00
Sherry hues, fugitive, 1-25 ct.	ct.	10.00-30.00
Colorless, 1-500 ct.	ct.	1.50-10.00
Colorless, rd. brills., 4-12 mm. (to 6 ct.)	ea.	2.50-15.00
Colorless, oct. step cuts, oval brills., 7x5-16x12 mm. (1-10 ct.)	ea.	4.00-50.00
Tumbled gems, yellow	lb.	40.00
Tumbled gems, good blue	lb.	40.00

TOURMALINATED QUARTZ, SEE QUARTZ

TOURMALINE

Extremely wide variety of hues, from colorless to brown, red, orange, yellow, green, blue; also with several colors in same gem. Order of desirability: reds, approaching fine ruby or spinel hues, lively blue-greens lacking any tinge of olive, rich yellow-greens, rich blues lacking tinges of gray. Colorless known as *achroite* and extremely rare, most gems actually containing some tinge of hue; reds are *rubellites*; medium to dark blues are *indicolites*; browns are *dravites*; black tourmaline is *schorl* but is seldom used in gems; other color phases are named according to the hue displayed. The best greens must not show tinges of olive; value drops markedly as olive appears because brilliance lessens due to strong absorption of light whenever this hue is present. Some green crystals which are strongly absorbent of light in one crystallographic direction are deliberately cut with excessively steep facets upon the ends of step-cut gems to prevent the lack of brilliance from appearing on top; they consequently display parallel step reflections from side facets only. Clean rubellites are difficult to find, most containing numerous reflective cracks and veil-type inclusions. Excellent catseye gems are not uncommon, the finest displaying brilliant sharp eyes upon a silky background, but sizes over 6 carats are rare in such high quality. "Bicolor" gems are those cut from crystals displaying two or more distinct hues, often in marked contrast, e.g., pink plus green, pink plus blue, etc.; exceptional examples are highly prized and very costly.

RUBELLITE

Purplish or violet-reds, medium dark, 3 ct.	ct.	125.00-180.00
Purplish or violet-reds, medium dark, 6 ct.	ct.	200.00-275.00
Purplish or violet-reds, medium dark, 10 ct.	ct.	250.00-400.00
Purplish or violet-reds, medium dark, 15 ct.	ct.	375.00-550.00
Same, medium intensity, 3 ct.	ct.	60.00-125.00
Same, medium intensity, 6 ct.	ct.	100.00-200.00
Same, medium intensity, 10 ct.	ct.	150.00-250.00
Same, medium intensity, 15 ct.	ct.	100.00-200.00
Same, light intensity, 3 ct.	ct.	15.00-25.00
Same, light intensity, 6-15 ct.	ct.	60.00-100.00
Maroon-red, "wine," 3-15 ct.	ct.	20.00-40.00

Brownish-red, 3-15 ct.	ct.	20.00-40.00

PINKS

Pink, high intensity, 3-15 ct.	ct.	135.00-350.00
Pink, medium intensity, 3-15 ct.	ct.	70.00-250.00
Pink, rd. brills., 3-12 mm. (to 6 ct.)	ea.	30.00-50.00
Pink, oct. step cuts, oval brills., 7x5-16x12 mm. (1-10 ct.)	ea.	15.00-225.00

GREENS

Fine bluish-green, medium dark, 3 ct.	ct.	75.00-100.00
Fine bluish-green, medium dark, 6 ct.	ct.	100.00-150.00
Fine bluish-green, medium dark, 10 ct.	ct.	150.00-200.00
Fine bluish-green, medium dark, 15 ct.	ct.	200.00-300.00
Same, medium intensity, 3 ct.	ct.	40.00-75.00
Same, medium intensity, 6 ct.	ct.	60.00-100.00
Same, medium intensity, 10 ct.	ct.	90.00-150.00
Same, medium intensity, 15 ct.	ct.	120.00-225.00
Same, light intensity, 3-15 ct.	ct.	10.00-50.00
Yellowish-green, no olive, medium dark, 3 ct.	ct.	10.00-20.00
Yellowish-green, no olive, medium dark, 6 ct.	ct.	15.00-30.00
Yellowish-green, no olive, medium dark, 10 ct.	ct.	25.00-50.00
Yellowish-green, no olive, medium dark, 15 ct.	ct.	25.00-50.00
Same, medium to light, 3-15 ct.	ct.	10.00-20.00
Yellow-green, no olive tinge, 3-25 ct.	ct.	10.00-30.00
Greens, olive-tinged, 3-45 ct.	ct.	1.00-20.00
Green, rd. brills., 3-12 mm. (to 6 ct.)	ea.	2.00-70.00
Green, oct. step cuts, oval brills., 7x5-16x12 mm. (1-10 ct.)	ea.	8.50-175.00
Green, melee, rds., 1-3½ mm.	ea.	1.50-5.00

INDICOLITE

Rich blues, pure or tinged with green, medium dark, 3 ct.	ct.	75.00-120.00
Rich blues, pure or tinged with green, medium dark, 6 ct.	ct.	125.00-200.00
Rich blues, pure or tinged with green, medium dark, 10 ct.	ct.	225.00-375.00
Rich blues, pure or tinged with green, medium dark, 15 ct.	ct.	350.00-550.00
Same, medium intensity, 3-15 ct.	ct.	75.00-350.00
Same, light intensity, 3-15 ct.	ct.	25.00-150.00
Same, dark or grayish, 3-15 ct.	ct.	10.00-80.00
Blues, rd. brills., 3-12 mm. (to 6 ct.)	ea.	5.00-65.00
Blues, oct. step cuts, oval brills., 7x5-16x12 mm. (1-10 ct.)	ea.	20.00-175.00
Blue catseye	ct	25.00

ACHROITE

Achroite, faceted rds. or step cuts, 1-5 ct.	ct.	5.00-25.00

DRAVITE

Dravite, Sri Lanka, 1-20 ct., faceted	ct.	5.00-20.00

MISCELLANEOUS

Bicolors, faceted, various grades, to 20 ct.	ct.	10.00-150.00
Catseyes, blue + pink, 1-5 ct.	ct.	10.00-25.00
Catseyes, green, blue, pink, etc., 1-15 ct.	ct.	10.00-35.00
Cabochons, red, rds., 4-25 mm.	ea.	1.00-50.00
Cabochons, red ovals, 7x5-22x16 mm.	ea.	1.00-35.00
Cabochons, pink, rds., 4-25 mm.	ea.	2.75-30.00

Cabochons, pink ovals, 7x5-22x16 mm.	ea.	5.00-25.00
Cabachons, green, rds., 4-25 mm.	ea.	2.70-25.00
Cabachons, green, ovals, 7x5-22x16 mm.	ea.	5.00-25.00
Tumbled gems, mixed colors, $1/4$"-$5/8$"	lb.	15.00-64.00
Tumbled gems, greens, blues, S. W. Africa, $1/8$"-$3/16$"	lb.	32.00-45.00

END OF TOURMALINE SECTION

TURQUOIS

Fine turquois remains popular with all segments of the jewelry-buying public; the best material is Persian, but by far the largest quantity used in jewelry is provided by the United States, some material approaching Persian in quality. In the trade, Persian refers to the top-grade material of pure medium blue color uniformly distributed within the gem, with no flaws, spots or inclusions, and so compact that a fine polish is possible; the gems are translucent on thin edges. *Persian spiderweb* is similar except that a network of fine black lines divides the surface of the gem into a mosaic of even patches; *Persian matrix* is a lesser grade with coarser lines or less regular patchwork. Value rapidly decline as greenish tinges appear or the material becomes too porous; porous to earthy material fails to take a good polish and displays no translucency; it is commonly treated with waxes, oils, or plastics to impregnate the pores and heighten the colors. Excessively porous material is detected with the "tongue test," that is, when the gem is touched by the tongue, a definite "sticking" occurs due to rapid drying of saliva by the highly absorbent turquois; this test is not effective against impregnated material. Clear Persian gems are sold mainly in the Near East and India (80 per cent) , the remainder being sold in Europe and U.S.; spiderweb and matrix grades sell mostly in Europe and U.S. (60 per cent), the rest being sold in the East. Most U.S. production is used locally in American Indian jewelry.

Persian, clear, "gem" grade, rds., 2-14 mm.	ct.	10.00-150.00
Persian, clear, "gem" grade, ovals, 6x4-15x13 mm.	ct.	10.00-75.00
Persian, clear, AA grade, rds., 2-14 mm.	ct.	5.00-25.00
Persian, clear, AA grade, ovals, 6x4-15x13 mm.	ct.	6.00-40.00
Persian, clear, BB grade, rds., 2-14 mm.	ct.	10.00-50.00
Persian, clear, BB grade, ovals, 6x4-15x13 mm.	ct.	10.00-35.00
Persian, clear, CC grade, rds., 2-14 mm.	ct.	2.50-20.00
Persian, clear, CC grade, ovals, 6x4-15x13 mm.	ct.	5.00-20.00
Persian, matrix grade A, rds., 4-12 mm., 9: ovals, 7x5-15x13 mm.	ct.	10.00-100.00
Persian matrix, grade B, same sizes as above	ct.	8.00-75.00
Persian matrix, grade C, same sizes as above	ct.	5.00-60.00
U.S. material, rds., 4-25 mm.	ea.	1.00-25.00
U.S. material, ovals, 7x5-22x16 mm.	ea.	1.50-25.00
U.S. material, small rds., 1-3$1/2$ mm.	ea.	1.00-3.00
U.S. matrix, blues & blue-greens, rds., 4-7 mm.	ea.	.90-5.00
U.S. matrix, blues & blue-greens, rd., 16 mm.	ea.	2.00-4.00
U.S. matrix, blues & blue-greens, ovals, 8x6-20x11 mm.	ea.	2.50-10.00
U.S. good blue, clean, 4-6 mm. rds.	ea.	1.50-7.50
U.S. tumbled, pale blue, $1/4$"-$3/4$"	lb.	24.00-40.00

U.S. fine grades, comparable to Persian, are sold by the carat at comparable prices.

ULEXITE

Fibrous ulexite, or "television stone," is sometimes cut into catseyes and spheres; while initially taking a good polish, any normally damp atmosphere alters the surface and destroys the polish. Very soft and fragile.

White, fine, 1$1/2$"-2$1/2$"	ea.	2.00-6.00

UNAKITE
A granitic rock which is commonly tumbled; fairly attractive gems are possible if the patches of pink feldspar and green epidote are of uniform size and contrast in color.

Cabochons, ovals, 18x13-40x30 mm.	ea.	2.50-20.00
Tumbled, ½"-1½"	lb.	10.00-25.00

UREYITE (Maw-Sit-Sit)
This material from Myanmar is a vibrant opaque green rock first reported by Dr. E. Gubelin. The green is a rare pyroxene mineral called ureyite. The lighter gren is natrolite. About $7 per carat. Cabs are cut from this material; sometimes mistaken for jadeite.

VARISCITE
The classic material from Fairfield, Utah, provides attractive cabochons displaying gray and yellow eyes and bands on a pale yellow-green background of variscite, but it is now quite scarce; recent finds of Utah and Nevada material provide cabochons ranging from pale to pure medium-dark green, some being quite translucent in the better grades.

Solid green, cabochons, rds., 4-25 mm.	ea.	10.00-20.00
Solid green, cabochons, ovals, 8x6-30x20 mm.	ea.	12.00-40.00
Fairfield material, patterned, ovals, 30x20 mm.	ea.	10.00-45.00
Facet, fine, 1-2 ct.	ct.	40.00

VESUVIANITE, see IDOCRASE

WILLEMITE
Attractive faceted gems have been cut only from transparent crystals from Franklin, New Jersey, deposits; also cabochons from more or less pure massive willemite and admixtures of willemite and other minerals; now extremely rare in faceted form; colors include orange, olive-green, vivid yellow-green, yellow, and, sometimes, straw-yellow; some olive-green material containing numerous platelets of orange-red hematite has been cut into interesting catseyes. Soft, brittle.

Faceted gems, usually ¼ -1½ ct., any color	ct.	50.00-695.00

WILLIAMSITE, see SERPENTINE

ZINCITE
Faceted gems cut only from transparent material from Franklin, New jersey; the best are deep orange-red in hue, resembling slightly orangy pyrope; poor zincites have been cut from very blackish-red material which is so dark that the gems cannot be over 2-3 mm. if they are to show any reflections. Extremely rare; specimens highly prized by collectors. Record gem in Smithsonian collections, just over 20 carats; however, any good color gem from ½ to 3 ct. is considered very desirable.

Deep orange-red, ½-3 ct.	ct.	100.00-400.000
Deep orange-red, 4-6 ct.	ct.	200.00-600.00
Blackish-red, very dark, ¼-½ ct.	ct.	25.00-50.00

ZIRCON
Most commercial gems, especially blues, are faceted in Thailand from local material; also in quantity from Sri Lanka; a few gems are supplied by Australia. From colorless to various shades of brown, red, green, yellow, gold, orange, blue, and purple. Color desirability as follows: rich red, orange-red, fine blue, green, orange, yellow, pale blue, and colorless. Considerable variation in asking prices among dealers, especially for blue gems. The metamict zircons from Sri Lanka are commonly various shades of green and cannot change color when heat treated; however, ordinary zircons from Thailand and Sri Lanka, usually some shade of brown or red-brown as recovered from gravel deposits, are heat-treated to colorless, blue, blue-green, yellow, etc., or the natural color lightened through successive shades of brown to red or yellow. Metamict

greens usually slightly milky. Some blues are light-sensitive, becoming mottled with whitish or greenish tinges after long exposure to light. Because of large double-refraction, best-quality gems are cut to minimize the "fuzziness" of reflections, especially in gems over 5 carats. Common defects are striated polishes, optical "fuzziness," interior milkiness, and chipped edges due to careless handling of gems.

Red, orange-red, medium dark, 1-5 ct.	ct.	18.00-70.00
Red, orange-red, medium dark, 10 ct.	ct.	70.00-100.00
Red, orange-red, medium dark, 15 ct.	ct.	75.00-125.00
Same, medium intensity, 1-15 ct.	ct.	12.00-70.00
Same, light intensity, 1-15 ct.	ct.	10.00-40.00
Purplish-red, medium, 1-15 ct.	ct.	7.00-50.00
Pure blue, medium dark, 1-5 ct.	ct.	50.00-100.00
Pure blue, medium dark, 10 ct.	ct.	150.00-250.00
Pure blue, medium dark, 15 ct.	ct.	200.00-300.00
Pure blue, medium, 1-15 ct.	ct.	15.00-150.00
Pure blue, light, 1-15 ct.	ct.	10.00-150.00
Blue, rd. brills., 3-12 mm. (to 6 ct.)	ea.	5.00-80.00
Blue, oct. step cuts, oval brills., 7x5-16x12 mm. (1-10 ct.)	ea.	10.00-150.00
Blue, tinged with green, medium dark, 1-5 ct.	ct.	15.00-45.00
Blue, tinged with green, medium dark, 110 ct.	ct.	20.00-60.00
Blue, tinged with green, medium dark, 115 ct.	ct.	40.00-100.00
Blue, tinged with green, etc., medium, 1-15 ct.	ct.	5.00-100.00
Blue, tinged with green, etc., light, 1-15 ct.	ct.	2.00-35.00
Green, medium dark, 1-5 ct.	ct.	10.00-40.00
Green, medium dark, 10 ct.	ct.	10.00-45.00
Green, medium dark, 15 ct.	ct.	10.00-40.00
Green, medium, 1-15 ct.	ct.	4.00-16.00
Green, light, 1-15 ct.	ct.	4.00-12.00
Orange, medium to light, 1-15 ct.	ct.	10.00-30.00
Yellow, medium to light, 1-15 ct.	ct.	5.00-15.00
Brown, medium to light, 1-15 ct.	ct.	5.00-12.00
Brown, rd. brills., 3-12 mm. (to 6 ct.)	ea.	5.00-75.00
Brown, oct. step cuts, oval brills., 7x5-16x12 mm. (1-10 ct.)	ea.	15.00-225.00

ZOISITE

The massive pink variety, thulite, is sometimes cut in cabochons but is soft and difficult to polish. Extremely beautiful faceted gems, resembling Kashmir sapphires, have been cut from the crystals recently found in Tanzania; faceted gems to 50 or 60 carats are known, flawless.

Cabochons, thulite, rds., 4-25 mm., ovals to 40x30 mm.	ea.	1.50-10.00
Tanzania, faceted, step cuts, 1-5 ct.	ct.	15.00-40.00
Tanzania, faceted, step cuts, 6-15 ct.	ct.	20.00-60.00
Tanzania, faceted, step cuts, 15-30 ct.	ct.	30.00-75.00

TANZANITE

Tanzanite was discovered in Tanzania, East Africa in the late 1960s. The East African zoisite is found in average stone sizes 3-10 carats. The gem displays a strongly violetish-blue color, the result of heat treatment to induce a permanent color change from brownish to bluish. The stone is strongly trichroic.

Purple, bluish purple, violet, very fine 1-3 cts.	ct.	185.00-575.00
Purple, bluish purple, violet, very fine 3-5 cts.	ct.	345.00-900.00
Purple, bluish purple, violet, very fine 5-10 cts.	ct.	420.00-1,200.00
Purple, bluish purple, violet, very fine 10-20 cts.	ct.	550.00-1,800.00
Good quality blue, moderate flaws, 1-3 cts.	ct.	60.00-290.00

Good quality blue, moderate flaws, 3-5 cts.	ct.	150.00-475.00
Good quality blue, moderate flaws, 5-10 cts.	ct.	200.00-675.00
Commercial quality, pale-medium color, 1-3 cts.	ct.	40.00-150.00
Commercial quality, pale-medium color, 3-5 cts.	ct.	80.00-250.00
Commercial quality, pale-medium color, 5-10 cts.	ct.	100.00-300.00

V

ENGRAVED GEMS

AMONG THE EXQUISITE PRODUCTIONS OF THE LAPIDARY ARTS are the miniature sculptures known as *engraved gems*. While some are as large as several inches in diameter, most are less than one inch. Despite their small size, skilled carvers specializing in this class of work are able to impart an astonishing wealth of detail in one of two major styles of carving, *cameo* or *intaglio*. When the subjects rise *above* the base of the gem in shallow relief carving, it is called cameo, and, conversely, when the subjects are created by scooping out material, that is, grinding away cavities *below* the surface of the gem, it is called intaglio. Both kinds of work are shown in the sketches of Figure 36. The *cuvette* combines features of both by creating a shallow relief sculpture resting in a depression of the gem, such that the sculpture does not rise above the top surface. *Seals* are intaglios incised with coats-of-arms or symbols, with the depressions left as-is or filled with metal. *Scarabs* are miniature representations of the sacred beetle of the ancient Egyptians, with or without symbolic engraving. They have some vogue today as stones for bracelets.

USE OF LAYERED GEMSTONES

Much of the effectiveness of engraved gems depends on the use of multi-colored layers in gemstones as also indicated in Figure 36. Strong contrasts are especially effective in cameos where the subjects are carved in a pale-colored layer resting upon a background of dark material. By careful thinning of the upper, pale-colored layer, the skilled artist is able to impart striking realism to portraits, particularly in the flesh tones of the human face. A fine example is shown in Figure 37, in this instance, a typical cameo in shell produced at the famous cameo center of Torre del Greco near Naples, Italy. Strong color contrasts are also obtained in banded chalcedonies, but useful material is more difficult to obtain than shell. Sometimes chalcedonies are found in which there are three or more layers of contrasting color, in which cases the engraver is able to take advantage of them

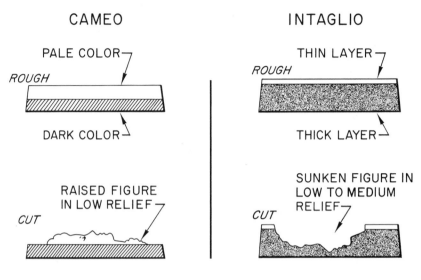

FIG. 36
The basic types of engraved gems shown in cross-sections.

to even greater effect than is possible with single- or double-color -material. In Figure 38, for example, the artist used the top layer for hair, a lower white layer for facial features, and a dark bottom layer for the background.

Contrasting colors are also used effectively in intaglios, either by piercing through a thin top layer of pale-colored material, or by reversing the layers to make the subjects appear light against dark backgrounds. However, most intaglios are cut from single-color material.

EVALUATION OF ENGRAVED GEMS

The factor of intrinsic value of the gem material itself is not as important in engraved gems as it is in either faceted or cabochon gems. Mainly the materials are selected for their ability to take the fine detail required for high-class work. While some cameos and intaglios have been made from such valuable materials as ruby, sapphire, emerald, and opal, by far most cameos are made from relatively inexpensive shell and intaglios from various types of chalcedony. Thus the cost of the basic material is seldom a major factor in the retail price, unless, as will be explained below, the material is hard and therefore requires the expenditure of much work to shape it. In other instances, the cost rises appreciably when an engraved

FIG. 37
A fine large cameo cut upon the exterior of a *Cassis madagascariensis* shell in Naples, Italy. The shell is about 7 inches tall.

gem is prepared from layered chalcedonies, because these are far less abundant in nature than ordinary single-color chalcedonies.

DESIGN EXECUTION

The shell cameo in Figure 37 shows how much exquisite detail can be imparted to the design, and even more important, how the very low relief can be made to project itself upward, as if the head of the subject actually rose much higher above its background than is really the case. The art of creating such illusions, coupled

FIG. 38
Two fine cameos cut in banded chalcedony. The artist has cleverly taken advantage of the different color layers to bring out the design.
(Courtesy Field Museum of Natural History, Chicago)

with taste in the choice of designs and a delicate touch in carving the gently sloping contours of facial and body features, is the essence of first-class gem engraving. It has been said that the true artist-engraver must know all that the professional sculptor knows, but unlike the latter, he must work within the confines of microscopic frame, using microscopic tools on microscopic subjects.

Therefore it is important to remember in judging engraved gems that the choice of design is of paramount importance, just as it is in the much larger studio sculptures. Next, the design must be executed with skill and careful attention to fine detail. If the subjects are meant to faithfully portray human figures, they must be anatomically correct. Finally, the details of the work should stand up to the closest scrutiny in regard to precision and quality of workmanship. The best work shows perfect gradations in slope upon facial and body features, crisp edges without "overshoots" caused by slips of the engraving tools, and surface finishes which are appropriate to the subject, that is, a glossy or matte finish for skin, a rougher texture for fur, clothing, or wood, or minute striations to simulate hair tresses or the bark of trees, to name a few examples.

Even if one is not sure of his ability to judge the artistic merits of a design upon an engraved gem, the fact remains that *the finest workmanship is usually expended on the best materials by the most skilled engravers, generally upon the most artistically meritorious designs that are possible to devise.* While it sometimes happens that a topnotch engraver is called upon to create a fine gem from a poor design, this occurs so rarely that this possibility can be discounted for all practical purposes.

Materials Used

Cameos are commonly carved from shell, usually the *Cassis*, or helmet, shell. Any kind of shell is vastly softer than those gemstones classed as "soft" by mineralogists, except for a few exceptions such as soapstone, alabaster, and calcite onyx which are comparable in softness to shells. In any event, shell is much softer than the hard and tough chalcedony gemstones which are commonly used in intaglios. Despite its softness, shell is uniform in texture, fairly tough, and also durable, if treated with reasonable care. Shell cameos are shaped with steel tools, gouges, and points, and finished with files and loose abrasive powders. The cheap "tourist souvenir" cameos, generally less than one inch in size, are given only the minimum detail, often very crudely. From a short distance they look good, but close examination shows sloppiness in execution. The better work appears on the larger cameos, with much more attention being paid to the quality of the shell, the kind of design, and the workmanship expended.

The natural size limitations of the *Cassis* shell prevent making cameos much larger than about 3" in diameter. Larger ones could be made, but the curvature of the shell would cause mountings to become so deep that brooches and pins would also become awkward to wear. The *Strombus gigas*, or West Indies conch, has also been used for cameos but the pink layer beneath the white outer layer affords only a weak color contrast, and for this reason the much stronger contrast in the *Cassis* shells is vastly preferred.

Hardness of Materials and Cost

In contrast to shell cameos, those carved in chalcedonies, moonstone, opal, and labradorite, to name a few that have been used, necessarily take much longer to carve because all of these materials are harder than steel and require the use of tedious and time-consuming abrasive processes. The engraver is therefore forced to use diamond powder as the abrasive, applied to a succession of small rotating copper wheels to achieve shaping. These initial shaping steps must then be followed by the use of finer powders upon another set of wheels to impart suitable finishes to all the surfaces. The time factor, plus the long training period required to merely learn the mastery of the tools, causes all work in hard gemstones to be much more expensive.

Other factors contributing to cost are the costliness of the diamond powder itself, the large variety of shaping tools which must be used, and the machinery necessary to hold and spin these points. Lastly, the cost of suitable chalcedonies is always a factor because very few natural examples either have the proper color to begin with, in which case they must be dyed, or lack color-contrasting layers. While *Cassis* shells are always the same in respect to coloring of layers, this cannot be said of chalcedonies.

The problem of obtaining suitable one-color material for intaglios is much less severe because any naturally or artificially pigmented gemstone will do, provided that it is uniform in texture and color, sufficiently tough and fine-grained, and free of disfiguring cracks and flaws.

QUALITY OF DETAIL

Shell cameos are often more precisely cut than mineral cameos or intaglios because the carver can keep his steel tools continually sharpened as the work progresses. This is not possible with diamond-impregnated metal wheels which must be used for shaping the much harder mineral gemstones, because once a wheel is charged with diamond its shape cannot be easily altered thereafter. However, extremely fine detail is possible, if the engraver carefully forms his wheels before they are charged with diamond, or uses specially mounted slivers of diamond to sculpt the finest details of the design. But this technique calls for much time and care, and is generally not used except in the highest-class work.

OPTICAL EFFECTS IN ENGRAVED GEMS

Engraved gems cut from moonstone, sunstone, tigereye, or labradorite should be cut to place the optical effect of each squarely on top. In cameos, the relief should be shallow so that the optical effect appears to best advantage; if the relief is too high, only an occasional glimmer will appear on those places which are nearly flat. This requirement is most critical in gemstones whose reflections appear in sharply defined planes or layers; it is less critical in sunstone and moonstone.

ANTIQUES AND FAKES

It is very unlikely that genuine antique engraved gems will be offered to the average buyer, because most known examples have long since made their way into museum collections. A few are found from time to time in building, road, and archeological excavations in Italy, Greece, and Near East countries, but these quickly pass into the hands of government officials responsible for preserving national treasures. Most so-called "antique" gems are really recent works, perhaps no older than the last century when engraved gems were produced in quantity to satisfy the demands of collectors who were more numerous than now. Many of the 19th-century gems were deliberate fakes, even to the point of employing ancient styles and subjects, simulating older tool marks, using the same materials, and producing artificial "aging" by various means. The tourist in the countries mentioned above may be offered such gems, but unless he is a keen student of the subject, he will certainly not be able to distinguish a fake from a real antique merely by a cursory examination. While shell cameos may be as much as several hundreds of years old, if they were carefully preserved to begin with, they cannot survive burial over centuries without disintegrating or decomposing. Any shell cameo offered as dating from Roman times, for example, is almost certain to be a modern specimen and should be rejected.

SIZE AND ITS EFFECTS ON PRICES

For all practical purposes, cameos and intaglios are approximately tabular or disk-like in shape, and the cost of engraving can be tied directly to the area. For rectangular shapes, the rise in price with increase in dimensions can be easily calculated by obtaining the dimensions and multiplying them to obtain the areas. For ovals or circles, the rise in price with increasing diameters can be calculated by using the formula for the area of a circle, *pi x r x r*, where *r* is one-half the diameter, and pi is 3.14. As an example, we wish to compare prices of two shell cameos, one two inches in diameter and the other three inches in diameter. How much more should the larger one cost if the smaller one costs $40? We find the answer as follows:

Multiply out the dimensions and pi as given in the formula above—

(a) 3.14 x 1 x 1 = 3.14 sq. in. for the first cameo, costing $40
(b) 3.14 x 1.5 x 1.5 = 7.1 sq. in. for the second cameo.

We now can readily see that the second cameo, while only one inch more in diameter than the first one, is actually over twice the area of the first and should therefore cost about $80, or perhaps even more. It is quite possible that the cost of the larger cameo will be appreciably greater than $80 because the nature of the *Cassis* shell is such that only one large flattish area exists upon which cameos can be cut without the excessive curvature mentioned earlier causing bulkiness in mounted jewelry. Thus it costs more to turn out one large cameo from the shell than it does to turn out smaller examples, of which more can be fitted into the same flattish area. We can therefore expect to pay a premium for the largest shell cameos, substantially over that required by the use of the area formula described above. A similar premium can be expected for cameos carved from mineral gemstones, because flawless large specimens are much rarer than smaller ones.

ENGRAVING CENTERS AND CHARGES FOR WORK

Practically all shell cameos are carved in the famous center of Torre Del Greco, not far from Naples, Italy. The smallest, and usually crudest, gems are turned out by apprentices, who rise through experience and improving skill into master workmen capable of executing the largest and finest gems. The production is marketed through dealers in Naples, who, in turn, export the cameos to foreign and domestic wholesalers and retailers. Work in hard gemstones, such as chalcedony, is rarely attempted, although some soft and porous volcanic rocks of local origin have been cut into excellent, high-relief cameos in years past.

The next major center is located in Idar-Oberstein, Germany, where a number of individual artists and a few specialty shops engrave, for the most part, intaglios in hard to soft gemstones. Much of the output is seal stones, produced either by the classical abrasion method or by acid etching. A much smaller quantity of true artistic works is produced by a few masters and their apprentices. Special commissions are executed on order, with details of materials, designs, sizes, etc., arranged between artist and customer. One well-known engraver produces high-quality cameos and intaglios in any kind of gemstone in the size range of 20 to 50 millimeters. The charges range from $200 to $1,000, depending on size and complexity of the design. Portraits are more costly because they must be recognizable likenesses acceptable to customers. They are prepared from one or more photographs taken from the desired angle. The charges for portrait gems from 20 to 50 millimeters in size are approximately $500 to $1,500, the charge depending on the difficulty of the portrait, a full face work being more difficult than a profile, for example, and the type of material used.

A very few individual artists work elsewhere in the world, but their numbers are decreasing because of the current indifference to fine-quality engraved gems and the relative cheapness and abundance of Italian shell cameos.

ULTRASONICALLY CARVED AGATE CAMEOS

Cameos and intaglios have been cut by ultrasonic methods since the 1970s in Idar-Oberstein. The Japanese learned to use the machinery and adopted this method of cameo cutting in the 1980s and have exported thousands of carats of machine-cut agate cameos into the U.S. market. The ultrasonic method of carving is only useful on hard materials with regular surfaces, therefore, is not used with shell. Most ultrasonically cut cameos today come from Idar-Oberstein, Japan and Hong Kong workshops.

Agate, blue and white woman's profile, 12x10-16x12 mm	ea.	38.00-58.00
Agate, black and white woman's profile, 12x10-16x12 mm.	ea.	35.00-70.00
Agate, blue and white, woman's profile, 18x13-25x18 mm.	ea.	75.00-88.00
Agate, black and white, woman's profile, 18x13-25x18 mm.	ea.	69.00-85.00
Agate, blue and white, woman's profile, 30x32-40x30 mm.	ea.	160.00-215.00
Agate, black and white, woman's profile, 30x32-40x30 mm.	ea.	140.00-185.00
Agate, blue and white, horse head, 18x13 mm.	ea.	40.00
Agate, blue and white, horse head, 30x22 mm.	ea.	100.00
Agate, blue and white, pair of running horses, 40x30 mm.	ea.	190.00

PAIR OF CAMEOS FOR EARRINGS (right and left facing designs)

Agate, blue and white, woman's head, 16x12 mm.	ea.	60.00
Agate, blue and white, woman's head, 25x18 mm.	ea.	40.00
Agate, blue and white, woman's head, 30x22 mm.	ea.	77.00
Agate, blue and white, woman's head, 40x30 mm.	ea.	150.00

IMITATIONS

Engraved gems have been imitated in plastics, glasses, and porcelain, generally by casting or molding in a master die. They can be easily distinguished by their lack of tool marks and crisp details. Many cameo-like porcelain imitations made by the famous china makers, Wedgwood, of England, are still available in the antique market.

PRICES OF ENGRAVED GEMS

The brief lists below provide information only on the easily obtainable shell cameos of Italy and the hardstone intaglios and cameos of Germany. Both countries mass-produce large numbers of relatively inexpensive engraved gems which are far less costly than either the special order gems described in a previous section, or the artistic works produced by a few individuals. Naturally they will not display the sharp detail, inspired designs, or the superb workmanship expected in the high-priced special-order gems. It also true, as a general rule, that one may find cameos and intaglios dating from the previous century which are of better quality than modern works. These are sometimes available in antique furniture or jewelry shops.

CAMEOS, HARDSTONE

Available in standard oval, octagon, and cushion shapes; the layered chalcedony gems are usually cut from dyed material and may be single-, double-, or triple-layer. The following are individually cut from a master gemstone carver in Idar-Oberstein.

Chalcedony, black/white "mother and child," 47x25 mm.	ea.	850.00
Chalcedony, blue/white "mother and child," 44x31.5 mm.	ea.	550.00
Chalcedony, green/white "mother and child," 46.5 mm.	ea.	1,000.00
Chalcedony, red/white "mother and child," 45x35 mm.	ea.	675.00
Chalcedony, black/white Woman's silhouette, 49x35 mm.	ea.	850.00
Round design, black/white, golf club and ball, 20 mm.	ea.	110.00
Round design, black/white, agate dinosaur design, 20 mm.	ea.	110.00
Round design, carnelian, brontosauraus design, 20 mm.	ea.	110.00

REGULAR PRODUCTION LINE:

Chalcedony, paired warrior heads, black, white, black 10x9-20x15 mm.	ea.	300.00-600.00
Chalcedony, paired warrior heads, black, white, red, 10x8-20x15 mm.	ea.	300.00-600.00
Chalcedony, single head, brown or black, 10x8-20x15 mm.	ea.	200.00-400.00
Chalcedony, paired head, brown or black, 10x8-20x15 mm.	ea.	250.00-450.00
Tigereye, single head, good, 10x8-20x 15 mm.	ea.	75.00-125.00
Tigereye, single head, fair, 10x8-20x 15 mm.	ea.	60.00-100.00
Tigereye, paired heads, good, 12x10-20x15 mm.	ea.	90.00-250.00
Tigereye, paired heads, fair, 12x10-20x15 mm.	ea.	60.00-150.00
Hematite, single heads, 12x10-20x15 mm.	ea.	25.00-50.00
Hematite, paired heads, 12x10-20x15 mm.	ea.	30.00-60.00
Amethyst, single head, 18x13 mm.	ea.	60.00-150.00
Various materials, designs to order, high quality, 20-50 mm.	ea.	35.00-350.00
Various materials, portraits to order, high quality, 20-50 mm.	ea.	550.00-1,500.00

CAMEOS, SHELL

Italian manufacture, from *Cassis rufa*, a helmet shell which provides a ground layer of brownish-red material and a yellowish-white top layer, or from *Cassis madagascarensis*, a helmet shell which is dark to medium brown in color with a pure white top layer.

Woman's head, single, good quality, 10x8-20x15 mm.	ea.	15.75-85.00
Woman's head, single, good quality, 25-35 mm. sizes	ea.	45.00-60.00
Woman's head, single, good quality, 30x40 mm. ovals	ea.	100.00-120.00
Woman's head, single, fair quality, 10x8-20x15 mm.	ea.	12.00-55.00
Woman's head, single, fair quality, 20-25 mm. sizes	ea.	45.00-60.00
Woman's head, single, poor quality, 10x8-25x18 mm.	ea.	6.00-45.00
Woman's head, single, good, modern hair styling, 15x20-19x25 mm.	ea.	60.00-85.00

CAMEOS, CORAL

Woman's head, single, 12x9-15x7 mm.	ea	20.00-45.00

Woman's head, boldly carved, fine quality, 30x25 mm.   ea.   100.00-200.00

MOTHER-OF-PEARL CAMEOS

Mother-of-pearl cameo heads, hand carved, black backgrounds, fair to crude carvings.

Mother- of-pearl cameos, 12x10-18x13 mm.	ea.	5.00-6.00
Mother-of-pearl cameos, 25x19-40x30 mm.	ea.	7.50-14.00

INTAGLIOS, HARDSTONE

Available in standard ovals, octagons, cushions, and antiques. Practically all are made from single-color material, but some are engraved to shallow depth and the design grooves filled with gold.

Chalcedony, black, warrior head,10x8-22x16 mm.	ea.	15.00-45.00
Carnelian, warrior head, 10x8-22x16 mm.	ea.	15.00-45.00
Hematite, warrior head, 10x8-22x16 mm.	ea.	15.00-45.00
Synthetic ruby, warrior head, 10x8-16x12 mm.	ea.	45.00-100.00
Synthetic ruby, blue spinel, warrior head, 10x8-16x12 mm.	ea.	25.00-65.00
Various materials, designs to order, high quality, 20-50 mm.	ea.	100.00-250.00
Various materials, portraits to order high quality, 20-50 mm.	ea.	550.00-1,800.00
Gold inlay, black chalcedony, warrior head, 10x8-20x15 mm.	ea.	10.00-65.00
Gold inlay, carnelian, warrior head, 10x8-20x15 mm.	ea.	20.00-90.00
Gold inlay, hematite, warrior head, 10x8-20x15 mm.	ea.	10.00-70.00
Gold inlay, synthetic ruby, warrior head, 10x8-18x13 mm.	ea.	25.00-125.00
Gold inlay, synthetic blue spinel, warrior head, 10x8-18x13 mm.	ca.	20.00-45.00
Gold inlay, nephrite, warrior head, rd., 21 mm.	ea.	15.00-35.00
Crests, arms, etc., plain or inlaid gold, to order	ea.	30.00-50.00
Zodiacal signs, cushion shape, gold inlaid, 12x10-16x12 mm.	ea.	20.00-40.00
Zodiacal signs, cushion shape, gold inlaid, jade rds., 18-25 mm.	ea.	10.00-40.00

SCARABS

According to material, 14x10 mm.	ea.	10.00-25.00

VI
CARVINGS AND
MISCELLANEOUS GEMSTONE
OBJECTS

THE USE OF THE TERM "CARVING" IS SOMEWHAT MISLEADING because gemstones, with a few exceptions, are far too hard to shape with chisels such as used by a wood carver in creating his sculptures. Instead, the gem carver is forced to grind away the stone in a tedious, time-consuming, and costly series of hand-directed operations until the carving is shaped. Even here his work is not complete, for all surfaces must be smoothed, fine details added, and the whole finished to perfection. Furthermore, when it is considered that gemstone carvings can be as artistically important as other types of fine art works, it is easy to understand why some skillfully fashioned and artistically meritorious carvings are so expensive.

Allied to carving, but seldom calling for the artistry and wondrous hand skills of the expert sculptor in gemstones, are the ornamental objects which are sold in large quantities every year. Among them are purely geometrical objects such as beads and spheres, paper weights, book ends, desk pen bases, and ash trays, and some, such as free-form bowls and trays, which are more difficult to make and therefore more costly.

The first part of this chapter describes various types of carvings and the other objects referred to, with remarks on quality, materials used, sources of supply, and other information of value to prospective purchasers, and ends with retail price listings.

Types of Carvings

The most difficult carvings are called *in-the-round* because they are fully shaped on all sides in three-dimensional representations. They are more challenging to the carver because they must look well from all aspects and not merely from the front. In most in-the-round work only the bottom is left unfinished, but some meticulous craftsmen even take the trouble to finish the details in this area which is normally hidden from view. A modification of in-the-round sculpture is seen in screens and panels, especially of Chinese origin, in which the carving is complete and interconnected on both sides, with pierced work as appropriate to the design. Other shallow carvings are in relief, which is to say that the sculpture is shallow and the objects portrayed appear to emerge from the background of solid stone. This kind of work is identical to the cameo work previously described, but is generally on a much larger scale. Incised work, or intaglio, is used in screens and panels, plaques, and other broad surfaces, sometimes in extremely delicate and complicated designs. There are many other carving variations possible, the only limits being the physical form of the rough, the kind of subjects the artist wishes to portray, and the techniques used to obtain desired results.

Artistic Value of Carvings

Unlike facet and cabochon gems which are shaped according to well established rules, the carver of gemstones is allowed the greatest freedom of expression. if his talents are equal to the task, he can produce works of art which are comparable in every respect, except in size, to those produced by the professional sculptor. Such gemstone sculptures are judged according to the same artistic rules, of which the most important is that the object of art should arouse an emotional response or "feeling" within the viewer. A few examples will clarify what is meant by such responses.

The Harvill carving shown in Figure 39 is much more than a realistic representation of a human being. It is, in fact, the story of life itself, and of man's faith in his own future. This is shown by the actions of the old man who plants a sapling, knowing full well that he will not live to see it mature. Yet, because of his faith in the future, he is happy to plant the sapling in his lifetime so that those who succeed him will reap the benefits of his actions. Thus, when we study Harvill's carving and let our minds think about what is being portrayed, we begin to identify ourselves with the subject and feel a sympathetic response, possibly because we remember past actions of our own that were based solely on our faith in the future.

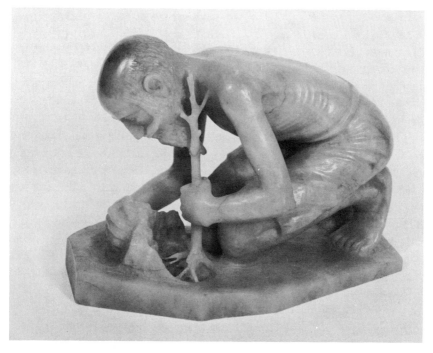

FIG. 39
The remarkable jadeite carving of R. S. Harvill of Sinton, Texas, entitled "Old Man Planting a Tree." (Courtesy R. S. Harvill)

Other emotional responses to the subjects portrayed in sculptures can range from serious to joyful. For example, the horse depicted in the rock crystal sculpture of Figure 40 cannot but help appeal to any admirer of horses and horsemanship. Merely viewing this miniature sculpture evokes memories of brisk canters through woods and fields, or other pleasurable activities associated with horses. Another response may be of an inspirational nature, depending upon the customs and traditions of the culture concerned. For example, the rock crystal sculpture of Turgenev (1818-1883), the celebrated Russian novelist, shown in Figure 41, could serve as a constant reminder to viewers of the qualities which made Turgenev an important historical figure in the world of literature. Inspiration may also be derived from carvings representing gods, deities, and saints, or popular folk tales and adventures based on the lives of important personages. Finally, an emotional response, as pointed out before under discussions of attractiveness in faceted and cabochon gems, may be a relatively simple reaction to a beautifully colored, patterned, or shaped carving.

Regardless of the exact nature of the emotional response evoked by a carving, the connoisseur of the fine arts or the learned collector is apt to judge a gemstone

FIG. 40
A horse cut in rock crystal by an unknown
Russian lapidary of the 19th century. The
detail and the use of matte finish is
particularly good.
(Courtesy Field Museum of Natural History, Chicago)

carving on the basis of its "message" or appeal to his sensibilities. If at the same
time the carving is made from suitable material and is skillfully executed, he may
accord it the highest possible marks in his personal esteem. On the other hand, if
the "message" is weak, trivial, or merely non-existent, the factor of artistic value
declines to the point where the object is judged solely on the basis of its ornamental or utilitarian value.

VALUE RELATED TO CHOICE OF SUBJECT

The selection of a meaningful subject or design for a carving strongly influ-
ences the price asked for it. Some subjects are far more difficult to execute convincingly than others, mainly because strict fidelity to the original is required if
they are to "look right." In this class are carvings portraying human beings. We
are so familiar with our fellow men that we feel uneasy whenever we see a carving which contains an anatomical error or some awkward pose. While we may
not be good enough students of anatomy to identify the place where the carver
went wrong, we know that something is amiss and react accordingly. Thus,
when the carver attempts a faithful human portrayal, his task is most demand-

FIG. 41
A bust of the Russian novelist Turgenev,
executed in rock crystal by an unknown
Russian lapidary of the 19th century. The
effect of dark velvet lapels is brought out by
the use of a polished surface.
(Courtesy Field Museum of Natural History, Chicago)

ing if his work is to escape criticism. Not many gemstone carvers are willing to take up the long training in art required to do human subjects, preferring instead to stick to "safer" subjects such as animals, plants, or inanimate objects with which more liberties can be taken. The least demanding works are those which have no particular meaning, such as book ends, bowls, spheres, and other geometrical forms.

Thus, in judging carvings, we may use the choice of subject as an evaluation factor, remembering that the order of difficulty proceeds downward from the undraped human figure, which is most difficult of all, to portraits, thence to draped figures, and then to animals. After these come subjects from plant life, followed by inanimate objects. This order is usually a good approximation of the amount of time spent in conceiving and sketching the design as well as in carving.

Closely related to this discussion is the *originality* of the design, a factor which is given great weight by art experts who have seen so many carvings that they are seldom surprised by a new carving remarkable for the freshness of its concept. Among Chinese snuff bottles, for example, there is a sameness about many of them because unimaginative carvers tended to reproduce certain designs, varying the designs a little, or the material, but essentially carving the same bottle over and over again. The same may be said for many modern carvings of animals and gods which are mass-produced in various centers throughout the world. In Kofu, the famous carving center of Japan, visitors report that they have seen carvers specialized to such a degree that one will turn out nothing but dogs, another lions, and still another, Kwan Yin goddesses. Such carvers soon become so efficient that they can literally turn out these subjects in their sleep. Naturally the artistic merits of such pieces are of a very low order and the prices asked reflect only the relatively small costs incurred for labor, material, and handling. To the other extreme lie the carvings which are specially commissioned, either carved by copying a careful sketch or small model supplied by the customer, or carved on speculation from an idea conceived by the artist-carver. Such objects will generally be carved from the highest-quality material suitable for the design and will show superb craftsmanship in all phases of lapidary work. In a following section, the hallmarks of high-quality work will be described and discussed, but for the moment it is enough to say that carvings of this kind are the most costly.

HISTORICAL AND ANTIQUE VALUES

It would not be far wrong to claim that few, if any, of the skills developed by carvers in past centuries cannot be achieved today. If necessary, it is still possible to arrange for duplicates to be made of older works, reproducing all details exactly, in the same gemstone material as used in the original. In fact, some experts claim that forgeries and skillful imitations of the famous, and now enormously expensive carvings of the Fabergé shops of Tsarist Russia, are in circulation and cannot be told from the genuine articles. Be that as it may, the fact remains that Fabergé carvings, and the much older Chinese carvings, represent bygone periods of art and culture, reflecting the customs and traditions of the times and therefore becoming important relics of interest to the archeologist and sociologist as well as to the art connoisseur and historian. Thus antique values are attached to many carvings which, in many instances, outweigh the artistic values, particularly if the pieces happen to be among the few surviving shreds of evidence as to the nature of some ancient civilization. It is for this reason that some rather poorly executed jade carvings from ancient Chinese tombs, or seals and intaglios from ancient Mediterranean and Near East cultures are valued far above modern copies made from better materials with better workmanship.

VALUE OF UNIQUE OR UNUSUAL MATERIALS

If any carving is unique in some respect, it will appeal to the connoisseur who recognizes this fact and is far more likely to place a much greater value upon it.

For example, there is in the Morgan Gem Hall of the American Museum of Natural History in New York City a lovely carving, less than a foot tall, of a nude young woman executing a ballet step, carved realistically and with impeccable skill, from a flawless block of pale blue-gray chalcedony. While the subject is not new, the connoisseur is aware of the fact that very few statues of this kind have ever been done in such a hard and recalcitrant material as chalcedony and, further, in such perfect chalcedony, whose delicate hue and evenness of texture enabled the artistry of the carver to appear at its best. This object is truly unique, a fact we could have assumed from its inclusion in a collection of worldwide fame.

The expert is well aware of the value of unique or unusual materials, examining each carving presented to him on this basis as well as upon the basis of artistic merit. Rare and beautiful materials often cause a drastic increase in price even if used in such commonplace objects as bowls and spheres, particularly if the material itself seldom occurs in large masses. We see this factor at work in the prices asked for flawless rock crystal spheres which are relatively simple to grind and polish to geometrical perfection. In nature, rock crystal occurs abundantly in sizes large enough to yield spheres from 1" to about 3" in diameter, but larger specimens containing suitable areas become increasingly rare until few are capable of furnishing perfect spheres of from 4" to 6" in diameter. Those which are larger still are practically unobtainable. It is for this reason that the officials of the Smithsonian Institution in Washington, D.C., are so proud of their flawless Warner rock crystal sphere with the astonishing diameter of 12½"! This object, possessing no more artistic merit than any other sphere of rock crystal, is nevertheless unique in respect to size and perfection of the material.

Other rare or unusual materials which excite interest whenever they appear in carvings are ruby, sapphire, precious opal, peridot, and spinel, because most of this rough is ordinarily cut up for facet or cabochon gems. Ruby and sapphire are particularly unusual because of their rarity in good material and the great difficulties encountered in shaping and polishing them. Among the species and varieties which occur in carving grade, the following are considered unusual when of good quality: rich blue aquamarine, fine chrysoprase, chrysocolla chalcedony, tourmalinated quartz, sagenitic quartz, and uniformly colored amethyst lacking conspicuous flaws or inclusions. More common materials include rock crystal, rose quartz, citrine, smoky quartz, tigereye, various chalcedonies, jaspers and agates, aventurine quartz, serpentine, rhodonite, nephrite, jadeite, and amazonite. For small carvings, tourmaline, moonstone, and turquois are also commonly employed.

SUITABILITY OF GEMSTONES FOR CARVING

Many gemstones are sufficiently fine-grained to accept the most delicate engraved detail. However, if strength is required also, the choices open to the carver narrow very quickly. For example, rock crystal obviously can be carved in fine detail, as shown in Figures 40 and 41, but if it were to be used in extremely thin-walled bowls, or in the Chinese vases decorated by delicate floral sprays, its lack of toughness could easily result in breakage during the carving process. For projects calling for very thin sections, slender projections, delicate chains and links, or other inherently weak sections, few gemstones can compare in strength to jadeite or nephrite. The physical properties of these jades account for the fact that so many carvings of great complexity with pierced and open work are made from them.

As a result of the differences in strength, grain size, presence or absence of cleavage, hardness, and other properties, coupled with the scarcity or abundance of suitable material in sizes sufficiently large for carvings, the kind of project undertaken by the carver is governed by the nature of the material itself. This imposes a "rarity" factor which the knowing collector also takes into account when judging the value of any carving. For example, a deep blue aquamarine snuff bottle, carved with raised floral decoration of considerable delicacy, may excite the admiration of the connoisseur for two reasons: first, the material is rarer than the usual kinds of jade, and, second, the material is far more brittle than jade, thus indicating that a skilled carver worked upon the bottle and exercised extreme care to prevent breaking projections during his shaping and polishing operations. While there are thousands of ordinary jade snuff bottles in existence, very few fine aquamarine examples exist, and fewer still with the dangerously delicate work just described. Needless to say, the collector will consider the aquamarine bottle much more valuable than the usual run of jade bottles, even though the latter, due to the nature of jade itself, may be carved in far finer detail.

The table on page 212 lists common carving gemstones according to their suitability, ranging from those of great strength and capable of accepting delicate detail, to those which are incapable of being carved except into relatively massive objects with coarse detail. If a carving jumps out of its class into a higher one, it may become more valuable for the reasons given above. The gemstones are arranged vertically according to relative strength.

CLEVER USE OF COLOR AND OPTICAL EFFECTS IN CARVINGS

While many carvings are made from uniformly colored material, others contain patches, spots, or streaks of color which the clever workman incorporates into

CARVING GEMSTONES ARRANGED ACCORDING TO ORDER OF STRENGTH AND SUITABILITY FOR DETAIL

Gemstone	Finest Detail	Delicate Detail	Moderate Detail	Coarsest Detail
Extremely Strong in Thin Section				
Nephrite	xx			
Jadeite	xx	x		
Very Strong				
Chalcedony	x	xx		
Agate	x	xx	x	
Tigereye		xx		
Serpentine	xx	x		
Jasper	x	xx	x	
Rhodonite		x	xx	
Idocrase		xx	x	
Grossular		xx	x	
Strong				
Beryl	x	xx		
Tourmaline	x	xx		
Quartz (Cryst.)	x	xx		
Weak				
Moonstone	x	xx		
Hematite	x	xx		
Turquois		x	xx	
Malachite		x	xx	x
Amazonite			x	xx
Labradorite			x	xx
Rhodochrosite			x	xx
Jet		x	xx	
Weak and/or Brittle				
Fluorite		x	x	xx
Obsidian		x	x	xx
Opal	x	xx	x	
Calcite onyx			xx	xx
Howlite			x	xx
Amber		x	xx	
Gypsum			x	xx

Note: The "x" symbol means that the material is sometimes used in the class listed, and the "xx" symbol means it is regularly used in the listed class.

FIG. 42
Brown and white nephrite are most effectively used in the same piece in this carving of the legendary "three sheep" of Chinese folklore. The base is teak inlaid with wires of silver. Overall length about 6 inches.

the design. A good example of Chinese work is shown in Figure 42 where three sheep are portrayed in nephrite, one of which is carved in a brown area and the others in a whitish area. By studying the rough, the carver was able to visualize a design that would take advantage of the markedly different hues and, as can be seen, he was most successful.

The Chinese carvers, as Figure 42 indicates, were particularly skilled in utilizing non-uniform color distribution. Other examples of such skill are small floral and fruit carvings in bicolored tourmaline, cameo-like figures carved in banded agate in such a way that the base material is light and the decoration is dark, belt buckles in jadeite with bright green or red on top and pale material beneath, and snuff bottles with raised figures in one color and bodies in another. There are many other examples that could be described, but these few are sufficient to alert the buyer to the fact that such work often enhances the value of a carving which would otherwise be considered quite ordinary.

FIG. 43
A shallow relief carving in precious Australian opal. The cap has been left plain to effectively display the strong colors in that section.
(Courtesy Ward's Natural Science Establishment, Rochester)

In a similar fashion, the skilled and imaginative carver also uses differing patterns of inclusions, striations, or other features to the best advantage. Exceptionally striking results occur when strong optical effects, such as the beautiful blue or silver sheen in moonstones, are made to appear upon the face of any carving portraying a human subject. Usually such carvings must be in rather low relief if the optical display is to appear to best advantage. For example, in the low-relief precious opal of Figure 43 greater depth would only serve to lessen the play of color, and the carver rightly chose to flatten the figure rather than to increase thickness to add more realism.

Disguise of Defects in Carvings

Allied to the clever use of color, as explained above, is the equally clever placement of defects to minimize their unsightliness. This is made necessary by such materials as amethyst, aquamarine, tourmaline, and rose quartz which often occur in crystals containing noticeable cracks and fissures. Unless the carver is satisfied to cut up such rough into much smaller and relatively clean pieces which can be carved without worrying about flaws, he is forced to select a design whose details will enable him to tuck away the more glaring flaws in inconspicuous places such as deep clothing folds, spaces between arms, legs and body, and other locations where the flaw is cut away bodily or removed from direct observation.

The General Quality Rule

Before describing the signs of quality in carvings that the alert buyer will look for, it is worth expounding again the general quality rule. This rule holds good in a remarkably consistent fashion for all forms of art work, including carvings. It is: *The best work is expended on the best materials by the best craftsmen following designs created by the best artists.*

If this rule is kept firmly in mind when buying carvings, or other lapidary objects for that matter, it is possible for the buyer to partly compensate for his personal uncertainties as to the artistic merits of a particular work by paying attention to those features which do not call for such expertise, namely, the *quality* of the gemstone materialused in the carving and the *skill* with which the lapidary shaped and polished this material. Since the rules for judging quality of gemstones have already been given, it remains only to discuss specific details of workmanship which should be looked for in judging lapidary quality.

Judging Workmanship in Carvings

Because deep sculpture calls for more work than shallow sculpture, poor carvings will commonly display, among other shaping defects, clothing folds which are not deep enough, facial features that are too rounded or even "puffy" in appearance, arms and legs which look more like cylinders than muscled members of the body, and others which will be described below. A good example of inadequate shaping is shown in the Kwan Yin goddess of Figure 44. While there is some general grace to the figure, the face is nearly featureless and the deep clothing, folds and depressions between fingers are indicated only by shallow

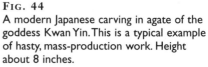

FIG. 44
A modern Japanese carving in agate of the
goddess Kwan Yin. This is a typical example
of hasty, mass-production work. Height
about 8 inches.

grooves. This carving is typical of hasty work in which reduction of labor cost
is the prime consideration.

Another short cut popular among carvers in cheap, mass-production work is
"slab-sidedness," a defect noted especially in animal carvings and due solely to the
workman not cutting away enough material to round off curved surfaces properly.
Elephants, for example, tend to show flat spots along their flanks which are the
smoothed and polished remnants of the sides of the block form which the carving
was prepared. Another sign of quality, or the lack of it, is evident in the narrow
grooves and channels which commonly appear in carvings to indicate hair or fur,
or which are used for shallow surface decoration; all striations and grooves should
be cut to uniform width and depth, with wheels fine enough to prevent fraying of
the edges. In poor work, these features easily betray the ineptness of the carver by
varying in width, overlapping or touching, or overshooting the obvious limits of
the design. Note the high quality of the grooves in the rock crystal carvings of
Figures 40 and 41.

FIG. 45
A brownish to pale greenish nephrite carved to represent a shell arising from curling waves and spray. The details are deeply incised. The carved stand matches the shape of the bottom. About 6 inches tall.

Where deep carving is attempted, the "cleaning up" of the recesses becomes a difficult and tedious task which many workmen avoid by giving only the minimum attention to the condition of the surfaces at the deepest points. High-quality treatment of recesses is shown in the nephrite carving of Figure 45

Fig. 46
The carving of Fig. 45 exposed along the bottom to show how the Chinese carver finished off the work.

where the bottoms of deep grooves and bore holes used to impart depth to the modeling have been carefully smoothed and polished. In this connection, carvers proud of their skill frequently finish off carvings completely, as shown in Figure 46, a view of the base of the carving of Figure 45. The carver carried the splashing wave motif of the upper part completely around the base and finished it off in a logical and esthetically pleasing manner. While many excellent carvings do not carry in-the-round treatment quite to this extreme, it still remains a useful indicator of quality.

POLISH AS A SIGN OF QUALITY

While a brilliant polish certainly calls for much labor, it does not necessarily mean that the carving is artistically meritorious. In fact, the opposite is often true, especially in modern mass-produced carvings which are given a dazzling finish to divert the prospective buyer's attention from serious shaping defects. In some instances, the artist's design is best brought out by a brilliant polish, but in others, particularly those in which form is all-important, as in nude sculpture, a semi-gloss to matte finish may be vastly preferable. Further, some carvings may increase in effectiveness if different finishes are applied to appropriate areas of the sculpture, as strikingly shown in the bust of Figure 41 where the then fashionable velvet lapels of men's jackets were cleverly simulated by making them much more smoothly finished than the rest of the carving. Here a better polish reduced reflections from the surfaces and made them appear black.

CARVING STANDS AS INDICATORS OF QUALITY

Many carvings are enhanced in appearance by providing them with pedestals or stands of suitable design and material. The idea is to set them off just like an important painting is set off by the use of an appropriate frame. In Figure 42, for example, the wooden stand is very plain but is ornamented with delicate inlays of silver wire. Its simplicity complements the relatively uncomplicated carving which rests upon it. On the other hand, the much more complex carving of Figures 45 and 46 is set off better by an ornately carved base which uses the same wave motif. In both examples, the stands are carefully hollowed out to exactly fit each carving.

It is obvious that previous owners of these carvings thought enough of them to provide matching stands of considerable cost, when we consider the effort that was involved in making them. While it is entirely possible that a valuable stand can be provided for a relatively poor piece of gemstone carving, it isn't very likely. In fact, in many cases, the experienced buyer of carvings finds that carvings have become separated from their bases, or sometimes a really good carving is placed upon a cheap base on the assumption that some base is better than none at all. Nevertheless, when one finds a carving fitted with an obviously "tailor made" base of excellent workmanship, it suggests that the carving itself is probably of high quality. Therefore, when buying a carving, ask to see the base and note whether it is made especially for the carving and how well it is executed in respect to design and workmanship. You may find that the stand provides valuable clues as to the true worth of the carving itself.

RULES FOR JUDGING CARVINGS

To summarize and to close the discussion on carvings, the following rules are formulated; they should be borne in mind when purchasing carvings.

ARTISTIC FACTORS

1. *Importance of the Subject.* The greatest values are ordinarily attached to carvings which portray subjects or ideas of considerable emotional appeal; somewhat lesser values are attached to portrayals of important personages or events. The individual "expression" of the artist, when characteristic of his work and appealing to our sensibilities, also increases value.

2. *Choice of Subject.* The most difficult subjects to execute are, in order, the undraped human figure, human facial features, the draped human figure, animal figures, plant life, and inanimate objects, with values usually assigned in the same order.

3. *Historical or Antique Value.* Increased value is often assigned to carvings which represent past cultures, particularly if such carvings are virtually all that remain, because more perishable evidences have been destroyed by the ravages of time. Good examples are the "tomb" jades of ancient Chinese dynasties, Middle East seal stones, and the jades of Meso-American Indian cultures.

4 *Choice of Materials.* The colors, patterns, transparency, optical effects, texture, and other properties of the gemstone materials employed by the carver must be appropriate to the subjects of the carvings.

WORKMANSHIP FACTORS

1. *Depth of Sculpture.* The finest effects appear in those carvings which are deeply carved in-the-round, with lesser values being assigned to shallower work, unless the use of the latter emphasizes some particularly handsome optical effect.

2. *Full Shaping.* The highest values for in-the-round carvings are given when all traces of the original rough block are removed; there must be no sign of *slab-sidedness*, and all recesses, such as clothing folds, seams, and wrinkles, are carved to suitable depth.

3. *Fine Details.* The accuracy, uniformity, and finish of fine details such as grooves, channels, and recesses are very useful clues as to the skill of the carver; overlapping or overshooting grooves are indicative of poor workmanship.

4. *Recess Treatment.* Deep recesses should be shaped precisely and with a surface finish appropriate to the rest of the carving.

5. *Polish.* The degree of polish must be appropriate to the subject; a brilliant glass-like polish should be regarded with suspicion because it may be an attempt to divert attention from serious deficiencies elsewhere in the carving.

6. *Disguise of Defects.* While the best carvings will ordinarily be made from the best material available, defective material can be used if the carver is sufficiently skilled to orient the rough or to adjust the design to place the defects where they will not show; how well this is done is a measure of the skill of the carver and of the value of the carving itself.

7. *Clever Use of Different Colored Areas.* Intriguing effects are produced by imaginative carvers when working with rough displaying different colored areas; if the rough is properly oriented, or the design adjusted to the rough, the value of the carving can be considerably increased.

8. *Treatment of Bottom Surfaces.* The bottom surfaces of high-class carvings, even though hidden from view, are carved and finished completely; cheaper work avoids this finishing touch.

STANDS

1. *Artistic Values.* Stands must complement the carvings and must be appropriate in respect to design, relative size, and material.

2. *Workmanship.* High-quality workmanship expended upon stands usually means that the carvings themselves are also of high quality.

OTHER TYPES OF CARVING WORK

The carver's techniques are also used to produce many decorative and utilitarian objects which are classed as carvings but are essentially non-representational. Among them are bowls, vases and urns, ash trays, boxes, pen bases, and paperweights, sometimes modeled along pure geometrical lines, or sometimes decorated with representational sculpture. On the whole, such objects call for far less artistic genius in their design and exeuction than do the true sculptures just discussed. However, graceful shaping, clever utilization of colored and patterned areas, careful attnetion to finish, and other factors, determine value just as they do in representational carvings.

The simplest objects in this class may consist of nothing more than blocks of rough gemstone material, partly shaped and polished to reveal an interesting design or pattern, or emphasizing some interesting geometrical form. From this elementary beginning they go on toward the very elaborate and skillfully carved bowls of wonderful thinness and grace which come to us from Chinese and German carvers. The prices of such objects advance step by step with the labor required to shape them, it being particularly costly to hollow out thin bowls or trays in such intractable materials as agate and jade. the difficulty in hollowing out gemstone materials, however, reaches its peak in the famous Chinese snuff bottles where all of the unwanted core material has to be removed by a tedious and time-consuming grinding process through a single opening at the top of the bottle, seldom over ⅜" in diameter. This is not an easy task even in soft gemstone rough, and accounts for the high value placed upon snuff bottles despite their small size. ˙

Bowls and vases may range from thick-walled objects to those which are thin-walled and often reduced to the point where the material becomes translucent or transparent. Beautiful results are possible with translucent agates displaying colored bands. However, because great care must be exercised during carving to prevent breakage, the work must progress slowly and cautiously and, accordingly, the price charged for such a bowl rises steeply. If decorations are added, the extra work required also reflects itself in the price, especially if the decorations take the form of raised figures whose creation requires that a great deal of material be removed from around the bowl to place the figures in relief.

The rules previously given, suitably modified for these simpler carvings, can be applied in judging their merits.

AVAILABILITY OF CARVINGS

The most consistently available high-class gemstone carvings are Chinese in origin, ranging from the ritualistic jades of several thousand years ago, to the symbolic and ornamental jades and decorative hardstone carvings produced in enormous quantity from the 17th century onward. The objects produced in this latter period are commonly offered for sale in antique stores in major cities all over the world. They range from very large urns and vases up to twenty-four inches in height, and costing many thousands of dollars, down to small pocket or "fondling" pieces of not more than two inches in diameter which sometimes can be purchased for as little as five or ten dollars.

In modern times, say in the last fifty years, an abundance of carvings has been and is still being produced in the Japanese carving center of Kofu, and more recently, in Hong Kong, to which city a number of skilled carvers have emigrated from the traditional carving centers in Peking and Canton in the mainland of China. Much work, generally sleazy, excessively fussy, and over-polished, is also available from Communist China, but is barred from the United States by customs regulations. Excellent carvings are produced in Germany but are comparatively more expensive because of the greater care and labor expended on them. The famous Russian works produced before World War I have practically vanished from the market except when some private collection is auctioned. The celebrated carvings from the Russian workshops of Fabergé are eagerly sought for and command astonishingly high prices, even for rather plain and obviously non-meritorious objects. Other examples of pricing being driven up to stratospheric levels because of keen competition occur in Chinese snuff bottles, which, amazingly enough in view of the disappearance of the snuff-taking habit, are now being carved again in Hong Kong and even in the United States! A similar situation holds true for the exquisitely carved miniature Japanese slide fasteners *netsuke* and *ojime*; these too are being turned out in goodly numbers in Japan to satisfy collectors who must have them, even though there is now no place on the Japanese costtume for these ornamental objects!

COMPOSITE WORK

In this class fall *inlays, overlays,* and *appliqués,* each type of work being characterized by the use of separate thin pieces of gemstone cemented together to form representational, symbolic, or merely geometrical designs. In most instances, a cheap but strong material is used for a backing or base upon which the colorful or patterned gemstone slabs are assembled and cemented. As the name implies, inlay work is done by scooping out depressions in the base material and insetting the pieces. Overlay work is similar to veneer work in furniture or floor parquetry because the base is entirely covered by a layer of gemstone pieces fitted together in checkerboard or jigsaw fashion. Appliqué work is that in which the base is only partly covered by numerous small pieces of gemstone assembled to create the appropriate design. The pieces are usually shallowly sculptured on top and flatted on the bottom. Appliqué work sometimes utilizes a base which may be wood or some other non-gemstone material as in the antique Chinese Coromandel screens.

INLAY WORK

The finest and most spectacular inlay work has been and is still being produced in Florence, Italy. An older example of this work, an ink stand, appears in Figure 47. It largely consists of a black stone base, soft enough to be easily chiseled out

FIG. 47
An ink stand of Florentine inlaid, or *pietre dure*, work. The basic stone, which is black slate, has been inlaid with malachite and serpentine leaves, and ivory flowers. This piece dates from the 19th century and measures 15 inches wide.

to provide the shallow recesses for the inset leaves of malachite (bright green) and serpentine (olive green) and the ivory blossoms. Minute grooves simulating twigs and stamens are filled with crushed stone of appropriate color. This kind of work is called *pietre dure* by the Italians and by art connoisseurs, or sometimes *intarsia*, although the latter term has been applied mainly to similir work in wood. The object shown in Figure 47 is a relatively simple Florentine production, others being far larger and more complex, sometimes portraying religious scenes, landscapes, or extremely ornate floral and geometrical designs. Other objects include brooch stones, popular in the Victorian era, box panels, paper weights, complete desk sets, and many others of decorative and/or utilitarian value. As a whole, the older and more carefully executed works are now scarce and considered collectors' items.

Inlay objects made from gemstones also include ring stones, usually flat or slightly curved on top, inset with color-contrasting bits of gemstone or sometimes squares of precious opal. These are manufactured mainly in Germany.

The most demanding inlays require the separate shaping of each thin slab of gemstone material, once the keen and appreciative eye of the workman has determined that its color and pattern are appropriate to the design. The work must progress slowly and carefully because a slight slip in shaping can result in an unsightly opening between two pieces. The *absence* of such openings is the chief sign of high-quality workmanship. In the best work, these joints are so narrow that only the difference in coloration or pattern between two adjacent pieces reveals the junction.

The choice of material is also demanding, and the Florentine shops scour the world to assemble rough which furnishes enough variety in respect to color, pattern, and texture to enable tliem to execute their designs. If the material chosen for any portion of the design is too hard or too soft in relation to neighboring pieces, an uneven surface is likely to result during polishing. How well this problem was solved can be easily discovered by sighting along the top surface of the object at a very low angle, when, in good reflected light, surface irregularities become apparent. Slight departures from level are acceptable, but definite shallow depressions indicate poor choice of materials and low-quality work.

OVERLAY WORK

Complete overlays are also prepared in the Florentine shops and are judged on the same basis as true inlay work. However, they generally cost less because recessing is not called for. Much less expensive are those overlays which consist of geometrical shapes such as squares and rectangles, fitted together without the time-consuming "cut and try" methods previously described. Examples are chess and checker boards made of squares, sometimes tigereye and other attractive materials which are usually set alternately to provide interesting optical effects. Very cheap boards are made in Italy from soft and easily carved gypsum. Overlay work also appears in ring and brooch stones, in box panels, and other objects.

APPLIQUÉS

Gemstone appliqués are much rarer than inlays or overlays and few appliqué objects are ever offered for sale. Occasionally small plaques and pendants of Chinese work appear in the antique market, most of them consisting of translucent whitish serpentine slabs of about ⅛" or less in thickness, decorated on one side by small leaves, flowers, and other motifs carved from bits of carnelian, lapis, jade, and other gemstones. Among larger objects are the Chinese Coromandel room-divider screens, consisting of a number of panels decorated on one or both sides by gemstone appliqués. These also are rare and most good examples have gravitated into museum collections.

SPHERES AND BEADS

As previously mentioned, spheres and spherical beads are easily manufactured in a simple mechanical process which insures accuracy and good production rates. As a class of lapidary objects they do not cost as much as other objects in which skilled handwork is necessary. However, the costs mount rapidly with increasing diameters because of the mathematical fact that the volumes are proportional to the cubes of the diameters while the surface areas are proportional to the squares of the diameters. Since the volume determines how much rough must be used to obtain a sphere, and the surface area determines how much lapidary work has to be expended, both factors must be considered by the manufacturer when fixing his costs.

DRILLING OF BEADS

A significant cost factor is the drilling of holes which may be half-drilled for beads meant to be cemented to small metal pegs, or full-drilled for necklace beads. Costs of drilling are proportional to length of hole and the materials. Some gemstones are drilled easily and quickly while others are drilled slowly and with difficulty.

Domestically, no one seems to drill beads for the public anymore. When someone does consent to take in a job, it is restricted to a very small project of a few beads, for which the fee may run $5.00 and up for a bead-drilled hole. Most companies with laser-drilling capabilities do not take outside work. On the other hand, with the advent of supersonic drilling machines which enormously shorten the time required for drilling, one now sees necklaces of drilled baroque tumbled stones that sell very cheaply. These are manufactured in the Far East where labor costs are very low.

NECKLACES
(see next chapter for Pearls)

Matched sets of drilled beads meant to be used in necklaces are commonly sold in *strings*. As such, they lack the strong cord, knotting between beads, and the clasps of ready-to-wear necklaces and are therefore allowed to enter the United States at lower rates of duty. Strings containing beads all of one diameter are called *uniform* strings, while those with smaller beads at the ends, gradually increasing in diameter toward a large central bead, are called *graduated* strings.

Graduations can increase rapidly or slowly, depending upon individual taste. Bead diameters are usually expressed in millimeters.

Necklace strings are available in many mineral gemstones and also in coral, shell, jet, amber, and ivory. Individual beads may be spheres, ovoids, cylinders, or other shapes, and plain-surfaced or faceted, or sometimes covered with shallow carving work. There are many variations and combinations possible.

From the lapidary viewpoint, the smallest labor charges are incurred for spherical beads because these can be mass-produced in specially designed "bead mills." Beads of other shapes must usually be done by hand methods, but sometimes the finish can be applied inexpensively by tumbling them in polishing barrels. In some Oriental countries, notably in India, hand-shaped beads are the rule, but they compete in price with mechanically produced beads only because of the cheapness of native labor. Faceted beads are also available from India, Japan, and Germany, with prices depending on the precision with which the faceting is executed, the best work usually being done in Germany, fair work in Japan, and poor work in India. The best class of faceted bead work demands as much attention as the faceting of other objects and is charged for accordingly. The most costly beads are those made from expensive gemstones which are partly or wholly carved.

Standards for judging the quality of beads are the same as those already given for facet, cabochon, and carving work, as appropriate. If beads are smoothly rounded, they may be judged as cabochons; if faceted, as faceted gems, etc. the only points worthy of further consideration are (1) closeness of match in respect to material, color, and pattern, (2) accuracy of size in the case of uniform beads, or smooth taper in the case of graduated beads, and (3) the quality of the bore holes.

For some materials, particularly for such rare gemstones as opal, emerald, ruby, and sapphire, it is very difficult to achieve a good match in respect to color and freedom from flaws, but it may also be difficult to obtain a good match when a necklace is being assembled from less expensive gemstones which, however, occur in a wide variety of hues such as tourmaline and beryl. On the other hand, it is easy to obtain perfect matches in beads made from gemstones which occur in large, uniformly colored masses such as citrine, smoky quartz, tigereye, and aventurine. The factors of size and smoothness of taper in strings of beads are easily judged and need no special remarks. However, it is pointed out that larger beads in the rarer materials are more difficult to match and consequently cost appreciably more than size alone would dictate. the workmanship displayed in the boring and finishing of the stringing holes is of considerable importance because beads which are inaccurately bored do not hang well upon the necklace cord and are instantly conspicuous on that account, while bore holes which are not smoothly finished upon their edges may chafe against the cord and cause it to break. All holes should be as narrow as possible so that when the necklace is examined the cord appears to enter each bead without any space between the cord and the bore hole. Transparent beads must have their bore holes smoothly finished upon the interior to present a neat appearance.

NECKLACE LENGTHS

There is considerable variation in the length of necklaces, even among those which are supposed to be of the same standard length. However, the following lengths are generally accepted in the trade but may vary somewhat according to the individual supplier. *Chokers* are about 16 inches in length, *regulars* are about 24 inches, *operas* about 28-32 inches, and *ropes* about 40-45 inches.

EGGS

While similar to beads in shape, eggs are much more difficult to make because the proper proportions are familiar to everyone and departures from the ideal form are easy to recognize. This requires more attention on the part of the lapidary, which, added to the cost of the hand labor that has to be expended on shaping and polishing, causes fine examples to fetch good prices. Small to large eggs are generally made from opaque massive materials, the smaller ones being used for pendants after a hole is drilled in one for insertion of a suspension fitting, and the larger ones for table ornaments. The rules used for judging cabochons apply here.

RINGS, CYLINDERS, AND TUBES

A variety of ring-like objects are made from gemstones, and, in small sizes, may be used as finger rings or as connectors in necklaces or pendants. Larger cylindrical objects, mainly fashioned from the left-over cores of hollowed-out vases and urns, are sometimes used in making small pill boxes. Most of the objects in this class can be judged according to cabochon rules, but some narrow rings meant for wear upon the fingers are faceted and therefore require the use of the appropriate faceting rules.

FLAT-SURFACED OBJECTS

Included in this class are book ends, paper weights, pen bases, plaques, thin slabs used for transparencies in lamp shades and windows, and cross-sections of petrified wood. the flat surfaces are easily and inexpensively created by sawing, followed by sanding or by pressing each surface against a whirling lap charged with loose abrasives to remove the marks left by the saw blade. Little artistic ability is required and the cost of such objects is mainly for the labor. The highest-quality work is done upon rotating laps, using a succession of abrasive powders until the surface is smooth enough to accept a polish. If the steps are carried out conscientiously, the result is a polished surface that resembles plate glass in quality. However, because it costs less to sand flat surfaces than to lap them, many cheaper items are done this way, with the result that the corners are less crisp and the surfaces always slightly wavy as compared to the geometrical flatness possible with lapping. The quality of surfaces therefore depends not only on the solidity of the raw material and its ability to take a good polish, but upon the lapidary technique used. A good way of judging quality is to hold the object up to a distant light and catch its reflection from the polished surface. If the surface is truly flat, the image of the light will not be distorted; if the surface is slightly wavy, as usually happens if it is sanded rather than lapsed, the reflection will be distorted in proportion to the irregularity of the surface. Rounded edges are almost always a sign of sanding and of course are less desirable than the sharp edges left by lapping. In respect to polish, the surfaces should be free of conspicuous scratches or the slight dimples caused by non-uniform polishing of certain gemstones like jacleite and nephrite.

Sections of petrified wood logs or limbs and agate nodules or geodes should be *complete*, showing a representative cross-section of the whole; partial sections are of less value. All sections should be sharp-edged, without chiping, and without removal of the outer natural "rind" or "bark."

CARVING VALUES

While it is impossible to list more than a few objects representative of each class of work in the price schedules below, sufficient information is given for each object to enable the reader to gain some idea of what a similar object of equivalent size and quality would be worth. Attention is particularly invited to the prices of "commercial" quality carvings, a term used to designate modern, mass-produced carving sold extensively to tourists. Their hallmarks are lack of detail, crude shaping, and brilliant, glass-like polishes. Older carvings, particularly those of Chinese origin, should be compared with these modern productions, side by side if possible, and if the quality is comparable, the prospective buyer would be better off to take the older carvings in preference to the new. In the long run, the values of the antique carvings are bound to appreciate at a greater rate than those of the modern examples, especially if the older pieces have genuine artistic merit.

HUMAN FIGURINES, BETTER GRADES

Amber, red-brown, antique, god, 2¾"x1¼"x½", good work	ea.	450.00-875.00
Bowenite serpentine, goddess, translucent yellow-green with some red areas, 8½"x4"x2", excellent work	ea.	525.00-1,500.00
Coral, pink-orange, man with wine jug and dog, 6½"x2¾", very good	ea.	400.00
Coral, white, fine, old man, 1½"x4"	ea.	275.00
Coral, good pink, slender girl, 4½" tall, good work	ea.	375.00
Ivory, Doctor's lady, 9" long	ea.	925.00
Ivory, the 8 immortals, gods, 10"x3"x2", Chien Lung, yellowed with age, very good, the set	ea.	4,700.00
Jadeite Doctor's lady, green & lavender, 9½" x 1¾", on wooden stand	ea.	2,000.00
Lapis Lazuli, Food Dog, carved from single piece, 4½"x9", very fine, on carved wooden stand	ea.	1,425.00
Lapis Lazuli, Dragon & Phoenix, 3"x5½", wooden stand	ea.	1,200.00
Lapis Lazuli, Buddhist Immortals, 6"x3¾" with Pyrite	ea.	1,000.00
Lapis Lazuli, Oriental King & Queen on wooden stands, 3x4¾"	ea.	1,000.00 pair
Lapis Lazuli, Dragon with removable lid, 2½"x4½"	ea.	1,400.00
Lapis Lazuli, Fighting dragons, 5½"x7" on wooden stand	ea.	950.00
Rock crystal, god kneeling, 2¾"x2½"x2", good	ea.	250.00
Quartz, woman, amethyst, 7¾" tall Kuan Yin work	ea.	750.00
Sugilite women and man, 5¼"x3¼", good	ea.	700.00
Turquois, ladies, 1"-3" tall	ea.	425.00-1,900.00
Turquois, Kwan Yin, 4"x3"	ea.	300.00

HUMAN FIGURINES, COMMERCIAL GRADE

Coral, pink, old man, standing, 1"-1½"good	ea.	2.00-250.00
Nephrite, Kuan Yin, 5½", good	ea.	600.00
Nephrite, Taiwan, gods, 2½"-7"	ea.	150.00-850.00
Obsidian, gods, ¾", crude	ea.	8.50-15.00
Obsidian, tikis, 3"-3½", simple, well-polished	ea.	10.00-20.00
Rock crystal, gods, 2½"-7"	ea.	75.00-250.00
Rock crystal, gods, ¾", crude	ea.	10.00
Tiger iron seated figure, wide man, 7¼", good	ea.	5.00
Tourmaline, blue-green, Dragon, 3", good	ea.	1,300.00
Tourmaline, pink, elephant, 2½"x2", good	ea.	1,000.00
Turquois, woman and child, 3" tall on wooden stand	ea.	450.00

ANIMALS, BETTER GRADES

Aventurine, snake 2½" on wooden stand	ea.	100.00
Carnelian, banded, fantail goldfish, 2"x1¼"x1", modern	ea.	85.00-125.00
Carnelian, banded, fantail goldfish, 2½"x1¾"x1¾", modern	ea.	125.00-175.00
Carnelian, milky, fantail goldfish, 2½"x1¾"x1¾", modern	ea.	100.00-125.00
Jadeite, dark green, white mottled, dragon, 4"x4", good work, modern	ea.	1,800.00

Jadeite, 2 grasshoppers, each in different color, with thin
partition of another color between, 7½"x4",
very skillfully done ..... ea. 1,475.00
Jadeite, lavender, some green spots, horses, 6"x3½"x2¾",
excellent work ..... ea. 1,000.00
Jadeite, lavender & green, elephant with baby elephant
on its back, excellent work, 4½"x3½" ..... ea. 1,150.00
Nephrite, mutton fat with red skin spots, 5"x2¼"x2",
exquisite work, antique ..... ea. 6,500.00
Nephrite, mythical monster (lion?), pale greenish white,
partly altered by burial or burning, Han, 10"x3½"x4" ..... ea. 6,500.00-8,000.00
Nephrite, yellow, with orangy spots, very rare type
nephrite, pair of camels, each 4½"x4"x2¾",
exquisite work, antique, the pair ..... ea. 5,000.00-7,500.00
Obsidian, snowflake, frog, 6½"x3"x4" ..... ea. 650.00
Rhodonite, cat, 2¾"x4" ..... ea. 350.00
Rose quartz, rabbit, long cars, 3"x3"x1½", modern ..... ea. 225.00
Sugilite Cranes & Trees, 5½"x3¾" ..... ea. 950.00
Turquois, elephant, 3½"x2⅛"x1¼", fair material ..... ea. 400.00

Animals, Commercial Grade
Amber, various animals, 2½"-5" ..... ea. 225.00-550.00
Agate, giraffe, 5" high, good ..... ea. 75.00-125.00
Amazonite, parrot on branch, 2½", good ..... ea. 75.00
Azurite-malachite, fish, 3", crude ..... ea. 50.00
Calcite, onyx, Mexican, animals, 1"-3", very crude ..... ea. .85-3.50
Calcite, onyx, Mexican, animals, 1"-3", more complex ..... ea. 3.00-9.00
Rhodonite, frogs ..... ea. 25.00
Rhodonite, bears, ½"-6" long, according to complexity ..... ea. 100.00-125.00
Jasper, bear, 2", good ..... ea. 45.00
Jasper, fish 2¾" (obiclar jasper) ..... ea. 35.00
Jasper, bird on branch, 2¾"x2" ..... ea. 150.00
Malachite, rabbits, turtles, birds, 2"-3", fair ..... ea. 30.00-50.00
Malachite, Sitting Dog, 2¼"-3", good ..... ea. 55.00
Malachite, Horse reclining, 2¾"x1½" tall ..... ea. 165.00
Nephrite, New Zealand, animals, ½"-2", good ..... ea. 6.00-70.00
Nephrite, New Zealand, animals, flat black, ¾", fair ..... ea. 3.50-5.00
Nephrite, N.Z. or Alaska, elephants, drilled,
20-22 mm., fair ..... ea. 10.00-20.00
Nephrite, Alaska, 3" scarab, good ..... ea. 65.00
Nephrite, mutton fat, horse, 2"x1½"x½", fair ..... ea. 65.00
Obsidian, standing cat, 2", according to complexity ..... ea. 20.00-35.00
Opal, precious, lizard on rock matrix, 33x19 mm., fine ..... ea. 295.00
Opal (Boulder) matrix, frogs, 4"x2¼", good ..... ea. 295.00
Quartzes, ½"-2", squat animals, fair ..... ea. 3.50-7.50
Quartzes, ½"-2", squat animals, good ..... ea. 4.00-30.00
Soapstone, 5½"x6¾", horses ..... ea. 10.00-12.00
Serpentine, turtles, 2"-4" ..... ea. 6.00-12.00

Fingering or Fondling Pieces, Disks, etc., Better Grades
Some of the most imaginative work of all has been expended on these small sculptures, most
of which were produced in China. Especially noteworthy are those which take advantage of sev-

eral color layers or zones to place some objects in relief in one color resting upon a base material of another color.

Aquamarine, bamboo section leaves, 2"x1¼"x½", good	ea.	250.00-450.00
Aquamarine, flowers & leaves, 2"x1"x½", good	ea.	275.00-425.00
Carnelian, fruits, leaves, 2"x1¼"x1⅝", very good	ea.	200.00-225.00
Chalcedony, particolored, animals, 1¼"x1¼"x¾", fair	ea.	65.00
Chalcedony, peach, 2"x1¾"x1⅝", fair	ea.	50.00
Malachite, fruits & leaves, 2½"x1½"x⅝", good	ea.	150.00-300.00
Nephrite, mutton fat, low relief plaque, 2½"x2"x2⅛", good	ea.	75.00-150.00
Nephrite, mutton fat, fruits, leaves, 2"x1½"x⅜", good	ea.	100.00
Nephrite, mutton fat, pebble, ornately carved, hollowed out, 3"x1¾"x1", very fine work	ea.	275.00
Nephrite, yellow-green bell, with loop, engraved, 2"x2"x½", very fine	ea.	275.00-350.00

FINGERING PIECES, DISKS, ETC., COMMERCIAL GRADE

Many of these are modern productions imitating older pieces, or are carved for the tourist trade in various foreign places, especially Hong Kong.

Jadeite, copies of coins, square holes, ¾"-1¼", good	ea.	5.00-10-00
Jadeite, flat ornamental pieces, low relief, 30-50 mm., good	ea.	12.00-15.00
Jadeite, low relief disks, excellent quality jadeite 12½ mm.	ea.	60.00
Jadeite, fingering pieces, 1¾"-2½", good sculpture	ea.	35.00-50.00
Jadeite, temple bell, flat back, ¾"-1", good	ea.	6.00-10.00
Jadeite, pagodas, ¾"-1", flat back	ea.	8.00-12.00
Onyx, worry stones, 1½"x1¾"	ea.	.50-1.00

BELT BUCKLES AND CLASPS, BETTER GRADES

These are typically Chinese work, and consist of two major types, the first being a one-piece curving hook, usually ornamented with mythical beasts or dragons on top, and the second, a two-piece buckle in which the separate pieces cleverly interlock. The two-piece buckles are generally more expensive because they are commonly carved in elaborate patterns from higher-class materials.

Jadeite, pale green with bright green spots 3"x½"x⅝", very good	ea.	200.00-350.00
Jadeite, white, with red top, 5"x¾"x⅝", good	ea.	175.00-300.00
Jadeite, linked pair, bright red top, with carved Chinese good luck characters, 1½"x1¾"x⅝", very fine	ea.	450.00-600.00
Nephrite, mutton fat, dragons on top in high relief, 3½"x4½" long, good work	ea.	85.00-250.00

HEADS, FACES, MASKS, TIKIS, COMMERCIAL GRADE

Amber, tiki, 1¼"x2½"	ea.	225.00
Calcite onyxes, Mexican, masks, 1½"x3¾", crude	ea.	1.50
Calcite onyxes, Mexican, gods, chess set, 2"-4", crude	set	40.00
Jet, head, 3", fair	ea.	20.00
Nephrite, New Zealand, tikis, ¾"x1¼", crude	ea.	2.25-10.00
Obsidians, mask, drilled, 1½", simple lines	ea.	3.50
Obsidians, mask, undrilled, 1½", simple lines	ea.	2.00
Serpentine, head, ¾"x1", simple	ea.	10.00-15.00
Tigereye, mask, ⅝"x 1¼", simple lines	ea.	10.00-15.00

BUDDHAS

Amethyst, very good, 5"x9" tall	ea.	1,200.00
Calcite onyx, Mexican, drilled, 1¼"x1", very crude	ea.	1.50-3.00

Coral, pink, drilled, ½"x1", good	ea.	2.00-10.00
Fluorite, pale green, crude, 3½"	ea.	75.00
Fluorite Buddha, standing purple & green, 3½" tall	ea.	50.00
Fluorite Buddha, lavender & green, 5¼"x5¼"x3¼"	ea.	180.00
Jadeite, various hues, flat back, 12x9-20x15 mm.	ca.	5.00-20.00
Jadeite, various hues, in-the-round, ¾"-1¼"	ea.	5.00-20.00
Nephrite, New Zealand or Alaska, drilled, 20-22 mm.	ea.	8.00-15.00
Rose quartz, 1½"x2¾", good	ea.	60.00
Rose quartz, 3¼"x6½" on stand	ea.	300.00

DECORATIVE PIECES OF BETTER GRADE

Amethyst, flower buds, on smoky quartz section, 3½"x1¾"x2¼", fair	225.00
Jadeite, Burmese, Screen, lavender & green, 10" tall on wooden stand, fine	7,500.00
Jadeite, Burmese, Screen, lavender & green, 9¾" tall, on wooden stand, fine	5,000.00
Jadeite, lavender Buddha, 9" tall, very fine	4,800.00
Jadeite, lavender, Chinese warrior, 7⁵⁄₁₆" tall,	1,750.00
Jadeite, lavender, Chinese lady, 5" tall	2,000.00
Malachite, large oval screen, covered on both sides by high relief dragons, etc., 9¼" tall, 8½" wide, 2½" thick overall, very good work	6,000.00-7,500.00
Nephrite, white jui scepter, bat, peaches, dragon, 10⅛" long	2,000.00
Serpentine, opaque green, lion on pedestal, the pedestal in several sections, 7"x4½"x3", fair	250.00
Sodalite, blue & white, dragon design, box with Foo Dog lid, 5½"x3"	400.00
Sodalite, tree with birds, 4"x7½"	400.00
Rock crystal, seal, 2⅞"x1⅝"x1", plain with round handle on top	150.00-350.00
Rock crystal, seals, similar, 2¾"x1¼" square, round handles, pr.	165.00-475.00
Steatite, seal or "chop," shallow carving on tops, set of three, 1" square, 3" tall, the set	150.00-350.00
Steatite, seal, 4½"x1¾"x1¾", carved top, fair	125.00-275.00
Steatite, seal, 1½"x11½", name carved	65.00-100.00

URNS, VASES, BOWLS, TRAYS, BETTER GRADES

Some of the finest Chinese carving work has been expended on containers of various types, ranging from those which are absolutely plain but depending upon graceful lines and fine material for their beauty, to those which are so elaborately decorated that the container portion is almost hidden from view. The price range is very wide.

Agate, brown, with filamental moss, teapot with lid, 6¼" tall, 6¾" wide overall, 3¾" deep, fair workmanship	2,500.00
Aventurine, green, flattish urn, with lid, loose rings on handles, shallow incised designs on flanks, overall height 13", 6½" wide, 3" thick, excellent work	4,700.00
Chalcedony, grayish with reddish patches, bowl, deeply hollowed with cross-over straps, ornate exterior floral work, 4¾"x3½"x2", fair	900.00
Chalcedony, grayish, with raised leaves & twigs in brownish material, 3½"x3½"x1", fair to crude work	350.00

Fluorite, green, bowl, 6" tall, 5½" dia., Chinese, good work	750.00
Jadeite, white jade vase and cover, Jiaqing, with a frieze of dragon motifs, 11" (antique), fine work	12,000.00
Jadeite, greenish-white, 6¾", genuine antique of 18th century	2,800.00
Jadeite, green with dark flecking, oval vessel with flared fluted sides, lid, 7⅞" antique	3,250.00
Jadeite, greenish-white Moghul-style, 18th/19th century carved with stylized flowers and petals, lid, 3½" tall, modern	7,250.00
Jadeite, vase with lid, pale green and lavender, relief or dragons chasing a flaming pearl, 10½" tall, modern	2,500.00
Jadeite, lavender with green mottling, good color, 10¾" long	10,000.00
Jadeite, white translucent material, with brilliant green spots, and some yellow and mauve, gourd tray, deeply carved, thin-walled, openwork on exterior, 6⅜"x5½"x2", very fine workmanship	1,200.00
Jadeite, fine white, with deep green slender veinings, bowl with lid, the body 8½" tall, 6"x3½" with plain sides and delicate relief work on front and back panels, carved handles; lid to match, superb workmanship	8,000.00
Lapis lazuli, dark with gray areas & pyrite, round box, with interlocked lid, carved in shallow geometrical patterns over all surface, 3¼" diam., 1¼" deep, good work	675.00
Nephrite, brownish mutton fat, wine ewer, with spout and handle, 3½"x2"x1¼", thin walled, fair	325.00
Nephrite, brownish-green, horn-shaped container, archaic design, protruding ring-type handles, incised patterns, partly altered material, 8"x4¼" diam., Chou	15,000.00-18,000.00
Nephrite, grayish-green, pitcher, with spout and ring-type handles, archaic design, 10½"x6"x2¾", Ming	12,000.00-20,000.00
Nephrite, perfectly uniform olive-green material, without flaw, urn, with matching lid, surrounded by ornate raised work, handles with loose rings, 7⅝" tall, overall 4⅛"x2", exquisite workmanship	5,000.00-8,000.00
Nephrite, green Turkestan material, univormly mottled with lighter areas, round bowl, 7½" diam., 3" tall, with walls ⅛" thick, beautifully polished	2,500.00
Rock crystal, urn, with lid, two handles, three feet, beautifully ornamented with dragon patterns, 8½" tall, 10"x7", very fine work	1,900.00
Tiger's eye, blue, rare, vases with lids, fine work, 4½"x4"	2,400.00/pair

SNUFF BOTTLES

Presently, snuff bottles are being eagerly collected and the prices have reached high values when compared to those placed upon other, equally complicated works of much larger size in similar gemstones. Nephrite, jadeite, and various members of the quartz family provided most of the raw material used, but amber, ivory and sometimes the very rare hornbill ivory were also employed. The quality of the material counts a great deal in setting prices, especially if the gemstone happens to be unique in some respect such as color, pattern, or layering. Thinness of walls is especially appreciated by connoisseurs, and prices asked for bottles rise sharply according to how well the hollowing-out job was performed. In very exceptional cases, the walls may be so thin that the bottle, despite being cut form a heavy gemstone such as jadeite, nephrite, or chalcedony, floats in water if the mouth is sealed with a strip of tape. Graceful shapes, spirited designs, and exquisite, finely detailed work also elevate prices.

Agate, banded, brown & white, plain, $2\frac{1}{4}$"x$1\frac{5}{8}$"x1"	100.00-275.00
Amber, with children and kite raised sides, $2\frac{1}{8}$"	400.00
Amber, 3" tall with all over ornamentation	1,100.00
Amber (Baltic), $2\frac{3}{4}$" tall with scenes both sides	975.00
Amethyst, fair color, $2\frac{1}{4}$" tall, $1\frac{3}{8}$"x$1\frac{1}{8}$", matching stopper, raised leaf ornamentation on sides, fair work	175.00
Amethyst, deep shaded purple, $2\frac{1}{4}$"x$1\frac{3}{8}$"x1", gods & trees in relief, excellent	700.00
Amethyst, medium purple, rectangular shape, with carved shoulders, $2\frac{1}{2}$"x$1\frac{5}{8}$"x$\frac{3}{4}$", very large for this size amethyst, very fine work	2,000.00
Aquamarine, pale blue, shallow carving over all surfaces, $2\frac{7}{8}$"x$\frac{7}{8}$"x$\frac{5}{8}$", very good work	1,650.00
Aquamarine, pale blue-green, miniature urn, poised on legs, with integral base, carved tourmaline cap, 2"x$1\frac{1}{8}$"x$\frac{7}{8}$", exquisite	2,500.00
Aquamarine, green-blue, shallow relief carving, $1\frac{3}{4}$"x$1\frac{1}{8}$"x$\frac{7}{8}$", very good	700.00
Azurite-malachite rock, "burnite," modern, plain ovoid shape, with cylindrical bore only, 2"x$1\frac{1}{2}$" diam.	350.00
Calcite onyx, white, with narrow bandings, simple ovoid, incised panels, $2\frac{1}{2}$"x$1\frac{7}{8}$"x$1\frac{1}{8}$", good	650.00
Calcite onyx, faintly grayish with brown patch, low relief carving, $2\frac{1}{2}$"x$1\frac{1}{4}$"x1", poor work	175.00
Carnelian, fine uniform red, ovoid, shoulder carving only, 2"x$1\frac{5}{8}$"x$\frac{5}{8}$", fine	425.00
Carnelian, dark brownish red, plain ovoid, with matching gold-rimmed stopper, 2"x$1\frac{3}{8}$"x$\frac{3}{4}$"	250.00
Chalcedony, stream pebble, natural shape and with abrasion marks, 2"x$1\frac{1}{2}$"x2"	200.00
Chalcedony, brown, black markings in material, shallow engraving of horse on front, $1\frac{1}{4}$"x$1\frac{7}{8}$"x$\frac{3}{4}$"	100.00
Chalcedony, translucent, whitish, well hollowed, shoulders carved only, $2\frac{1}{4}$"x2"x1", good	150.00
Chalcedony, pale gray-brown, with dark brown stains in old cracks, shallow engraved, carved shoulders, $2\frac{3}{4}$"x2"x$1\frac{1}{2}$", fair	90.00
Chalcedony, very pale brown, dark brown crack stains, well hollowed, plain, $2\frac{1}{4}$"x2"x$1\frac{1}{8}$", good	95.00
Chalcedony, pale gray translucent, with deep green inclusion cut away in shallow relief, 2"x$1\frac{1}{2}$"x$\frac{5}{8}$", unusual	500.00
Chalcedony, brown, with overlay of whitish material cut away to provide figures in relief, 2"x$1\frac{3}{4}$"x$1\frac{1}{8}$", very good	425.00
Chalcedony, pale brown, translucent, with finely-detailed dark brown dendrites,	

thin-walled, circular, $2\frac{5}{8}$"x$1\frac{1}{8}$" diam.   575.00

Chalcedony, pale gray, highly translucent, ovoid,
painted inside with scenes, $2\frac{1}{8}$"x$1\frac{3}{4}$"x$1\frac{3}{8}$", fine   425.00

Chalcedony, pale brown, with reddish raised relief
figures on one panel, $2\frac{1}{8}$"x$2\frac{1}{8}$"x$1\frac{1}{8}$", good   275.00

Citrine, smoky, fruit, with raised leaves, thin-walled,
$2\frac{1}{8}$"x$1\frac{1}{4}$"x$1\frac{3}{8}$"   425.00

Coral, deep red, flowering tree stump,
$2\frac{1}{8}$"x$1\frac{5}{8}$"x$\frac{3}{4}$", very good   1,600.00

Hornbill ivory, pale yellow-brown with red,
narrow carving, 2"x$\frac{7}{8}$"x$\frac{3}{8}$", rare   2,800.00

Ivory, two fish, deeply sculptured with fine
details, $2\frac{3}{8}$"x$1\frac{1}{4}$"x$\frac{5}{8}$", fair   200.00

Ivory, two fish, finely carved, $2\frac{1}{2}$"x$1\frac{1}{2}$"x$\frac{5}{8}$"   150.00

Ivory, square, tapered vase shape, engraved and
lines stained with ink, 2"x $1\frac{1}{2}$"x $\frac{1}{2}$", fine   100.00

Ivory, overall shallow incised patterns, matching
stopper, $2\frac{1}{4}$"x$1\frac{1}{4}$"x$\frac{3}{4}$", excellent work   110.00

Ivory, walrus, dyed malachite green, plain, $2\frac{1}{4}$"x$1\frac{1}{8}$"x1"   275.00

Jadeite, fine white, crane, with matching stopper,
$2\frac{7}{8}$"x $2\frac{1}{4}$"x1"   650.00

Jadeite, double white with emerald-green veinings,
plain ovoid shape with figures and coins, $2\frac{1}{2}$" tall   500.00

Jadeite, pale green with white mottlings, squirrel
and pine trees, circular, 3" tall   950.00

Jadeite, one half bright brown-red, other half
pale green, with shallow engraving,
$2\frac{1}{8}$"x$1\frac{3}{8}$"x$1\frac{1}{8}$" good   450.00

Jadeite, white body with patches of bright green,
the latter carved in lotus leaves with
engraving, circular, 2"x2"x$\frac{3}{4}$", fair work   135.00-175.00

Jadeite, mauve, squat ovoid, very shallow incised
decorations, $2\frac{1}{8}$"x$1\frac{7}{8}$"x$\frac{3}{4}$", matching
stopper, very good work   750.00

Jadeite, good green with slight veinings, plain
ovoid, 2"x$1\frac{5}{8}$"x$\frac{7}{8}$", well hollowed   1,800.00

Jadeite, white, ovoid, plain, extremely thin walls,
2"x $1\frac{3}{4}$"x$1\frac{1}{8}$"; this bottle floats   625.00

Jadeite, deep green, exquisitely chiseled bead
pattern, 2x"$1\frac{7}{8}$"x$1\frac{1}{8}$"   975.00

Jadeite, good green, veined, ovoid, with low relief
patterns, thin walled, 2"x$1\frac{3}{4}$"x1"   1,000.00

Lapis lazuli, dark blue, with gray areas of small
size, ornate raised carving,
$2\frac{1}{4}$"x$1\frac{1}{4}$"x$\frac{5}{8}$" matching stopper   350.00

Lapis lazuli, dark blue, good quality material,
rectangular cross-section, with nicely incised
archaic motifs, $2\frac{3}{8}$"x$1\frac{7}{8}$"x$\frac{7}{8}$", fine work   600.00

Moss agate, brownish, octagonal shape, faceted
shoulders, 2"x2"x $1\frac{1}{4}$", good work   250.00

Moss agate, reddish, with fine green moss, carved
shoulders only, very thin-walled, 2"x$1\frac{5}{8}$"x1"   225.00

Malachite, rectangular cross-section, deeply incised panels, $2\frac{1}{2}$"x$1\frac{1}{4}$"x$\frac{1}{2}$", fair workmanship	125.00
Malachite, well banded, urn with raised twigs, leaves & fruit surround, stopper to match, $1\frac{1}{4}$"x$1\frac{3}{4}$"x$1\frac{1}{8}$", good	400.00-550.00
Mother-of-pearl, shallow incised patterns on front and back, $2\frac{1}{4}$"x$1\frac{1}{4}$"x$\frac{1}{2}$", worn with use	150.00-225.00
Nephrite, mutton fat, shallow incised characters on sides, 2"x $1\frac{1}{4}$"x$\frac{3}{4}$"	50.00-175.00
Nephrite, mutton fat, plain ovoid, decorated shoulders, 2"x$1\frac{1}{2}$"x$\frac{1}{2}$", good	150.00
Nephrite, mutton fat, discoid shape, completely covered by fine geometrical patterns, $2\frac{1}{8}$"x2"x$\frac{3}{4}$"	225.00
Nephrite, mutton fat, rectangular cross-section, shallow cut dragons oil one face in reddish nephrite, $2\frac{1}{4}$"x$1\frac{1}{4}$"x1", good	150.00-275.00
Nephrite, grayish, overall incised archaic patterns, $2\frac{3}{8}$"x$1\frac{3}{4}$"x$1\frac{1}{8}$"	125.00-165.00
Nephrite, mutton fat, nearly white, octagonal shape, overall shallow relief carving, $2\frac{1}{2}$"x$1\frac{1}{2}$"x$1\frac{1}{8}$" good	200.00
Nephrite, pale brown, with raised design iii darker brown, $2\frac{5}{8}$"x$1\frac{3}{8}$"x1", good	180.00
Nephrite, white, gourd carving, with raised leaves partly red-brown, $2\frac{1}{4}$"x $1\frac{3}{4}$"x$1\frac{1}{4}$", good	150.00
Nephrite, greenish, raised leaf pattern, $2\frac{5}{8}$"x $1\frac{1}{4}$"x$1\frac{1}{2}$", good	185.00
Nephrite, mutton fat, curious pumpkin profile, with very fine fluting & pttterns, $2\frac{1}{2}$" tall, $3\frac{1}{4}$" wide, $\frac{3}{4}$" thick	350.00
Nephrite, white, shallow carving on all sides, exquisitely done, $2\frac{1}{8}$"x$1\frac{1}{4}$"x$\frac{3}{8}$"	800.00
Nephrite, mutton fat, one side with raised design in red-brown, $2\frac{1}{4}$"x$1\frac{1}{2}$"x$\frac{3}{4}$", very good	350.00
Nephrite, white opaque "chicken bone" material, tapered vase shape, shallow relief Nephrite, ornament, $2\frac{1}{2}$"x$1\frac{1}{2}$"x$1\frac{1}{8}$", very good	675.00
Nephrite, bright green with small black specks, plain, thin-walled, $2\frac{3}{8}$"x$1\frac{3}{4}$"x$1\frac{1}{8}$", very good	600.00
Nephrite, yellowish, plain, ovoid, $2\frac{5}{8}$"x$\frac{3}{4}$" x$\frac{3}{4}$", good	450.00
Nephrite, whitish, rectangular cross-section urn shape, with exquisite carved panels composed of numerous minute geometrical inclusions, $2\frac{1}{8}$"x$1\frac{1}{4}$"x$\frac{7}{8}$", very fine	600.00
Nephrite, dark gyay, with deep carving in white on front panel, ovoid, $2\frac{7}{8}$"x$2\frac{3}{4}$"x$1\frac{1}{4}$", rare type nephrite	3,500.00
Nephrite, tomb material, recut, ovoid, with deep dragons overall, brown & green stainings, $2\frac{1}{8}$"x2"x$1\frac{1}{8}$", very good	1,000.00-1,500.00
Nephrite, mutton fat, with outer layer of green cut away in relief, $2\frac{3}{4}$"x$1\frac{1}{4}$"x$1\frac{1}{4}$"	350.00

Nephrite, dark green, with outer panels of dark
red-brown, carved with dragons,
$2\frac{7}{8}$"x$1\frac{7}{8}$"x$1\frac{1}{8}$", crude work 500.00

Pearl, baroque, silver-white, iridescent, with
overlay of imperial jadeite leaves at top, red
tourmaline stopper; reputed to have belonged
to the Dowager Empress, $1\frac{5}{8}$"x$1\frac{1}{8}$"x$1\frac{1}{8}$" 6,500.00

Quartzite, stained red, plain, heart-shaped
bottle, 2"x$1\frac{1}{2}$"x$\frac{3}{4}$" 115.00

Quartzite, stained deep brownish-red, squarish
bottle, with incised pattern of beads covering
exterior, $2\frac{1}{4}$"x$1\frac{1}{2}$"x1", excellent work 375.00

Rock crystal, ovoid, diamond patterns, $3\frac{1}{4}$" tall 225.00

Rock crystal, flower shape, $2\frac{1}{4}$" tall 200.00

Rock crystal, uniformly filled with attractive white
veils of inclusions, plain panels oil sides,
$2\frac{3}{4}$"x$1\frac{7}{8}$"x$\frac{3}{4}$" 375.00

Rock crystal, flawless, plain, inside well-hollowed
and polished, $2\frac{5}{8}$"x2"x$\frac{7}{8}$" 375.00

Rose quartz, ornate vase-like bottle, with raised
carving, matching stopper, 3" overall,
2"x$1\frac{1}{4}$", fair work 125.00

Ruby corundum, purplish, plain, $1\frac{5}{8}$"x$1\frac{3}{8}$"x$\frac{7}{8}$",
green jadeite stopper, fair work 1,650.00-2,000.00

Ruby in zoisite, horse shape, $2\frac{1}{8}$" tall 150.00

Ruby in zoisite, bird in flowering tree, $2\frac{1}{8}$" tall ... 950.00

Rhodochrosite, bottle with crane, 2" tall 125.00

Rhodochrosite, bottle with rabbit, $2\frac{1}{4}$" tall 135.00

Rhodonite, bottle with elephant carving, $2\frac{1}{4}$" tall 85.00

Rhodonite, carved village scene and mountains, 3" tall ... 100.00

Smoky quartz, crudely hollowed bottle, plain,
3"x$1\frac{1}{2}$"x$\frac{5}{8}$" 45.00-75.00

Smoky quartz, plain, with delicately incised
scenes upon pinels, the incisions filled
with gold, $2\frac{1}{8}$"x$1\frac{3}{4}$"x$\frac{3}{4}$" 175.00-200.00

Smoky quartz, thin-walled, plain, scenes painted
inside, $2\frac{3}{8}$"x$1\frac{5}{8}$"x$\frac{5}{8}$", good 300.00

Smoky quartz, shallow incised designs on both
sides, well hollowed, $2\frac{1}{2}$"x$1\frac{1}{2}$"x$\frac{3}{4}$" 150.00

Smoky quartz, dark, octagonal bottle, with
incised yang-yin symbol on both panels,
plus decorative grooves, 2"x$1\frac{3}{4}$"x$1\frac{1}{8}$" 185.00

Tourmaline, pink, ornately & beautifully carved
leaves & vines, moderate hollowing, gourd
shape, very good, 3" tall 1,425.00

Tourmaline, pink, with ducks design, $2\frac{1}{2}$" tall 800.00

Tourmaline, pink, overall shallow relief carving,
$1\frac{3}{4}$"x2"x$\frac{1}{2}$" 425.00

Tourmalized quartz, plain ovoid, $2\frac{1}{2}$"x$1\frac{1}{2}$"x$\frac{3}{4}$" 375.00

Turquois, flowers & leaves in raised relief, $2\frac{1}{2}$" tall ... 450.00

Turquois, greenish, exquisite work, with small goat
heads on shoulders, raised panels, $1\frac{5}{8}$"x$1\frac{1}{4}$"x$\frac{3}{4}$" ... 400.00

Turquois, Persian black matrix, plain, (rare now) $1\frac{3}{4}$"x$1\frac{3}{8}$"x$\frac{3}{4}$"	700.00

IVORY, MISCELLANEOUS CARVINGS OF BETTER GRADES

Tusk section, hollowed, with elaborate figures and scenes inside, $5\frac{1}{2}$"x$2\frac{3}{4}$"x1", very fine work	1,500.00-2,500.00
Tusk section, similar to above, Japanese work, exquisitely detailed, $9\frac{3}{4}$"x$2\frac{1}{2}$"x1"	2,500.00-5,000.00
Vase, with lid, ornately carved, immortals & Meiji period, $15\frac{3}{4}$" tall	2,600.00
Netsukes, authentic Japanese antiques, 1"-$2\frac{1}{2}$" by acknowledged carvers	150.00-1,500.00

CARVED LEAVES, FLOWERS

Leaves generally very simple in shape, many of the precious gemstone kinds being crude approximations with veinings indicated only by shallow scores; larger leaves and flowers tend to be more deeply sculptured with considerable curvature; expensive gemstone leaves sold by carat.

Abalone, leaves, flowers, $\frac{3}{4}$"-3", crude	ea.	.75-4.00
Amethyst, leaves, $\frac{3}{8}$"-$\frac{3}{4}$", fair	ct.	1.00-3.00
Aquamarine, leaves, blue 12-13 mm.	ct.	16.00
Citrine, leaves, flowers, $\frac{3}{8}$"-$\frac{3}{4}$", good yellow	ea.	1.00-3.00
Coral, pink, flowers, 2", fine detail	ea.	55.00
Emerald, leaves, $\frac{1}{4}$"-$\frac{1}{2}$", good green, many flaws	ct.	6.00-12.00
Garnet, rhodolite, leaves, 12"x9"	ea.	8.00-12.00
Iolite, $\frac{1}{2}$"-1", dark blue	ct.	1.00-3.50
Jadeite, flowers, leaves, fruits, $\frac{1}{2}$"-$1\frac{1}{2}$", good	ea.	12.00-100.00
Mother-of-pearl, flowers, leaves, 17 mm., fair	ea.	5.00
Mother-of-pearl, flowers, leaves, 42x39 mm., fair	ea.	15.00
Nephrite, New Zealand, leaves, 22-50 mm., fine details	ea.	12.00-25.00
Peridot, 10"-2x5"	ea.	10.00
Ruby, leaves, $\frac{1}{4}$"-$\frac{1}{2}$", deep red, flawed	ct.	6.00-10.00
Sapphire, leaves, dark blue, $\frac{1}{4}$"-$\frac{1}{2}$"	ct.	4.00-10.00
Tigereye, flowers, 2"x1", fair	ea.	6.00
Tourmaline, purple, 15.5"x12"	ea.	14.00

CARVED CABOCHONS, COMMERCIAL GRADE

Mostly ovals, the tops carved with floral motifs, deeply incised and pierced in the better classes of work; mainly modern Chinese and Japanese work.

Amethyst, ovals, 14x10-10x8 mm.	ea.	2.00-15.00
Carnelian, ovals, 14x10-6x4 mm.	ea.	2.00-10.00
Chrysoprase, Australian, ovals, 12x10-18x13 mm.	ea.	12.00-50.00
Coral, white, rd. buttons, $\frac{1}{2}$"	ea.	6.00
Coral, pink, ovals, 6x4-8x6 mm.	ea.	6.00-45.00
Ivory, ovals, 14x10-25x18 mm.	ea.	1.50-2.50
Jadeite, ovals, 14x12-30x20 mm.	ea.	6.00-40.00
Jadeite, dark green, 18x 13 mm.	ea.	12.00-15.00
Jadeite, earring drops, drilled, 37x15 mm., good	ea.	40.00
Lapis lazuli, Afghan., ovals, 14x12-25x18 mm.	ea.	15.00-60.00
Lapis lazuli, Chile, ovals, 14x12-25x18 mm.	ea.	5.00-12.00
Moonstone, India, ovals, 16x12 mm.	ea.	35.00
Moonstone, Ceylon, ovals, 14x10-20x15 mm., fine	ea.	20.00-45.00
Moonstone, Ceylon, tie-tack rds., 4-10 mm.	ea.	2.00-3.00
Nephrite, ovals, 10x8-30x22 mm.	ea.	15.00

Rose quartz, ovals, 14x12-30x20 mm.	ea.	2.00-10.00
Tourmaline, pink, ovals, 6x4-9x7 mm.	ea.	14.00-45.00

BOWLS, COMMERCIAL GRADE

A specialty of the Idar-Oberstein center in Germany is the production of thin-walled agate bowls which are highly translucent and display beautiful bandings and patterns; the difficulty of making such delicate objects and the rarity of suitable rough is reflected in the prices.

Agate, banded, about 6½"x5½"x3", walls about ⅛"-³⁄₁₆" thick	ea.	350.00-3,500.00

ASHTRAYS, COMMERCIAL GRADE

The simplest types are merely slabs of rough, untrimmed, with top surfaces and scooped-out depression polished; others are completely polished or crudely faceted upon the edges; prices increase mainly with labor expended but some materials also influence cost; produced in Germany and Brazil.

Agate, natural rim, 4"x3", ⅝" thick	ea.	9.00-25.00
Agate, natural rim, 8"x4", 1¼" thick	ea.	25.00-65.00
Agate, round, polished rim, 4"x3", ⅝" thick	ea.	12.00-25.00
Agate, round, polished rim, 2" diam.	ea.	15.00
Agate, oval, polished rim, 2" diam.	ea.	16.00
Amazonite, 2½"x2", ¾" thick	ea.	10.00-25.00
Obsidian, 2½"x2", ¾" thick	ea.	6.00-12.00
Onyx, 5½"-7½" square	ea.	10.00-20.00
Onyx, 5½"-7½" round	ea.	10.00-20.00
Rhodochrosite, 2¾"x2¼", ¾" thick	ea.	15.00-35.00
Rose quartz, 3"x2"-4"x3", 1¼" thick	ea.	12.00-35.00
Tigereye, 2½"x2", ¾" thick	ea.	9.00-18.00

INLAID RING AND BROOCH STONES

Quartz & other gemstones, parquetry, 18x18-18x13 mm.	ea.	5.00
Precious opal in black-dyed chalcedony, rds., 10-12 mm.	ea.	10.00-15.00
Same, ovals, 10x8-14x2 mm.	ea.	12.00-15.00
Same, pears, navettes, 10x8-16x8 mm.	ea.	8.50-15.00

SPHERES

Agates, 1"-3"	lb.	20.00-25.00
Agates, 3"-4"	lb.	25.00-30.00
Amethyst, 40-50 mm.	ea.	16.00
Calcite onyxes, 2"-4"	ea.	5.00-20.00
Calcite onyxes, 4"-5"	ea.	15.00-30.00
Howlite, black veined, 2½"-4"	lb.	15.00-25.00
Jasper, 4"	lb.	20.00-25.00
Malachite, 1¼"	ea.	20.00
Nephrite, California, 3½"-	lb.	35.00-40.00
Obsidians, flow types, 4"	lb.	15.00-25.00
Rock crystal, cloudy, asteriated, 3½"	lb.	40.00-70.00
Rock crystal, clean, 1"-2"	lb.	30.00-70.00
Rock crystal, 2½"-3"	lb.	30.00-70.00
Rose Quartz, 40-50 mm.	ea.	16.00
Smoky quartz, clean, 1"-3"	lb.	40.00-60.00
Rutilated quartz, 1"-3"	lb.	40.00-90.00
Rutilated quartz, 4¾", fine	ea.	600.00-800.00
Rhodonite, black veined, 3½"	lb.	30.00-50.00
Rhyolite, orbicular, 2½"-4"	lb.	30.00-50.00
Variscite, pale green, 4"	lb.	45.00-75.00

BEADS, UNDRILLED AND DRILLED

The list below shows *undrilled* prices, followed by *one-half drilled* and *full-drilled* prices, if these are known. One-half drilled beads are used mainly for cementing to small studs in various types of jewelry.

		Undrilled	*One-half drilled*	*Full-drilled*
Agate, 4-10 mm.	ea.	.20-1.35.	.60-1.60	.80-1.80
Agate, dyed, 8-12 mm.	ea.	.50-1.00		
Amazonite, 3-20 mm.	ea.			.75-6.00
Amethyst, good grade, 4-10 mm.	ea.	.45-1.50	1.70-4.10	1.85-4.90
Aventurine, India, 4-10 mm.	ea.	.16-1.25	.60-1.60	.80-1.80
Bloodstone, 4-20 mm.	ea.			.50-5.25
Carnelian, 4-10 mm.	ea.	.25-.80	.60-1.60	.80-1.80
Chalcedony, dyed, 2-3½ mm.	ea.	.25-.30	.60-1.60	.80-1.80
Citrine, 4-10 mm.	ea.		.60-2.60	.80-3.00
Coral, pink, 4-10 mm.	ea.		2.00-8.00	2.25-8.25
Garnet, 4-10 mm.	ea.		1.00-4.00	1.25-4.25
Goldstone, 4-10 mm.	ea.		.60-1.60	.80-1.90
Hematite, 4-10 mm.	ea.	.50-4.00	.60-1.50	.80-1.90
Jadeite, 4-10 mm., poor grade	ea.		.60-1.60	.80-1.80
Jasper, 4-10 mm.	ea.	.90-2.00	1.00-2.40	1.25-2.80
Lapis, Afghan, 5-10 mm., good grade	ea.		2.00-6.00	2.70-9.00
Labradorite, 4-10 mm.	ea.		1.00-4.00	1.25-4.25
Malachite, 4-10 mm.	ea.		1.00-4.00	1.25-4.25
Mother-of-pearl, 7-12 mm.	ea.			.25-.75
Nephrite, Wyoming, 4-10 mm., poor grade	ea.	.20-.65	.60-1.60	.80-1.80
Nephrite, New Zealand, 4-10 mm.	ea.			.90-2.50
Rhodochrosite, 8 mm.	ea.			1.25
Rhodonite, 4-20 mm.	ea.	.26-3.20	.31-3.25	.35-3.50
Rock crystal, 4-20 mm.	ea.	.16-3.25	.21-3.30	.25-3.50
Rose quartz, 4-10 mm.	ea.		.60-1.60	.80-1.80
Smoky quartz., 4-10 mm.	ea.		.60-1.60	.80-1.80
Sodalite, 4-10 mm.	ea.		.60-1.60	.80-1.80
Tigereye, 3-20 mm.	ea.		.85-2.10	1.10-2.25
Tourmaline, 4-12 mm.	ea.			1.00 7.00
Turquois, 4-10 mm.	ea.		.60-1.60	.80-1.80

NECKLACE STRINGS, GOOD QUALITY

These necklaces are strung on temporary cord and are without clasps or fittings. Most of the beads are spherical in shape and made by bead mill processes in Germany to insure accuracy and high polish. The coral beads are mainly from rough material fished from Japanese waters and cut in Japan.

Agates, uniform, 4-10 mm., 15"-16"	ea.	10.00-20.00
Amazonite, uniform, 8-10 mm., 15"-16"	ca.	45.00-60.00
Amber, cloudy, uniform, 8-10 mm., 15"-16"	ea.	100.00-500.00
Amber, clear, faceted, uniform, 8-10 mm., 15"-16"	ea.	60.00-120.00
Amber, cloudy, grad., 7-15 mm., 15"-16"	ea.	250.00 +
Amber, clear, faceted, 7-16 mm., 15"-16"	ea.	350.00 +
Amethyst, uniform, 8-10 mm., 15"-16"	ea.	80.00-150.00
Amethyst, uniform, high quality, 8-10 mm., 15"-16"	ea.	150.00 350.00
Amethyst, grad., faceted, 7-12 mm., 15"-16"	ea.	200.00

Amethyst, grad., 7-12 mm., 15"-16"	ea.	100.00
Amethyst, uniform 4-12 mm., fair	ea.	15.00-45.00
Aquamarine, grad., 2-5 mm., 15"-16", fair	ea.	25.00-100.00
Aventurine, round shapes, 16"	ea.	16.00-24.00
Azurite, 4-12 mm, 16"	ea.	40.00-180.00
Bloodstone, uniform, 4-15 mm., 15"-16"	ea.	40.00-65.00
Carnelian, uniform, 5-12 mm., 15"-16"	ea.	28.00-50.00
Chalcedony, dyed, uniform, 5-12 mm., 15"-16"	ea.	28.00-50.00
Citrine, uniform, faceted, 8 mm., 15"-16"	ea.	150.00
Citrine, grad., faceted, 6-12 mm., 15"-16"	ea.	125.00
Coral, white, uniform, 5-8 mm., 15"- 1 6"	ea.	18.00-100.00
Coral, white, grad., 6-12 mm., 15"-16"	ea.	75.00
Coral, orange, grad.	ea.	75.00
Coral, pink, uniform, 5-8 mm., 15"-16"	ea.	20.00-140.00
Coral, pink, 6 mm., 15"-16"	ea.	15.00-75.00
Coral, dark pink, uniform, 8 mm.	ea.	35.00-125.00
Coral, pink, uniform, 10 mm.	ea.	65.00-200.00
Coral, pink, uniform, 12 mm.	ea.	100.00-300.00
Coral, angel's skin pink, uniform	ea.	250.00-300.00
Coral, light red, uniform, 10-12 mm.	ea.	120.00-150.00
Coral, fine red, grad.	ea.	160.00-250.00
Coral, red mottled, uniform, 17", 42 bds.	ea.	90.00-150.00
Coral, ox-blood red, grad.	ea.	200.00-400.00
Coral, twig sections, ⅜" twigs, 24"-32" long	ea.	15.00-45.00
Coral, black, ½" twig sections, uniform, 16"	ea.	9.00-12.00
Garnet, almandite, grad., 3½-7 mm., 15"-16"	ea.	10.00-60.00
Ivory, uniform, 6-10 mm., 15"- 1 6"	ea.	28.00-50.00
Ivory, grad., 7-14 mm., 15"-16"	ea.	30.00-45.00
Ivory, grad., carved, 5-9 mm., 15"-16"	ea.	40.00-65.00
Ivory, uniform, with 2" pendant, 16"	ea.	40.00-50.00
Jadeite, green, uniform, 9 mm., 1	ea.	100.00-375.00
Jadeite, light green, uniform, 12 mm., 14"	ea.	250.00
Jadeite, dark green, uniform, 6 mm., 14"	ea.	150.00
Jadeite, uniform, 6-8 mm., 15"-16"	ea.	60.00-150.00
Jadeite, grad., 4½-10 mm., 15"-16", good qualitv	ea.	250.00
Jadeite, uniform, 8-10 mm., 15"-16", good quality	ea.	300.00-500.00
Jaspers, also dyed blue, uniform, 5-12 mm., 15"-1 6"	ea.	28.00-50.00
Jaspers, also dyed blue, grad., 7-13 mm., 15"-16"	ea.	35.00
Jaspers, grad., 6-12 mm., 15"-16"	ea.	40.00
Jet, uniform, 16", 3 mm. (imitation)	ea.	16.00
Lapis, Afghan., grad., 4-1 0 mm., 15"-l 6"	ea.	300.00
Lapis, Chile, uniform, 8-12 mm., 15"-1 6"	ea.	80.00-275.00
Lapis, Chile, grad., 6-12 mm., 15"-16"	ea.	50.00-100.00
Labradorite, uniform, 4-12 mm., 15"-16"	ea.	15.00-65.00
Malachite, uniform, 6-8 mm., 15"-16"	ea.	120.00-140.00
Malachite, grad., 5-10 mm., 15"-16"	ea.	150.00
Moonstone, India, grad., 8-14 mm., 15"-16"	ea.	60.00
Moss agate, green or red, grad., 4-12 mm., 15-16"	ea.	20.00-45.00
Mother-of-pearl, uniform, 6 mm., 17"-28"	ea.	8.00-10.00
Nephrite, uniform, 8-10 mm., 15"-16"	ea.	75.00-80.00
Nephrite, grad., 6-12 mm., 15"- 16"	ea.	100.00
Obsidian, black, faceted, uniform, 16", 12 mm.	ea.	15.00

Opal, crystal, 3 mm., 143 beads		375.00
Opal, crystal, 3-6 mm. 107 beads		4,000.00
Opal, crystal, 4-7 mm., 87 beads		850.00
Opal, crystal, 5-9 mm., 63 beads		1,200.00
Opal, crystal, 7-15 mm., 39 beads		12,500.00
Opal, gray-base, 8-10 mm., 43 beads		2,500.00
Opal, white-base, 8-13 mm. 44 beads		1,500.00
Opal, jelly, 7-15 mm., 49 beads		1,500.00
Opal, black, good color, 7-13 mm., 44 beads		3,500.00
Rhodochrosite, uniform, 8-10 mm., 15"-16"	ea.	50.00-60.00
Rhodochrosite, grad., 7-15 mm., 15"-16"	ea.	50.00
Rhodonite, uniform, 8-10 mm., 15"-16"	ea.	50.00-65.00
Rhodonite, grad., 7-15 mm., 15"-16"	ea.	40.00
Rock crystal, uniform, faceted, 6-10 mm., 15"-16"	ea.	16.00-30.00
Rock crystal, grad., faceted, 6-10 mm., 15"-16"	ea.	10.00-25.00
Rose quartz, baroque shapes, 18"	ea.	16.00-24.00
Rose quartz, uniform, 10 mm., 15"-16"	ea.	30.00
Rose quartz, grad., 7-13 mm., 15"-16"	ea.	35.00
Smoky quartz, uniform, faceted, 10 mm., 15"-16"	ea.	30.00
Sodalite, uniform, 12 mm., 15"-16"	ea.	25.00-40.00
Sodalite, 15"-16" pebble	ea.	10.00
Tigereye, uniform, 6-10 mm., 15"-16"	ea.	30.00-48.00
Tigereye, grad., 7-13 mm., 15"-16"	ea.	35.00-40.00
Tigereye, red, 10 mm.	ea.	16.00-24.00
Tigereye, blue, uniform, 6-10 mm., 15"-16"	ea.	28.00-50.00
Turquois, uniform, 5-8 mm., 15"-16"	ea.	350.00-775.00
Turquois, uniform, 8 mm., 15"-16"	ea.	335.00
Turquois, tumbled, ½", 15"-16", color-treated and stabilized	ea.	20.00

INDIAN QUALITY NECKLACES

The necklaces below are cut in India, mainly from Indian gemstones. They are characteristically non-uniform because the shaping and finishing are done by hand. The faceted beads are crude. Ready to wear, with inexpensive fittings and spacers.

Agates, "beggar beads", banded, elongated beads, 26"	ea.	6.50-15.00
Agates, brownish, elongated beads, 17"	ea.	8.00-15.00
Agates, milky banded, round beads, 17"	ea.	7.00-15.00
Amethyst, round beads, 17"	ea.	32.00-40.00
Amethyst, faceted beads, 17"	ea.	50.00-60.00
Amethyst, carved beads, 17"	ea.	50.00-60.00
Aventurine, round beads, 17"	ea.	9.00-15.00
Aventurine, round beads, 26"	ea.	18.00-24.00
Bloodstone, round beads, 17"	ea.	7.00-10.00
Bloodstone, mixed shapes, 26"	ea.	9.00-13.00
Bloodstone, elongated beads, 17"	ea.	8.00-12.00
Carnelian, mixed beads, 26"	ea.	10.00-15.00
Carnelian, elongated beads, 17"	ea.	8.00-12.00
Carnelian, round beads, 17"	ea.	7.00-15.00
Emerald, round beads, 17"	ea.	300.00 +
Garnet, almandite, round beads, 17"	ea.	14.00-40.00
Garnet, almandite, round beads, larger size, 17"	ea.`	40.00-50.00
Lapis lazuli, Afghan., poor grade, rd. beads, 17"	ea.	32.00-40.00

Lapis lazuli, Afghan., good grade, rd. beads, 17"	ea.	60.00-70.00
Moonstone, round beads, 17"	ea.	12.00-25.00
Moss agate, mixed shapes, 17"	ea.	9.00-11.00
Moss agate, mixed shpaes, 26"	ea.	12.00-15.00
Ruby, round beads, 17" (approx. $450 ea. strand)	ct.	.50
Sapphire, round beads, 17" (approx. $450 ea. strand)	ct.	.50
Tigereye, round beads, 17"	ea.	18.00-24.00
Tigereye, round beads, 26"	ea.	25.00-35.00

EGGS

Hand shaping required, consequently inaccuracies can result; from small pigeon-egg to large hen's-egg sizes; the smaller eggs are often drilled for suspension as pendants.

Agate, 2" long, high quality	ea.	30.00
Amethyst, 2"-2½"	ea.	60.00-70.00
Calcite onyx, Mexico, hen's-egg sizes, crude	ea.	3.00
Bloodstone, India	ea.	45.00
Carnelian, banded, 2", high quality	ea.	50.00
Carnelian, banded, ½"-1½" long, fine quality	ea.	20.00-50.00
Jasper, picture, 5"	ea.	200.00
Jadeite, 2" long, fair-good quality	ea.	30.00-75.00
Lapis, Chile, 2"	ea.	100.00
Malachite, 2"x2¼"	ea.	40.00
Obsidian, 1½"x½"	ea.	10.00
Rhodonite, 2", good	ea.	50.00

RINGS

Usually created by core-drilling cylinders and slicing into sections of suitable length; such cores are often by-products of hollowing vessels; can be worn as finger rings but most are used for pendants or earring hoops.

Chalcedony, dyed, faceted edges, slender, ½" diam.	ea.	2.00-5.00
Jadeite, 5/16"-½", wide, finger ring sizes	ea.	12.50-25.00
Jadeite, ⅛"-¼", wide, finger ring sizes	ea.	10.00-20.00
Jadeite, 3 interlocking rings, for pendants or earrings	set	25.00-40.00
Jadeite, heavy rings, ¾"-1½" diam., fair quality	ea.	6.75-25.00
Jadeite, disks, with center hole, 20 mm. diam.	ea.	10.00-20.00
Nephrite, black or green, heavy rings, ¼"-⅜" wide	ea.	7.50-15.00
Tigereye, rounded edge rings, ¾"-1" diam.	ea.	3.00-6.00

CYLINDERS

Gavel heads, ½" hole for handle, common gemstones, 3"-1½"	ea.	7.50
Buttons, suit size, common materials, 1" diam.	ea.	5.00-7.50
Buttons, coat size, common materials, 1¼" diam.	ea.	3.00-10.00
Rods, agate, tigereye, ¾"-1", ¼" thick	ea.	1.00-5.00

AGATE ENHYDROS

These agate carvings and geodes have the unique feature of having water trapped in a hollow cavity inside the stone. The water can be seen within the cavity when the geode or carving is tilted. direct light helps highlight this unusual feature.

All on wooden stands:

Agate, enhydro, gray, birds, 5½"x4"x1½"	ea.	2,500.00
Agate, enhydro, gray and white, cricket, 5"x4"x1¾"	ea.	900.00
Agate, enhydro, bluish-gray, birds and fruit, 5"x4"x1½"	ea.	1,500.00
Agate, enhydro, bluish-gray, grape cluster, 5"x4"x1¾"	ea.	750.00

Agate, enhydro, gray and white, birds, 7"x5"x1½" ea. 1,500.00

FLAT-SURFACED OBJECTS

Book-ends, carnelian, 9"x6½"	pr.	70.00
Book-ends, gray agate, 9"x6½"	pr.	50.00
Book-ends, rose quartz, 8"x5½"	pr.	60.00
Book-ends, petrified woods, 6"x4"-12"x6"	pr.	85.00-95.00
Book-ends, calcite onyxes, 6"x5"-11"x6"	pr.	40.00
Crosses, quartzes, drilled, 1½"x¾"	ea.	7.00-10.00
Crosses, nephrite, 1"-1½"	ea.	8.00-12.00
Crosses, nephrite, undrilled, ¾"x1¼"	ea.	5.00-10.00
Cubes, one face polished, various materials, ¾"	ea.	5.00-15.00
Paperweights, polished, fluorite materials, 2"-3" square	ea.	50.00
Paperweights, polished, chrysocolla materials, 2"-3" square	ea.	75.00
Paperweights, polished, amethyst materials, 2"-3" square	ea.	15.00-30.00

PAGODAS

Triangular tapered prisms, usually of rock crystal but also imitated in glass and plastics, with the back edge notched to create multiple reflections of Chinese pagodas; abundantly produced in Japan.

Rock crystal, drilled at apex, ¾"-2"	ea.	5.00-10.00
Rock crystal, undrilled, 2"-8"	ea.	6.00-60.00

VII

PEARLS

ALTHOUGH FINE NATURAL PEARLS STILL APPEAR ON THE MARKET, their place in jewelry has been largely taken over by the Japanese cultured pearls which are supplied by the millions each year. The decline of salt-water and fresh-water pearl fisheries can be attributed to over-fishing and destruction of the oyster beds in salt waters, the pollution of suitable fresh-water streams which formerly supplied pearl-bearing mussels in enormous quantities, and the lessened demand for mother-of-pearl, the shell material which mostly paid for the costs of fishing.

The scarcity of natural pearls has caused them to become true rarities in the gem world, with very high prices being asked for fine examples. Some attempts are being made to grow non-nucleated pearls in both salt- and fresh-water pearly mollusks, with good results being reported from Japan, where non-nucleated fresh-water pearls are being successfully produced. However, it is not likely that such pearls will ever be furnished in quantities large enough to disturb the preeminent position now held by the Japanese cultured pearl. For practical purposes, this chapter will therefore devote some space to natural pearls, but will place most emphasis on cultured pearls.

NATURAL SALT-WATER PEARLS

Most natural salt-water pearls are found in the mollusks *Pinctada vulgaris* of the Persian Gulf, Red Sea, and the Gulf of Manaar between Ceylon and India, the *Pinctada margaritifera* and *Pinctada maxima* inhabiting the waters around northern Australia and the South Sea Islands, and to a lesser extent, in the *Pinctada radiata* of Venezuelan waters, the *Pinctada margaritifera* (*mazatlanica*) of the Gulf of California, and the *Pinctada squamulosa* of the Gulf of Panama. The best of these pearls are generally conceded to come from the *P. vulgaris* and the *P. radiata*, although the largest specimens occur in the *P. Margaritifera* and *maxima*. Colorful pearls sometimes occur in the various species of the abalone (*Haliotis*), and non-iridescent, but still attractive, pink pearls in the giant conch (*Strombus gigas*) of the West Indies. Pearls from ordinary salt-water mussels, clams, and edible oysters are completely without value.

A very large number of species of fresh-water mussels (*Unio*) produce attractive pearls, mainly of small size and many of highly irregular or baroque shape. They were once recovered in large numbers from the mussels inhabiting the rivers and streams of the Mississippi River drainage basin, but industrial pollution and silting behind dams has destroyed most of the formerly productive beds. Excellent pearls are still being taken from the fresh-water mussels of the British Isles and Europe, while in Japan, one species is being cultivated to produce non-nucleated pearls of good quality.

CULTURED PEARLS

Practically all cultured pearls upon the market are produced by the Japanese species *Pinctada martensi* which is carefully farmed in protected waters off the Japanese islands. The pearls consist of mother-of-pearl spherical nuclei which are implanted in the flesh of the mollusk, and, in time, are coated by concentric layers of nacre by the host. Partially successful attempts are being made to grow cultured pearls in the *P. maxima* in Australian waters, some of the pearls being of enormous size as compared to those of the *P. martensi*, which seldom exceed 12 mm. in diameter. Blister pearls are also being produced in the *P. maxima*, by inserting a hemispherical nucleus against the inner wall of the shellfish. These *mabé* pearls, as they are called, sometimes reach one inch in diameter and now have considerable vogue as half-pearls in earrings and brooches. The fresh water mussel *Hyriopsis schlegeli* is being successfully induced to grow non-nucleated pearls in Lake Biwa, Honshu, Japan. The pearls tend to be rather irregular in shape, but the colors are attractive and the industry appears sure of a successful future.

IRIDESCENCE

True pearls are prized mainly because of the iridescence which arises from the diffraction of light from the translucent outer layers of the pearls. It is promoted by greater translucency and, conversely, decreased by less translucency. Those pearls which are "chalky" white usually have poor iridescence while those which look as if one can see beneath the surface and hence are highly translucent, are the best. Thus one of the tests for quality, particularly for cultured pearls. is to make a round hole in a slip of cardboard, somewhat smaller than the pearl itself, and hold the pearl against a strong light while it is resting in the hole. If the entire material of the pearl is highly translucent, one will be able to see some light passing through even the thicker portions. On the other hand, if only a thin outer layer is translucent, as is commonly the case with poorer cultured pearls, the light will only pass through along the periphery of the pearl. Good cultured pearls are those in which this translucent outer layer is fairly thick, at least over one-half millimeter, and in which the growers of the pearls have taken the trouble to use high quality translucent natural pearl shell for the nuclei.

PEARL SHAPES AND SURFACE QUALITY

The next consideration is the shape of the pearls, the prized shapes being perfect spheres, followed by symmetrical pear or drop shapes. Somewhat flattened pearls are less prized, while those which are irregular in shape, sometimes fantastically so, and called *baroques*, are considerably less prized. The surfaces of pearls should be perfectly smooth, lacking pits, raised areas, ridges, or other physical deformities. Black, discolored, or chalky spots are also serious defects. If the pearls are drilled, the holes must be just large enough to accommodate the necklace stringing cord or nylon filament, and the edges of the holes must not be chipped.

PEARL COLORS AND THEIR DESIRABILITY

The *body color* of a pearl is that which one sees when the pearl is placed upon perfectly white paper or cotton in natural north daylight. It is surprising how the subtle colors stand out clearly when a number of pearls of differing body hue are compared side by side under precisely the same lighting conditions. Even differences in hue from one pearl to the next in a strand of pearls are not difficult to detect. In general, the body colors that are highly prized are white, pink, cream, gold, and black, the last not really being black at all but pale steel-gray or bluish-gray. The colors of salt-water pearls tend to be delicate in tint, but rather rich colors are encountered in fresh-water pearls, particularly those from Mississippi River tributaries. The natural pearls of Southwest Pacific waters are largely silvery-white, as are the extremely large blister-pearl mabés, which are cultured in the pearly mollusks of those waters. Black pearls occur in the Bay of Panama and in the Gulf of California, but very few are found now. Pearls from the Persian

Gulf, Red Sea, and the waters between Sri Lanka and India are ordinarily yellow-ish in tinge.

In the United States, cultured pearl merchants have found that the greatest de-mand is for pink, or *rosé*, as it is commonly called, or for a slightly yellowish-pink called *cream-rosé*. On the other hand, the European prefers the cream-rosé to pure pink while the buyers in the Near East and India, among other Asiatic countries, seem to prefer yellow and gold tints.

DYED PEARLS

The use of staining agents to impart color to cultured pearls is a common prac-tice and warrants careful examination of high-priced strings of black or rosé pearls. In most instances, a suspect pearl examined under moderate magnification shows minute specks or concentrations of color in surface layers, indicating that a staining agent was used. If the color were natural, it would be diffused evenly and would not be detectable by simple optical means.

SIZES OF PEARLS

Size is of crucial importance in establishing prices because very few natural pearls exceed about 6 mm. in diameter, while even among the cultured pearls, specimens in excess of 12 mm. are rarely found in sufficient number to market them except as individual rarities. just as in gemstones, rarity of large specimens exacts its toll in respect to price. Pearls are considered *very small* when they are less than 3 mm. in diameter, *small* when from 3 to 4½ mm., *medium* from 5 to 6 mm., and *large* when from 7 to 8 mm. in diameter; *very large* pearls are over 8 mm., but, among Japanese cultured pearls, not usually over 12 mm. South Seas pearls reach diameters up to 15 mm., while mabé half-pearls may reach as much as 25 mm. in diameter.

PEARL NECKLACES

The principal use of round or nearly round pearls is in necklaces which may contain pearls all of the same size, or perhaps a few at each end which are slightly smaller, or may contain pearls of increasing size from each end to a large cen-trally-located pearl. The first kind is called a *uniform* necklace, and the second a *graduated* necklace. Uniform necklaces contain pearls from as small as 3 mm. to as large as 12 mm. in diameter; the standard length, or *choker*, is about 16 inches, but also sold are *princess* (18"), *matinee* (20-24"), *opera* (28-32"), and *rope* (40-45") necklaces. Graduated necklaces range from 16 to 18 inches in length, with the 17-inch length being most popular.

To avoid duty on ready-to-wear necklaces, most dealers import strands of carefully matched pearls, strung on temporary cords. The customer may buy such strands and arrange for the final stringing and application of terminal fittings, or ask the dealer to do this for him.

TABLES OF STANDARD JAPANESE CULTURED PEARL STRANDS

Uniform Type-16-inch Length

Pearl Diameter in Millimeters	Weight in Grams
3	3.75
5	12.36
6	18.75
7	26.25
8	30.00
9	33.75
10	37.50

Graduated Type-17-inch Length

Pearl Diameters (Center & Ends), in mm.	Weight in Grams
7-3	13.12
7.5-3.5	15.00
8-4	18.75
8.5-3.75	22.50
9-5.5	28.13
9-6 (18-inch length)	30.00
9.5-6.5 (18-inch length)	35.63

Data supplied by Japan Pearl Exporters' Association.

OTHER PEARL USES

Pearls are commonly used in earrings and in small jewelry pieces. They are secured by cementing them in sockets or upon pins which fit holes drilled about half way through the pearls, or are secured in place by bentover prongs. Large baroque pearls are prized for jewelry in which the pearl serves as the body of a bird, a human torso, or some other object, with the rest of the design being made from precious metals decorated with gems or enamels in various colors. Small baroque pearls, especially those resembling flower petals, are used in naturalistic jewelry designs, in which they are very attractive. Mabé pearls, being hemispherical in shape, are most commonly used in button-type earrings but also provide beautiful settings in brooches, pins, and pendants.

NATURAL PEARLS AND PRICES

The classical salt-water natural pearls are enormously expensive when compared to cultured pearls of equal quality. For example, a single natural pearl of fine quality 4 mm. size will be priced about $110.00; 6 mm. pearl $675.00; 8 mm. pearl $3,200.00; and 9 mm. pearl as much as $5,500.00. While it is nearly impossible for the average layman to detect any appreciable differences between natural and cultured pearls of fair to good quality, and only slightly less difficult for the expert who is often forced to use advanced testing methods to be certain, it is obvious that the factor of rarity is of great importance in the case of natural pearls-and fashion too. We see both these value factors working in the case of natural versus synthetic sapphires and rubies, and should not be surprised to see them being equally effective in setting prices between natural and cultured pearls.

Unlike cultured pearls which are sold in quantity by the Japanese *momme*, a weight measure equivalent to 3.75 grams, natural pearls are sold by the grain, a measure equivalent to one-fourth of a metric carat. However, some cheaper natural pearls are sold by the carat.

ABALONE PEARLS

These are surprisingly rare despite the large numbers of abalones fished from the Pacific Ocean waters of Mexico, the United States, and Japan. Most specimens are baroque shapes, usually flattened buttons or elongated and irregular pear shapes, ranging from 4 to 25 millimeters in length. Many are hollow. Colors are beautiful but the iridescence is only skin-deep. Effective in modern "free-form" jewelry, tic-tacks, and pendants.

Undrilled, baroques, 15-30 cts.   ct.   300.00-500.00

CONCH PEARLS

Produced occasionally by the large queen conch (*Strombus gigas*) of the West Indies and Florida; the color is the same pink as the inner lining of the shell, with a delicate graining of fibrous texture, and glossy rather than glassy luster; uncommon. Sizes sometimes to 20 mm.

Pink, West Indies or Florida, to 12 cts.	ct.	75.00-300.00

Exceptional Pink to $500.00 per carat

FRESH-WATER PEARLS (*UNIO*)

Now regularly obtainable only in small numbers except from the Lake Biwa, Japan, beds where, strictly speaking, the pearls are cultured, although natural specimens do occur. The stream pearls of the United States, Canada, Europe, and Asia are noted for their wide color range, although white to nearly white specimens are also found. Some typical colors are pink, copper, pale brown, gold, gray, blue-gray, purplish, and green, but these are n ever intense. Many United states specimens are highly irregular baroques, common shapes being *wings*, which resemble a single insect wing in shape, *buttons*, and flattened baroque shapes resembling flower petals. Due to the general scarcity of these pearls, especially of good shapes and similar hues, it is nearly impossible to find enough of them to assemble even a short necklace of reasonably matching specimens. Most of them are used inividually in jewelry, sometimes in earrings where a reasonable match is satisfactory, and in moderate-priced jewelry where flower and leaf motifs are developed by the use of wing baroques.

U.S., fresh-water pearls, white	ct.	1.00-15.00
U.S., tinted, ¼-¾ carat	ct.	1.00-15.00
U.S., various colors, round pearls	ct.	15.00-125.00
U.S., various colors, baroques	ct.	5.00-50.00

SALT-WATER PEARLS (*PINCTADA*)

Generally scarce; fished from the waters of the Persian Gulf, Red Sea, and the Gulf of Manaar; small quantities sent to market from Australian and South Seas waters as recovered incidental to fishing for mother-of-pearl *Pinctada* species. Prices vary considerably according to size and quality, the highly translucent pearls from the Near East and Indian waters generally commanding better prices than the larger but less translucent specimens from Australian and South Seas waters. Commonly size-classified according to letters of the alphabet, ranging from "D," or about 2½ mm. in diameter, to "Y," or about 6 mm. in diameter. The prices below are merely indicative of general trends.

Single pearls, good quality, 2½ mm. to 6 mm. diameter	ea.	25.00-1,000.00
Strand, graduated, 2½-3½ mm., fair to good quality	ea.	25.00-3,000.00
Strand, uniform, 6-7 mm., fair to good quality	ea.	25,000.00-90,000.00

CULTURED PEARLS

FRESH-WATER, JAPANESE

These are the Lake Biwa pearls previously referred to; they have been marketed since about 1961; colors include near-white, pale rosé, pink, orange, cream, very pale blue, and very pale green; baroque shapes are most common but many pearls are nearly spherical; in sizes to 7½ mm.

Grayish, button shaped, good quality	grain	4.00-5.00
Grayish, nearly spherical, good quality	grain	2.00-10.00
Bronze, nearly spherical, 2½-5 mm.	ea.	3.75-5.00
Pink, 4 mm., baroques	ea.	1.50-4.500

Pink, baroques, 8-8½ mm.	ea.	10.00-85.00
White, 4-5 mm., baroques	ea.	4.00-5.00
Necklace, 18", baroques, various colors, 5-6 mm.	ea.	200.00-230.00

SALT-WATER, JAPANESE

There are wide price ranges due to the fact that larger pearls are more difficult to grow and nacre production varies markedly from one shellfish to the next. As a consequence, and despite the enormous numbers of pearls removed each year from the mature shellfish, much time must be spent in grading the pearls according to body color, degree and quality of iridescence, perfection of shape, absence of flaws, thickness of nacre, and finally, closeness of match in the case of necklace strands. For necklaces particularly, retail prices are basically established in Japan where the experts in selecting matched pearls assemble the strands and set the wholesale costs; the quality statements, and the accompanying prices, are accepted at face value by buyers or importers who then pass on the necklaces to retailers. After suitable markups, according to these basic cost figures, retailers place the necklaces on sale to the general public. In respect to the buyer being able to judge quality, this is a far more difficult task for pearls than is true for many gemstones where color quality, accuracy of cut, and presence or absence of flaws are not too difficult to judge. The subtle colors of pearls, the degree of translucency, quality of iridescence, and other important factors, are not learned overnight, and, in effect, the buyer must place his trust upon the pearl grader who initially assembled the necklace strand in Japan. The Japanese Pearl Exporters' Association is aware of this state of affairs, and has taken steps to maintain controls over pearl production and to set standards of quality. Once the pearl strands reach the United States, prices can and do vary according to the amount of profit realized by wholesalers and retailers, but generally speaking, retail prices tend to standardize because of the large quantities of necklaces sold and the highly competitive nature of the business.

SINGLE JAPANESE CULTURED PEARLS

These are sold in all sizes and qualities, either whole, drilled through, or half-drilled in the event that they are to be mounted on pegs. The charge for drilling the relatively soft calcareous substance of which pearls are made is considerably less than for ordinary hard gemstones, and ranges from about $.25 to $.50 per hole.

SPHERICAL

Top grades, fine rosé, 2-6 mm., ½ drilled	ea.	2.50-15.00
Top grades, fine rosé, 6½-10 mm., ½ drilled	ea.	20.00-500.00
Top grades, fine rosé, 10½-12 mm., ½ drilled	ea.	500.00-1,500.00
Medium grades, good rosé, 2-6 mm.,½ drilled	ea.	2.25-9.50
Medium grades, good rosé, 6½-10 mm., ½ drilled	ea.	12.00-600.00
Medium grades, good rosé, 10½-12 mm., ½ drilled	ea.	100.00-900.00
Fair grades, rosé, 2-6 mm., ½ drilled	ea.	2.00-7.25
Fair grades, rosé, 6½-10 mm., ½ drilled	ea.	7.25-375.00
Fair grades, rosé, 10½-12 mm., ½ drilled	ea.	325.00-600.00
Lesser grade, rosé, 4-5 mm., ½ drilled	ea.	1.50-2.00
Lesser grade, rosé, 5-6 mm., ½ drilled	ea.	2.00-2.25
Lesser grade, rosé, 7-9 mm., ½ drilled	ea.	5.00-45.00
Grey, fair, 5-9 mm., ½ drilled	ea.	11.75-200.00
White, matched pairs, 5-6 mm., ½ drilled	pr.	5.00-15.00
Black dyed, ordinary grade, 3-5 mm., ½ drilled	ea.	5.90-10.00
Black dyed, ordinary grade, 5-9 mm., ½ drilled	ea.	10.00-170.00

BLACK CULTURED PEARLS

Tahitian black cultured pearls are natural black color. Imitations can be colored by dye or irradiation. Prices are for natural color black only. The black lipped oyster is harvested in the outer island of French Polynesia. Colors can range from black to silver gray, copper and gold. Sizes are generally from 8-14 mm. and shapes are round, drop, button, circle and baroque. *Prices are per pearl.*

Black cultured pearl, round, 8-10 mm., fine	ea.	250.00-1,050.00
Black cultured pearl, round, 10-12 mm., fine	ea.	1,080.00-2,900.00
Black cultured pearl, drop, 8-10 mm.	ea.	215.00-900.00
Black cultured pearl, drop, 10-12 mm.	ea.	925.00-2,700.00
Black cultured pearl, circle, 8-10 mm.	ea.	100.00-200.00
Black cultured pearl, circle, 10-12 mm.	ea.	200.00-290.00
Black cultured pearl, baroque, to 9 mm.	ea.	60.00-75.00
Black cultured pearl, baroque, 9-10 mm.	ea.	90.00-125.00
Black cultured pearl, baroque, 10 mm. +	ea.	150.00-200.00

MABÉ OR BLISTER PEARLS

These are large blister pearl, consisting of a thin hemispherical shell of nacre, carefully cleaned on the inside, filled with a backing material, and a close-fitting closure cemented to the bottom; they are grown in Australia but are sent to Japan for processing and marketing.

White or cream, fair grades, 11-18 mm.	ea.	65.00-100.00
Grays of various hues, fair grades, 12-20 mm.	ea.	45.00-150.00

NECKLACE STRANDS

Figures below are given in price ranges with variations due to differences in quality and accuracy of matching individual pearls in either uniform or graduated strands. The diameters given in the *uniform* section are size ranges in which the individual pearls in any given strand can occur; they do not imply that the strand tapers. However, for *graduated* strands, the sizes are for the end pearls (low figure) and the largest pearl in the center of the strand (high figure). The taper in graduated strands may be a *straight* taper or a *compound* taper. A straight taper means that when the strand is laid in a suitable groove to hold the pearls steady, a ruler placed along one half of the necklace will touch every pearl from the smallest on the end, to the largest in the center. On the other hand, repeating this operation with a compound tapered strand will disclose the fact that the ruler may touch only the largest central pearl and one of the end pearls, with a "sag" between, or may touch some pearls between the largest pearl and one of the end pearls because of a "bulge" between. All varieties of taper are made, some being more pleasing to customers than others, it being a matter of individual taste as to which is preferred.

UNIFORM (16")

Top grades, rosé, 2-4 mm.	ea.	350.00-500.00
Top grades, rosé, 4½-6 mm.	ea.	450.00-1,000.00
Top grades, rosé, 6½-8 mm.	ea.	675.00-3,500.00
Top grades, rosé, 8½-10 mm.	ea.	3,000.00-19,000.00
Top grades, rosé, 10½-12 mm.	ea.	8,000.00-19,000.00
Fine grades, rosé, 2-4 mm.	ea.	240.00-395.00

Fine grades, rosé, 4½-6 mm.	ea.	300.00-500.00
Fine grades, rosé, 6½-8 mm.	ea.	675.00-1,900.00
Fine grades, rosé, 8½-10 mm.	ea.	1,100.00-16,000.00
Fine grades, rosé, 10½-12 mm.	ea.	1,500.00-20,000.00
Good grades, rosé, 2-4 mm.	ea.	125.00-250.00
Good grades, rosé, 4½-6 mrn.	ea.	225.00-400.00
Good grades, rosé, 6½-8 mm.	ea.	500.00-1,500.00
Good grades, rosé, 8½-10 mm.	ea.	2,500.00-8,000.00
Good grades, rosé, 10½-12 mm.	ea.	8,500.00-15,000.00
Fair grades, rosé, 2-4 mm.	ea.	170.00-185.00
Fair grades, rosé, 4½-6 mm.	ea.	170.00-240.00
Fair grades, rosé, 6½-8 mm.	ea.	300.00-600.00
Fair grades, rosé, 8½-10 mm.	ea.	1,100.00-6,000.00
Fair grades, rosé, 10½-12 mm.	ea.	5,000.00-9,000.00
Top grades, golden, 2-6 mm.	ea.	175.00-800.00
Top grades, golden, 6½-10 mm.	ea.	850.00-6,500.00
Top grades, golden, 10½-12 mm.	ea.	3,500.00-15,000.00
Fine grades, golden, 2-6 mm.	ea.	100.00-600.00
Fine grades, golden, 6½-10 mm.	ea.	250.00-2,600.00
Fine grades, golden, 10½-12 mm.	ea.	3,000.00-5,300.00
Good grades, golden, 2-6 mm.	ea.	90.00-150.00
Good grades, golden, 6½-10 mm.	ea.	180.00-850.00
Good grades, golden, 10½-12 mm.	ea.	500.00-2,000.00
Fair grades, golden, 2-6 mm.	ea.	50.00-125.00
Fair grades, golden, 6½-10 mm.	ea.	125.00-250.00
Fair grades, golden, 10½-12 mm.	ea.	250.00-575.00
Good grades, white, 3-4 mm.	ea.	125.00-350.00
Good grades, white, 4½-6 mm.	ea.	75.00-425.00
Good grades, white, 6½-7 mm.	ea.	375.00-450.00
Good grades, white, 7½-9 min.	ea.	550.00-2,200.00
Ordinary grades, white, 3-4 mm.	ea.	90.00-125.00
Ordinary grades, white, 4½-6 mm.	ea.	100.00-225.00
Ordinary grades, white, 6½-7 mm.	ea.	275.00-450.00
Ordinary grades, white, 7½-9 mm.	ea.	450.00-1,200.00
Fair grades, white, 3-4 mm.	ea.	50.00-100.00
Fair grades, white, 4½-6 mm.	ea.	70.00-125.00
Fair grades, white, 6½-7 mm.	ea.	125.00-390.00
Good grades, black, 6-6½ mm.	ea.	400.00-625.00
Good grades, black, 6½-7 mm.	ea.	600.00-850.00
Fair grades, black, 3-4 mm.	ea.	50.00-75.00
Fair grades, black, 4½-6 mm.	ea.	75.00-125.00
Fair grades, black, 6½-7 mm.	ea.	125.00-600.00
Baroques, white, 16" strands, approx. 6½-7 mm.	ea.	250.00-395.00
Baroques, white, 16" strands, approx. 7½-8 mm.	ea.	490.00-800.00

CULTURED SALT-WATER PEARL NECKLACES, 16" LENGTH, WHITE

PRICED PER STRAND

	AAA	AA	A	COMMERCIAL
2-2½ mm.	350.00-475.00	250.00-350.00	190.00-250.00	110.00-175.00
2½-3 mm.	350.00-450.00	250.00-350.00	175.00-250.00	95.00-135.00
3-3½ mm.	350.00-450.00	250.00-350.00	165.00-225.00	95.00-145.00
4-4½ mm.	350.00-475.00	250.00-390.00	170.00-235.00	90.00-150.00
5-5½ mm.	450.00-650.00	300.00-450.00	190.00-300.00	110.00-175.00

SALT-WATER PEARL NECKLACES, 18" LENGTH

	AAA	AA	A	COMMERCIAL
6-6½ mm.	675.00-875.00	400.00-675.00	250.00-400.00	170.00-225.00
7-7½ mm.	1,100.00-1,800.00	600.00-1,100.00	350.00-595.00	210.00-325.00
8-8½ mm.	3,000.00-4,500.00	1,500.00-2,900.00	725.00-1,400.00	360.00-600.00
8½-9 mm.	4,000.00-5,500.00	2,000.00-3,800.00	900.00-1,900.00	450.00-750.00
9-9½ mm.	7,500.00-11,000.00	4,500.00-7,400.00	2,200.00-4,200.00	1,000.00-2,000.00
9½-10 mm.	14,000.00-19,000.00	8,000.00-13,500.00	4,000.00-7,000.00	1,200.00-3,500.00

MATINEE LENGTH, 20-24"

	AAA	AA	A	COMMERCIAL
4½-5 mm.	550.00-825.00	400.00-550.00	255.00-390.00	135.00-250.00
5½-6 mm.	725.00-1,175.00	490.00-750.00	300.00-475.00	180.00-295.00
6½-7 mm.	1,175.00-1,950.00	750.00-1,175.00	450.00-750.00	265.00-400.00
7½-8 mm.	3,000.00-5,250.00	1,800.00-2,850.00	790.00-1,650.00	490.00-750.00
8½-9 mm.	6,000.00-8,250.00	3,000.00-5,700.00	1,350.00-2,850.00	675.00-1,125.00
9½-10 mm.	21,000.00-28,500.00	12,000.00-19,500.00	6,000.00-10,500.00	1,800.00-5,000.00

OPERA LENGTH 28"-32"

	AAA	AA	A	COMMERCIAL
5½-6 mm.	950.00-1,550.00	650.00-950.00	450.00-635.00	240.00-390.00
6½-7 mm.	1,550.00-2,600.00	990.00-1,550.00	590.00-990.00	350.00-550.00
8-8½ mm.	6,000.00-9,000.00	3,000.00-5,800.00	1,400.00-2,800.00	700.00-1,200.00
9-9½ mm.	15,000.00-22,000.00	9,000.00-14,800.00	4,400.00-8,400.00	2,000.00-4,000.00
9½-10 mm.	28,000.00-38,000.00	16,000.00-26,000.00	8,000.00-14,000.00	2,400.00-7,000.00

GRADUATED 18" LENGTH, WHITE CULTURED SALT-WATER PEARLS

	AAA	AA	A	COMMERCIAL
3x7 mm.	450.00-800.00	350.00-450.00	250.00-350.00	150.00-190.00
4x8 mm.	590.00-850.00	390.00-575.00	200.00-395.00	175.00-225.00

Baroque cultured White Salt-Water Pearls, 16" Length			
6-6½ mm.	250.00-275.00	200.00-240.00	100.00-195.00	70.00-100.00
7-7½ mm.	400.00-475.00	265.00-400.00	125.00-250.00	90.00-115.00
8-8½₂ mm.	600.00-700.00	375.00-600.00	200.00-375.00	165.00-185.00
9-9½ mm.	1,725.00-2,000.00	750.00-1,800.00	450.00-750.00	340.00-400.00
9½-10 mm.	2,250.00-2,700.00	1,750.00-2,375.00	900.00-1,800.00	600.00-875.00

Fresh-Water Rice Pearl Necklaces, 16", Temporarily Strung (no clasp)			
3-3½ mm.	21.00-3.00	1.50-2.00	1.00-1.50
3½-4 mm.	3.00-6.00	2.00-3.00	1.50-2.00
4-5 mm.	3.50-10.00	2.50-3.50	2.00-2.50

VIII
SELECTED BOOKS ON GEMS

GENERAL

AREM, J. E. *Color Encyclopedia of Gems*, 2nd ed. New York: Chapman & Hall, 1987, 288 pp., illust. Continually useful; includes many rare gemstones.

AREM, J. E. *Gems and Jewelry*, 2nd ed. Tucson, AZ: Geoscience Press, 1992, 176 pp., illust. Handy, very useful quick reference; easy to read.

FEDERMAN, D. and HAMMID, T. *Modern Jewelers' Consumer Guide to Colored Gemstones*. New York: Van Nostrand Reinhold, 1989, 256 pp. Notable for superb color plates of the finest gems.

GEMOLOGICAL INSTITUTE OF AMERICA. *The GIA Jeweler's Manual*. 3rd ed. Santa Monica, CA: Gemological Institute of America, 1989, 321 pp., illust. Covers all aspects from gems to jewels.

LYMAN, K., editor. *Simon & Schuster's Guide to Gems and Precious Stones*. New York: Simon & Schuster, 1986, 384 pp., illust. Full of useful and interesting information.

MCNEIL, D. S. *Jewelers Dictionary*, 3rd ed. Radnor, PA: Jewelers' Circular-Keystone, 1976, 268 pp. Standard reference.

NASSAU, K. *Gems Made by Man*. Radnor, PA: Chilton, 1980, 382 pp., illust. Covers all synthetics and other kinds of manufactured stones.

NASSAU, K. *Gemstone Enhancement*. London: Butterworths, 1984, 216 pp., illust. What has been done to gemstones to make them look better, and how you can tell.

NEWMAN, H. *An Illustrated Dictionary of Jewelry*. London: Thames & Hudson, 1987, 334 pp. Standard.

SCHUMANN, W. *Gemstones of the World*. New York: Sterling, 1977, 256 pp., illust. Very helpful, full of facts, figures and excellent illustrations.

WEBSTER, R. and ANDERSON, B. W. *Gems: Their Sources, Description and Identification*, 4th ed. London: Butterworths, 1983, 1006 pp., illust. The encyclopedic reference of lasting value. A 5th ed. in press in 1994.

GEM IDENTIFICATION

ANDERSON, B. W. and JOBBINS, E.A. *Gem Testing*, 10th ed. London: Newness-Butterworths, 1990, 390 pp., illust. Standard textbook, clearly written.

HURLBUT, C. S. and KAMMERLING, R. C. *Gemology*, 2nd ed. New York: Wiley, 1991, 353 pp., illust. Standard textbook: principles and applications.

LIDDICOAT, R. T. *Handbook of Gem Identification*, 12th ed. Santa Monica, CA: Gemological Institute of America, 1987, 362 pp., illust. The standard textbook in the U.S.

MATLINS, A. L. and BONANNO, A. C. *Gem Identification Made Easy*. S. Woodstock, VT: Gemstone Press, 1989, 279 pp., illust. Intelligent use of a few instruments in simple tests.

SINKANKAS, J. *Gemstone and Mineral Data Book*. Tucson, AZ: Geoscience Press, 1988, 352 pp. Facts gathered from many sources for a handy workshop reference.

SINKANKAS, J. *Gemology: An Annotated Bibliography*, 2 vol. Metuchen, NJ: Scarecrow Press, 1993, 1179 pp., illust. The only complete reference ever published on gemstones.

WEBSTER, R. *Practical Gemmology*, 6th ed. London: N.A.G. Press, 1976, 209 pp., illust. Best quick introduction available.

WEBSTER, R. and JOBBINS, E. A. *Gemmologist's Compendium*, 6th ed. London: N.A.G. Press, 1979, 240 pp., illust. Miniature encyclopedia of basic facts.

GEM GUTTING

KRAUS, P. *Introduction to Lapidary*. Radnor, PA: Chilton, 1987, 224 pp., illust. Basic instructions for all types of work.

SINKANKAS, J. *Gem Cutting, A Lapidary's Manual*, 3rd ed. New York: Chapman & Hall, 1984, 365 pp., illust. The standard textbook.

VARGAS, G. and VARGAS, M., *Descriptions of Gem Materials*. Palm Desert, CA: (privately published), 1985, 180 pp. Basic data on features and properties for gem cutters.

INDIVIDUAL GEMSTONES

BRANSON, O. T. *Turquoise: The Gem of the Centuries*. Tucson, AZ: Treasure Chest, 1975, 62 pp., illust. Worldwide treatment, but emphasizes Southwest U.S.A.

BRUTON, E. *Diamonds*, 2nd ed. Radnor, PA: Chilton, 1978, 550 pp., illust. Standard coverage of all aspects.

DOWNING, P. B. *Opal Identification and Value*. Tallahassee, FL: Majestic Press, 1992, 210 pp., illust. Describes all varieties; worldwide coverage.

FARN, A. E. *Pearls: Natural, Cultured and Imitation*. London: Butterworths, 1986, 150 pp., illust.

FRAQUET, H. *Amber*. London: Butterworths, 1987, 176 pp., illust. Interesting discussions of history, lore, sources, etc.

HOOVER, D. B. *Topaz*. London: Butterworths, 1992, 207 pp., illust. History, lore, sources, etc.

HUGHES, R. W. *Corundum*. London: Butterworths, 1990, 314 pp., illust. Most complete study of gem varieties, such as ruby, sapphire, star stones, etc.

KEVERNE, R., Editor. *Jade*. London: Anness Publishing, 1991, 368 pp., illust. Worldwide coverage from deposits to carvings and lore, with splendid color photographs.

KUNZ, G. F. and STEVENSON, C. H. *The Book of the Pearl*. New York: Dover, 1993, 672 pp., illust. Reprint of the unsuperseded classic of 1908. Best pearl reference.

MULLER, H. *Jet*. London: Butterworths, 1987, 149 pp., illust. Sources, manufacturers, jewelry, etc.

O'DONOGHUE, M. *Quartz*. London: Butterworths, 1987, 110 pp., illust. Mostly about the gem varieties.

RICE, P. C. *Amber: The Golden Gem of the Ages*. New York: Kosciuszko Foundation, revised 1987, 304 pp., illust. The standard work.

ROSE, J. D. *Garnet*. London: Butterworths, 1986, 134 pp., illust. Worldwide coverage garnet deposits and types, plus much other information.

SINKANKAS, J. *Emerald and Other Beryls*. Tucson, AZ: Geoscience Press, 1989, 665 pp., illust. Standard reference on this mineral and its gem varieties.

SINKANKAS, J. and READ, P. G. *Beryl*. London: Butterworths, 1986, 225 pp., illust. Abridgment of above.

MISCELLANEOUS

DUBIN, L. S. *The History of Beads: From 30,000 B.C., to the Present*. New York: Abrams, 1987, 368 pp., illust. Outstanding work, with much information on gemstones.

EVANS, J. *A History of Jewellery*, 2nd ed. London: Faber & Faber, 1989, 432 pp., illust. Standard.

KUNZ, G. F. *Rings for the Finger*. New York: Dover, 1973, 512 pp., illust. Reprint of the great classic of 1917.

KUNZ, G. F. *Curious Lore of Precious Stones*. New York: Dover, 1989, 406 pp., illust. Reprint of the great classic of 1913.

MATLINS, A. L. and BONANNO, A. C. *Jewelry & Gems: The Buying Guide*. S. Woodstsock, VT: Gemstones Press, 1993, 272 pp., illust.

MILLER, A. M. *Gems and Jewelry Appraising: Techniques of Professional Practice*. New York: Chapman & Hall, 1988, 198 pp., tables, worksheets.

MILLER, A. M. *Cameos Old and New.* New York: Chapman & Hall, 1991, 216 pp., illust. The only comprehensive book on the subject that is currently available.

Index